A Short Introduction to English Grammar

❧ A Short Introduction to English Grammar

JAMES SLEDD, UNIVERSITY OF CALIFORNIA

SCOTT, FORESMAN AND COMPANY

CHICAGO,   ATLANTA,   DALLAS,   PALO ALTO,   FAIR LAWN, N. J.

Contents

Introduction 2

part one

Introduction

If a great book is a great evil, a long "Introduction" to a *Short Introduction* is an ungodly backsliding; yet this little grammar needs a big explanation. It was written in particular circumstances to meet particular needs, and its origin and intent have determined its nature and its possible uses.

The demands of the situation

Three features of the situation which prompted the composition of this book must be discussed: (1) the persistence, in American schools, colleges, and universities, of an eighteenth-century grammatical tradition; (2) the development, in the nineteenth and twentieth centuries, of a modern linguistics whose rejection of the earlier tradition and whose failure to influence that tradition have at least been comparable, though not equally complete; (3) recent attempts to make a linguistically respectable description of English available for classroom use.

❧ The tradition

A typical eighteenth-century grammarian provides the borrowed title of the present book. In 1762, Robert Lowth, Bishop of London, Hebraic scholar, and Oxford's professor of poetry, published *A Short Introduction to English Grammar*. The work was tremendously successful, and not without some reason; its influence can still be seen in twentieth-century handbooks and in controversies among twentieth-century schoolmen. In many ways, however, the *Short Introduction* was misguided and misleading.

Lowth was persuaded that the English used by even the best speakers and writers was full of grammatical errors, but it is a little hard to say what was his notion of an error. Perhaps he meant a violation of universal grammar, an arbitrary set of linguistic principles allegedly grounded in the nature of things or in the nature of the divine or human mind; perhaps he meant the failure to get rid of grammatical irregularities by extending the simplest and most general structural patterns of the language to all its parts. In any case, his remedy was not to follow the usage of acknowledged masters of English speech and writing but to investigate the supposed principles of the language so that one might judge every utterance as correct or incorrect and bring one's own speech and writing into accord with true propriety.

Lowth's characteristic technique was to teach what is right by showing what is wrong. He filled his footnotes with supposed blunders from the works of famous writers, and he completed the conservative pattern of his work by reintroducing, into the description of English, a good deal of the machinery of Latin grammar which some earlier writers on the vernacular had sensibly discarded. Despite all this, the *Short Introduction* provided a syntax of sorts when a syntax was needed; it has kept Lowth's name alive for two hundred years; and we might temper our sense of intellectual superiority by asking where, in America today, we might discover an eminent literary critic who is also, by contemporary standards, a competent grammarian. Lowth, in his century, was such a man.

Readers familiar with conventional American handbooks of English grammar will realize that the pattern which Lowth helped set has never been broken. It was perpetuated, especially in this country, by his successors in public favor, men like Lindley Murray and Samuel Kirkham, who in recent years have suffered as much condemnation as once they received praise. Perhaps the condemnation has been a bit overdone. The old grammarians did provide, for example, the set of terms and distinctions in which all of us first learned to talk about our language and which, on occasion, most of us still use; and the handbooks make many statements which will appear, with modifications, in any description of English. But though some elements of the schoolroom tradition are worth preserving, the old-fashioned grammars for American schools and colleges are hardly distinguished works. They remain typically normative and give much of their space to correcting error; but their standards are not always reasoned or reasonable. Their attempts at description are also distorted by errors in fact and method. The handbooks still try to transfer the categories of Latin to so different a language as English; they continue to neglect phonology, the basic study of the sounds of speech, and sometimes to confuse speech with writing; and their continued acceptance of ready-made logical and psychological categories still prevents them from accurately and fully stating the real forms of English. Two hundred years of pedagogic labor should have produced something better.

❧ Revolution in linguistics

Toward the end of the eighteenth century, at the very time when schoolroom grammarians like Murray were establishing their dominance over the popular mind, a great change took place in those more serious linguistic studies from which the schoolroom tradition was henceforth virtually insulated. Increasing familiarity with Sanskrit forced the recognition of its similarity to most of the languages of Europe; and with this recognition came the hypothesis that Sanskrit, Greek, Latin, the Germanic and Celtic languages, and a number of others must all have developed from a common ancestor. A widely spoken language, it became apparent, may change differently in different places until ultimately there emerges a set or family of languages which are different but historically related. Historical and comparative linguistics then underwent a century of very rapid and extensive development. It turned out to be possible, with the help of written records, to trace the history of individual languages for centuries, showing the processes by which they had been transformed; and when written records failed, comparison of the earliest recorded stages of the individual languages allowed the partial reconstruction of their common ancestors. In the last quarter of the nineteenth century, the attempt to confirm certain hypotheses of historical linguistics by the study of living dialects led to the development of linguistic geography, which deals with regional variations in speech and their historical explanation. As the changes in vocabulary and in linguistic structure came to be recorded in the great historical dictionaries and grammars, so regional variations came to be recorded in linguistic atlases.

Within the last seventy-five years, progress in linguistics has been less in linguistic history than in linguistic description. Historical linguists came to see that without at least two good descriptions of different stages in the development of a language, they could not write a good history; and the attempt to describe not just Indo-European languages, but languages of the most diverse structure all over the world, finally showed that it was worse than useless to try to force every language into the Latin mold. New descriptive concepts and techniques were elaborated, especially in phonology; and the principle was established that every language must be described as it is, not as if it were Latin and not as some grammarian might think it ought to be.

While the schoolroom grammarians, then, were perpetuating the pattern of books like Lowth's *Short Introduction,* more serious students of languages were mapping the fields of descriptive linguistics, historical linguistics, linguistic geography, and historical lexicography. The linguists learned to work inductively and to describe each language in and for itself, to distinguish speech from writing, to avoid rash value judgments and uncontrolled speculation, and to reject the easy circularities and evasions of pseudodefinitions in grammar. They came to demand at least two things of everyone who wished to lay down laws for the use of language:

first, a precise knowledge of how people actually do speak and write; second, a reasoned justification for statements of how people *should* speak and write. Since most schoolroom grammars did not meet these standards, they fell into disrepute among competent linguists.

That same disrepute, among the careless or arrogant, seems sometimes to involve all books about English not written within the last twenty-five years. It is almost impertinent to say that criticism properly directed at the average contemporary handbook for American freshmen does not apply to the great standard grammars of our language, most of which were not written in America. Linguists like Henry Sweet the Englishman and Otto Jespersen the Dane, and grammarians like the Dutchmen Kruisinga and Poutsma were not unaware of the deficiencies of the common schoolbooks. Their own imposing collections of material, and, to some extent, their descriptive statements, remain extremely valuable to every student of English grammar. Ideally, they should be as familiar to handbook writers as the American linguists Bloomfield and Sapir.

☞ Popularizers and their problems

The recognition that traditional English grammar is more than somewhat unsound has been slow and painful; the suggestion that it *is* unsound is still disturbing to many teachers, students, and laymen. No one likes to confess ignorance and error, to write off a large investment of time and energy as an intellectual loss, or to surrender his status as a medicine man. That is what classroom grammarians have been asked to do, often by propagandists for linguistics whose claims to peculiar wisdom were rather dubious. And there have been other, less personal reasons why linguistics has not much affected American education or touched the popular mind. For one thing, descriptive or structural linguistics is a relatively late development. Leonard Bloomfield's great book *Language,* the most important American work in the field, was not published until 1933; and the next dozen years were filled with wars. Even in more favorable circumstances, the inertia of institutions for mass education and the reluctance of commercial publishers to move ahead of their markets would have been hard to overcome. The opposition of humanists, moreover, to anything called *science* naturally extended to linguistic science. Somewhat less than devoted to the advancement of knowledge for its own sake, English departments in particular (in American universities, the largest humanistic departments) have held obstinately to the old ways. The linguistic training of most of their members has been a combination of the eighteenth-century prescriptive tradition with the historical linguistics of the late nineteenth century, and few professors of English have contributed notably to the development of American linguistics within the last generation. Since English departments and schools of education control the training of secondary-school teachers, advocates of the teaching of an English grammar which linguists might respect have not lacked sparring partners.

THE DEBATE OVER USAGE. The first round of the battle was fought over standards of usage and was pretty well finished by the late thirties. It had been obvious, for a good long time, that the grammatical lawmakers often provided no convincing justification for the *do*'s and *don't*'s of their handbooks and that a distressing number of good speakers and writers violated the handbook rules. Combative linguists and their combative disciples, armed with the *Oxford English Dictionary,* the greatest historical dictionary of a modern language, took some pleasure in pointing out these exemplifications of false philology; and although some heroic purists took the position that rules are rules no matter who violates them, it was hard to defend a rule which great writers did not observe, which a considerable number of educated people thought ridiculous or unnecessary, and for which the principal argument was bare authority. The rules had gradually to be modified so that they did not prescribe usages which were alien to standard English or forbid usages which were established there.

Not all the results, however, of this first conflict were so happy. Since the linguists and their followers quite rightly insisted on defining standard English as the actual language habits of the ruling classes, they could easily be accused, with a little strategic misrepresentation, of teaching that in language, whatever is is right; and since the more dogmatic handbooks were rather generally discredited, it could also be argued, by another moderately dishonest maneuver, that *all* grammatical training had been proved useless. To the latter argument, it seemed a somewhat feeble answer that a good grammar could not be discredited by the failure of a bad one, that sound grammatical training would certainly not damage a student's speech and writing, and that such training, undoubtedly a good end in itself, might very probably have beneficial practical effects. Unfortunately there is no substantial body of experimental evidence that a conscious, organized knowledge of the structure of English makes students speak better or write better.

CRITICISM OF TRADITIONAL DESCRIPTIONS. When the second great shooting war was over, the second battle in the grammatical war began. In the debate over usage, methods of grammatical description had not been the main issue. Principles and methods of *prescription* had been involved, and matters of factual accuracy; but the charge had not been generally made that the schoolroom grammarians were wrong in their whole approach to language, in their notion of what a language is and how it may be adequately described. Now the lines of battle changed. Structural linguistics, in the late forties, was a well-established discipline, still young enough to be brash, too young or too vigorous to be free from internal controversy, but mature enough to have accomplished notable things. American linguists, like their European colleagues, had done a great deal of excellent work in describing many of the world's less well-known languages, especially American Indian languages; they had made fine contributions to English grammar; and they were eager to reach a larger public than they had reached so far. For a variety of reasons, a number of them turned their attention to English and to the teaching of English, so that studies of English structure and critiques of the traditional descriptions increased together.

A good many of the linguists' criticisms have already been repeated here, but two more must now be mentioned. The words *structure* and *structural* suggest the first. A language, the linguists said, is first of all a structure, a system, an elaborate set of patterns; and a system can only be described systematically. The schoolroom grammars did no such thing. Instead, they dealt with bits and pieces of the English language—those bits where native speakers disagreed among themselves, so that a choice among conflicting customs had to be made. The bad results of this method were exemplified by the fact that American students memorized rules about *shall* and *will* and *between you and I* but learned little or nothing about the sound patterns of their own speech, the way their words were formed, or the selection and ordering of their words in phrases and sentences. The linguists argued, second, that a good description of a language must be a description of its *forms*. They objected violently to semantic definitions of grammatical classes ("A noun is the name of a person, place, or thing") because, they said, the traditional definitions are logically indefensible and useless in practice, because it would be extremely difficult to frame *better* semantic definitions, because linguistic forms, on the other hand, can be made the subject of very precise statements, and because, in language, meanings are communicated only by the forms that bear them, so that the only access to the meanings is through the forms.

This attack on the schoolroom grammarians was much more damaging than any that had been made before. It was an attack on the foundations, not the superstructure, and if it succeeded, a revolution in grammar was inevitable. Since few of the traditionalists had kept up with developments in linguistics, they were under something of a disadvantage. To answer their opponents among the linguists, they had to learn what their opponents were doing and what their opponents meant. At the least, the linguists were sure to win a wider audience, and there was always the possibility that the reading of their work, if only to refute it, might actually make converts. That is what happened. Interest in structural linguistics increased sharply among English teachers, and a number of them undertook to pass on their newly acquired knowledge to their students.

THE MAKING OF NEW TEXTS. In 1951 and 1952, two books appeared which strengthened the hands of the linguistic popularizers. So far, the attempts of the popularizers had suffered from one obvious weakness: they had had no textbooks of English grammar which embodied the principles for which they were contending. The publication, in 1951, of *An Outline of English Structure,* by George L. Trager and Henry Lee Smith, Jr., and, in 1952, of *The Structure of English,* by Charles Carpenter Fries, provided excellent materials for such texts. In a concise and highly systematic description of English phonology, Trager and Smith summed up the work of a whole generation of American linguists in that field; they also described the English inflectional system and made some valuable suggestions concerning methods of describing English syntax. Fries, on his part, said little of phonology and not a great deal about morphology, but devoted most of his book to the basic structure of English sentences and to the theoretical and practical bearings of his work. The materials of the two books thus seemed neatly complementary, and several popularizers, including the present writer, set out immediately to combine them.

They encountered a number of difficulties. The statements by Trager and Smith and by Fries were neither so harmonious, so inclusive, nor so final as they first seemed to naïvely enthusiastic readers; and the popularizers, who were largely self-trained in linguistics (since they were members of English departments), found that they had much more to do than to assemble prefabricated grammars. They had not only to adapt the linguists' statements, with their often forbidding terminology, for use in the classroom; they had also to fill up gaps in all the descriptions which the structuralists could offer, and to choose among *competing* descriptions and methods of description where the linguists disagreed among themselves. These problems were not always easily solved or solved at all, and even a friendly audience will find the new textbooks often crude, sometimes inconsistent, and never definitive. Their authors believe that at least the new texts are steps in the right direction.

⌁ Summary

What now, in summary, does the present situation demand of a grammarian who believes that English grammar should be an important part of the general education of American citizens and of the special education of English teachers? The general direction in which he should move is clear: the conventional schoolroom grammar is defective and must be brought more nearly in line with the principles and methods of contemporary linguistics. The movement in this direction is already too strong to be resisted, even if resistance were wise. Yet the schoolroom tradition is the only grammatical tradition which many teachers, students, and laymen now know; it is not totally false or misguided; and since contemporary linguistics is not monolithic but various, alive, and changing, no one can offer a new description of English as a grammatical faith in which the untutored may finally and safely rest. Only the light-minded opponents of *any* grammatical training will profit if the change from old grammars to new is attempted arrogantly or too rapidly.

To the writer of this book, it seems to follow from all this that not merely one or two but a number of interim textbooks are needed. They should embody careful efforts to maintain some continuity in learning and teaching, to avoid the mere substitution of new dogma for old, and (since they must seek approval not only from grammarians) to show both the extrinsic and the intrinsic value of English grammar: some emphasis on practical applications is necessary. Compromise with ignorance or bigotry is *not* necessary. This particular textbook is one attempt, undoubtedly quite imperfect, to meet the demands of the present situation; but its writer does not believe that a prudential mixture of supposed truth with known falsehood is a workable transition from anything to anything. He has tried to relate his description of English to other descriptions in less ambiguous ways.

A description of this book

The title, *A Short Introduction to English Grammar,* was not borrowed merely as a joke. It is meant to suggest a certain conservatism, a desire to link the present with the past; and, since Lowth is currently despised by just those American linguists on whose work this book is built, the borrowing might ironically announce a modicum both of diffidence and independence.

⁌ Traditional features

Another attempt at a workable transition from old to new grammar for students in American colleges and universities, the present *Introduction* preserves as much of the schoolroom tradition as its author thought possible—not enough for thoroughgoing traditionalists, too much for many linguists. With some modifications, the familiar subject-predicate definition of the sentence is retained, along with the classifications of sentences into simple, compound, complex, and compound-complex and into statements, questions, commands, and exclamations. The first classification presupposes distinctions, which are duly stated, between independent and dependent clauses and between clauses and phrases. Most of the familiar constructions, including three kinds of objects, are also distinguished, and wherever possible the familiar names are used. Nouns, verbs, adjectives, and adverbs are here nouns, verbs, adjectives, and adverbs—not words of Classes 1, 2, 3, and 4 respectively; the present tense is called the present tense, not the non-past; and neologisms like *resultative phase, inchoative aspect,* and *negative status* are avoided. In content and in appearance, the book is more traditional than most of the other interim texts.

⁌ Departures from tradition

What appears, however, to be traditional may in fact be sometimes rather new; for though a conscious effort has been made to avoid unnecessary innovation or the appearance of it, the primary intent has always been a linguistically honest description of English. For example, though the terms *phoneme* and *phonemic* seldom if ever occur, the first chapter outlines the English phonemic system, and the chapters on syntax make more use of the phonology than some modern linguists have done. The discussion of parts of speech breaks sharply with tradition. There, two sets of classes, one morphologic and one syntactic, are formally defined, so that the traditional terms are given new meanings; and a careful attempt is made throughout at formal definition of larger units by reference to previously established smaller ones. This step-by-step progression from sound to sentence, in the writer's opinion, is clearer and more teachable than other organizations.

Perhaps it might be said that if this grammar is more traditional than most others like it, it is also in some respects more independent: if it is bad, it is bad in its own way. Everywhere in the book, current linguistic doctrines, like the traditional pronouncements, are treated as hypotheses to be tested, not as ultimate truths. So in the first chapter the reader will not find the analysis of English vowels which was completed and made popular by Trager and Smith, and in the pages on syntax he will find none of the elaborate but incomplete and largely arbitrary analyses into immediate constituents which make a considerable part of several recent grammars. The combination of old and new, it is hoped, is neither a covert plagiarism from a calumniated tradition, nor an uncritical repetition of the newest statements by well-known linguists, nor yet an impossible compromise. But of all this the reader will judge. He will find in Chapter Seven, "A Glossary of Grammatical Terms," direct statements of many relations between the analysis in this book and the schoolroom tradition.

⌥ Outline

The glossary follows the six chapters which constitute the grammar proper: "The Sounds of English," "Parts of Speech," "Nominal Sequences," "Verbal Sequences," "Subjects and Predicates," "The Sentence and Its Kinds." An eighth and final chapter, "Applied Grammar: Some Notes on English Prose Style," attempts one application of grammatical knowledge. The numerous exercises in Chapters One–Six and in Chapter Eight should make the book almost self-teaching, while the short bibliographies for the first six chapters provide guides to further reading.

AN INDEPENDENT PHONOLOGY. Detailed comments on individual chapters may usefully supplement this statement of general organization. Chapter One begins with the English systems of pitch and stress—those subsets of our distinctive sounds, or phonemes, which are most important in syntactic analysis. The description here is taken directly from Trager and Smith. A brief and conventional description of the speech organs and of methods for the articulatory classification of vowels and consonants then precedes the section on vowels and consonants themselves. The enumeration of twenty-four consonants simply repeats the most widely accepted theory, but the treatment of the vowels and diphthongs is an independent modification of John S. Kenyon's familiar analysis. Short vowels and long vowels, both treated as unit phonemes or single sounds, are recognized, as well as short and long diphthongs, both treated as sequences of two sounds. The short diphthongs consist of two short vowels, of which the second is always either /ɪ/ (as in *pit*), /ʊ/ (as in *put*), or /ə/ (as in *but*). The rare long diphthongs consist of a long vowel and —in the dialects which the writer knows—a following /ə/.

This complicated and even messy system is offered tentatively. The writer wishes to avoid any commitment to a theory of overall pattern, a phonemic super-system which will accommodate all the individual systems of particular dialects; but for teaching purposes some general statement is necessary. The Trager-Smith analysis, which recognizes nine short vowels and twenty-seven possible combinations of short vowels with the semivowels /y/, /w/, and /h/, does not provide for all the contrasting sounds in well-known American dialects. Despite its acknowledged value, then, the writer has rejected it, hesitantly, for a system which does make room for the facts of American English pronunciation, as he knows them. His modification of Kenyon's much earlier statement has the further advantages that it is familiar in its elements, close to prevalent British descriptions, and—incidentally—broadly like the sound systems described in standard historical grammars of English.

Perhaps fortunately, the analysis of the vowels, like that of the consonants, is not so important for the rest of the book as is the description of stress and pitch. Without some statement concerning these latter features of the sound system, a good English syntax is hardly possible; but the strongest reason for describing the sounds of English in Chapter One is the necessity for keeping speech and writing distinct from the beginning. The maintenance of the distinction between speech and writing and some knowledge of the relations between the two in English are essential both in grammar and in composition courses, where many students must learn the conventions of the writing system as well as the distinctive characteristics of those kinds of speech which we normally write down. These matters are further touched upon in the chapter on style.

TWO SETS OF PARTS OF SPEECH. The second chapter, "Parts of Speech," includes the widest departure from traditional statements in the entire grammar. Though it does keep many traditional labels, including *noun, verb, pronoun, adjective,* and *adverb,* Chapter Two modifies the usual definitions very extensively. Instead of the traditional eight parts of speech, it recognizes one set of classes distinguished by their suffixes and another set distinguished by their positions in sentences. *Nouns,* for example, are defined as words inflected like *man, boy, James,* or *root; nominals* are defined as words, phrases, or clauses standing in sentence positions which nouns typically occupy. This recognition of distinct morphological and syntactic classes might be avoided, as it usually is, by ranking morphological and syntactic criteria according to their importance. So Fries, who does not make the distinction, defines his Class 1 words both morphologically and syntactically but gives precedence to the syntactic criteria. The result is only that the same distinction turns up, more obscurely, in another guise. Since the distinction, that is, between the morphologic and syntactic classes is built into the English language, either the grammarian can define a morphologic class of nouns by its inflections and a syntactic class of nominals by the occurrence of its members in noun positions, or he can use both criteria to define a single class of nouns and then say that some nouns satisfy just one of the two conditions while others satisfy both. The choice is whether to violate tradition by insisting on the distinction or to risk obscuring the distinction by following tradition. Clarity seems preferable.

And there is actually some support for the two sets of classes in traditional grammar (to say nothing of the *Outline of English Structure,* from which the idea is taken). In sentences like *The poor despise the rich because they envy them,* one says conventionally that *poor* and *rich* are adjectives used as nouns. This is much the same as to say that *poor* and *rich* are adjectives because they are inflected with *-er* and *-est* but that in this sentence they are also nominals since they occupy noun positions. The nominal is very like the traditional substantive.

Whether or not support from traditional grammar is an advantage, classes like the nominal do have peculiar value because they include not just words but larger forms as well. This makes it easy to analyze complicated structures by showing their equivalence to simple ones. For instance, since the subject position is typically occupied by nouns, all forms in that position, whether words, phrases, or clauses, are members of the nominal class; and so the structure is the same though the subject may be a noun, a pronoun, a noun with its modifiers, an adjective preceded by *the,* an infinitive, a clause, or any other eligible form.

In addition to the morphologic-syntactic distinction, two other features of Chapter Two may be mentioned more briefly. First, stress and pitch are made regular parts of the testing frames for syntactic classes. If our orthography allowed us to write these phonemes, every grammarian would have followed the same practice, which allows us to avoid obvious orthographic confusions like that between the two phrases *moving van* "a van for moving" and *moving van* "a van in motion." Second, the chapter includes a discussion of the *word,* a concept which is usually left unexamined in elementary grammars. Though the discussion is inconclusive and perhaps forbidding, it contributes to the clarity and consistency of later chapters and might have a further, independent value in the discussions of word formation which frequently make a part of efforts at vocabulary building.

CHAPTER THREE: NOMINAL PHRASES. Chapters Three and Four lead on from words toward sentences. The third chapter might be variously but synonymously described as an analysis of certain nominal phrases, an analysis of the possible expansions of noun heads, or an analysis of the nature and position of the most common modifiers of nouns, including noun adjuncts and appositives. The third description, which refers to appositives as modifiers, suggests the difficulties inherent in the concept of modification. Any definition of modification which the writer knows, whether semantic or formal, makes appositives into modifiers of nouns and objects into modifiers of verbs. Traditionally, appositives then become adjectives, and objects become adverbs—unwanted classifications which traditional grammarians have avoided only by being inconsistent. Linguistically oriented textbooks also have their difficulties with modification, such as the question what part, if any, of verbal phrases like *would have been talking* is modified and what parts are modifiers. Since these and similar problems remain unsolved, no direct and extended analysis of modification is undertaken in this book. It turns out that no great loss is involved.

CHAPTER FOUR: VERBAL PHRASES. Chapter Four does for verbal phrases what Chapter Three does for nominal phrases. It attempts no extended analysis of the complicated class of adverbials (Fries's Class 4), and it keeps the traditional array of complements, including three kinds of objects; but as usual the familiar terms are formally and not semantically defined. Recent arguments that the different objects are incapable of formal definition are unconvincing results of a too narrow definition of formal definition. It is plain, for example, that a sentence containing an indirect object and a direct object has two passive equivalents, while a sentence containing a direct object and an object complement has just one; and this kind of comparison of the different sentences in which a set of forms occurs is a formal and not a semantic technique.

CHAPTER FIVE: SUBJECTS AND PREDICATES. Since the basic English sentence pattern consists of a nominal phrase followed by a verbal phrase, Chapters Three and Four are the foundation for the discussion of subjects (a subset of nominals) and predicates (a subset of verbals) in Chapter Five. Here the advantages of a progression from sounds through words and phrases to clauses and sentences become very clear. The definition of subjects and predicates and still more the definition of the sentence depend on previous definitions of the smaller units which these structures include; but if the successively larger units have been carefully defined, even the term *sentence* is no bugaboo. Chapter Five concludes with formulas which schematically represent a number of the constructions distinguished in that and the two preceding chapters. The model for such formulas is in Fries's *Structure of English*.

CHAPTER SIX: THE SENTENCE. The concluding chapter in the grammar proper, Chapter Six, gives the chosen definition of the sentence and the two quite conventional classifications of sentences which have been mentioned. The increasingly traditional aspect of the grammar reflects the writer's conviction that modern American linguists have accomplished more in phonology than in syntax and that considerable parts of the conventional syntactic analysis of English may be usefully preserved. Thus, for the purposes of this book, the usual subject-predicate definition of the sentence is basically acceptable. It is easily stated (see the glossary), not hard to apply, and well adapted to the practical needs which an English grammar is expected to meet in English departments. But the definition is not alone defensible on practical grounds and should not be defended only so. The traditional term *sentence fragment* suggests a theoretical defense that many utterances which do not have the subject-predicate form may be described in terms of the smaller units on which the sentence definition rests.

Something more should also be said of the refusal, in this grammar, to attempt any overt analysis of sentences into their immediate constituents. Linguists often say that English sentences can be analyzed by successive dichotomy until the individual morphemes, roughly the smallest meaningful units, have been reached; it is sometimes argued that further constituent analysis, into phonemes and sequences of phonemes, is also possible. Such analysis by twos works very well on some sentences and sentence parts, but there is no reason to believe that it is applicable to all sentences. Nothing is lost by avoiding so dubious a procedure.

CHAPTER SEVEN: A GLOSSARY WITH A DIFFERENCE. Matters of this kind (immediate constituents, the definition of the sentence, modification) are rather fully discussed in Chapter Seven, the glossary of grammatical terms, which further provides a selective index to the first six chapters, sums up their important statements, and indicates the relation of those statements to the schoolroom tradition. At the least, the glossary is no mere appendix but an integral part of the book; and if entries like that on "Parts of Speech" accomplish their purposes, it may well be the most important part. The writer hopes it may serve as a model for the sort of translation between systems which every student of English grammar, for many years to come, should be prepared to make.

CHAPTER EIGHT: A PRACTICAL APPLICATION. The final chapter, the notes on style, is more loosely attached and of less general interest. Its practical nature should not suggest that the first purpose of the grammar is anything other than the intrinsically valuable understanding of the speech which makes us human; and for this purpose Chapter Eight is not especially significant. Instead, it illustrates one of the extrinsic values of grammatical study, its usefulness to students and teachers of writing, particularly the writing of simple exposition and argument. The chapter rests on a definition of style as the manner of saying what is said. Style in language is then synonymous with linguistic choice and rejection; the study of style becomes basically comparative; and the necessary instruments of comparison are grammars and dictionaries. In the light of this theory, the chapter considers a variety of familiar topics, emphasizing structural elements of style more than vocabulary and closing with a section on those standards of good and bad writing which linguists are often falsely said to deny. The chapter is not intended, however, as a handbook of correction.

❧ Audience and use

The book as a whole should not be too difficult for college freshmen, but it will not be dismissed, the writer hopes, as too elementary for more advanced students: it contains much information which many graduate students, at least in English departments, do not but should control. Specifically, the writer believes the book might well be used in courses in Modern English grammar, especially courses for prospective teachers of English; in courses in the history of the language, where the history will hardly be understood without a previous analysis of the students' own speech; and in beginning courses in linguistics, since the best introduction to linguistics must also include some description of the students' native language. Teachers of undergraduate composition courses might also use the book, either systematically or for the occasional reference which the glossary facilitates.

Details of the use of any textbook are of course for teachers to decide, but one or two suggestions may be in order. Chapters One through Six would be best taught in sequence and might be taught without the introduction and the last two chapters. The glossary could be used alone, but Chapter Eight presupposes the grammar. The introduction might or might not be assigned in connection with any other part of the book. A possible objection to its assignment is its inevitable presupposition of some knowledge which most students will lack. Its frankness in presenting grammatical controversies, however, is no reason not to assign it. Students should know the state of their field, and teachers should know that controversies cannot be hidden from students.

The one thing absolutely essential in any teaching of any English grammar is participation by the student. Lectures may be useful, especially on subjects not treated in the text, but neither text nor lectures will be of much use to the average student unless he shares in the inquiry. Hence the numerous exercises in all parts of this book except the introduction and the glossary. Without them, or without other exercises of the teacher's devising, the book will not be fully understood.

Acknowledgments

To write the following paragraphs is at once a pleasure and an embarrassment—a pleasure because they acknowledge much kindness freely bestowed, an embarrassment because so many obligations should be repaid with a better book.

To begin with, the book could never have been written without the *Outline of English Structure,* by George L. Trager and Henry Lee Smith, Jr., and *The Structure of English,* by Charles Carpenter Fries. To both books and to all three men, the writer is most deeply indebted. He has also learned and borrowed from published works by Bernard Bloch, Leonard Bloomfield, H. A. Gleason, Jr., Zellig S. Harris, Archibald A. Hill, John S. Kenyon, Hans Kurath, Albert H. Marckwardt, and Kenneth L. Pike, and from the unpublished dissertations of C. Westbrook Barritt, Eugene A. Nida, and Mrs. Aileen Traver Kitchin. In the chapter on style, he is indebted for examples to Cleanth Brooks and Robert Penn Warren, John C. Hodges, James B. McMillan, Porter G. Perrin, Stuart Robertson and Frederic G. Cassidy, Kendall Taft and his colleagues John Francis McDermott and Dana O. Jensen.

At various times, the writing of the book has been supported, knowingly or unknowingly, by the American Council of Learned Societies and the Guggenheim and Rockefeller foundations. Much assistance was given, in the earlier stages of composition, by colleagues at the University of Chicago, especially Eric Hamp, Robert B. Lees, Norman A. McQuown, and George Metcalf. Of the numerous readers of the original typescript or its revisions, special thanks are due to Harold B. Allen, William Card, Karl Dykema, H. A. Gleason, Jr., W. C. Greet, Archibald A. Hill, Sumner Ives, Raven I. McDavid, Jr., Albert H. Marckwardt, Arthur Norman, Porter G. Perrin, Henry Lee Smith, Jr., George L. Trager, and Francis Lee Utley.

Another Chicago colleague and friend, Mrs. Wilma R. Ebbitt, has generously given assistance which amounts really to collaboration. From the beginning, her advice, criticism, and encouragement have been of the utmost value.

Thanks are also due to many students at the University of Chicago and the University of California (Berkeley). Their helpful suggestions are gratefully acknowledged, particularly those of my friends Sheldon Sacks and Karl Teeter.

To wife and sons, the writer can give no adequate thanks for their forbearance; he can only ask their pardon, as he asks pardon of any teachers and friends whose help he has inadvertently failed to mention.

No one but himself, he should add, is responsible for his statements or misstatements. His linguist friends, particularly A. A. Hill, have encouraged him to be critical, so that he has felt at liberty to disagree even with those from whom the framework of his book is borrowed, Fries and Trager and Smith. At times he has followed a source quite closely, as in the outline of verb phrases which he takes from Nida; at times he has exercised considerable freedom, as in the discussion of the English vowels; but any mistakes are always his own.

In conclusion, thanks are due to the authors and publishers who have granted permission for the use of illustrative quotations. Specific acknowledgments accompany the selections.

CHAPTER ONE The

Sounds of
English

Intonation

⤳ Why start with speech?

"It wasn't what he said that got my goat; it was the way he said it." Probably most college students, at one time or another, have made this faintly sour remark, and probably they had good reason to make it. Every speaker of English knows that by changing his "tone of voice," he can turn the politest words into an insult or turn an insult into a friendly joke. Even a simple greeting like *hello* can be made to convey half a dozen attitudes, from active dislike, to indifference, to warm friendship, as anyone can hear for himself by making the experiment. What very few people know, however, is just how they use their "tone of voice" to make the same words mean so many different things; for we learn to speak our language by using it, not by reasoning about it, and the grammar which we have learned in school is usually the grammar of written English, not of speech. Most of us have little consciously organized knowledge of the way we talk.

Our ignorance hinders us in learning to write. Men talked long before they wrote; and ideally, if we want to understand the tools of communication and expression which our writing system gives us, we should first understand the resources of our speech, from which our writing is derived. Otherwise we are likely to forget that the marks which we make on paper when we write do not completely and accurately represent the sounds which we make when we talk; and we are likely to have trouble in learning both the devices of written English which substitute for those features of our speech that we cannot record in normal spelling, and the distinctive resources of the literary language. The problems of writing, therefore, to whose study this book may serve as a partial introduction, are best approached through speech.

This chapter will describe or illustrate all or most of the distinctive sounds which speakers of American English normally hear or use, and will outline a system of spelling which will enable us to record these sounds in a simple and easy way.

Exercise one. Choose some common greeting, like *Good morning, Mr. Jones* or *How do you do, Mr. Smith?* and say it as many different ways as you easily can. Try to explain what each way would mean or in what situation each way would be appropriate.

Exercise two. Here are five passages describing a farewell. Read them aloud to a friend, and ask the friend to read them aloud to you.

1. "Good-by, Mr. Brown," she said; and he knew from the way her voice fell and faded into silence that she hoped she would never see him again.
2. *"Good*-by, Mr. Brown," she chirped, with a lilt in her voice that was much too cheerful for Monday morning.
3. "GOOD-BY, Mr. Brown!" she almost shouted, as she stalked angrily from the room.
4. " 'Good-by, Mr. Brown?' " he repeated, incredulously; "do you really mean to leave like this?"
5. "G'by, Mr. Brown," she said carelessly, and her voice rose a little on his name as if to reassure him that the parting was not final.

What are the signs, in each written passage, that tell you how to read it? (For example, in the third passage, *good-by* is written in capitals.) Except for personal, individual differences in the quality of your voices, do you and your friend read all the passages in the same way? If not, can you describe some of the differences between your readings? (Common differences might be that the voice of one reader would rise on a word where the voice of the other reader would fall; that one reader might pronounce a word more loudly than the other would; that one reading might be more singsong than another; etc.)

Exercise three. Each of the following sentences can be read in more ways than one. Read each sentence aloud in at least two ways. Try to control your voice so that each reading of a sentence will make one of its possible meanings quite clear. (For example, the first sentence can mean either that the son of the daughter of Pharaoh is the son of the daughter of Pharaoh, or that the daughter of the son of Pharaoh is the daughter of the son of Pharaoh, or that the son of the daughter of Pharaoh is the daughter of the son of Pharaoh, or that the daughter of the son of Pharaoh is the son of the daughter of Pharaoh.)

1. The son of Pharaoh's daughter is the daughter of Pharaoh's son.
2. He wrote after each word that he knew a definition of its central meaning.
3. I have a message to report.
4. He doesn't talk to anybody.
5. Grammar helps us to understand meanings precisely because it describes their formal signals.
6. He attended a small boys' school.
7. The people have refused altogether to obey their leaders.
8. The number called for required use of the old sheets.
9. There would soon be published proposals for a reprint.
10. Our theory develops further notions already widely accepted.

❧ Tone of voice

We will begin our description of the sounds of English with "tone of voice." That phrase is used to refer to a good many things that go on in talk. One of the things it may refer to is the distinctive, individual quality of a person's speech, which we can recognize on the telephone or radio even though we cannot see the speaker. Another element in "tone of voice" is the difference in the stress with which we pronounce different syllables, as when we distinguish *objéct*, the verb, from *óbject*, the noun: *I object to that object*. These differences in stress are often accompanied by differences in pitch, in the speech tune to which the words are set; and "tone of voice" may also refer to such patterns or sequences of pitch, with the "pauses" that mark where one tune or pattern ends and another one begins. For example, *I objéct to that óbject* may be read with a high pitch on the second syllable of the verb *objéct* and on the first syllable of the noun *óbject;* the sentence is likely to end with a falling pitch and a fading out of the voice into silence; and a good many hearers are likely to report that they hear a "pause" after the verb. The first two of the preceding exercises, finally, should have reminded us that any speaker, while he keeps the basic patterns of stress and pitch unchanged and while the distinctive quality of his individual speech remains recognizably the same, can still change his "tone of voice" into a shout, a whisper, a singsong, a whine, or a chuckle. It is worth repeating that we all constantly say things which we could never write in ordinary spelling.

The common idea, then, of "tone of voice" is so broad and vague that we must limit it to avoid confusion. We will not discuss the distinctive, individual qualities which are normally present in every speaker's utterances, whether he wants them to be there or not. These qualities are socially important, and to some extent they can be modified; but it is not very helpful to say that one man's voice is squeaky and that another man talks through his nose. We will not discuss the *voice qualifiers,* either— the shouting, whispering, singing, whining, chuckling, and the like which we use to qualify utterances that in other respects are pretty much the same. The voice qualifiers are also important socially, and much more easily controlled than the individual features of a person's speech; but they seem not to be a part of the basic structure of English, and since they have not been studied very long or systematically, little can be said about them. We *will* discuss the two remaining elements in "tone of voice," the distinct though related systems of stress and pitch; for as essential parts of English structure, they are of the greatest importance to speakers and writers of English. We could not build a satisfactory grammar without them.

Exercise four. List the four elements in "tone of voice" which we have distinguished. Then:

1. As precisely as you can, tell how you distinguish the voices of two members of your family from each other and from the voices of other people.
2. Repeat the following sentence in a whisper, in a normal tone, and in a shout: "Let me go, Charley."
3. Which syllable of the word *Charley* was stressed in each repetition? In the second and third repetitions, was the pitch on *Charley* higher or lower than the pitch on *go?* (For most speakers and situations, it will regularly be lower.) Can you relate your answers to the statement that the systems of stress and pitch are parts of the basic structure of English, while the voice qualifiers are not?
4. In the following sentence, the italics indicate that the word *such* is to be emphasized: "Your father was *such* a gentleman!" Repeat the sentence twice, stressing *such* both times; but in the first repetition use a high pitch on *such* and in the second a low pitch. Do stress and pitch ever vary independently?

❧ Intonation patterns

The importance of speech tunes, or *intonation patterns,* including the "pauses," or *terminals,* which mark their ends, is demonstrated by one simple fact: though we cannot really write a single intonation pattern in ordinary English spelling, we cannot pronounce a single English word without *using* such a pattern. To some extent, our punctuation is an attempt to overcome this defect in our writing system, but an attempt which never quite succeeds. A very simple sentence can be used as a first example.

Suppose we write

the cat caught the bird

and write it without capitals or italics and without punctuation at the end. Our reader will not know just how we would say the words which we have written, and since he will not know how we would say them, he will not know whether we are asking a question or making a statement, whether we are surprised and pleased or shocked and disgusted. He could make a fair guess if we punctuated the sentence, and he would know for sure, the moment he heard us *speak* it; for then he would have our intonation pattern, among other things, to guide him.

Very often, when this sentence is spoken as a statement, the pitch of the speaker's voice will first rise, and then fall rather sharply, on the word *bird:*

the cat caught the $^{\text{b.}}\text{ir}_{\text{d}}$

"The cat caught the bird."

If, on the other hand, the sentence is spoken as a question, often the pitch will first rise on *bird* and then, instead of falling, rise again:

the cat caught the bi^{rd}

"The cat caught the bird?"

It is mainly this second rise in pitch which distinguishes the sentence as a question from the sentence as a statement.

Other questions also make good illustrations of the nature and use of intonation patterns, particularly if the situations in which the questions are asked are described as well. For instance, we may imagine that Tom and Bill are roommates and that Bill regularly goes to a dance on Saturday night. One Saturday at supper, however, Tom unaccountably asks Bill,

what are you doing tonight   are you going to the dance

Bill is so surprised that he echoes the question:

am I going to the dance   of course I am

Though there are various intonations that Tom and Bill may use in these sentences, the number of patterns which they are really likely to use is rather small. In asking his first question,

what are you doing tonight

Tom may mean one of at least two different things. He may want to know what Bill is doing on this *particular* night, this Saturday night as opposed to Friday or Sunday. If this is what Tom means, his voice is likely to rise on *night* and then fall quickly and fade away:

what are you doing to^{ni}gh$_{\text{t}}$

"What are you doing *tonight?*"

The rise in pitch on *night* is one sign to Bill that Tom wants to know about this *particular* night.

On the other hand, Tom may simply be absent-minded for the moment; he may be asking only what Bill will be *doing* in the next few hours, without any intention of contrasting Saturday night with Friday night or

Sunday night. In this situation, the pitch of Tom's voice is likely to rise, not on *night*, but on *do*. By the end of the sentence, and before the fading out of the voice, the pitch will have fallen to Tom's lowest pitch level, so that now the word *doing* is made to stand out:

what are you ^{do}ing to$_{night}$

"What are you *doing* tonight?"

Tom is asking what Bill is *doing*, not what Bill is doing *tonight*.

Bill, in turn, will probably use one of two intonation patterns in his echo question,

am I going to the dance

and his choice will depend largely on how impatient he is at a question which a stranger might ask, but hardly his own roommate. If he is only a little surprised but not really irritated, the pitch of his voice is likely to rise on *dance* and then rise slightly again before the end of the word:

am I going to the da^{nce}

"Am I going to the dance?"

But if Bill is disgusted at Tom's stupidity and wants Tom to know it, he will probably use a different pattern:

am I going to the ^{da}n$_{ce}$

"Am I going to the dance!"

Here the pitch first rises on *dance,* as in the other way of asking the question, but rises further; it then falls sharply instead of rising once more, but it does not fall all the way to Bill's lowest pitch level. Bill's voice then fades into silence. Tom will certainly get his meaning: he won't mind what Bill says, but he won't like the way he says it.

Intonation patterns, indeed, very often rouse strong feelings, particularly when the pattern used is not what the hearer expects in the circumstances. Different ways of giving the common greeting,

how are you

make good examples. In many parts of the United States, including the Middle West, the first of two speakers to use this greeting will often raise his pitch on *are* and let it fall again and fade on *you:*

how ^{are}y$_o$$_u$

"How are you?"

The second speaker, if he thinks that his acquaintance is not really asking for information but merely passing the time of day, may repeat

how ^{are} y$_{o_u}$

with this same intonation pattern; but if he takes the remark for a real question, he may reply

fi$_{n_e}$ how are ^{y}o$_u$

In his repetition of the question, he raises his pitch on *you* and then lets it fall and fade once more:

"Fine. How are you?"

Such a pattern brings the word *you* into the center of attention, and the meaning of the second speaker's whole utterance will be something like this: "I'm fine; and how are *you* as contrasted with *me?*"

Persons, however, from other parts of the country, including much of the Southeast, might be considerably irritated by our first speaker's imagined words, since they will expect, as the initial greeting, the form which our imagined second speaker uses in answer to a real question. That is, they will expect their friends to greet them with

how are ^{y}o$_u$

Failure to give prominence to the word *you* by raising the pitch will strike this second group of speakers as gross rudeness. "He asked how I was," they will feel, "but I could tell from his tone of voice that he didn't care."

Exercise five. One of the commonest intonation patterns in English is the one which we used in the statement,

the cat caught the ^{b}ir$_d$

Repeat the following sentences, using this level-rise-fall-fade pattern.
1. Dogs eat meat.
2. The fish took the bait.
3. The game's a tie.
4. He answered the letter.
5. You'll be ready.
Now change each of these five statements to a question by replacing the final fall-and-fade with a final slight rise in pitch, thus:

1. Dogs eat me^{at} "Dogs eat meat?"

Exercise six. Repeat the sentence, *What are you doing tonight?* five times. Each time put the main stress and high pitch on a different word. Tell how the meaning changes with the changes in stress and pitch.

One more example, and enough preparation will have been given for a systematic statement about English intonation patterns. Intonation sometimes allows the local wit to perpetrate corny jokes, and though the jokes may not be very funny, inventing them is good practice in recognizing different intonation patterns. The following paired sentences are notorious specimens:

what's that in the road a^{he}a$_d$

"What's that in the road ahead?"

what's that in the ^{ro}ad a^{he}^{ad}

"What's that in the road—a head?"

And again:

what are we having for ^{din}ner tonight moth^{er}

"What are we having for dinner tonight, Mother?"

what are we having for ^{din}ner tonight moth^{er}

"What are we having for dinner tonight—mother?"

❧ Pitch levels

The intonation patterns which we have illustrated so far, and most other such patterns in English, can be fairly well described in terms of four different levels of pitch and three different kinds of pattern-ending terminals ("pauses"). The pitch levels may be conveniently numbered from /^{1}/, the lowest pitch which a speaker uses, to /^{4}/, the highest. Pitch /^{2}/, a little higher than pitch /^{1}/, is often a beginning pitch in American English and is a kind of base line for normal conversation; words pronounced on this level are normally not forced upon our attention. Pitch /^{3}/, which lies between /^{2}/ and /^{4}/, often does give words special attention, and /^{4}/ is likely to give them greater attention still. For example, in Bill's surprised but unirritated echo question,

am I going to the da^{nce}

the pitches may be numbered like this:

^{2}am I going to the ^{3}dance^3

In this writing, the slight second rise on *dance* is ignored for the moment. The number *2* indicates that the first five words of the sentence are spoken with the pitch which serves Bill as a base line, and the *3* indicates the rise to the next higher pitch on *dance*. In the irritated echo question

$$\text{am I going to the } \quad {}^{da}{}_{n}{}_{ce}$$

the pitches are different, so that they would be numbered

$${}^{2}\text{am I going to the } {}^{4}\text{dance}^{2}$$

Here the fade at the end of *dance* is ignored, as the second rise on *dance* was ignored in the previous numbering. What should be noted is that when Bill is irritated, he may raise his pitch on *dance* not just to level /3/, but all the way up to /4/. Only the lowest level, /1/, now remains unnumbered. It occurs in the greeting:

$$\text{how } {}^{are}\, {}^{y}{}_{o}{}_{u}$$

$${}^{2}\text{how } {}^{3}\text{are you}^{1}$$

in which the fall on *you* carries the pitch down to the speaker's very lowest level before the terminal "fade."

Exercise seven. Number the pitch levels in the ten sentences in Exercise five, ignoring the final slight rise in pitch in the five questions and the terminal fade in the five statements. Follow these rules of thumb:
1. Never write less than two numbers in a single intonation pattern. Three or four numbers will usually be needed, and sometimes five.
2. Write a number at the beginning of the pattern.
3. Write a number before the syllable that gets the strongest stress.
4. Write a number at the end of the pattern.
5. Write a number at any other point where a significant rise or fall in pitch occurs.

Note: Often, where the voice falls from a higher pitch somewhere within the pattern to a lower pitch at the end, the fall is gradual and not precisely localized. For such patterns, the number at the end is enough to mark the gradual fall. There are patterns, however, for which a number must be written between the syllable that gets the strongest stress and the end; and there are still other patterns for which a number must be written between the beginning and the syllable that gets the strongest stress. Thus:

a. Gradual fall not precisely localized:
$${}^{2}\text{What are you } {}^{3}\text{dóing tonight}^{1}?$$

b. Significant change of pitch between the strongest stress and the end of the pattern:
$${}^{1}\text{Éat } {}^{3}\text{your lunch}^{2}.$$

(This is a rather irritated command to a child playing with his food.)
c. Significant change of pitch between the beginning of the pattern and the strongest stress:

²It's ³ri¹dículous¹.

(This is a snippy, self-satisfied condemnation.)
The sentences in Exercise five involve no special complications. The first statement is simply

²Dogs eat ³méat¹.

The corresponding question is

²Dogs eat ³méat³?

↱ Terminals

Even the little practice which has been given in the preceding examples and exercises should make a native speaker rather sensitive to the four pitch levels. The three kinds of terminal may give a bit more difficulty. One of the three occurs at the end of the unirritated echo question,

am I going to the da^{nce}

and can be recognized by the slight rise in pitch just before the end of the last word:

²am I going to the ³dance³↗

The upward arrow is a convenient way of writing this terminal.
A second kind occurs at the end of the greeting,

how ^{are} y_{o_u}

²how ³are you¹↘

This terminal, conveniently written with the downward arrow, often follows a falling pitch but itself involves no further fall to a distinctively lower pitch level; it is marked, instead, by the fading away of the voice into silence.

am I going to the da_{n}ce

²am I going to the ⁴dance²↘

The fading of the voice into silence is distinct from the fall in pitch which often precedes it.

The third terminal is sometimes represented in conventional writing by a comma, as in the sentence,

I ^{called} him but he didn't ^{an}sw_{er}

"I called him, but he didn't answer."

Here the pitches and terminals would be marked in this way:

²I ³called him²—→²but he didn't ³answer¹↘

There is a terminal (a "pause") after *him;* but as the level arrow indicates, there is no rise in pitch and no fading of the voice into silence. At this third kind of terminal, the loudness of speech is often reduced, and the speed is slowed down; but the pitch remains unchanged until the next intonation pattern begins. Two points should be particularly noted. First, after the level arrow, when the next intonation pattern does begin, the pitch may change with great rapidity:

²I ³called him²—→¹he ¹said¹↗²but he didn't ³answer¹↘

"I called him," he said, "but he didn't answer."

In this sentence, pitch /²/ is sustained for a moment as the word *him* is slowed down almost to a drawl, but the quick change that follows makes the word *he* begin with pitch /¹/. Second, although the terminal that we write with the level arrow *is* a terminal in the sense that it concludes an intonation pattern, *another* pattern regularly begins immediately afterwards. That is, the terminal written with the level arrow marks the end of important *parts* of sentences rather than the ends of sentences themselves.

Exercise eight. Read the following greetings aloud. Be sure to make your intonation patterns follow the markings.

1. (Rather formal) ²Good ³morning²—→¹Mister ¹Jones¹↘
2. (A bit more friendly) ²Good ³morning²—→¹Mister ¹Jones¹↗
3. (Polite, though colorless) ²Good ³morning¹↘
4. (An exclamation of shocked surprise) ²Good ⁴morning²↘
5. (Very lively and kittenish) ⁴Good ¹morning¹—→¹Mister ¹Jones¹↗

Exercise nine. Read the following sentences from Exercise three so as to give them the indicated meanings. Try to mark the intonation patterns which you use.

1. Sentence: I have a message to report
   Meaning: I have a message which I am to report.
2. Sentence: He doesn't talk to anybody
   Meaning: He talks to just no one at all.
3. Sentence: The people have refused altogether to obey their leaders
   Meaning: The people have completely refused to obey their leaders.
4. Sentence: The number called for required use of the old sheets
   Meaning: The number which was called for required the old sheets to be used.

5. Sentence: There would soon be published proposals for a reprint
   Meaning: Proposals for a reprint would soon be published.

Now compare your markings with those which the writer of this book would use:

1. ²I have a ³message to report¹↘
2. ²He doesn't talk to ³anybody¹↘
3. ²The people have refused alto³gether²→²to obey their ³leaders¹↘
4. ²The number ³called for²→²required use of the old ³sheets¹↘
5. ²There would soon be ³published²→²proposals for a ³reprint¹↘

Do your markings and the writer's coincide? Where they differ, are you convinced that you have accurately represented your speech? Can you read the sentences as the writer would?

Exercise ten. Mark the intonation patterns in the two pairs of sentences which we quoted on p. 27.

1. What's that in the road ahead?
   What's that in the road—a head?
2. What are we having for dinner tonight, Mother?
   What are we having for dinner tonight—mother?

Stress and transition

With so much for an explanation of the intonation patterns of English, we may go on, as we planned, to a second element in "tone of voice" and a second part of the English sound system, the patterns of stress and transition. Just as discussion of the four pitches led to discussion of the three terminals which combine with the pitches to make up intonation patterns, so stress and transition go together both in fact and in analysis. Of the two, stress is the more familiar subject.

↰ Stress and stresses

When we compare words like *cónduct* (noun) with *condúct* (verb), *cón-flict* (noun) with *conflíct* (verb), *cóntrast* and *éxtract* with *contrást* and *extráct*, we hear immediately that some syllables are pronounced more prominently than others and that these differences in prominence can distinguish one word from another. Similar pairs of nouns and verbs include *ímport* and *impórt*, *óbject* and *objéct*, *rébel* and *rebél*, *récord* and *recórd*, *réject* and *rejéct*, *súspect* and *suspéct;* and other parts of speech are sometimes similarly distinguished, as in the sentences

His *íntĭmăte* friends are there

and

They *íntĭmàte* that the results are good.

Such relative prominence is what we mean by *stress,* and if we push our comparisons far enough, we will find some evidence that most of us recognize four degrees of prominence, four stresses, in our talk. We can call them *strongest stress, second stress, third stress,* and *weakest stress.* Other common names are primary or loudest stress, secondary, tertiary, and minimal stress.

Strongest stress is heard whenever we pronounce a word of one syllable by itself: *cóme; gó; sít; stánd.* We will mark strongest stress by placing an acute accent (´) over the vowel of the strongly stressed syllable. If, now, we pronounce certain words of two syllables, like *cómĭng, góĭng, síttĭng, stándĭng,* we hear a great difference in the prominence with which the two syllables of each word are pronounced. The first syllable of each of these words has strongest stress; the second has weakest stress. In the words *súbjĕct* (noun) and *sŭbjéct* (verb), we get a direct contrast between the two, with strongest stress on the first syllable of the first word and the second syllable of the second word. Weakest stress will be marked by a breve (˘) over the vowel of the weakly stressed syllable.

Between the two extremes of strongest stress and weakest, there seem to lie at least one other stress and probably two. The weaker of these intermediate degrees, which we are calling third stress, may be heard in contrast with strongest stress in the words *cóntènt* (noun) and *cŏntént* (verb). The noun, *cóntènt,* has strongest stress on its first syllable, third stress on its second syllable. *Cŏntént,* the verb, has weakest stress on its first syllable, strongest on its second syllable. Apparently, between the second syllable of the noun and the second syllable of the verb we hear a contrast between third stress, which we will mark with a grave accent (`), and strongest stress. Third stress contrasts with weakest stress in the last syllables of *réfŭgeè* and *éffĭgў,* or in the last syllables of the verbal *ánĭmàte* and the adjectival *ánĭmăte.* (Some people, of course, say *rèfŭgée,* not *réfŭgeè;* but they may still find the contrast between third and weakest stress in other words, like *rèfŭgée* and *rĕfúse.*)

A couple of bad linguistic jokes, of the sort which we used in our discussion of English intonation, will introduce second stress, the only one of the presumed four stresses which we have not yet exemplified. The President of the United States lives in the White House, which happens to be what its name suggests, a white house. We can say, then,

²Thàt whîte ³hóuse²—→²is thĕ ³Whíte Hoùse¹↘

or

²Thĕ ³Whíte Hoùse²—→²is ă whîte ³hóuse¹↘

There seems to be a contrast between second stress (marked with a circumflex accent: ⌃) on the *white* of ²whîte ³hóuse²→ and strongest stress on the *White* of ³White Hoùse¹↘. We can even use the same words, *white* and *house,* to mean still a third thing. A house which belongs to a family named White may be called ²thĕ ³White hôuse²→, with strongest stress on *White* and second stress on *house.*

The same sort of game can be played with the words *light, house,* and *keeper,* which can be put together in that order, but under different stress patterns, to mean three different things:

(1) the man who keeps a lighthouse—³líghthoùse-kêepĕr¹↘

(2) a woman who does the kind of housekeeping which is called light—²lìght-³hóusekeèpĕr¹↘

(3) a housekeeper who is light, who doesn't weigh much— ²lîght ³hóusekeèpĕr¹↘

In our description, then, we will recognize these four stresses: strongest (/´/), second (/⌃/), third (/ˋ/), and weakest (/˘/). All four may be heard in ³élĕvàtŏr-ôpĕràtŏr¹↘. Like pitches and terminals, from which, however, we have described them as distinct, the stresses are very important in English grammar. Failure to observe them would often prevent communication or cause ridiculous blunders. A ²Spânĭsh ³stúdĕnt²→, unless he studies his native language, is not a ⁴Spánĭsh stûdĕnt¹↘; a ²môvĭng ³ván²→ is not necessarily a ⁴móvĭng vân¹↘; and a ²fîshĭng ³wórm²→ would be a very strange spectacle indeed. On the other hand, if we get the stresses right, some things that look very odd and confusing when written will be perfectly clear in speech. For example, a student of English who is both an Englishman and a lover of his native customs will be ²ă vèrў Ênglĭsh Ênglĭsh ³Énglĭsh mâjŏr¹↘, but unless he is a military man, he will not be ²ăn Ênglĭsh ⁴májŏr²→ at all.

Exercise one. In the following words, put an acute accent (´) over the vowel of the syllable that has the strongest stress:

1. nitrate	6. remain	11. illegal
2. grammar	7. expander	12. basketry
3. arrest	8. parachute	13. introduce
4. doctor	9. rhinoceros	14. hyena
5. defy	10. exposition	15. eyeful

Exercise two. Pronounce each of the following words twice. The first time, put strongest stress on the first syllable. The second time, put it on the second syllable. Tell what each word means each time you pronounce it.

1. compact	6. desert	11. perfect
2. compound	7. entrance	12. permit
3. contest	8. frequent	13. present
4. contract	9. incense	14. progress
5. convict	10. increase	15. refuse

Exercise three. In the following words, put a grave accent (ˋ) over the vowel of each syllable that has third stress.

1. alternate (verb)	6. influential
2. associate (verb)	7. observation
3. competition	8. reprimand
4. estimate (verb)	9. resolution
5. exclamation	10. transfer (verb)

Exercise four. Read the following items aloud, using the indicated stresses. State the meaning of each item.

1. ă dâncĭng gírl; ă dáncĭng gîrl
2. ă crîmĭnăl láwyĕr; ă crímĭnăl lâwyĕr
3. ă plâin áccĭdĕnt; ă pláne âccĭdĕnt
4. côokĭng ápplĕs; cóokĭng àpplĕs
5. àn ĭnsáne ăsỳlŭm; àn ĭnsâne ăsýlŭm
6. ă dêaf ănd dûmb téachĕr; ă deàf ănd dúmb têachĕr
7. ă blâck bírd; ă bláckbìrd
8. ă gôld físh; ă góldfish
9. ă strông bóx; ă stróngbòx
10. ă râbĭd dóg; ă rábbĭt dôg

◇ Transition: open and close

What we are calling *transition* is often called juncture, but we have chosen the name *transition* since many students of language object to the other label; the names are of no importance in themselves. The nature of the thing, moreover, to which the names refer is not much harder to grasp than the nature of pitch and stress. If we think of transition as a way of getting from one sound to another when we talk, then transition is no stranger than the fact that we write spaces between the last letter of one word and the first letter of the next and yet do not write spaces between the letters within a word (*a name* but *an aim*). Since writing is in part a representation of speech, we might expect that sometimes the spacing of letters should correspond to features of our talk. Our expectation is justified. Often the space between words corresponds to what we will call *open transition,* and the absence of a space to *close transition.* Open transition occurs, then, mostly between words or between two meaningful parts of a single word. At these points the way of getting from one sound to the next is often different from the *close* transition between sounds at other points. The word *nìtràte,* for example, has just the same vowels and consonants and almost the same stresses as *night-ràte,* and the two items can be spoken with the same intonation pattern; but the ways of getting from /t/ to /r/ in *nitrate* and in *night-rate* are different. After the /t/ of *nitrate,* there is a puff of breath and a whistling sound of friction which we do not make or hear in *night-rate.*

      The nitrate is cheaper.

      The night-rate is cheaper.

The way of getting from /t/ to /r/ in *nitrate* is the close transition between these two sounds, which we will indicate by writing the letters with no space and no mark between them. To show the *open* transition in *night-rate,* we will write a plus (⁺) where ordinary spelling has the hyphen: *night ⁺ rate.*

    We cannot assume, however, that open transition occurs *only* where in ordinary spelling we use a hyphen or put a space between letters. Sometimes it occurs where ordinary spelling puts two letters side by side, as in the "made-up" word *myness* and in some pronunciations of *slyness.* After the *my* of *myness* and the *sly* of *slyness* (when *slyness* is pronounced so that the two words rhyme), we must write a plus to mark the contrast with words like *minus.* The "I"-sounds in the first syllables of *myness* and *slyness* are longer than in the first syllable of *minus,* and we associate this difference in length with an open transition in *myness* and *slyness* and a close transition in *minus.* We can hear the same kind of difference between *trayful,* with open transition before *ful,* and *playful,* with close transition. On the other hand, we sometimes put a space between letters, in ordinary spelling, when the transition in speech is close. If we say, *I'll take 'er,* the sounds which we represent by *take 'er* are identical with the sounds which we represent by *taker* in *He was the only taker.* There is close transition in both cases.

Exercise five. In each of the following pairs, one open transition in the first item is marked with a plus (there may be other open transitions, unmarked, in either item of a pair). At the corresponding point in the second item, the letters are written with neither a plus nor a space between, since the transition there is close. Read the contrasting pairs aloud and listen for the differences between them.

1. *B* + *for Brown; Beefer Brown.* (Notice the length of the "bee"-sound in *B* + *for Brown.* You may ignore the open transition after *Beefer* in the second item, since there is also an open transition after *for* in the first and the two do not contrast.)
2. *(He) docked* + *a workman; Doctor Workman.* (*Docked* is longer than *Doct-* in this pair. The transitions before *workman* and *Workman* do not contrast.)
3. *Due* + *to call; duty calls.* (*Due* is longer than *du-* here, and there is a puff of breath after the /t/ of *to.* After the /t/ of *duty,* which sounds more like a /d/, there is no such puff. Thus the presence of open transition is recognized by what it does to the sounds on either side of it. It does different things, of course, to different sounds.)
4. *Eiffel; eye* + *ful.* (The "I"-sound in *eye* + *ful* is much the longer of the two.)
5. *Ill* + *eagle; illegal.* (Despite the spelling, we pronounce only one *l*-sound where we write the double *l*'s in these items. The *l*-sound of *ill* is not only longer than the corresponding /l/ of *illegal;* the /l/ of *ill* sounds "dark," almost like an "uh"-sound, while the corresponding /l/ of *illegal* sounds "light" or "clear," like a sound pronounced in the front and not the back of the mouth.)
6. *Lin* + *seed; rancid.* (Which is the longer /n/?)
7. *Book* + *case; hoecake.* (In *book* + *case,* the speaker's tongue remains in the /k/-position a long time, without moving; but hearers usually report not just one *k*-sound but two. We will treat such overlong consonants as double, with open transition between them. Compare the overlong /n/ of *pen-knife,* the overlong /t/ of *rat-trap,* and the overlong /b/ of *scrub-bucket.* The first *k*-sound in *hoecake* is quite short. Do not let the spelling mislead you: there is no *k*-sound in *pen-knife,* and there are two in *hoecake.*)
8. *Row* + *boat; robot.* (What difference in length makes the open transition different from the close?)
9. *Win* + *today; winter day.* (Of the two /n/'s, that in *win* is much the longer. There is a slight puff of breath after the /t/ of *today.* For many speakers, the contrasting /nt/ of *winter* will seem to be "run together" in a very quick sort of "flapped" sound.)
10. *New* + *deal; nude* + *eel.* (There is an open transition in both these items, but at different points. The difference will be clearest in dialects where *news* rhymes with *snooze.* What *is* the main difference?)

The organs of speech

So far, we have said nothing of the way we make our English sounds— nothing of the organs of speech and their uses in speaking. The reason is simple: it is not possible, in the present state of knowledge, to say just how the pitches, terminals, stresses, and transitions are produced. We know, for example, that the diaphragm and the muscles of the chest pump air from the lungs, and we know that we adjust the vocal cords in various ways to control the pitch; but after a few obvious statements like these, we would have to rely on guesses. Of the vowels and consonants, however, the sounds which we will discuss in the following section, we know a good deal more. We know roughly what organs are used, and how they are moved or placed, to make each consonant and each vowel, so that these sounds are best described in terms of their physical production. It is time, therefore, for a brief description of the speech organs.

✢ The larynx

English sounds are normally produced by a stream of air pumped outward from the lungs and modified, in various ways, in its outward pas-

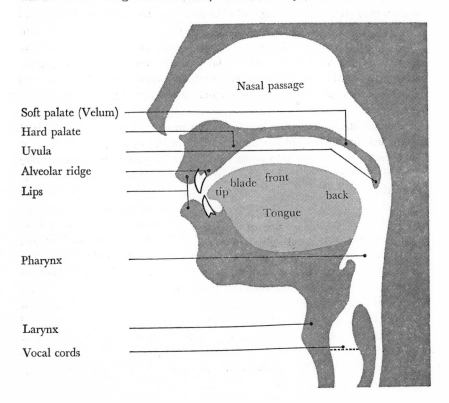

sage. First, at the top of the windpipe, the air passes through the Adam's apple or voice box, technically known as the *larynx*. Inside the larynx are the *vocal cords*, which we have mentioned as essential to the control of pitch. They are a pair of bands which run from front to back along the side walls of the larynx; the opening between them is called the *glottis*. By bringing the vocal cords together, we can completely close the glottis and so cut off the breath stream at that point; by leaving the cords wide apart, we can give the breath free passage; and by bringing the cords almost together, we can set them in vibration in the outward stream of air. This vibration produces the musical hum which is called *voice* and which characterizes all English vowels and some of the English consonants.

❧ The mouth

In the front wall of the throat, above the larynx, there are openings into the mouth and into the nose, through either or both of which the breath may pass. The passage into the nose may be closed by raising and drawing back the *soft palate* or *velum*, the boneless back part of the roof of the mouth; the mouth passage may be closed at various points by movements of the tongue or lips. The resulting sounds are distinguished as *oral*, when the nasal passage is closed, and *nasal*, when it is open. No American English vowels are distinguished by nasality, but some of the consonants are nasal and others oral.

The modifications of the breath stream within the mouth may be best described if we represent the upper surface of the tongue, like the roof of the mouth, as divided into parts from front to back. The area directly behind the *tip* of the tongue may be called the *blade;* it lies below the hard ridge behind the upper front teeth (the *alveolar ridge*). Behind the blade is the *front* of the tongue, beneath the bony *hard palate,* and behind the front of the tongue is the *back,* which is closest to the velum.

The movements of the lower jaw and of the flexible lips and tongue, with its various areas, can narrow, impede, or cut off the breath stream in a number of ways. The lips may be spread wide, or closed, or rounded and protruded; the lower lip may touch or approach the upper front teeth; the tip of the tongue may be placed between the teeth, near or against them, or near or against the alveolar ridge; the blade, front, and back of the tongue may touch or approach the corresponding portions of the roof of the mouth; and the lower jaw may be raised or lowered to different heights. The products of all these articulations are a large number of distinct sounds.

Exercise one. Read the description of the speech organs again. As you reread it, examine your own mouth, nose, and throat with a hand mirror and a small flashlight.

Exercise two. Stop your ears with your fingers, and pronounce first the sound which the letter *f* usually represents, then the sound of the letter *v* (*not* the names of the letters!). Which of the two sounds is distinguished by voice? While you pronounce the *v*, hold your thumb and first finger against your Adam's apple. Can you feel any vibration? Next compare the *v* with the sound (not the name) of the letter *m*. Which sound is nasal? Do you make a nasal or an oral sound when you say *ah* as a doctor examines your throat?

Exercise three. Practice all the movements which are described in the paragraph just preceding this exercise. Watch yourself in the mirror while you do it.

⌇ Describing the consonants

Using our description of the organs of speech and a few bits of incidental information which we will provide as they are needed, we may now assemble a set of terms and distinctions with which to characterize English consonants and vowels.

VOICED AND VOICELESS. For the consonants, we need first the opposition between *voiced* sounds, like the first consonant in *bit,* and *voiceless* sounds, like the first in *pit.* In the production of a voiced sound, the vocal cords vibrate, so that one feature of the sound is the musical hum, or voice, from the larynx; voiceless sounds lack this feature.

NASAL AND ORAL. Second, we need the opposition between *nasal* consonants, in whose production the breath stream passes out through the nose only, and all other consonants, which may be called *oral.* An English consonant may be presumed to be oral unless it is specifically described as nasal; the nasals include the final consonants in *rum, run,* and *rung.*

POINTS OF ARTICULATION. Third, we need terms to indicate the points at which the outgoing breath is stopped or impeded. If the stoppage or impediment is formed by the two lips, we will call the consonant *bilabial* (for example, the *b*-sound in *bin*); if the lower lip touches or approaches the edges of the upper front teeth, the consonant is *labiodental* (the *f*-sound in *fin*); if the tip of the tongue is placed lightly *between* the front teeth, the consonant is *interdental* (the sound represented by *th* in *thin*); the term *dental* is appropriate if the tip of the tongue approaches or touches the *backs* of the front teeth (some kinds of *t*-sound); for an *alveolar* consonant, the tongue tip touches or approaches the hard tooth ridge (the *s*-sound in *sin*); if the front of the tongue nears or touches the hard palate, or if the back of the tongue nears or touches the soft palate, the consonant is *palatal* or *velar,* respectively (the *k*-sounds in *key* and *coo*); if the blade and front of the tongue touch or approach the alveolar ridge and the hard palate, we may use either of the compound names *palato-alveolar* or *alveolo-palatal* (the *sh*-sound in *shin*); and if the stoppage or impediment is at the glottis, we will call the consonant *glottal* (some speakers have a glottal consonant in the middle of the word *bottle*).

KINDS OF ARTICULATION. Fourth, having established terms for the *places* of the obstruction to the breath stream, we need terms for the different *manners* or *kinds* of obstruction: *stop,* if the breath is quite cut off by a complete closure (the first and last consonants of *dot*); *continuant,* if the sound is not momentary, like a stop, but can be continued or prolonged (any of the nasals); *fricative,* for a continuant where the obstruction to the breath creates audible friction (the *s*-sound in *set*); and *affricate,* for a continuant made by opening the closure for a stop so slowly that friction is heard at the widening aperture (the first consonant in *jet*).

Finally, we add the terms *lateral,* for a consonant (the *l*-sound) in whose production a closure along the center line of the tongue allows the breath to escape only over one or both of the tongue's sides, and *retroflex,* for use when the tip of the tongue is turned back toward the roof of the mouth (a common kind of *r*-sound).

SUMMARY. In short, we distinguish among consonants mainly by the presence or absence of voice (*voiced, voiceless*), by the presence or absence of nasality (*nasal, oral*), by the place of the obstruction to the breath stream (*bilabial, labiodental, interdental, dental, alveolar, palatal, velar, palato-alveolar* or *alveolo-palatal, glottal*), and by the manner of the obstruction to the breath (*stop, continuant, fricative, affricate*). To these terms we add *lateral* and *retroflex,* which may be said to indicate both place and manner of obstruction.

Ზ Describing the vowels

To characterize the English vowels, we do not need so many terms. All the English vowels are voiced, oral sounds; and in making them we do not stop the breath stream or hinder it so as to create audible friction, but only narrow it at various points within the mouth or at the lips. We therefore distinguish among the vowels by the place where the breath stream is narrowed, by the extent or degree of that narrowing, and by the presence or absence of lip-rounding. For a *front* vowel, the tongue is bunched up to narrow the breath stream in the front of the mouth; for a *back* vowel, the tongue is bunched up to narrow the breath stream in the back; and for a *central* vowel, the narrowing is neither back nor front but in between. If the tongue is high in the mouth so that the breath stream is narrowed considerably, we have a *high* vowel; if the tongue is low in the mouth, the vowel is *low;* while for a *mid* vowel the tongue is neither high nor low but in a middle position. Finally, vowels marked by rounded lips are called *round,* and those for which the lips are at rest or spread are called *unround.*

Our three sets of labels for vowels are therefore *front* (as in *beet*), *back* (as in *boot*), and *central* (as in *but*); *high* (*sit*), *low* (*sat*), and *mid* (*set*); and *round* (*boat*) and *unround* (*bait*). We will also use the term *diphthong* to indicate a succession of two vowels joined in a single syllable under a single stress by a continuous, smooth glide of the tongue from one vowel position to the other (as in *bite*). If successions of three such vowels occur, they may be called *triphthongs* (sometimes in *our*).

Exercise four. Collect the descriptive terms for English vowels and consonants which we have defined in the last few paragraphs. Write each term, with its definition, on a 3 x 5 card. Alphabetize the cards, and memorize the definitions. Before reading the next section, see if you can provide additional consonants or vowels to illustrate each term.

Vowels and consonants

↻ Sounds and letters

We have said that ordinary writing is in part a representation of speech but that it is not a complete or accurate representation. This statement holds just as good for vowels and consonants as it does for pitches, terminals, stresses, and transitions. Often we use the same letter for different sounds, as in *cat* and *palm, rage* and *want;* and we indicate the same sound by different letters, as in *meat* and *meet, priest* and *key.* To make our discussion of the sounds of English as complete as we need make it, we must now list, illustrate, and label the most important of the

English vowels and consonants; and to make possible a precise representation of those sounds in writing for those occasions when we may need precision, we must match each consonant or vowel with a single letter and each letter with a single consonant or vowel.

We will begin by providing, for each of twenty-four consonants, the single letter which we will always use for that consonant and for no other sound. To get our list of consonants, we make another series of comparisons, much as we did in finding the four stresses. The first part of the word *pill*, for example, is different from the first part of *bill*, and the last part of *pill* is different from the last part of *pit*. By comparing just these three words, we can see that three of our consonants are the sounds which we can most conveniently represent by the letters *p*, *b*, and *l*. We choose these letters because they are often used with these same sound values in ordinary spelling; but since we have more consonants and vowels in English than we have letters in our alphabet, we will sometimes have to adopt letters from other alphabets, or add diacritical marks to familiar letters. Otherwise we cannot establish the one-to-one correspondence of letters and sounds which we need for our more precise way of writing. What we write in that more precise way will be enclosed in slant lines (/ /), so that we will not be misled, in our study of the *sounds* of English, by the peculiarities of English orthography. When we talk about a letter, that letter will be italicized; when we talk about a sound, the letter representing that sound will be placed within the slants. Occasionally, we have already used these conventions as means to the unobtrusive insistence on the distinction between writing and speech.

❧ A list of English consonants

Here, then, are the twenty-four letters for the twenty-four consonants:

1. /p/. The letter *p* will represent the voiceless bilabial stop which is heard at the beginning of the word *pill*, in the middle of the word *rapid*, and at the end of the word *lap*.

2. /t/. The letter *t* will represent the initial consonant in *till*, the medial consonant (there is only one) in *batted*, and the final consonant in *let:* a voiceless dental or alveolar stop.

3. /k/. Initial—*kill;* medial—*backing;* final—*lack*. In ordinary spelling, of course, the two letters *ck* here represent just one sound, a voiceless palatal or velar stop.

4. /b/. *Bill; rabid; lab*. Voiced bilabial stop.

5. /d/. *Dill; ladder; lad*. Voiced dental or alveolar stop.

6. /g/. *Gill; baggy; lag.* Voiced palatal or velar stop.

7. /č/. *Chill; ratchet; latch.* Voiceless palato-alveolar affricate. Three things should be noted here. First, ordinary spelling is again misleading. Second, the tick on top of the *c* is our first diacritical mark. Third, the stretch of speech which we are treating as a single sound and writing with the one letter *č* is often treated as a sequence of *two* sounds: the sound /t/ followed by the initial sound in *show.* If we had chosen to consider this stretch of speech as two sounds, we would of course have had to write it with two letters: *tš.* For the letter *š,* see No. 12 below.

8. /ǰ/. *Jill; ridges; ledge.* Voiced palato-alveolar affricate. In *ledge,* the letters *dge* stand for what we are treating as a single consonant sound and writing with the one letter *ǰ.* It should not be necessary to give further warnings against the peculiarities of ordinary spelling; but it *should* be said that our single sound /ǰ/, like our /č/, is often treated as a sequence and written with two letters such as *dž.* See No. 5 above and No. 16 below.

9. /f/. *Fill; siphon; laugh.* Voiceless labiodental fricative.

10. /θ/. *Thill, thin; pithy; path.* Voiceless dental or interdental fricative. Our letter *θ* is the Greek theta. A thill is a part of a wagon.

11. /s/. *Sill; passing; lass.* Voiceless alveolar fricative.

12. /š/. *Shill, shin; washing; lash.* Voiceless palato-alveolar fricative. Some books use the long *s,* ʃ, for this sound. *Shill* is a gambling term.

13. /v/. *Village; gavel; have.* Voiced labiodental fricative.

14. /ð/. *Then; bathing; bathe.* Voiced dental or interdental fricative. The crossed *d* is an Old English letter; its name, *eth,* is pronounced with the vowel of *pet* followed by the first consonant of *then:* /εð/ in our writing.

15. /z/. *Zeal; lazy; maze.* Voiced alveolar fricative.

16. /ž/. *Jeanne* (for speakers who use the "French" pronunciation of this name); *measure, vision; garage* (for some speakers, who end this word with the sound that regularly occurs in the middle of *measure*). Voiced palato-alveolar fricative, sometimes written with the letter ʒ.

17. /m/. *Mill; hammer; lamb.* Voiced bilabial nasal continuant.

18. /n/. *Nil, kneel; banner; ban.* Voiced alveolar nasal continuant.

19. /ŋ/. This consonant, a voiced velar nasal continuant, does not occur initially in English. It occurs medially in *singer,* finally in *wing.*

20. /l/. *Lit; salad; pal.* Voiced alveolar lateral continuant.
21. /r/. *Rill; mirage; pair.* Commonly a voiced retroflex continuant. Some speakers in the Southeast and some in New England do not have a final /r/.
22. /w/. *Will; away.* This consonant requires special description as a tongue-and-lip glide, usually voiced, from a mid or high back round position to the position of a following vowel. Like the next two consonants, /y/ and /h/, /w/ does not occur, in our analysis, at the end of a word or syllable.
23. /y/. *Yes; beyond.* A voiced glide from a mid or high front unround position to the position of a following vowel. Sometimes written with the letter *j*.
24. /h/. *Hill; ahead.* A glottal fricative, generally voiceless, /h/ might also be defined as a voiceless anticipation of a following vowel or glide.

With these twenty-four letters, the twenty-four principal consonant sounds of English can be represented simply and precisely; native speakers are not likely to have much trouble with the symbols for the consonants.

Exercise one. On each 3 x 5 card of Exercise four, page 41, list now all the consonants that illustrate the technical term on that particular card. Memorize the lists. Some of the terms for vowels will not, of course, be illustrated by consonants.

Exercise two. In the space beside each of the following items, write the symbol for its initial consonant.

1. pig__	17. Mig__	33. chocks__
2. tick__	18. nick__	34. ghost__
3. keg__	19. lick__	35. toast__
4. big__	20. rig__	36. mow__
5. dig__	21. wig__	37. woe__
6. gig__	22. yegg__	38. Joe__
7. chick__	23. hick__	39. threat__
8. jig__	24. box__	40. yet__
9. fig__	25. fox__	41. vet__
10. thick__	26. Cox__	42. that__
11. signal__	27. knocks__	43. shall__
12. ship__	28. hocks__	44. hall__
13. victory__	29. rocks__	45. zero__
14. this__	30. sox__	46. cough__
15. zigzag__	31. docks__	47. through__
16. treasure__	32. locks__	48. though__

Exercise three. In the space beside each of the following items, write the symbol for its medial consonant.

1. ahead__	9. sobbing__	17. itches__
2. battle__	10. rather__	18. legging__
3. badger__	11. penny__	19. mythic__
4. simmer__	12. ringer__	20. vicious__
5. column__	13. berry__	21. acid__
6. lacquer__	14. bewitch__	22. thorough__
7. bosom__	15. jiffy__	23. hiccough__
8. oven__	16. headed__	24. magic__

❧ Some problems with English vowels

The English vowels (like the middle part of *bit*) and diphthongs (like the middle part of *bout*) are harder to describe than the consonants, since in the use of the vowels and diphthongs there are greater differences among speakers of different dialects than there are in the use of the consonants. A Texan, for instance, may not have the same vowel in the word *rock* as an eastern New Englander, and a Chicagoan may not say *news* as an Atlantan does. Moreover, students of English pronunciation disagree in their *analysis* of the vowels and diphthongs. The word *day* provides a simple example. Different students might write it as /de/, /de:/, /dee/, /dei/, or /dey/, making differences in the writing which would not all be due to differences in pronunciation from dialect to dialect. It has not even been proved that a single analysis, or a single kind of analysis, can be used for all the varieties of American speech. Maybe no "overall pattern" of vowels exists in American pronunciation.

We need not concern ourselves very much with these differences in analysis or in dialect, though we cannot ignore them. Using one of the several possible descriptions, we will outline a vowel system for American English, as we outlined systems of pitch and stress, only in enough detail to meet the needs of an elementary grammar.

❧ Short vowels

Probably most native speakers of American English use from seven to ten "short" or "simple" vowels; but in particular dialects one or two of the total number may be rare, and the distribution of the vowels varies markedly from dialect to dialect. That is, in different dialects the same vowels will not always occur in the same words. As a result, there is some difficulty in finding illustrations which will be generally satisfactory throughout the United States, and the student must be prepared to find that some of his classmates distinguish *marry* from *merry* while others do not, that some pronounce *pin* and *pen* in just the same way, that *dog* and *hog* and *fog* may or may not rhyme for a given speaker, etc. If he accepts such differences as perfectly natural among educated Americans, the student can get on with the job of learning how he talks, supplying his own examples in case of need.

FIVE EASY ONES. Most of us can quickly and easily distinguish five of the vowels which we are calling "short." They occur in the words *pit, pet, pat, putt* (or *cut*), and *put*, which we will write (without marking stress, pitch, or terminals here) as follows:

1. /ɪ/—*pit* /pɪt/. To make this vowel, the tongue is bunched up high in the front of the mouth, but not quite so high as it is for the vowel of *peat;* the lips are spread, not pursed or protruded. Thus /ɪ/ may be described as lower high front unround.

2. /ɛ/—*pet* /pɛt/. For this vowel, the tongue is raised to a middle height in the front of the mouth, but remains somewhat lower than for the vowel of *pate;* again there is no rounding of the lips. /ɛ/ differs from /ɪ/, then, primarily in the height of the tongue and may be described as lower mid front unround.

3. /æ/—*pat* /pæt/. From this point on, detailed explanation of the descriptive labels should not be necessary. The vowel /æ/ is low front unround.

4. /ə/—*putt* /pət/, *cut* /kət/. For the mid central unround vowel /ə/, the tongue is close to its position of rest—neither high nor low, neither front nor back. (Some books restrict the use of this symbol to syllables with weakest stress; but the vowel /ə/ actually occurs under all stresses, from weakest to strongest.)

5. /ʊ/—*put* /pʊt/. For /ʊ/, the tongue is bunched up high in the back of the mouth, but not quite so high as for the vowel of *boot;* since the lips are slightly rounded, the proper description is lower high back round.

A SIXTH. Though every native speaker of American English has more than five short vowels, the difficulty of illustration increases beyond this number. In most American speech, a sixth vowel occurs in the word *pot:*

6. /ɑ/—*pot* /pɑt/. Commonly, the vowel of *pot* is low central unround; but many New Englanders will have still another vowel in this word, a low back round (/ɔ/—*pot* /pɔt/), and they will have to look elsewhere for a short vowel "halfway between" their back vowel in *pot*

/pɔt/ and the front /æ/ in *pat* /pæt/. For example, they might find their low central /ɑ/ in the first syllable of *máma*.

A HARD ONE. A seventh short vowel, which we will write /ɨ/, is even harder to illustrate, since it is used in different words in different dialects and since many speakers find it rather difficult to distinguish from the front /ɪ/ of *pit* and the back /ʊ/ of *put:*

7. /ɨ/—*just*, adverb /jɨst/. For /ɨ/, the lips are spread, and the tongue is bunched up relatively high in the mouth, but neither pushed to the front nor pulled to the back. The word in which this high central un-round vowel is most likely to be heard is our adverb *just*, as in the sentence *He's just come* (contrast the /ɪ/ of *gist* in *the gist of it*). If we say *just* by itself, we usually pronounce it /jəst/, with the mid central vowel of *cut;* but if we put it into our sentence, we often do say /jɨst/, with the high vowel halfway between the vowels of *pit* /pɪt/ and *put* /pʊt/. Writers of dialect stories sometimes indicate the pronunciation /jɨst/ with the spelling *jist*, but it is not a vulgar or illiterate pronunciation; it is common among highly educated people. In the Southeastern states, /ɨ/ frequently occurs in a number of other words, such as *children, dinner, milk, pillow,* and *wish.* In that area, moreover, the words *bilious, city,* and *filling* will have /ɪ/ in their stressed syllables; *pillar, sitter,* and *filler* are likely to have /ɨ/; *and buller, sooty* (sometimes), and *fuller* will have /ʊ/; so that the contrast among the three vowels can be clearly heard. Speakers who make the contrast in this way may also distinguish *lyric*, with /ɪ/, from *jury*, with /ɨ/. Speakers in other parts of the United States may perhaps find /ɨ/ most easily in syllables with weakest stress; the second syllable of *roses* commonly has /ɨ/, which is different from the /ə/ in the second syllable of *Rosa's*.

NUMBER EIGHT. Our comment on the pronunciation of words like *pot* in some sections of New England has already indicated one region where an eighth vowel may occur:

8. /ɔ/—New England *pot* /pɔt/, low back round.

AND NINE. In the old-fashioned New England pronunciation of *home, road, stone,* and *whole,* a ninth vowel may be heard:

9. /o/—Old-fashioned New England *home* /hom/, mid back round. Other dialects often have this ninth vowel in *gonna* /gonə/, as in the sentence *I'm gonna tell my daddy.* For some speakers, however, seven or eight short vowels apparently exhaust the list; and for many, our eighth and ninth vowels, /ɔ/ and /o/, may not be distinguished at all. Speakers who keep *horse* and *hoarse* apart do commonly have /ɔ/ as

the first vowel of a diphthong in *horse* /hɔərs/ or /hɔəs/, and /o/ similarly in *hoarse* /hoərs/ or /hoəs/. For these people, *war* and *wore*, *morning* and *mourning*, will be distinguished in the same way: *war* with /ɔə/, *wore* with /oə/, etc. Southeastern speakers sometimes have /oə/ in *pork* /poək/ and /oɪ/ in *porch* /poɪč/, pronounced as if it were spelled *poych;* contrasting words with /ɔ/, for these speakers, will be *cork* /kɔək/ and *scorch* /skɔɪč/. Other words in which the difference between /ɔ/ and /o/ is sometimes heard, in various parts of the United States, are *angora, boric, chloroform, Cora, Flora,* and *oral* (all with /o/), but *aural, aureate, aurochs,* and *warrior* (all with /ɔ/).

SUMMARY. In these words or others, many Americans, with enough patience, can find the /ɔ/—/o/ distinction in their own speech; but the student should not assume that he *must* have any one given number of short vowels—seven, eight, nine, ten, or more, or less. If Southeasterners are likely to have ten, many Midwesterners are likely to have just seven or eight: 1. *pit* /pɪt/; 2. *pet* /pɛt/; 3. *pat* /pæt/; 4. *cut* /kət/; 5. *put* /pʊt/; 6. *pot* /pɑt/; 7. *just,* adverb /jɨst/, the second syllable of *roses* —/ɨz/ (if /ɪ/ is treated as a separate vowel, as it probably should be); 8. *one* other vowel where other dialects may have the two, /ɔ/ in *aural* and /o/ in *oral.* The Midwestern eighth vowel may conveniently be written /o/, although this writing should not suggest a contrast with /ɔ/ if none exists.

FOOTNOTE FOR REBELS. The Southeastern tenth vowel should not be overlooked. It frequently occurs in words like *fire* and may be written /a/:

10. /a/—Southeastern *fire* /faə/, *hire* /haə/, *tire* /taə/, etc. Readers familiar with such pronunciations will recognize /a/ as a low, unround vowel. It is front, but not quite so far front as the /æ/ of *pat:* to make /a/, the tongue is pulled back a little from the front position for /æ/ toward the central position for the /ɑ/ of *pot.* A convenient description for /a/, then, is low front unround, somewhat retracted.

Exercise four. Study the following table of ten short vowels and the illustrations which follow it. After each symbol, a convenient name for it is given in quotation marks; learn these names so that you can use them in talking about pronunciation.

/ɪ/ "*i*"	/ɨ/ "barred *i*"	/ʊ/ "*u*"
/ɛ/ "*e*"	/ə/ "schwa" (rhymes with *pa*)	/o/ "close *o*"
/æ/ "digraph"	/ɑ/ "*a*"	/ɔ/ "open *o*"
/a/ "Confederate *a*"		

/ɪ/—*bit, fit, hit*
/ɛ/—*bet, let, met*
/æ/—*bat, fat, hat*
/a/—as first vowel in the diphthong /aə/ in *fire, hire, tire,* etc. (for some Southeasterners)
/ɨ/—commonly in the *just* of *He's just come;* in the unstressed syllables in *roses, bushes, bridges,* etc. (for many speakers); in the stressed syllables in *children, dinner, filler, jury, milk, minnow, pillar, pillow, river, silk, sitter, wish* (for some speakers, especially in the Southeast)
/ə/—*but, hut, nut*
/ɑ/—*pot, hot, lot* (for most Americans outside New England); in the stressed syllables in *máma, pápa*
/ʊ/—*put, bull, full*
/o/—old-fashioned New England *home, road, stone, whole; gonna* (often); *angora, boric, chloroform, Cora, Flora, oral* (sometimes); in the diphthong /oə/ in *hoarse, mourning, pork, wore* (for speakers who distinguish *hoarse* from *horse*); in the diphthong /oɪ/ in *porch* (for some Southeasterners)
/ɔ/—*pot* (in some New England speech); *aural, aureate, aurochs, warrior* (sometimes); in the diphthong /ɔə/ in *cork, horse, morning, war* (for speakers who distinguish *horse* from *hoarse*); in the diphthong /ɔɪ/ in *gorge, George, scorch* (for some Southeasterners)

Exercise five. Study the following vowel chart:

	Front	Central	Back
High	/ɪ/	/ɨ/	/ʊ/
Mid	/ɛ/	/ə/	/o/
Low	/æ/ /a/	/ɑ/	/ɔ/
	Unround		*Round*

If you do not clearly remember what the labels mean, review Exercise four, page 41.

Exercise six. Try to find series like *bit-bet-bat, roses-Rosa's,* and *aural-oral* which will show all the contrasts among the short vowels in your own dialect. Compare your list with a list made by a friend from a different part of the country.

Exercise seven. Using the vowel and consonant symbols which we have established so far, transcribe the following items:

1. Philip /_____/
2. then /_____/
3. fraction /_____/
4. children /_____/
5. hiccough /_____/

6. mama /_____/
7. bulrush /_____/
8. gonna /_____/
9. forest /_____/
10. badges /_____/

❧ Long vowels and diphthongs

So far, we have dealt only with vowels which we have called "short" or "simple." We have said little or nothing about the "long" vowels, as in *beet* and *boot,* or the diphthongs, as in *bite* and *bout,* or the possible triphthongs, as sometimes in *fire, our,* or *trial.* No generally accepted analysis of these sounds has yet been made, as we saw when we listed different respellings of the word *day:* /de/, /de:/, /dee/, /dei/, /dey/.

Some students treat the so-called long vowels, and even the diphthongs, as single sounds, just as they treat the vowels of *pit* and *pet* as single sounds. For such students, the vowel of *day* is a unit, and so are those parts of *beet* and *boot, bite* and *bout* which come between the initial /b/ and the final /t/. The respellings /de/ and /de:/, with a single letter, *e,* for the vowel, usually indicate that the vowel is being treated as a single sound, which the colon marks as long. Other students, who treat the long vowels and diphthongs as sequences of *two* sounds, write /dee/, /dei/, or /dey/, representing the two sounds by two letters. The different spellings show that these students do not all agree on the identity of the second sound, which some consider a consonant, /y/, and others a vowel, /i/. Finally, some students believe that a word like *day* has a unit vowel, which they generally write with one letter, but that a word like *bite* should be written with four letters, perhaps as /bait/ or /bayt/, to indicate that there are two sounds between the /b/ and the /t/.

Thus the long vowels and diphthongs may be treated as units (one sound each), or as sequences (two sounds each), or some in one way and some in the other; and if any of them are treated as sequences, the student must decide, in each case, whether the second sound in the sequence shall be treated as a vowel or as a consonant.

DISTINCTIONS OF LENGTH. Part of the difficulty is that not all the "long" vowels are distinguished from the corresponding "short" vowels in the same way. Sometimes the distinction is quite literally the distinction between long and short. In some dialects, for example, the stressed vowel of *father* is just like the stressed vowel of *fodder,* but longer: *father* has the long vowel, /ɑ:/, and *fodder* has the short vowel, /ɑ/. Similar pairs, in one dialect or another, would include the following:

SHORT VOWEL	LONG VOWEL
bombing /bɑmɪn/	*balmy* /bɑ:mɪ/ (no /l/)
comic /kɑmɪk/	*calming* /kɑ:mɪn/ (no /l/)
Commie /kɑmɪ/	*Carmen* /kɑ:mɪn/ (no /r/)

SHORT VOWEL	LONG VOWEL
sorry /sɑrɪ/	*starry* /stɑːrɪ/
sovereign /sɑvrɪn/	*solving* /sɑːvɪn/ (no /l/)

The contrasting pairs are not limited to short /ɑ/ and long /ɑː/. Some Southeasterners, including the writer of this book, also contrast short /æ/ with long /æː/:

SHORT VOWEL	LONG VOWEL
Alice /ælɪs/	*alleys* /æːlɪz/
avid /ævɪd/	*lavish* /læːvɪš/
cavil /kævəl/	*cavern* /kyæːvən/ (no /r/)
Hallie /hælɪ/	*galley* /gyæːlɪ/
having /hævɪn/	*tavern* /tæːvən/ (no /r/)
laggard /lægəd/ (no /r/)	*lagger* /læːgə/ (no /r/)
mallet /mælɪt/	*valley* /væːlɪ/

In the same dialect, short /ə/ and long /əː/ are opposed:

SHORT VOWEL	LONG VOWEL
bub /bəb/	*bulb* /bəːb/ (no /l/)
bud /bəd/	*burred* /bəːd/ (no /r/)
stirrup /stərəp/	*stirring* /stəːrɪn/
stud /stəd/	*stirred* /stəːd/ (no /r/)

These pairs, and a good many others like them, prove that sometimes the distinction between a long and a short vowel is simply length; the two vowels sound alike, but one is longer than the other.

OTHER DISTINCTIONS. Sometimes, however, the difference between so-called long and short vowels is *not* primarily a difference in length; the two vowels are not opposed just as long and short varieties of the same sound. Thus the vowel of *beat* is not a mere lengthening of the vowel of *bit,* and the vowel of *pool* is not a lengthening of the vowel of *pull.* On the contrary, the vowels of *beat* and *pool* differ from those in *bit* and *pull* not just in quantity but in quality, in the very nature of the sounds. *Beat* and *pool* have higher vowels, for one thing, than *bit* and *pull.*

Some of the vowels which are called long are not indeed "pure" sounds at all. Many speakers pronounce the word *day,* for instance, with something like the vowel of *bet* (/ɛ/) followed by a gliding movement of the tongue which makes a sound like the vowel of *bit* (/ɪ/). This is why *day* may be respelled as /dei/ or /dey/ by students who do not distinguish between long vowels and diphthongs but treat them both as sequences.

OUR METHOD. Admitting the difficulties, in this book we will recognize both long vowels (treated as units) and diphthongs (treated as sequences of two vowels). The first vowel in a diphthong may be either short or long. We will ignore possible triphthongs in our elementary discussion.

A LIST OF LONG VOWELS. Some of the commonest long vowels, which we will mark with colons to distinguish them from the short vowels, may be illustrated by the following words:

1. Short vowel: lower high front unround /ɪ/, as in *bit, bid.*
   Long vowel: high front unround /i:/, as in *beat, feed, heat, mead, seat.*
2. Short vowel: lower mid front unround /ɛ/, as in *bet, bed.*
   Long vowel: mid front unround /e:/, as in *bait, fade, gate, hate, made.*
3. Short vowel: lower high back round /ʊ/, as in *pull, put.*
   Long vowel: high back round /u:/, as in *boot, food, hoot, mood, pool.*
4. Short vowel: mid back round /o/. For examples, see pp. 47–49.
   Long vowel: long mid back round /o:/, as in *boat, goat, mode, note, pole.*
5. Short vowel: low back round /ɔ/. For examples, see pp. 47–49.
   Long vowel: long low back round /ɔ:/, as (in some dialects) in *bought, fought, Maud, nought, Paul.*

Though these are perhaps the commonest long vowels, at least three others occur, as we have pointed out, in one or more American dialects (/æ:/, /ə:/, /ɑ:/). The long mid central vowel /ə:/ is actually not uncommon in words spelled with *er, ir,* or *ur,* like *herd, bird, furred.* These may be transcribed, for some dialects where /r/ is pronounced after a vowel and before a consonant, as /hə:rd/, /bə:rd/, /fə:rd/, and for some dialects where /r/ is not pronounced in those positions, as /hə:d/, /bə:d/, /fə:d/. The long /ə:r/ or /ə:/ is different from the short /ər/ or /ə/ in the second syllable of a word like *mother.* Other pronunciations for *herd, bird, furred* are /ər/, /ɨr/, and also /ɨ:r/ or /ɨ:/. The last two pronunciations illustrate still another long vowel.

THREE SETS OF DIPHTHONGS. Most diphthongs may be said to consist of a short vowel followed by an /ɪ/, /ə/, or /ʊ/. Diphthongs whose second vowel is /ɪ/ include /ɑɪ/ or /aɪ/, /ʊɪ/, and /ɔɪ/ or /oɪ/, which many speakers use in the following sets of words: /ɑɪ/ or /aɪ/ in *buy, fight, guide, height, sign;* /ʊɪ/ in *buoy, ruin, suet;* /ɔɪ/ or /oɪ/ in *boy, coin, Hoyt, joy, toyed.* In the next two sets, many speakers use diphthongs whose second vowel is /ʊ/: /ɪʊ/ or /ɨʊ/ in *dew, feud, Hugh, new, tune;* /ɑʊ/ or /aʊ/ in *bough, cowed, down, gout, now.* Diphthongs whose second vowel is /ə/ occur most frequently in words which are spelled with an *r*, whether or not an /r/ is actually pronounced. In various dialects, at least seven diphthongs of this type occur: /ɪə/ in *beard, beer, dear, feared, gear;* /ɛə/ or /æə/ in *air, bared, care, fared, scare;* /ɑə/ in *are, barred, car, far, scar;* /ʊə/ in *boor, moored, poor;* /oə/ in *bored, core, door, soared, wore;* /ɔə/ in *for, or, ward, war.*

Obviously, no one speaker will have all these long vowels and diphthongs or have them in just the words which we have chosen as illustrations. Some will have /ɔɪ/ not /ʊɪ/ in *buoy;* some will pronounce *new* and *tune* not with a diphthong but with the long vowel, /u:/, of *noose* and *noon;* some will have /ɛə/ and others /æə/ in *air*, etc.; many will not distinguish *wore* from *war*. From time to time, however, everyone will *hear* all the long vowels and diphthongs which we have listed, even if he does not use them all himself; and a good listener will hear even more, such as the diphthongs /əɪ/ and /əʊ/ in some pronunciations of *wife* and *house*. Our list is not meant to be exhaustive.

LONG DIPHTHONGS. Two additions will make it full enough for our purposes. In some dialects there are not only diphthongs whose first vowels are short but diphthongs whose first vowels are long. Two of the clearest examples are /i:ə/ and /e:ə/, which sometimes occur in items like the following: /i:ə/ in *eon* (or *Ian*), *see 'em, see 'er, via, we're;* /e:ə/ in *gayer, layer, mayor, player, slayer.* Since some speakers who use these pronunciations will not rhyme *we're* with *weir* (a dam) or *mayor* with *care* or *mare,* and since *we're, weir, mayor, care,* and *mare* may all have the same number of syllables, our system must include long diphthongs as well as long vowels.

OUR SYSTEM ILLUSTRATED. We can now illustrate the full range of the system (possible triphthongs excepted) by two sets of contrasting forms, drawn from the writer's Southeastern dialect where /r/ does not occur before consonants or at the ends of words:
1. Short vowel /ɪ/: *bid, hip, limb, pin, sit*
   Long vowel /i:/: *bead, gleam, heap, peat, sea*
   Short diphthong /ɪə/: *beard, idea, seer, veer, weir*
   Long diphthong /i:ə/: *eon, see 'em, see 'er, via, we're*
   Short vowel /ɪ/ before /r/ and another vowel: *cereal, irrigate, lyric, period, satiric*
   Long vowel /i:/ before /r/ and another vowel: *Erie, hero, Nero, series, zero*
   Short diphthong /ɪə/ before /r/ and another vowel: *cheery, clearer, dearest, fearing, peering*

2. Short vowel /ɛ/: *bed, let, met, net, pep*
   Long vowel /e:/: *bayed, fame, grape, late, may*
   Short diphthong /ɛə/: *cared, hear, here, ne'er-do-well, scared*
   Long diphthong /e:ə/: *gayer, layer, mayor, player, slayer*
   Short vowel /ɛ/ before /r/ and another vowel: *berry, ferry, heron, merry, terror*
   Long vowel /e:/ before /r/ and another vowel: *dairy, Gary, Mary, prairie, vary*
   Short diphthong /ɛə/ before /r/ and another vowel: *caring, hearing, scaring.*

The great advantage of an analysis which recognizes long and short vowels and long and short diphthongs is precisely that it gives us the means of recording and describing such forms as these. Simpler and more elegant systems have been constructed, but are untrue to the enormous variety of American speech. Our analysis is complicated—for some dialects, unnecessarily complicated; but probably there is not much in the speech of any American which cannot be described by this or a similar method.

Exercise eight. Study the following table of common long vowels, short diphthongs, and long diphthongs. Learn the names of the long vowels. You can then call any diphthong by the names of its two vowels; for example, /ʊɪ/ "short *ui*." Note that the position of items on the page indicates their articulatory position on the chart of Exercise five.

Long vowels
/i:/ "long *i*"   /u:/ "long *u*"
/e:/ "long *e*"   /o:/ "long close *o*"
                                                    /ɔ:/ "long open *o*"
Short diphthongs ending in /ɪ/
                                                    /ʊɪ/
                                                    /oɪ/
                    /aɪ/   /ɑɪ/   /ɔɪ/
Short diphthongs ending in /ʊ/
/ɪʊ/   /ɨʊ/
                    /aʊ/   /ɑʊ/
Short diphthongs ending in /ə/
/ɪə/   /ʊə/
/ɛə/   /oə/
/æə/   /ɑə/   /ɔə/
Long diphthongs
/i:ə/
/e:ə/

Exercise nine. Pronounce the following items. Write them in ordinary spelling.

1. /³fí:t¹↘/ _____
2. /³dé:t¹↘/ _____
3. /³bú:t¹↘/ _____
4. /³kó:t¹↘/ _____
5. /³tɔ́:t¹↘/ _____

6. /³pám¹↘/ _____
7. /³rúm¹↘/ _____
8. /³čɔ́ɪs¹↘/ _____
9. /³gáʊt¹↘/ _____
10. /³jíʊn¹↘/ _____

Exercise ten. Pronounce the two following sets of items just as they are transcribed. The first set might be heard in parts of the Middle West, the second in parts of the Southeast. For some items, variant pronunciations are given within a single set.

1. *beer* /³bíər¹↘/
2. *air* /³ɛ́ər¹↘/
3. *air* /³ǽər¹↘/
4. *are* /³d́ər¹↘/
5. *poor* /³púər¹↘/
6. *wore* /³wóər¹↘/
7. *we're* /³wí:ər¹↘/
8. *they're* /³ðé:ər¹↘/
9. *bird* /³bɔ́:rd¹↘/

1. *ear* /³íə¹↘/
2. *ere* /³ɛ́ə¹↘/
3. *air* /³ǽə¹↘/
4. *ire* /³áə¹↘/
5. *poor* /³púə¹↘/
6. *ore* /³óə¹↘/
7. *or* /³ɔ́ə¹↘/
8. *bur* /³bɔ́:¹↘/
9. *are* /³á:¹↘/
10. *we're* /³wí:ə¹↘/
11. *they're* /³ðé:ə¹↘/

Exercise eleven. Transcribe the following items as you pronounce them. Use the intonation pattern (/³¹↘/) of Exercises nine and ten. Be sure to mark the stresses on all items.

1. hit	9. mutt	17. woo	25. due	33. out
2. heat	10. our	18. poor	26. louse	34. turn
3. beer	11. pot	19. joke	27. mountain	35. suet
4. bet	12. mama	20. soy	28. pass	36. home
5. bait	13. sight	21. store	29. chair	37. oral
6. there	14. shout	22. aural	30. moon	38. yaw
7. bat	15. tar	23. Roy	31. bee	39. horse
8. dinner	16. full	24. cawed	32. third	40. gore

Note: In transcribing the unstressed syllables of words like *dinner, mother, bothered,* etc., most speakers should use /ər/ if they have a final and preconsonantal /r/, and /ə/ if they have no /r/ in these positions. In transcribing words like *third* and *turn,* more difficulty may be encountered. Either these words will contain an /r/, or they will not. The vowel will usually be either mid central or high central (though some /r/-less dialects will have a diphthong, /ɚɪ/). And the vowel in /r/-ful dialects may be either short (/ər/, /ɪr/), or long (/ə:r/, /ɪ:r/). Those /r/-pronouncing speakers who contrast short and long vowels in pairs like *sorry* (/ɑ/) and *starry* (/ɑ:/), *hurry* (/ə/) and *furry* (/ə:/), should normally write a long vowel; speakers with no such contrasts should normally write a short vowel. The commonest American pronunciations are probably /θə:rd/, /tə:rn/, etc.

Summary

Though writing is derived from speech and is in part a representation of speech, conventional English writing is by no means a complete and accurate representation. Since a knowledge of the distinctive sounds of English is the essential foundation for a discussion of the rest of English grammar, we must not only learn what those sounds are but devise or adopt a system of writing which will represent them precisely.

In our analysis, the distinctive *pitches* and *terminals* of English compose its *intonation patterns*. We have recognized four pitches: /¹/ (lowest), /²/, /³/, and /⁴/ (highest). We have recognized three terminals: /↗/ is marked by a slight rise in pitch, not enough to reach the next higher pitch level; /→/ is marked by reduced loudness and reduced speed, with no change in pitch; /↘/ is marked by a quick dying away of the voice.

We have recognized four *stresses* and one open *transition*. The stresses may be called *strongest* (/´/), *second* (/ˆ/), *third* (/ˋ/), and *weakest* stress (/˘/). Open transition (/+/) occurs mostly between words or between two meaningful parts of a single word; but it does not always occur where we write spaces or a hyphen in ordinary spelling, and sometimes it is heard where the letters of ordinary spelling are written side by side with nothing between them.

Our list of distinctive sounds in the various dialects of American English also includes twenty-four *consonants;* a varying number of *short vowels,* usually from seven to ten; a varying number of *long vowels,* of which most dialects have five or more; and a considerably larger number of *diphthongs.* The diphthongs consist of a vowel, short or long, followed by /ɪ/, /ʊ/, or /ə/. The long diphthongs are not so numerous as the short diphthongs, which may amount to ten or more in a single dialect. The consonants and vowels, and hence the diphthongs, may be conveniently described by reference to the movements of the vocal organs which produce them.

Bibliography

BLOCH, BERNARD, and GEORGE L. TRAGER, *Outline of Linguistic Analysis*. Baltimore: Linguistic Society of America, 1942. Ch. ii, "Phonetics," pp. 10–37; Ch. iii, "Phonemics," pp. 38–52.

FRANCIS, W. NELSON, *The Structure of American English*. New York: The Ronald Press Company, 1958. Ch. ii, "The Sounds of Speech: Phonetics," pp. 51–118; Ch. iii, "The Significant Sounds of Speech: Phonemics," pp. 119–161.

GLEASON, H. A., JR., *An Introduction to Descriptive Linguistics*. New York: Henry Holt and Company, 1955. Ch. ii, "English Consonants," pp. 14–26; Ch. iii, "The English Vowel System," pp. 27–39; Ch. iv, "English Stress and Intonation," pp. 40–50; Ch. xvi, "Interpretations of English Phonemics," pp. 221–237.

HILL, ARCHIBALD A., *Introduction to Linguistic Structures*. New York: Harcourt, Brace and Company, 1958. Ch. ii, "Stress, Juncture, Pitch," pp. 13–30; Ch. iii, "Consonants," pp. 31–46; Ch. iv, "Phoneme and Allophone," pp. 47–61; Ch. v, "Vowels and Vowel Nuclei," pp. 62–67.

HOCKETT, CHARLES F., *A Course in Modern Linguistics*. New York: The Macmillan Company, 1958. "Signalling via Sound: Phonology," pp. 15–119; Ch. 40, "American English Stressed Syllabics," pp. 339–350.

KENYON, JOHN S., *American Pronunciation,* 10th ed. Ann Arbor: George Wahr, 1951.

THOMAS, CHARLES K., *An Introduction to the Phonetics of American English,* 2d ed. New York: The Ronald Press Company, 1958.

TRAGER, GEORGE L., and HENRY LEE SMITH, JR., *An Outline of English Structure*. Norman, Okla.: Battenburg Press, 1951. Part I, "Phonology," pp. 11–52.

Note: The interpretation of the English sound system in the present book combines and modifies two main traditions, one represented by Kenyon and Thomas, the other by Bloch, Trager, and Smith. Francis, Gleason, Hill, and Hockett follow the latter tradition, as this book does too in its treatment of stress and pitch. There is general agreement concerning the consonants, but analyses of the vowels differ rather widely, as the preceding chapter has indicated. The analysis here given is closest to Kenyon's.

CHAPTER TWO Parts
of Speech

Methods

❧ The familiar definitions

We have all been told at one time or another that there are eight parts of speech: noun, pronoun, verb, adverb, adjective, preposition, conjunction, and interjection. Some of us have probably spent a good deal of time learning the familiar definitions:

"A noun is the name of a person, place, or thing.

"A pronoun is a word that takes the place of a noun.

"An adjective is a word that modifies a noun or pronoun.

"A verb is a word that expresses action, being, or condition.

"An adverb is a word that modifies a verb, an adjective, or another adverb.

"A preposition is a word that shows the relationship between its object and some other word in the sentence.

"A conjunction is a word that connects words, phrases, or clauses.

"An interjection is a word that expresses strong feeling."

Using these definitions, we have probably been asked to mark the parts of speech in numerous sentences, and we may actually have developed considerable skill in such exercises. Our natural reaction is to accept the traditional terms and their definitions and to leave well enough alone.

AN EXERCISE IN FUTILITY. Unfortunately, if we really want to understand our language and the way it works, we cannot take this comfortable line of least resistance. The familiar definitions are definitions that do not define. Suppose we accept the statement that a preposition is a word showing the relationship between its object and some other word in the sentence. Then we are given the sentence, *I dislike John,* and we are asked to tell what part of speech *dislike* is. Quite logically, we can say that *dislike* is a preposition, because it shows the relationship between *John,* its object, and another word in the sentence, *I;* yet if we call *dislike* a preposition, disaster awaits us. We must say that *dislike* is a verb; it expresses action, being, or condition.

Suppose we accept that definition of a verb and proceed to compare two sentences which mean roughly the same thing:

The good news made us rejoice.

The good news made us joyful.

If *rejoice* is a verb (an "unmarked infinitive"), as our dictionaries and grammars instruct us to call it, how shall we classify *joyful?* It expresses condition, but we will certainly be told that it is an adjective and no verb.

Giving up the verb as a bad job, we go on to the conjunction, which "connects words, phrases, or clauses." Two very easy sentences land us in total confusion:

> He went to Chicago.
>
> The man who went to Chicago regretted it.

In the first sentence, we will not be allowed to call *to* a conjunction, al-though it certainly connects *went* and *Chicago;* and in the second sen-tence, we cannot call *who* a conjunction, although it connects two clauses. *To* is a preposition, we will be reminded, and *who* a relative pronoun.

(**ɪ**) SHIFTINESS OF THE OLD DEFINITIONS. Hard as the statement may seem, the traditional definitions plainly do not enable us to classify our words as belonging to one part of speech rather than another. For one thing, definitions like that of the noun are in terms of meaning, while others, like that of the pronoun, are in terms of function or use. Nouns and verbs are defined by what they mean, but the other parts of speech (except the in-terjection, which really does not fit into the system) are defined by what they do—ultimately by what they do with respect to nouns and verbs. This difference in the principle of classification causes some of our trouble. If we stick to meaning in our definitions, shall we say that *red* is a noun, because it is the name of a color? Certainly it is a noun in a phrase like *the hectic red of the autumn leaves;* but in the sentence,

> The red book is on the table,

most of us will want to say that *red* is an adjective. Here use determines meaning, and it might seem simpler to define the parts of speech directly in terms of their use than indirectly in terms of the meanings which that use determines.

(**2**) THEIR VAGUENESS. Turning to the definition of the pronoun, however, we see that even when the traditional definitions are based on use, they are not really satisfactory. In the following sentences, it would be very hard to say what words should be called pronouns because they "take the place of nouns":

> *I* hope *you* understand.
>
> *It* is hard to define these things.
>
> The detective learned *what* he wanted to know.
>
> From *here* to New York is a thousand miles.

In the first sentence, for example, what nouns do *I* and *you* take the place of; and in the second, what noun could stand where *it* stands? The defi-nition fails, not because it is based on use, but because it is too vague.

A second objection, then, to the old definitions is that they do not state either meaning or use clearly enough. Whether we take the definition of an interjection to be in terms of use or in terms of meaning, it is so broad that words of any class can be called interjections (*Rats! Broken! Quick! Here!*). Similarly, the definition of the adverb, which is based on use, does not allow us to exclude *Orion* from the class of adverbs in the sentence,

> I see Orion.

Orion "modifies" *see*, as we can tell by dropping *Orion* from the sentence and comparing simple *I see* with *I see Orion*. The presence of the direct object clearly modifies the meaning of the verb, but direct objects, we have been taught, are not adverbs.

NEGLECT OF FORM. A third difficulty with the usual definitions is even more serious: they neglect form for meaning, although it is precisely through the *form* of our words and sentences that we communicate our meanings. An imaginary sentence will clarify this objection immediately. If someone walked up to us and said in a loud, clear voice,

> ^{2}Hĕ + blûrped + ^{3}smítchlў^1↘

and if he continued his odd behavior by asking us what part of speech *blurped* is and when the blurping took place, we would all be able to answer him. We would say that *blurped* is a verb in the past tense and that the blurping took place in past time. We would say so, not because we know the meaning of *blurped* and *smitchly*, but because we recognize such familiar forms of our language as the "*-ed* ending" and the suffix *-ly*.

We cannot accept definitions which neglect these all-important formal signs. We must simply face the fact that our familiar schoolroom grammar needs drastic modification and try to frame definitions of the parts of speech which will be genuinely useful.

Exercise one. To what parts of speech would you assign the italicized words in the following nonsense sentences?

1. ^{2}Hĕ + gâve + thĕ + ^{3}téachĕr$^{2\rightarrow 2}$ă + *blân* + ^{3}ápplĕ^1↘
   ^{2}Thĕ + ^{3}ápplĕ$^{2\rightarrow 2}$wăs + ^{3}*blánnĕr*$^{2\rightarrow 2}$thàn + thĕ + ^{3}órănge^1↘

2. ^{3}Yéstĕrdày^2↗^{2}Í + câught + ă + ^{3}*rónk*^{1}↘
   ^{2}Nò + ^{3}óthĕr + *rônks*^{2}↗^{2}wĕre + ^{3}cáught^1↘

3. ^{2}Thĕ + ^{2}rónk$^{2\rightarrow 2}$*gróoled* + ănd + ^{3}*grábbĕred*^{1}↘
   ^{2}Fŏr + âll + ^{3}Í + knôw^2↗^{2}hè's + *grábbĕring* + ^{3}stíll^1↘

Exercise two. On the basis of the preceding sentences, what endings would you feel free to add to the words *blan, ronk,* and *grabber?*

Exercise three. For each italicized word in each sentence, list five real English words which could replace it. So in the first sentence, *red* could replace *blan.*

✺ Words and their parts

Since the first parts of speech which we will define are classes of *words,* we must begin our process of definition with the term *word* itself; but we will not attempt a rigidly scientific statement. Instead, we will look briefly at a few examples.

THE "-FIXES." In the following sentences, most of us would agree that *ùnkíndnĕss* and *kíndnĕssĕs* are words:

His ùnkíndnĕss angered her.

He did her many kíndnĕssĕs.

Comparing the two words, we note that -*kíndnĕss*- is common to both, that *ùnkíndnĕss* contains one form, *un*-, which is not in *kíndnĕssĕs,* that *kíndnĕssĕs* contains one form, -*es,* which is not in *ùnkíndnĕss,* and that each word, in isolation, has its distinctive stress pattern. The form *un*-, we can agree, is a *prefix,* -*es* is a *suffix,* and the stress patterns may be called *superfixes.* Prefixes, suffixes, and superfixes of this sort are not words, but parts of words.

PREFIXES. In English, the parts of words which we call prefixes could be defined by listing, although the list would be rather long. On it we would find *un*-, *con*-, *pre*-, *dis*-, *in*-, *ex*-, *re*-, and many other familiar forms which we have used or will use in these pages. Examining these items, we would discover that they share many distinctive characteristics. Thus, two or more prefixes may occur in sequence, as *un*- and -*im*- do in *ùnìmpréssed;* but when they do, they occur in a fixed order, and *all* prefixes will precede such forms as -*press* and *kínd.* The distribution of prefixes is further limited in other ways. Though *un*- and *in*-, for example, mean much the same thing, native speakers of modern English regularly say *ùnkínd* but *ìncéssănt;* and they would reject *ùncéssănt* and *ìnkínd* as "odd" or "not English." Most notably, except as names for themselves in linguistic discussion, prefixes usually do not occur alone (as "free forms") or directly before suffixes like the -*ness* of *ùnkíndnĕss* or the -*es* of *kíndnĕssĕs.* Even in a grammar where *pre*- and *un*- may stand alone as items on a list, we will hardly find a noun *únnĕss* or a plural *prés.*

TWO KINDS OF SUFFIX. Distribution, it would appear, the positions in which a form stands with respect to other forms, is the best criterion for determining whether or not a form is a prefix; "what goes with what" is a basic question for the student of language. Applying this criterion to the two *suffixes* in our initial examples, *ùnkíndnéss* and *kíndnĕssĕs,* we can see at once that not all suffixes occur in the same positions. As the prefix *un-* stands before the prefix *-im-* in *ùnimprésséd,* so the suffix *-ness-* precedes the *-es* in *kíndnĕssĕs.* This difference will help us to divide suffixes into two groups, *derivational* and *inflectional.*

Like prefixes, the members of both groups could be exhaustively listed; but again listing would be less helpful than analysis. Both groups follow forms like *-press-* and *kínd,* are more or less limited in their distribution with respect to the forms that precede them, and usually do not occur as free forms or directly after prefixes. For instance, of the limited number of suffixes which make nouns from adjectives, we add *-th* /θ/ to *trúe* (*trúth*) but *-ness* to *kínd;* and though we say *ùntrúth* and *ùntrúths,* we do not talk about *únth* or say "a *íth.*" The derivational and inflectional suffixes have all these things in common.

INFLECTION VS. DERIVATION. What distinguishes the two groups is partly their relative position, as we have said. Inflectional suffixes follow derivational suffixes and often close the constructions in which they occur, so that when one inflectional suffix has been added to a form, often no further suffix will follow. Returning to our first examples, we see that the inflectional suffix *-es* follows the derivational suffix *-ness-* and that normally we would not add another suffix to the whole construction *kíndnĕssĕs.* Similarly, from *móràl* we can form *móràlìze,* and from *móràlìze* we can form *móràlìzed;* but to *móràlìzed* we can add no other ending.

At least two other distinctions may be drawn between inflectional and derivational suffixes. One is the fact that a derivational suffix commonly changes the class of the form to which it is added. That is, *kínd* is adjectival and so is *kíndĕr; kínd* occurs in constructions like *the kind man,* where *kíndĕr* can replace it. *Kíndnĕss,* on the other hand, is nominal: it regularly occurs where nouns occur, as in *She liked his kindness,* and not in constructions like *the kind man* or *the kinder man. Kíndĕr,* with the inflectional suffix *-er,* belongs like *kínd* to the adjectival class; but *kíndnĕss,* with the derivational suffix *-ness,* is a noun.

The other, final distinction to which we have referred is that in English, there are numerous derivational suffixes but few inflectional suffixes. It is not surprising, then, that as a rule only a restricted list of forms will precede a given *derivational* suffix, while large classes of forms may actually be defined by their occurrence before one or more of the *inflectional* suffixes. Again the word *kíndněssěs* will provide our illustration. We have already pointed out that *-ness* is just one of a number of derivational suffixes which make nouns from adjectives, as in the pairs *kínd—kíndněss, trúe—trúth, áblě—ăbílĭtў, hárd—hárdshìp,* and *fálse—fálsehoòd.* We need now to emphasize that we cannot freely shift these five derivational suffixes around to make *kíndhoòd, trúeshìp,* or the like. We have to observe quite narrow and unpredictable limitations, making both *fálsehoòd* and *fálsĭtў* from *fálse* but *ăbílĭtў* and not *áblěhoòd* from *áblě,* using *-th* with only one of the five adjectives but *-ness* with three or more. The case is quite different with the "*-s* ending" which we write *-es* in *kíndněssěs.* We can use this *inflectional* suffix to form the plurals *kíndněssěs, trúths, ăbílĭties, hárdshìps,* and *fálsehoòds,* just as we can add the inflectional suffixes *-er* and *-est* to *kínd* and *trúe* and *áblě* and *hárd* and *fálse.* In the whole English language, only a handful of words occur with the suffix *-th,* but hundreds occur with *-er* and *-est* and thousands with the "*-s* ending" of plural nouns. We will soon see that this difference between inflectional and derivational suffixes is very important in defining parts of speech.

BASES. Meanwhile we go on with our attempt to explain what is meant by the label *word.* The prefixes and suffixes *un-, -ness-,* and *-es,* we have agreed, are not complete words but only parts of words. *Ùnkíndněss* and *kíndněssěs,* however, like *kínd* itself, *ùnkínd,* and the singular *kíndněss, are* words; they can stand alone in positions where *un-, -ness-,* or *-es* would be impossible. When we compare the five words to the one prefix and the two suffixes, we see that the one form which occurs in all the words, the form *kínd,* is neither a suffix nor a prefix, but something different. *Kínd* belongs to a class of forms which follow prefixes and precede suffixes and which constitute the most obviously and concretely meaningful parts of English words. These forms we will call *bases,* emphasizing that they are sometimes free forms (*kínd*), but not always (the *-tain* of *cŏntáin*); that it would be impossible to list them exhaustively, since new ones are constantly being introduced and old ones growing obsolete; that their distribution is very different from that of prefixes and suffixes; and that, as the "centers" of English words, they constitute much the most numerous class of meaningful forms in the language.

❧ Our sense of the word

We may conclude that any free form which consists of a single base, with or without accompanying prefixes or suffixes but with a superfix, is a word. Of course, as we have said, this is not a complete definition. We have said little or nothing about the superfixes or stress patterns which are parts of *all* our words, and it may be that there are other, multi-base forms which, in a full description, might usefully be placed in the word category—*whòévĕr*, for example, or *póstmăn, stráwbèrrў,* or *Spánĭsh ⁺ stûdĕnt,* meaning "a student of Spanish." Though all these forms contain two bases, they have all been called words in one grammatical description or another; and we will not argue here that they may not usefully be so called. The difficulty is in knowing precisely where to draw the line. If *Spánĭsh ⁺ stûdĕnt* is a word, what label shall we give to *Spânĭsh ⁺ ănd ⁺ Frénch ⁺ stûdĕnts?* If *Spânĭsh ⁺ ănd ⁺ Frénch ⁺ stûdĕnts* is a word, what of *deàf ⁺ ănd ⁺ dúmb ⁺ teâchĕr?* It is precisely such difficulties which we wish to avoid.

To avoid them, we will generally limit our use of the term *word* to free forms containing a single base; but when it seems particularly convenient, we may occasionally give the label *words* to certain forms containing two or more bases, like *póstmăn,* which are used in English very much like forms containing only one. The formula for our typical use of *word* is therefore as follows: prefix (or prefixes) plus base plus derivational suffix (or suffixes) plus inflectional suffix (rarely suffixes) plus superfix extending over the whole. The essential elements are the single base and the superfix. Other elements—prefixes and suffixes—may or may not be present, in any of their possible combinations, thus:

> *kínd*—base plus superfix;
> *ùnkínd*—prefix plus base plus superfix;
> *ùnkíndnĕss*—prefix plus base plus derivational suffix plus superfix;
> *ùnkíndĕst*—prefix plus base plus inflectional suffix plus superfix;
> *ùnkíndnĕssĕs*—prefix plus base plus derivational suffix plus inflectional suffix plus superfix;
> *kíndnĕss*—base plus derivational suffix plus superfix;
> *kíndĕr*—base plus inflectional suffix plus superfix;
> *kíndnĕssĕs*—base plus derivational suffix plus inflectional suffix plus superfix.

Exercise four. We have noted the following characteristics of prefixes: 1. Although prefixes are numerous, their number is still so much less than the number of bases that all the prefixes in English could be listed. 2. Prefixes occur before bases or other prefixes, not alone (as free forms) or directly before suffixes. 3. When two prefixes occur in sequence, they stand in a fixed order. 4. Any given prefix can precede only certain bases; not just any prefix can be used with any base. Using these criteria, select the prefix or prefixes in each of the following sets of forms, arrange each set of forms in a single word, and mark the stresses. For example:

1. *please; un; ing.* The prefix is *un.* The word is *ŭnpléasĭng.* Note that in assembling the complete words of this exercise, you may have either to add letters which do not appear in the separate elements of the words or to drop letters which do appear there.
2. *be; ed; witch.*
3. *ceive; de; un.*
4. *er; pose; com.*
5. *s; graph; para.*
6. *gon; poly; al.*
7. *ment; peach; im.*
8. *mit; ad; ance.*
9. *ic; anti; type; al.*
10. *bide; ness; a; ing.*

Exercise five. We have noted the following characteristics of suffixes: 1. All the suffixes in English could be listed. 2. Suffixes occur after bases or other suffixes, not alone or directly after prefixes. 3. When two suffixes occur in sequence, they stand in a fixed order. 4. Any given suffix can follow only certain bases; though some suffixes can follow any of a very large class of bases, not just any suffix can be used with any base. Using these criteria, sort out the bases and suffixes from the following list of forms, and make words by using each suffix with as many of the bases as it will combine with. Mark the stress pattern for each word.

1. boy	11. sing
2. tall	12. let /lɪt/
3. ness /nɨs/	13. pig
4. dom	14. ing
5. satire	15. green
6. ish	16. shrink
7. wood	17. bride
8. al	18. en
9. age /ɨj/	19. ize
10. king	20. round

Exercise six. We have noted the following distinctions between derivational and inflectional suffixes: 1. Inflectional suffixes follow derivational suffixes and often close the constructions in which they occur. 2. Derivational suffixes commonly (not always) change the class of the forms to which they are added. 3. There are more derivational than inflectional suffixes, and a given derivational suffix usually occurs with fewer bases than a given inflectional suffix. Using these criteria, sort out the derivational from the inflectional suffixes in the following words:

1. bricks
2. cleanliest
3. pained
4. riotousness
5. beautifiers

6. naughtily
7. growths
8. atheistic
9. activities
10. formalizing

Exercise seven. List the bases in the following items. Which of the items may be called words in the sense that they are free forms and contain only one base?

1. containers
2. prefixation
3. baseball
4. lighthouse-keeper
5. embankment

6. footman
7. unbelieving
8. anybody
9. night watchman
10. invader

❧ Two sets of parts of speech

Our discussion of the English word and of its parts has not been an irrelevant digression. As we have said, the first parts of speech which we will define are classes of words, and in defining them we will use the distinction between derivational and inflectional suffixes. We will then establish a second set of classes, to which not only items containing single bases but items containing two bases or more may also typically belong. Of the many different classes of forms which actually exist in English, we will thus recognize two clearly different kinds, whose definition will depend in part on what we have said about bases, prefixes, suffixes, and words.

INFLECTIONAL CLASSES. Our first method of definition will be to ask what suffixes, and especially what inflectional suffixes, a word is used with. The word *man*, for example, appears in the series *man, man's, men, men's;* the word *boy* appears in the parallel series *boy, boy's, boys, boys';* and we can establish one large and important class of words (one part of speech) by grouping together all members of such series. To this class, there will belong *man* and all other members of the inflectional series in which it appears, *boy* and all other members of *its* series, together with all members of all other series which are built on the relation of singular number to plural number (like *man, men; boy, boys*) or of common case to possessive or genitive case (like *man, man's; boy, boy's*). That is, we will class *cat* and *table* and *hedge* with *man* and *boy* because of the correspondences among the following series:

man	boy	cat	table	hedge
man's	boy's	cat's	table's	hedge's
men	boys	cats	tables	hedges
men's	boys'	cats'	tables'	hedges'

These twenty words belong together in a single class.

POSITIONAL CLASSES. Our second method of definition will be to consider, not the inflectional suffixes with which words are used, but the positions which are occupied by words and larger forms, with respect to other words and larger forms, in complete utterances. Using this method, we can put in a single class all forms, whether they contain one base or several, which fill the blank in the sentence,

$$^2\text{Thĕ} + \underline{\quad\wedge\quad} + \text{wĭll} + \text{bĕ} + {}^3\text{góod}^1\searrow$$

The words *man* and *boy,* which we group together because of their endings, will again be grouped together because they both fill this blank; but we should note that a word like *poor,* which can also fill the blank in our sentence, has endings quite different from those of *man* and *boy.* We say *poor, poorer, poorest,* but we cannot say *boy, boyer, boyest.* If we call *man* and *boy* nouns and *poor* an adjective because of their respective inflections, we have made a distinction which the structure of our language justifies; but we must be equally prepared to put all three words into a single class when we find them occurring in the same position in sentences. We will not get confused if we simply remember that our two methods of classification will produce two different sets of classes.

Parts of speech distinguished by suffixes

By the first method, considering particularly the inflectional suffixes with which words are used, we can establish four parts of speech, and we can give these four classes the familiar names of noun, pronoun, verb, and adjective. If we do not forget what we are doing and do not obscure valuable distinctions by carelessness, we can also note some important relations between the occurrence of inflectional suffixes and the occurrence of derivational suffixes. That is, words formed with particular derivational suffixes, like the *-dom* in *kingdom,* will often be limited to particular inflectional suffixes—in this case, the genitive or possessive ending (*kingdom's*) and the plural ending (*kingdoms*). This is another way of saying that since words in *-dom* are inflected like *man* and *boy*, they belong to the same class as *man* and *boy*. Ultimately, however, our classification is based on inflection, not derivation, and we will establish only one class, the adverb, by the use of a derivational ending. Logically, our adverb will not have the same status as our noun, pronoun, verb, and adjective.

⌗ The noun

We have already suggested our definition of the first of these four classes, the noun. A noun is any word belonging to an inflectional series which is built, like *man, man's, men, men's* or *boy, boy's, boys, boys'*, on *either* or *both* of the contrasts between singular and plural numbers and between common and possessive or genitive cases, and on no other contrasts. The words *man, boy, cat, table,* and *hedge,* their inflected forms, and thousands of other English words are therefore nouns, whether or not they are all the names of persons, things, or places.

NUMBER. To this simple definition, several explanatory comments must be added, the first of them being the explanation of the terms *number* and *case*. Roughly, the distinction between singular and plural numbers marks the difference between one and more than one; *man* is singular, and *men* is plural. If a noun is singular, we can often add derivational endings to it which we cannot add to its plural form (*boy, boyish; man, manly;* but not *boysish, menly*). We put *this* and *that* before singular nouns, which we also use in sentences as the subjects of singular verbs; but we put *these* and *those* before plural nouns, which we use as the subjects of plural verbs. Finally, if we use a personal pronoun as a substitute for a singular noun, we use *he, she,* or *it,* not *they,* which substitutes for plurals.

CASE. As for case, we need say only that the forms of nouns which correspond to *man, boy, men,* and *boys* are in the common case, and that the forms which correspond to *man's, boy's, men's,* and *boys'* are in the possessive. When we speak of the case of a noun, then, we are referring to its form, not its meaning; but since the common case forms and the possessive case forms do not occupy the same set of positions in sentences, a difference in case usually marks a difference in the relationship of the noun to other words with which it is used. The name *possessive* comes from the idea of possession which the form sometimes conveys, as in the sentence,

The *man's* hat is in the ring;

but the name is perhaps a little misleading, since the idea involved is often not possession at all. *The king's picture* may mean a picture representing the king as well as a picture owned by the king, and *the president's assassination* would usually refer to an action of someone other than the unfortunate executive. For this reason, some students prefer the label *genitive. Common case* is simply a general term for the forms of a noun which are not possessive (or genitive) and which do not occupy the same set of positions as the possessive forms.

THE PLURAL ENDING. The second comment on our definition of the noun has to do with the inflections on which the definition is based. The usual formal sign of the plural is the "*-s* ending," which is pronounced in three different ways. When the singular common form of the noun ends in /s/, /z/, /š/, /ž/, /č/, or /ǰ/, then the plural ending is a full syllable, which speakers of different dialects will pronounce /ɨz/, /əz/, or /ɪz/; examples are *hiss—hisses, maze—mazes, bush—bushes, rouge—rouges* (*rouge* ends in /ž/ in some dialects), *hitch—hitches,* and *ridge—ridges.* When the singular common form ends in any *voiceless* sound except /s/, /š/, or /č/, the plural ending is pronounced /s/, as in *caps, hats, backs.* When the singular common form ends in any *voiced* sound except /z/, /ž/, or /ǰ/, the plural ending is pronounced /z/, as in *cabs, cads,* and *bags.*

The "*-s* ending" in its three types is not, of course, the only form of the plural sign. Others appear in the words *oxen, children, sheep, geese, criteria* (the singular is *criterion*), *bases* /béː sìːz/ (sometimes; the singular is *basis*), *alumni, alumnae,* etc. Most of these will give no trouble to native speakers, who can always consult a good dictionary when they are in doubt about an uncommon word like *criterion;* and precise statement of the varieties of the plural ending and its accompanying changes of form is a good linguistic exercise. For example, in the word *houses* the ending is obviously the syllabic /ɨz əz ɪz/, but the base to which this ending is added is /hauz/, not /haus/. For nouns like *sheep,* which are pronounced in the plural just as they are in the singular, it is convenient to say that the plural ending is "zero." By setting up such zero forms, we can often make our statements about our language more general and so more compact. Thus, if we say that the ending of nouns like *sheep,* in the plural common form, is a zero, we can also say without exception that those English nouns which have plurals form them by adding some variety of the plural ending to the proper bases. Students who prefer to say that *sheep* has no ending in the plural will sacrifice generality to common sense in describing the same facts.

THE POSSESSIVE ENDING. Unlike the plural ending, the possessive or genitive ending has relatively few different shapes. Its varieties are /s/, /z/, /ɪz əz ɪz/, and zero, which are added to the common case forms of singular and plural.

COMMON CASE FORM		POSSESSIVE CASE FORM	
Singular:	*cat* /kæt/	plus /s/	*cat's* /kæts/
Plural:	*cats* /kæts/	plus zero	*cats'* /kæts/
Singular:	*cad* /kæd/	plus /z/	*cad's* /kædz/
Plural:	*cads* /kædz/	plus zero	*cads'* /kædz/
Singular:	*horse* /hɔərs/	plus /ɪz/	*horse's* /hɔərsɪz/
Plural:	*horses*/hɔərsɪz/	plus zero	*horses'* /hɔərsɪz/
Plural:	*sheep* /ši:p/	plus /s/	*sheep's* /ši:ps/
Plural:	*men* /mɛn/	plus /z/	*men's* /mɛnz/
Plural:	*mice* /maɪs/	plus /ɪz/	*mice's* /maɪsɪz/
Singular:	*James* /ǰe:mz/	plus /ɪz/	*James's* /ǰe:mzɪz/
Singular:	*James* /ǰe:mz/	plus zero	*James'* /ǰe:mz/

It should be noted that some speakers use the zero form of the possessive ending with singular nouns, like *James* or *Fritz*, which end in /z/ or /s/, and that the zero form is regular in the possessive plural of nouns like *cat, cad,* and *horse,* which all take the appropriate shape of the "-s ending" as the sign of their plurality. That is, we will hear both *James',* with zero possessive ending, and *James's,* with -/ɪz əz ɪz/; and the pairs *cats—cats', cads—cads', horses—horses'* are pronounced alike. The apostrophe, of course, belongs altogether to spelling, not to speech. Its proper use is none the less important for that.

DERIVATIONAL SUFFIXES WITH NOUNS. As a final comment on the noun, we may list some of the most common derivational suffixes which occur between bases and the noun-marking inflectional suffixes. They include *-age, -ance, -dom, -ess, -hood, -ism, -ist, -ity, -let, -ment, -ness, -ster,* and *-tion;* and their use is illustrated in the following pairs: *short—shortage, annoy—annoyance, king—kingdom, lion—lioness, boy—boyhood, true—truism, manner—mannerism, art—artist, odd—oddity, ring—ringlet, judge—judgment, kind—kindness, young—youngster, gang—gangster, convene—convention.* The second item of each pair is a noun, not because it includes a particular derivational suffix, but because, like other words with this suffix, it takes noun-marking inflections. Such items, in which one or more derivational suffixes have been added to a base, are known as *stems.*

Exercise one. Which of the following words are nouns? That is, which belong to series like *man, man's, men, men's?* (Warning: A single word may belong to two different parts of speech, like *fish,* which is both noun and verb. And a word is still a noun even though it has only two or three of the four forms that would parallel the forms of *man; scissors* is one example, because it has no singular, and *flesh,* which has a possessive but no plural, is another.

1. bottle	6. package	11. meat	16. own
2. easy	7. quickly	12. foot	17. trout
3. seize	8. bury	13. they	18. index
4. I	9. now	14. foolish	19. there
5. define	10. mat	15. oats	20. during

Exercise two. After each of the following nouns, write the variety of the "*-s* ending" which is used with it. For example, *whiff* takes /s/, *rum* takes /z/, and *miss* takes /ɨz əz ɪz/.

1. hop _____	6. boot _____
2. lung _____	7. work _____
3. ridge _____	8. lie _____
4. bar _____	9. gush _____
5. wheeze _____	10. wall _____

❧ The verb and its forms

Like the English noun, the English verb is relatively easy to define, but the forms of some verbs are so complicated that a full description would be confusing and not very useful here. A verb is any word belonging to an inflectional series which marks the difference between *present* and *past* *tense* and whose members will fit into a pattern like *sing, sings, sang, sung, singing* or *play, plays, played, played, playing.* The uninflected forms, or name forms, like *sing* and *play,* are given various labels in their various uses, which we will examine later: *infinitives* (*He likes to play ball*), *imperatives* (*Play ball*), etc. Forms like *plays* and *sings* are said traditionally to be in the *singular number, third person, present tense;* that is, they are used when the subject is *singular* and is neither speaker (*first person*) nor spoken to (*second person*) and when the action is not represented as preceding the moment of speaking (*non-past,* or *present*). Although the traditional terms are open to a number of objections, no generally satisfactory substitutes have yet been proposed. Forms like *sang* and the first *played* are called *past tense,* because they usually indicate an action before the moment of speaking; *sung* and the second *played* are called *past participles;* and *singing* and *playing* are *present participles.*

EXAMPLES. The complications in the inflectional forms of English verbs may be suggested by a representative list. First there is the verb *be,* which has eight forms instead of five like *sing:*

sing	be, am, are
sings	is
sang	was, were
sung	been
singing	being

Be is the name form; *am, are, is* are all present tense; *was* and *were* are past tense; and the participles are *been* and *being.* Several other important verbs have not more but less than five forms; for example, *can, could; may, might; shall, should; will, would.* Like *be,* all these can be considered verbs since they are inflected for tense; but if we follow our method of definition, we cannot treat *must* and *ought* as verbs, since they each have only one form. Later, of course, we can classify *must* and *ought* on the basis of the positions which they occupy in sentences, and we will find then that they fill much the same distinctive positions as certain of our verbs (*couldn't, wouldn't, shouldn't; mustn't, oughtn't;* etc.).

A much larger number of other verbs would have to be discussed if we hoped to describe English verb inflection completely. The following table includes some typical specimens, which can be distinguished one from the other by the forms of their endings and by the varying bases to which those endings are added:

BASE	PRESENT	PAST	PAST PPLE.	PRESENT PPLE.
make	makes	made	made	making
say	says	said	said	saying
dwell	dwells	dwelt, dwelled	dwelt, dwelled	dwelling
bring	brings	brought	brought	bringing
beat	beats	beat	beaten	beating
know	knows	knew	known	knowing
break	breaks	broke	broken	breaking
fly	flies	flew	flown	flying
hit	hits	hit	hit	hitting
run	runs	ran	run	running
meet	meets	met	met	meeting
swim	swims	swam	swum	swimming

BASE	PRESENT	PAST	PAST PPLE.	PRESENT PPLE.
prove	proves	proved	proved, proven	proving
do	does	did	done	doing
dive	dives	dived, dove	dived	diving
need	needs, need (with *not*)	needed	needed	needing
have	has	had	had	having

ENDINGS. From this table a few alternate forms have been omitted, but for our purposes only two remarks on it are necessary. (1) The usual sign of the third person singular, present tense, is another "*-s* ending," whose varieties (/s/, /z/, /ɪz əz ɪz/) are distributed like the plural "*-s* ending" of nouns: *he hits, he runs, he catches.* (2) Of the past tense, the commonest sign is the "*-ed* ending," which also has three varieties: /t/, /d/, and /ɪd əd ɪd/. When the uninflected form of the verb ends in /d/ or /t/, the full syllabic ending is usual: *fade, faded; wait, waited.* Otherwise, /t/ is usual when the uninflected form ends in a voiceless sound, as in *miss, missed* /mɪst/, and /d/ is usual when the uninflected form ends in a voiced sound, as in *brag, bragged* /brægd/. As we might expect by now, English spelling does not indicate how these varieties of the verbal endings are used in speech.

DERIVATIONAL SUFFIXES WITH VERBS. English spelling again is not ideally suited to represent the forms of bases and of derivational or stem-forming suffixes which combine in certain verbs. In the pair *stable* and *stabilize* it suggests a nonexistent difference in pronunciation between *stable* and *stabil-*, but in *solid* and *solidify* it does not indicate a real difference in the position of the stress. To native speakers, this causes no great difficulty, partly because the number of common derivational suffixes which form verb stems is not very large. Among the commonest are *-ize* (*-ise*) and *-fy* (or *-ify*).

Exercise three. Sort out the following list of verb forms. Put all the forms of a single verb together, and arrange them in the following order: uninflected form (name form), third person singular present tense, past tense, past participle, present participle. It will be easiest to use a separate note card for each verb. On the card, list each form of the verb as you come to it. When you have listed all the forms, arrange them as directed.

bit, writing, find, lost, digging, holds, wrote, win, chosen, glided, read, written, carved, fight, lain, giving, shoot, melts, fell, catches, gotten, heard, goes, standing, sat, write, took, seen, come, eating, help, laid, spoken, sells, costing, creep, found, hears, bite, falling, writes, won, losing, carved, biting, helps, get, spoke, sees, take, coming, eaten, sit, catching, stands, choose, glided, shot, cost, lay, selling, creeps, read, given, lie, leaving, go, held, left, dig, fighting, lose, takes, melt, reading, see, winning, carve, fought, catch, chooses, fallen, finding, lies, leave, speaking, stand, gives, held, melted, bitten, sell, gliding, shooting, came, eat, gone, bites, sitting, found, taken, carving, fall, wins, speak, costs, dug, hear, caught, saw, sold, melting, creeping, caught, shoots, taking, chose, comes, crept, won, stood, getting, give, fights, lost, stood, sat, cost, digs, got, lying, glide, leaves, read, eats, speaks, carves, sits, lay, gets, holding, shot, choosing, dug, loses, left, sold, fought, glides, come, melted, crept, ate, cost, lays, helping, finds, laying, reads, falls, seeing, laid, gave, helped, going, hearing, helped, heard, went, hold.

Exercise four. Classify the verbs in the preceding exercise according to the variety of the "*-s* ending" which they take in the third singular present.

Exercise five. After each of the following verbs, write the variety of the "*-ed* ending" which is used with it in the past tense. For example, *wish* takes /t/, *breathe* takes /d/, and *hate* takes /ɪd əd ɪd/.

1. rate _____	6. troop _____
2. trace _____	7. awe _____
3. goad _____	8. dart _____
4. bill _____	9. mob _____
5. hug _____	10. sniff _____

❧ The pronoun and its forms

The English pronoun is in one sense very easy and in another sense very difficult to define. In this book, we will give the name *pronoun* only to what are usually called *personal* pronouns and to the *relative* and *interrogative* pronoun *who*. The forms of the personal pronouns are familiar to us all.

SINGULAR

	Subject form	Object form	1st possessive	2nd possessive
First person	I	me	my	mine
Second person	you	you	your	yours
Third person				
Masculine	he	him	his	his
Feminine	she	her	her	hers
Neuter	it	it	its	its

PLURAL

	Subject form	*Object form*	*1st possessive*	*2nd possessive*
First person	we	us	our	ours
Second person	you	you	your	yours
Third person	they	them	their	theirs

We should note here that most of the personal pronouns, unlike the nouns, have object forms which are different from their subject forms and that most of them also have two possessive or genitive forms which are not related one to the other as singular to plural. That is, we say *I like them,* using a subject form (*I*) in subject position and an object form (*them*) in object position; and we say *her book* but *The book is hers,* choosing *her* for one position but a second possessive, *hers,* for another. With nouns, we cannot make these distinctions. Since there are no separate noun forms for subject and object, we say *Dogs fight cats* and *Cats fight dogs,* putting the same forms in both positions; and we use *Mary's* both in *Mary's book* and *The book is Mary's.* The difference between *man's* and *men's* is parallel to that between *her* and *their,* not that between *her* and *hers.*

The forms of *who,* on the other hand, show at least one significant parallel to the forms of the personal pronouns. Just as most of the personals have distinct subject and object forms, so this relative and interrogative pronoun has not only the possessive or genitive form *whose* but the subject form *who* and the object form *whom.* The isolation of these relative-interrogative forms within a class which otherwise includes only the personals helps to explain why so many of us have difficulty in using *whom;* but the fact that *whom* exists justifies us in placing *who/whose/ whom* with the other pronouns.

❧ Traditional pronouns

What shall we do with the many other words which traditionally are called pronouns? The simple fact is that any description and classification which we might give would seem involved and arbitrary, just because English is the kind of language it is. Probably the best solution for us is a list, with a few comments.

REFLEXIVES AND INTENSIVES. Forms like *myself, yourself, himself, herself, itself, ourselves, yourselves,* and *themselves* are traditionally called *reflexive* and *intensive* pronouns. They are said to be reflexive when they are used in sentences like *He cut himself,* and intensive when they occur

in positions like *The teacher herself didn't know.* Obviously, this classification depends on position in sentences, not on inflectional endings. If
we wished to fit the reflexives and intensives strictly into our word classes,
we might say that the first base in each (*my,* etc.) is a pronoun and that
the second base (*self, selves*) is a noun; *myself, ourselves,* etc. would not
as units be placed in *any* word class, since they all contain two bases.

RELATIVES AND INTERROGATIVES. The word *who,* which we do classify
as a pronoun, suggests another group of words which are usually known as
relatives and *interrogatives.* *Which* and *that* are usually called relative
pronouns in sentences like *The glove which/that he bought has been lost;*
which and *what* are usually called interrogative pronouns in such sentences as *What happened?* and *Which did he say?* Similarly, *who* suggests
the forms *whoever, whichever,* and *whatever.* For us, none of the forms
which, that, what, whoever, whichever, or *whatever* is a pronoun, since
which, that, and *what* do not have distinctive object forms and since the
forms with *ever* consist of two bases.

RECIPROCALS AND INDEFINITES. Other forms, consisting like *whoever*
of more than one base but traditionally classed as pronouns, include *an-*
other, each other, one another; anybody, everybody, nobody, somebody;
anyone, everyone, no one, someone; and *anything, everything, nothing,*
something. Each other and *one another,* which are used as objects in certain sentences having plural subjects (*They helped each other / one an-*
other), are sometimes called *reciprocal* pronouns. The rest of the forms
here listed are often known as *indefinite* pronouns, along with forms like
all, any, both, each, either, neither, none, one, other, several, and *some.*

DIFFICULTY OF SUCH CLASSIFICATION. We cannot use the term *pronoun*
in this catchall fashion. In the traditional descriptions, words like *all* and
each, which take no endings, are grouped with words like *one* and *other,*
which are inflected as nouns; and forms consisting of two or even three
bases (*another, one another*) are grouped with forms consisting of just
one (*both, some*). The principle of such haphazard classification seems in
part to be position in sentences and in part to be an old-fashioned attempt
to classify English forms according to the Latin forms which they translate. Some order may be brought into a confused situation by separating
the single-base forms, classifying at least four of them as nouns because
of their endings (*one, other, body, thing*), but postponing discussion of
most of the items until we come to talk about the positions which various
classes of forms can occupy in English sentences. It will then appear that
many traditional pronouns do "take the place of nouns" in the sense that

they frequently stand in positions which nouns also consistently occupy (*They like each other; They like apples*). This fact will allow their classification as *nominals,* forms which are nounlike in their distributions; but we will call none of them pronouns.

DEMONSTRATIVES. Finally, we must deny the label *pronoun* to the traditional *demonstrative* pronouns, *this* and *these, that* and *those,* which show the contrast between singular and plural but not between subject form and object form or between two kinds of possessive. If we call the forms *basis* and *bases* /bé:sì:z/ nouns because they are parallel to *man* and *men,* we must apply the same reasoning to *this, these, that,* and *those.* In our grammatical system they are nouns.

Exercise six. In religious language, English has another personal pronoun, *thou.* Is it singular or plural? What are its forms? Where does the form *ye* fit into the inflectional series of the second personal pronouns?

❧ Adjectives and adverbs

It is hardly possible, in English, to distinguish a class of adjectives from a class of adverbs by their inflectional endings; in defining our nouns, verbs, and pronouns, we have already used most of the inflections, and the remaining ones, -*er* and -*est,* will allow us to set up one more class but not two more. For this reason, some grammarians would say that English has no adverbs inflectionally defined, but only nouns, pronouns, verbs, and adjectives (compared words like *tall, taller, tallest*). A class like the traditional adverbs would not be established, in such a system, until the position of words and larger forms in sentences was considered.

COMPARED WORDS. Recognizing the possibility of this treatment, we still prefer to distinguish the adjective from the adverb as quickly as we can, partly because to do so will make our later positional classification easier. The first step is to set up the class of compared words. Traditionally, forms like *tall* are known as the *positive degree;* forms like *taller,* with the "-*er* ending," as the *comparative degree;* and forms like *tallest,* with the "-*est* ending," as the *superlative degree.* Words like *beautiful* do not belong in the class of compared words, since we do not say *beautifuller* or *beautifullest;* but such words as *good* (*better, best*) and *bad* (*worse, worst*) do belong in this class, since their forms make a series like *tall, taller, tallest.*

THE SUFFIX -LY. Within the class of compared words which we have now established, there are a number to whose uninflected form (the positive degree) the *derivational suffix -ly* is often added: *dead, deadly; good, goodly; quick, quickly;* etc. We intend to use this suffix, although it is derivational and not inflectional, to define our adverbs. If the second item in a pair like *dead—deadly* can itself be compared (*deadlier, deadliest*), then both the paired items are *adjectives: dead* is an adjective, and so is *deadly*. The same thing is true of *clean, cleanly* (/klí:n/, /klénlĭ/); *good, goodly; kind, kindly; live, lively* (/láɪv/, /láɪvlĭ/); *low, lowly; poor, poorly;* and a few others. On the other hand, in pairs like *quick, quickly,* the second item is not compared; we do not say *quicklier*. In pairs of this sort, we will say, the first item is an adjective, and the second an *adverb*. In short, we will define adjectives, by their inflectional suffixes, as compared words; but we will define adverbs, using a derivational suffix, as words which cannot be compared but which consist of the positive degree of an adjective plus *-ly*.

๙ Summary

Having made this decision, we have completed the definition of four "parts of speech" by their inflectional suffixes and one "part of speech" by a derivational suffix: nouns, whose forms fit into a series like *man, man's, men, men's;* verbs, whose forms fit into a series like *sing, sings, sang, sung, singing;* adjectives, words which are compared like *tall, taller, tallest;* pronouns, including the personals and *who,* most of which have distinct subject and object forms and two possessives like *my, mine;* and adverbs, uncompared words formed from the positive degree of adjectives by adding the derivational suffix *-ly*. We have also noted certain derivational suffixes to which the inflectional suffixes of nouns or of verbs may be added, and there are one or two derivational suffixes, like the *-y* of *speedy,* which frequently enter into adjectives (compared words); but, with the exception of the adverb, it is the *inflectional* suffix on which we have depended for our definitions. Our remarks on derivation in the noun, verb, and adjective simply note that stems formed with a given derivational suffix are commonly used with one of the specified sets of inflections: *artist* with noun inflections, *stabilize* with verb inflections, *speedy* with adjective inflections, etc.

๙ Preview

Our definitions by no means correspond to the traditional ones, and we will have to have another set of classes positionally defined; but our method at least allows us to recognize nouns, pronouns, verbs, adjectives, and adverbs when we hear or read them. Its efficiency in making important statements about English should compensate for the slight discomfort which some of us may experience when we are told that in our grammar *beautiful* is not an adjective nor *beautifully* an adverb, any more than *chaos*, in our grammar, is a noun or *must* a verb; and when we come to consider the positions which words and larger forms can occupy in English sentences, we will be able to classify all these words rather well, though not, of course, according to the endings which they do not have.

We will then say, essentially, that although *beautiful* is not an adjective it often *is* an *adjectival*, since it often fills the same positions that adjectives typically fill: for *big* in $^2th\breve{e}$ + *very* + *big* + $^3b\acute{o}ok^2 \rightarrow$ we can substitute *beautiful*. Similar reasoning will make *beautifully* an *adverbial*, *chaos* a *nominal*, and *must* a *verbal;* they often stand, respectively, in positions where we regularly find adverbs, nouns, and verbs.

Our double classification will actually get us out of some familiar difficulties. For example, what is *poor* in *The poor are always with us?* Is it an adjective, a noun, or an adjective "used as a noun"? We will answer, using a definition in terms of inflection, that *poor* is always and everywhere an *adjective*, since it fits into the series *poor, poorer, poorest*, but that in this sentence it is a *nominal*, since it fills a position which nouns usually occupy (*The men are always with us, The boys are always with us*, etc.). Our answer will be a complete and precise indication of what is vaguely suggested by the label "adjective used as noun."

Exercise seven. Separate the adjectives from the adverbs in the following list: *sickly, slowly, fast, slow, sick, chilly, dully, easily, hard, friendly.*

Exercise eight. Why, according to our definitions, is *beautiful* no adjective, *beautifully* no adverb, *chaos* no noun, and *must* no verb?

Parts of speech distinguished by position
↶ Method again

Defining parts of speech by their positions with respect to other words or other larger forms is at least a partially familiar procedure to most of us. When we say traditionally that a word like *steel* is a noun in one sentence (*The steel glistened in the sun*) and an adjective, or "a noun used as an adjective," in another (*The steel bridge collapsed*), we are really using position in the sentences as part of our customary definitions of "noun" and "adjective." Here is another difficulty with the usual definitions: to some extent, they are what we will call "positional" definitions, but they are not clearly and consistently so. The grammars which most of us have used do not make many precise statements about word order, and they confuse definitions in terms of positions in sentences with definitions by other criteria.

If we are to remove this confusion, we must be very careful to remember that we are using two different ways of defining "parts of speech," and that neither way is precisely like the old ways of definition. First, we have defined five classes of *words* according to their endings, but this method has given new and different meanings to the old terms *noun, verb, pronoun, adjective,* and *adverb,* which we have chosen to retain because they are familiar and convenient. Now, as the second main step in our process of definition, we will set up positional classes. These classes will be *quite different* from the five which we have already established, and we will have to give our second set of classes different names. In particular, the second set will include not only words but *larger forms than words,* as we will see later. We will call these larger forms *phrases* if they do not constitute a subject-predicate combination, and *clauses* if they do.

We do not throw away our first set of classes and forget about them when we establish the second set. The second set will be built, in part, with the help of the first, in a fairly simple way. We want now to find large classes of forms which occupy the same positions in sentences, for our sentences have to be described as arrangements of clauses, phrases, and words *belonging to definite classes,* not as sequences of isolated forms each of which is a law to itself. *Classes* of words and of larger forms, not individual items, are the building blocks, as we can easily see by making substitutions in almost any sentence.

> *Cash* talks.
> *Money* talks.
> *The money* talks.
> *The big money* talks.

After each substitution, the sentence still makes sense and still has the same basic grammatical structure; for the words and phrases *cash, money, the money,* and *the big money* all occur regularly in the same or similar positions. That is, our substitution works because we substitute one member of a certain positional class for another member of the same class, and so the substitution does not change the basic form of our sen tence any more than the sculptor changes the form of a bust when he copies it in bronze or plaster or clay rather than in marble.

℣ From noun to nominal

We take, therefore, the class of nouns, one of the classes which we have set up by considering the endings of words, and we ask what positions nouns typically occupy in English sentences. As native speakers, we know that nouns typically occur after any one of a group of words which we will later define as *determiners* and which include *a, an, the, your, our, their,* etc. To discover the items which occur in this position, we choose a sentence which we can use as a testing frame:

²Thĕ + ²___↗___²→²sêemed + ³góod¹↘

Any native speaker can quickly produce hundreds of forms that will fill the blank in this frame—among others, *speaker, hundred, form, blank, frame,* and *other.*

²Thĕ + ²spéakĕr²→²sêemed + ³góod¹↘
²Thĕ + ²húndrĕd²→²sêemed + ³góod¹↘
²Thĕ + ²óthĕr²→²sêemed + ³góod¹↘

Here five of our listed words are nouns, and the sixth, *other,* is traditionally, as we have said, an "indefinite pronoun"; but if we keep all the other features of our testing frame constant and change only the form which fills the blank, the structure of the sentence remains basically the same no matter which of the six we choose. For the single words, of course, we can also substitute phrases, forms which contain more than one base but do not constitute a combination of subject with predicate:

²Thĕ + fîrst + ²spéakĕr²→²sêemed + ³góod¹↘

We will call all such words and phrases *nominals,* and part of our definition of the nominal will be this: any form which fills the blank in our testing frame is a nominal. Though in another position the form may belong to another class, it is a nominal in *this* position; and though a phrase may contain within itself forms that are *not* nominals, the nominal label may still be given to the phrase as a whole.

THE DEFINITION EXTENDED. Our definition is not yet complete, however, and we have still to explain its use and usefulness. Earlier comments on substitution in a frame should have made it clear that our test sentence is not really changed if we replace *the* by another determiner, but it *is* changed somewhat if we omit the determiner altogether. Despite this fact, we will extend our definition of the nominal by saying that any form is a nominal if it fills the blank in the frame either with the determiner or without it: either

or

$$^2\underline{\quad\diagup\quad}{}^{2\rightarrow2}\text{s}\hat{\text{e}}\text{emed} + {}^3\text{g\'ood}^1\searrow$$

$$^2\text{Th\u{e}} + {}^2\underline{\quad\diagup\quad}{}^{2\rightarrow2}\text{s}\hat{\text{e}}\text{emed} + {}^3\text{g\'ood}^1\searrow$$

This extension immediately allows us to classify as nominals a number of words which usually do not follow determiners—words like *James, English,* and *July;* they are traditionally "proper nouns." We can also call most of the traditional pronouns nominals, since they too will fit into our frame, if we omit the determiner and allow for certain statable changes in stress and pitch, without disturbing its structure. Thus we can say,

$$^2\text{E\'ach}^{2\rightarrow2}\text{s}\hat{\text{e}}\text{emed} + {}^3\text{g\'ood}^1\searrow$$

or, with changes in stress and pitch,

$$^2\text{H\`e} + \text{s}\hat{\text{e}}\text{emed} + {}^3\text{g\'ood}^1\searrow$$

Our list of potential nominals (potential because some of them belong to other classes in other positions) will therefore include the common and possessive case forms of our nouns, the participles of our verbs, all three forms of our adjectives, the subject forms and one of the possessive forms of our personal pronouns, many other *traditional* pronouns, a variety of phrases, and some clauses. It will not include our adverbs or most forms of our verbs. Many uninflected words, but not all of them, will be nominals as well; *chaos* fits the frame, but *ought* does not.

SUBCLASSES OF NOMINALS. Having got so long a list of potential nominals, we can subdivide it in various ways. We can base one subclassification on occurrence in the frame with or without the determiner, as we have just seen; and we can make another subdivision by changing *seemed* to *seems* or *seem* and noting which nominals appear with the singular verb and which with the plural. For example, *James* occurs without a determiner and with a singular verb; *pliers* occurs either with or without a determiner but with a plural verb; *hat* has a determiner and a singular verb; etc.

Exercise one. In the sentence, *Games are fun,* place a determiner before the noun *games.* Insert an adjective after the determiner. Add a prepositional phrase after the noun (a prepositional phrase consists of a form like *at, in, on,* or *with,* followed by a nominal: *in the evening, at school,* etc.). Note that in each sentence which you make by following these instructions, the part of the sentence before *are fun* is a nominal. Can nominal phrases include words which themselves are not nominals?

Exercise two. List twenty words which can fill the blank in the testing frame,

$$^2\text{Thĕ} + {}^2\underline{\quad\nearrow\quad}{}^2{\rightarrow}{}^2\text{sêemed} + {}^3\text{góod}^1\searrow$$

List ten words which can fill the blank in the frame without the determiner:

$$^2\underline{\quad\nearrow\quad}{}^2{\rightarrow}{}^2\text{sêemed} + {}^3\text{góod}^1\searrow$$

How many of your thirty words are nouns?

Exercise three. In the blank in the first frame in Exercise two, insert the following forms (not all at once, but one at a time): the common case form of a noun; the possessive case form of a noun; the past participle of a verb; all three forms of an adjective; a phrase consisting of an adjective followed by a noun. In the blank in the second frame (the one without the determiner), insert the subject form of a personal pronoun; the second possessive of the same pronoun; the form *another*. Note that we can say either

$$^2\text{Hé}^2{\rightarrow}{}^2\text{sêemed} + {}^3\text{góod}^1\searrow$$

or

$$^2\text{Hè} + \text{sêemed} + {}^3\text{góod}^1\searrow$$

How do the two sentences differ in meaning? Which one might be written with *he* in italics?

USING POSITIONAL DEFINITIONS. One apparent difficulty in our definition of the nominal may already have suggested itself. We have used what is essentially a single position to define this class, so that we cannot yet include among the nominals some forms which we feel belong there, like the object forms of the personal pronouns. Moreover, some forms that can fill our one specified position can fill many other positions, too. We can say *The poor seemed good,* but we can also say *The poor man seemed good;* and we certainly do not want to say that *poor* belongs to the same positional class in both sentences. In fact, we might almost use the second of these sentences,

$$^2\text{Thĕ} + \underline{\quad\wedge\quad} + {}^3\text{mán}^2{\rightarrow}{}^2\text{sêemed} + {}^3\text{góod}^1\searrow$$

as a preliminary testing frame to discover the class of forms which we will later define as *adjectivals.* To make our statements consistent, we will have to say that now we are not classifying forms in isolation; *poor* can be either a nominal or an adjectival, but it actually *is* a nominal only when it occurs in a nominal position, and it *is* an adjectival only when it occurs in an adjectival position.

Does it follow that we must isolate all the positions in English sentences and label each of them as nominal, adjectival, or the like before we can classify forms in sentences positionally? Fortunately, the answer is no, and the reason is that English, like other languages, is a *system* and not just a conglomeration. Forms which appear together in one important position will usually appear together in other positions as well, so that if we isolate and label the important positions, we can establish a set of classes which we can expect to be fairly stable.

For example, when we have labeled the most important positions, we will discover that some forms, like *sang* and *wrote* and the corresponding forms of other verbs, appear always and only in positions to which we will have given the same label—in this instance, verbal positions. Such forms will always belong to the same positional class. Other forms, like *poor* and *steel,* appear in positions to which several different labels will have been given—*steel,* for instance, in nominal and verbal positions, *poor* in nominal and adjectival positions. So long as such a form appears in a position which we have labeled, its positional classification will be clear. When it appears in a less important, unlabeled position, its classification, though not immediately clear, will not be too hard to determine. Since we have chosen, as our nominal positions, those which most typically are occupied by nouns, and since we will choose our verbal, adjectival, and adverbial positions similarly, a good initial guess will be that a noun in an unlabeled position is a nominal, an adjective an adjectival, etc. We would make a guess like this if we were asked to classify *poor* in the sentence,

The farmer, poor but proud, worked hard for a living.

In this sentence, we would guess, *poor* is an *adjectival,* since by its inflections we know that it is an *adjective.*

Our initial guess could then be tested by substitution in the same sentence as a testing frame. The forms which can be substituted for *poor* when it appears in a position labeled adjectival can regularly be substituted for *poor* in this sentence, too. In the sentence,

The poor man seemed good,

poor occupies a labeled adjectival position. We can also say, for example,

The sickly man seemed good,

replacing *poor* by *sickly.* Returning to our original sentence,

The farmer, poor but proud, worked hard for a living,

we can make the same substitution once again and put *sickly* for *poor* in the position we are examining:

The farmer, sickly but proud, worked hard for a living.

Further experiment would confirm the conclusion that forms which else-where appear regularly in labeled adjectival positions can regularly be substituted for *poor* in our sentence.

On the other hand, many of the forms which can replace *poor* when it appears in a position labeled nominal cannot regularly replace it in *The farmer, poor but proud. . . . Poor* is labeled nominal, for example, in the sentence,

> The poor seemed good.

In that nominal position, we can substitute forms like *lawyer,* a noun:

> The lawyer seemed good.

We cannot, however, replace *poor* by *lawyer* in our unlabeled position; we do not say,

> The farmer, lawyer but proud, worked hard for a living.

Our initial guess would therefore be confirmed. The unlabeled position is regularly occupied by adjectives and other forms which elsewhere are adjectivals, not by nouns and other forms which elsewhere are nominals, and so the label *adjectival* may be given to the new position and to the forms that fill it.

MORE NOMINAL POSITIONS. Returning, now, to our definition of the nominal, we can apply to it the principle of uniformity which we have just explained. If, in a position which we have not overtly labeled, we find only or mainly forms which elsewhere occur consistently in positions that we have labeled nominal, we will be justified in labeling the new position nominal, and the forms that occur in it will still be nominals. Thus we can say immediately that the following positions are nominal positions:

$$^2\text{Th\u{e}} + {}^2\underline{\quad\nearrow\quad} {}^{2\rightarrow2}\text{c\u{o}ns\u{i}d\u{e}red} + \text{th\u{e}} + {}^3\underline{\quad\nearrow\quad}{}^1\searrow$$

$$^2\text{Th\u{e}} + {}^2\underline{\quad\nearrow\quad} {}^{2\rightarrow2}\text{g\^ave} + \text{th\u{e}} + \underline{\quad\wedge\quad} + \u{a} + {}^3\underline{\quad\nearrow\quad}{}^1\searrow$$

We can sum up our definition by saying that a form is a nominal when it occurs in any one of the positions which we have labeled nominal or in any unlabeled position consistently occupied by forms which consistently occupy the labeled nominal positions.

PROPER NOUNS AND OBJECT FORMS. The object forms of the personal pronouns, which we have not yet dealt with, are easy to classify according to this definition. One of our labeled nominal positions is consistently occupied by forms like *James*—"proper nouns."

$$^2\underline{\quad\nearrow\quad}{}^{2\rightarrow2}\text{s\^eemed} + {}^3\text{g\u{o}od}{}^1\searrow$$

$$^2\text{J\u{a}mes}{}^{2\rightarrow2}\text{s\^eemed} + {}^3\text{g\u{o}od}{}^1\searrow$$

For a proper noun in this position, a subject form of a personal pronoun may be substituted (often, however, with a change of stress):

$$^2\text{Hè} + \text{sêemed} + {}^3\text{góod}^1\searrow$$

Proper nouns also occur *after* the verb in sentences like

$$^2\text{Jóhn}^{2\rightarrow2}\text{sâw} + {}^3\text{Jámes}^1\searrow$$

In this post-verb position, the *object* form of a personal pronoun may be substituted (again with a change of stress, which this time is accompanied by a change in intonation):

$$^2\text{Jôhn} + {}^3\text{sáw hĭm}^1\searrow$$

The combined distribution of the subject and object forms of a personal pronoun, it appears, is parallel to the distribution of the common case form of a proper noun, and we may add the object forms of personal pronouns to our list of nominals. They occur so consistently in nominal positions that we can predict their classification even before we encounter them in actual utterances. We can make no such prediction, obviously, for forms like *steel* and *poor;* and it is well to remember that for most forms, we can give a positional classification only when we *are* dealing with actual utterances. A positional classification is not a classification of isolated forms.

Exercise four. We have defined the nominal as follows: "A form is a nominal when it occurs in any one of the positions which we have labeled nominal or in any unlabeled position consistently occupied by forms which consistently occupy the labeled nominal positions." This exercise is intended to clarify our definition and its use.

a. Study the following testing frames. The blanks indicate positions which we have labeled nominal.

$$^2\text{Thĕ} + {}^2\underline{\quad\nearrow\quad}^{2\rightarrow2}\text{sêemed} + {}^3\text{góod}^1\searrow$$

$$^2\underline{\quad\nearrow\quad}^{2\rightarrow2}\text{sêemed} + {}^3\text{góod}^1\searrow$$

$$^2\text{Thĕ} + {}^2\underline{\quad\nearrow\quad}^{2\rightarrow2}\text{cŏnsĭdĕred} + \text{thĕ} + {}^3\underline{\quad\nearrow\quad}^1\searrow$$

$$^2\text{Thĕ} + {}^2\underline{\quad\nearrow\quad}^{2\rightarrow2}\text{gâve} + \text{thĕ} + \underline{\quad\wedge\quad} + \text{ă} + {}^3\underline{\quad\nearrow\quad}^1\searrow$$

b. Underline the words which are used as nominals in the following sentences. All the nominals occur in positions which we have labeled.

The explanation seemed dull.

Chicago looked good.

The principal considered the suggestion.

The boy gave his dog a bone.

He felt bad.

The apple was sweet.
The class copied the assignment.
Our hero taught the bully a lesson.
You look sick.
The ball cleared the fence.

c. Underline the *nouns* in the following sentences.
The weather got hotter.
John, my friend, looked unhappy.
The driver of the truck gave the policemen some trouble.
The agent examined his papers closely.

d. Which of the nouns in *c* are in labeled nominal positions? Which are in positions which we have not labeled?

e. In the sentence *John, my friend, looked unhappy,* we can replace *friend* with these forms, among others: *teacher, brother, pal, buddy, rival, enemy, companion, instructor, catcher, guard.* Are these words nouns? Do they regularly fill the positions after the determiners in the testing frames in *a*? Note that we do not say things like *John, my poor, looked unhappy* or *John, my tell, looked unhappy* or *John, my they, looked unhappy* or *John, my quickly, looked unhappy.* To what positional class does *friend* belong in the original sentence?

f. How would you prove that *truck,* in the third sentence in *c,* is also a nominal?

❧ From verb to verbal

Just as we have used our class of nouns (words inflected like *man*) to help establish a related but different class of nominals, so we will next use our class of verbs (words inflected like *sing*) in establishing a positional class of *verbals.* The term *verbal* will be related to the term *verb* much as *nominal* is related to *noun;* but to find our verbals we will use, from the very beginning, three testing frames instead of one, and we will present these frames as sequences of positional classes, not sequences of individual forms.

    (1) ^{2}Detĕrminer + ^{3}nóminal$^{2\rightarrow2}$____ $\widehat{}$ + adjec^{3}tíval^1↘
    (2) ^{2}Detĕrminer + ^{3}nóminal$^{2\rightarrow2}$____ $\widehat{}$ + detĕrminer +
      ^{3}nóminal^1↘
    (3) ^{2}Detĕrminer + ^{3}nóminal$^{2\rightarrow2}$____ $\wedge$ + ad^{3}vérbial^1↘

Specific examples of these frames are the sentences:

    (1) ^{2}Thĕ + ^{3}mán$^{2\rightarrow2}$*wăs* + ^{3}góod^1↘
      ^{2}Yoŭr + ^{3}fóod$^{2\rightarrow2}$*seèms* + ^{3}góod^1↘

^{2}Hïs + ^{3}cómmènts^2→^{2}*rĕmâin* + ^{3}góod^1↘

(2) ^{2}Thĕ + ^{3}mán^2→^{2}*is* + ă + ^{3}fármĕr^1↘

^{2}Ă + ^{3}tráctŏr^2→^{2}*hĭt* + thĕ + ^{3}fármĕr^1↘

(3) ^{2}Thĕ + ^{3}gámes^2→^{2}*bĕgân* + ^{3}quícklў^1↘

THE INTENT OF THE VERBAL FRAMES. The examples clarify the intent of the frames in several ways. First, and most important, the frames are unchanged no matter what particular members of the indicated positional classes are used in specific sentences; thus we have used *a, his, the,* and *your* to fill the positions of the determiner. Second, the indicated stresses may fall on any syllables of the nominals, verbals, adjectivals, and adverbials, so that the stresses on their other syllables need not be specified; for example, *comments* has its stronger stress on the first syllable, while *remain* is stressed on the second. Third, in the first two frames the verbals may have any stress but the strongest, so that the variation from weakest stress on *was* through third stress on *seems* to second stress on *remain* is quite normal. Fourth, strongest stress will fall on the last word in the frames and will coincide with pitch /^{3}/ in the intonation pattern /^{231}↘/, as it does in ^{3}*góod*^{1}↘, ^{3}*fármĕr*^{1}↘, ^{3}*quícklў*^{1}↘. Finally, the nominals and verbals may be either singular or plural, but the verbal must agree in number with the first nominal: *man—was, comments—remain.* With these explanations, we may say that any word or larger form is a verbal if it fills the blank in any one of these three frames or if it fills any unlabeled position consistently occupied by forms which consistently fill these frames.

POSITIONAL CLASSIFICATION OF VERB FORMS. In effect, by our last statement we have said mainly that the present and past tense forms of verbs, and larger forms that can be substituted for these present and past tense forms, are verbals when they are used in sentences. We have not yet made any provision for positional classification of the other three forms of verbs, forms like *sing* (when it is not a present tense with subject expressed), *sung,* or *singing.* The name form (*be, sing,* etc.) may always be called a verbal; it occupies distinctive positions not occupied by any other group of forms. (Of course, the verb *sing,* which fits into a series with *sung* and *singing,* is not the same as the noun *sing,* whose plural appears in sentences like *We enjoyed the community sings;* and though the verb *sing* is itself always a verbal, it may occur in phrases like *to sing,* which *as whole phrases* may not be verbal at all.)

The participles, like *sung* and *playing,* are sometimes nominal, sometimes verbal, sometimes adjectival. They are nominals if they satisfy our earlier definition of that class, and adjectivals if they occur in certain positions which we will describe in the next paragraphs; but they are verbals if they occur in sequences of verb forms which, *as sequences,* fill the blanks in our testing frames for verbals. For example, *living* is a nominal in the sentence:

$$^3\text{Lívĭng}^{2\rightarrow2}\text{sêemed} + {}^3\text{góod}^1\searrow$$

It is an adjectival in the sentence:

$$^2\text{Thĕ} + \text{lívĭng} + {}^3\text{mán}^{2\rightarrow2}\text{sêemed} + {}^3\text{góod}^1\searrow$$

But it is a verbal in the sentence:

$$^2\text{Thĕ} + {}^3\text{mán}^{2\rightarrow2}\text{hăs} + \text{bĕen} + \text{lívĭng} + {}^3\text{háppĭlў}^1\searrow$$

More generally, in a sequence of verb forms that fills the blank in any of our testing frames for verbals, every word, including *must* and *ought* but not *to,* is itself a verbal. A full account of the positions which participles may occupy in these sequences and elsewhere in sentences would be too complex for our purposes, but in cases of doubt whether a participle should be called a verbal or an adjectival, a satisfactory rule of thumb is this: Substitute other forms in the doubtful position to see whether it can regularly be filled by both adjectives and participles or by participles only. If both adjectives and participles can regularly be substituted, then the doubtful participle is an adjectival; otherwise it is a verbal. Participles used as nominals will be easily recognized.

Exercise five. Make up ten sentences to fit each of the three testing frames for verbals.

Exercise six. In the following sentences, classify the underlined participles as nominal, verbal, or adjectival. Give reasons for each of your decisions.
1. Rubbing his arm, he left the game.
2. He had bruised his foot the preceding day.
3. The paintings, dusty and faded, hung in the attic.
4. His favorite sports, tennis and fishing, had begun to bore him.
5. The weather being bad, we didn't enjoy sailing.
6. Quite disappointed, the contractor withdrew his offer.

Note the difference between *rubbing* in Sentence 1 and *disappointed* in Sentence 6. What is the positional class of the whole phrases *rubbing his arm* and *quite disappointed?* It is different from the positional class of *rubbing* but the same as the positional class of *disappointed.*

⸙ From adjective to adjectival

Like the nominal, the verbal is such a large class that within it various subclasses may be distinguished, as we have suggested by our comments on the uses of the different forms of verbs; but such further distinctions as are necessary can be made later, after we have broadly characterized the most important positional classes.

The next main class to consider is the *adjectival,* which we name after the adjective, as we named the nominal and the verbal after the noun and verb. Were it not for one difficulty, the testing frame for the adjectival would be very simple:

$$^2\text{detĕrminer} + \underline{\quad ^\wedge \quad} + {}^3\text{nóun}^1\searrow$$
$$^2\text{thĕ} + g\hat{o}od + {}^3\text{dóg}^1\searrow$$

If we used this testing frame, we could define an adjectival as any form that fills it—that is, which stands under second stress between a weakest-stressed determiner and a strongest-stressed noun—or that occupies some unlabeled position consistently occupied by forms that consistently fill this frame.

The difficulty would be that the use of so simple a frame would make *stone* an adjectival in $^2\text{thĕ} + st\hat{o}ne + {}^3\text{wáll}^2\rightarrow$ and *man's* an adjectival in $^2\check{a} + m\hat{a}n's + {}^3h\acute{o}use^1\searrow$. Presumably the same classifications would be made in *the little stone wall* and in *a man's own house;* if *stone* and *man* are adjectivals in one pair of phrases, they are presumably adjectivals in both pairs. In *the little stone wall,* however, *stone* and *little* cannot change places, so that one hesitates to call the position of *stone* in that phrase an adjectival position; and, similarly, only nouns or pronouns in the possessive (genitive) can be used before *own,* as in *a man's own house.*

Since we do not want to say that *stone* and *man's* are adjectival in *the stone wall* and *a man's house* but that they are nominal in *the little stone wall* and *a man's own house,* we add a footnote to the proposed testing frame for adjectivals. We will label as adjectival any form which stands under second stress between a weakest-stressed determiner and a strongest-stressed noun, *unless* that form is itself a noun. *Good* is therefore an adjectival in

$$^2\text{thĕ} + g\hat{o}od + {}^3\text{dóg}^1\searrow$$

but *stone* and *man's* are nominals in

$$^2\text{thĕ} + st\hat{o}ne + {}^3\text{wáll}^1\searrow$$

and

$$^2\text{thĕ} + m\hat{a}n's + {}^3h\acute{o}use^1\searrow$$

We will add, naturally, that if items like *good* or *vicious,* which pass this amended test for adjectivals, can typically be substituted for a form in some unlabeled position, the unlabeled form is adjectival too. Thus in the sentence *He was very thirsty,* we will call *thirsty* an adjectival because forms like *good* and *vicious* can regularly replace it. In rare sentences, like *He was very Labor* (meaning that he was devoted to the Labor Party), consistency will force us to call such a noun as *Labor* an adjectival; but such a classification will surprise no one who remembers that participles, for example, may be adjectival, nominal, or verbal.

SUBCLASSES OF ADJECTIVALS. Having established the general class of adjectivals, we go on to note that positionally, the class can be rather extensively subdivided. In a long sequence like *those same four inferior French houses,* none of the forms between *those* and *houses* is likely to be shifted about; but despite the fact that their relative positions differ in detail, all these forms are here adjectivals, and all of them can appear under second stress between a weakly stressed determiner and a strongly stressed noun. It is just this stress pattern which is one of the best markers of an adjectival, and if the stress pattern is changed, the classification of the forms involved may change with it. $^2Th\breve{e}$ $^+$ $^3Sp\acute{a}n\breve{i}sh$ $^+$ $st\hat{u}d\breve{e}nts^2 \nearrow$, for example, means "the students of Spanish," while $^2th\breve{e}$ $^+$ $Sp\hat{a}n\breve{i}sh$ $^+$ $^4st\acute{u}d\breve{e}nts^2 \rightarrow$ means "the students from Spain." In this book, then, we will say that items of the first type consist of a determiner plus a compound nominal, while items of the second type consist of determiner plus adjectival plus (uncompounded) nominal.

Exercise seven. Among the items which are most commonly adjectivals are all three forms of adjectives, both participles, and many uninflected words. Underline the words which are adjectivals in the following sentences, and be prepared to explain your decisions.

1. The woman's hair was long and black.
2. A tired salesman wrapped three yards of cotton cloth.
3. When the trains began running again, the best service was given by the new line.
4. The nurse, laughing and crying at the same time, was plainly growing hysterical.
5. In our chaotic situation, the chairman placidly deceives himself with the notion that things are better than they were.

Exercise eight. Five sets of jumbled forms are given below. Each set includes one determiner and one noun in the common case. Arrange the forms in each set in normal English order, with the determiner first and the noun in the common case last. Once or twice you may have a choice between different possible arrangements.

1. his, first, old, ships, Cuban, six, own
2. good, men, the, ten, same, young
3. quite, few, battered, wagons, a
4. buildings, our, wooden, many, and, sturdy, strong
5. brazen, highly, next, bowls, polished, four, the

❧ From adverb to adverbial

The last of the four most important positional classes which we need to establish is the *adverbial.* It is not easy to define simply, since its members occupy many different positions and fall into a number of distinct positional subclasses and since a number of forms which often fill nominal and adjectival positions also appear as adverbials. To illustrate the variety of the adverbial positions, we may use the adverb *quickly,* which can stand initially, medially, or finally:

> Quickly she replied.
> She quickly replied.
> She replied quickly.

In contrast, the positions of *never* and *not,* when they are used as adverbials, show rather sharp limitations: if we try to replace *quickly* with *never* in our examples, we find that the replacement is possible in only one of the three (*She never replied*); and if we try to put *not* with *She replied,* we have to change *replied* to *did reply* (*She did not reply,* or *She didn't reply*). Other limitations appear when we use two or more adverbials together, as in the following sentences:

> He came back earlier.
> He came back quietly.
> He came quietly back.
> He came quietly and quickly.

We should note that we put *and* between *quietly* and *quickly* and that we put *earlier* after *back,* although we can shift *back* and *quietly* around. A further complication results, as we have suggested, from the fact that *earlier,* which we are using to illustrate certain properties of adverbials, is an adjective and can also be used in adjectival and nominal positions.

We can, however, make at least a few useful general statements about adverbials as a separate class. To begin with, we may obviously say that we do not want our classes to overlap; no nominal, verbal, or adjectival position should also be labeled adverbial. When we discover, by using our testing frames for nominals, verbals, and adjectivals, that adverbs fit none of them, we can go on to say that just as the noun is the typical nominal, so the adverb is the typical adverbial. We defined the adverb in order precisely that we might make this statement, which helps us to identify adverbials by the usual procedure of substitution. Adverbs, we have said, are uninflected; and in general, adverbials will be forms consistently replaceable by adverbs and other uninflected words (such as *then, there, thus*) but usually not by members of our inflected classes. One position in which adverbials commonly occur is under strongest stress after a nominal at the end of a sentence:

$$^2\text{Thĕ} + {}^3\text{mán}^{2 \rightarrow 2}\text{mâde} + \text{mônĕy} + {}^3\text{quícklў}^1\searrow$$
$$^2\text{Hĕ} + \text{bûrnt} + \text{thĕ} + \text{hôûse} + {}^3\text{úp}^1\searrow$$

APPLICATION OF THE DESCRIPTION. Assembling the elements of our description, we conclude that the adverbial is the positional class which includes no forms in nominal, verbal, or adjectival positions but only adverbs and forms typically replaceable by adverbs or by such uninflected words as *then, there, thus.* The application of this description may be illustrated by the following examples:

$$(1)\ ^2\text{Shĕ} + \text{reâd} + \text{thĕ} + \text{pâpĕr} + {}^3\text{yéstĕrdày}^1\searrow$$

Yesterday is of course a phrase, since it includes two bases. The second base, *day*, is a noun, but we are here concerned with positional classification. Since *yesterday* is not in a position which we have labeled as nominal or verbal or adjectival, since on the other hand it stands under strongest stress after a nominal at the end of a sentence, and since it is replaceable by adverbs like *slowly* and by the uninflected word *then*, we classify *yesterday* in this sentence as an adverbial. That decision is confirmed by attempts to replace *yesterday* with nouns, verbs, adjectives, or pronouns. Some participles and some adjectives seem indeed to be possible replacements, as in *She read the paper smiling* or *She read the paper fast;* but the suggestion that *yesterday* might be an adjectival seems hardly likely, since the general distribution of the form is quite unlike the distribution of adjectives but quite like that of adverbs. We cannot say *the yesterday paper,* but we *can* put *yesterday* in much the same positions as we can put a form like *quickly:*

Yesterday she replied.

She yesterday replied to the letter I had sent.

She replied yesterday.

(2) **²**Hĕ + tälked + tòo + **³**lóud¹﹨

We will not be able to classify *loud* in this sentence as easily and surely as we classified *yesterday* in Sentence 1. *Loud* is an adjective; is it an adjectival or an adverbial? We can consistently replace it with adverbs, like *slowly* and *loudly*, but we can also replace it consistently with certain adjectives, like *fast* and *low*. Since the evidence is not conclusive for either interpretation, our decision must be arbitrary. In this book, we will label *loud* and other forms which occur in this position *adverbial*, remembering, of course, that in other positions they may belong to other classes.

(3) **²**Fîne + **³**clóthes**²→²**mâde + thĕ + gîrl + **³**béautïfŭl¹﹨

Beautiful is an uninflected word under strongest stress after a nominal at the end of a sentence, yet it is not an adverbial. In all our substitutions, we have taken care that the structural meaning of the sentence should be the same both before the substitution and after it; but if we replace *beautiful* with an adverb, the replacement will change the structural meaning very drastically (*Fine clothes made the girl quickly*). On the other hand, we can replace *beautiful* with any number of adjectives and leave the structural meaning of the sentence quite unchanged: *Fine clothes made the girl happy, Fine clothes made the girl proud*, etc. We conclude, therefore, that in this sentence *beautiful* is an adjectival—not an adjective, since it is not inflected with *-er* and *-est*, but an adjectival because of its structural position.

Exercise nine. Review the definitions of noun, verb, pronoun, adjective, and adverb (pp. 68–81) and the testing frames for nominals, verbals, and adjectivals (pp. 83–96).

Exercise ten. In the following sentences, draw a line under the adverbs and over the adverbials. Which forms belong to both classes?

1. He hardly works hard.
2. It was never working well.
3. He certainly goes home tomorrow.
4. Probably he always wrote skillfully.
5. They weren't happily married.

❧ Smaller positional classes

With a little practice, we can classify most of the words, phrases, and clauses in English sentences as nominals, verbals, adjectivals, or adverbials, and since this book is not intended as a complete grammar, it need not offer a system by which every form in every sentence may be classified. Even for a minimal description of English, however, we do need several smaller positional classes; otherwise we will not be able to deal with many very common forms like *the, and,* or *at.* We will therefore conclude our scheme of parts of speech by isolating these smaller sets of frequently occurring forms, some of them quite distinct from our four large positional classes, some of them unusually important subclasses of the four large sets.

Most of the smaller sets, it should be noted, are *closed* classes; that is, their membership is fixed and slow to change. Thus any important new invention is likely to bring several new nominals into the language as names for itself and its parts and uses, but it is hard to conceive of a situation which would give us a series of new words of the same kind as *and* or *but* or *for.* Since this is true, in dealing with our small closed classes we can make considerable use of simple lists. Without at least partial lists of the forms in these smaller classes, it would indeed be very difficult to describe them; for they show no such relations to classes defined by inflection as nominals show to nouns, verbals to verbs, etc. The fact that the typical nominal is a noun and that nouns have distinctive inflections helps us to recognize nominals even though they are far too numerous to be listed; but since forms like *and* have no distinctive endings, we can recognize and classify them only by listing typical specimens and the frames in which they typically occur.

DETERMINERS. We should first define the determiners, a set which we have exemplified and used already in our discussion. Since *a, an, the, your, our,* and *their* are always determiners, we may get our testing frame by considering a position which these words consistently occupy. Regularly, they stand under third stress or weakest stress before a following nominal, as in the frame:

$$2 \quad \textbackslash \quad + {}^2\text{nóminal}^2 \rightarrow {}^2\text{vĕrbal} + \text{adjec}^3\text{tíval}^1 \searrow$$
$$^2\text{Thĕ} + {}^2\text{mán}^2 \rightarrow {}^2\text{sĕemed} + {}^3\text{góod}^1 \searrow$$

We may also class as determiners certain forms, both words and phrases, which are excluded from prenominal position by the presence of a word like *the;* if *the* stands before a nominal, none of these other forms appears there, and if one of these other forms appears, *the* is excluded. We can say, for example, *another man,* and we can say *the man,* but we cannot say *another the man* or *the another man.* In at least some of their uses, then, the following forms are all determiners: *another* (not a word but a phrase, with two bases), *any, each, either, every, her, his, its, my, neither, no, one, some, that, those, this, these.* Many English nouns do not appear in the singular unless they are accompanied by some such form.

A number of the determiners, it will be seen, are pronouns when we classify them by their inflections and not by their position. Since we have established no positional class of pronominals, no difficulty results when we say that in some positions pronouns are nominals, in others determiners. We can even go a step further and say that determiners may be considered a subclass of adjectivals. The forms *that, those, this,* and *these* do require, however, some additional remarks. By their inflections, they are nouns, and we have used the typical positions of nouns in sentences to define our class of nominals. If we say that *that, those, this,* and *these,* when they are used as determiners, are adjectivals, then we must remind ourselves that just as adjectives may rather commonly be used as nominals, so these four nouns are commonly placed in adjectival positions. Their forms and distribution are not representative of the various classes to which we have assigned them.

Exercise eleven. Summarize the general remarks which we have made on the smaller positional classes of English forms. Show in detail how these remarks apply to the determiners. Note particularly that although forms like *your, their, these,* and *those* do have inflections, the inflections do not help us to establish the class of determiners. Why not?

Exercise twelve. Which of the determiners that we have listed are personal pronouns? Of the following personal pronouns, which can be used not only as determiners but as nominals: *her, his, its, my, our?* Make five sentences in which *that* and *those, this* and *these* are used as determiners (a subclass of adjectivals), and five in which they are used as nominals.

PREPOSITIONS. Two other smaller positional classes which should promptly be defined might be given the slightly altered names of *prepositionals* and *conjunctionals,* since we are using the suffix *-al,* as in *nominal,* to distinguish positional classes from classes established in terms of endings, such as *nouns;* but most students will be more comfortable with the traditional names *prepositions* and *conjunctions.* Typical prepositions are *at, by, for, from, in, of, on, to,* and *with,* in at least some of the uses of these words. Often they follow a nominal, a verbal, or an adjectival and precede a nominal:

> The man *at* home was impatient.
> He lives *in* Wilmington.
> The box was full *of* toys.

In this position, prepositions usually have weakest stress; at the ends of sentences, they have third stress:

^{2}Hĕ $+$ lĭves $+$ ĭn $+$ ^{3}Pórtlănd^1↘

^{2}Thĭs $+$ ĭs $+$ thĕ $+$ ^{2}hóuse^2→^{2}hĕ $+$ ^{3}lĭved $+$ ĭn^1↘

Since most prepositions and many adverbials have no distinctive endings, the two classes can sometimes be distinguished *primarily* by their different stresses:

Adverbial: ^{2}Shè $+$ câme $+$ ^{3}tó^1↘ ("recovered consciousness")

Preposition: . . . ^{2}thĕ $+$ ^{2}tówn^2→^{2}wĕ $+$ ^{3}cáme $+$ tò^1↘ ("reached")

A preposition, then, is a form, usually uninflected, which regularly occurs with third or weakest stress in positions regularly filled by *at, by, for,* etc.

AND CONJUNCTIONS. Like the prepositions, the conjunctions are "connecting" forms, usually uninflected, and often occurring with third or weakest stress; but the positions in which the conjunctions occur are different from the prepositional positions, so that the two classes can and must be distinguished, although sometimes the same form in different positions may be now a preposition and now a conjunction (even, at times, an adverbial). One important difference between conjunctions, on the one hand, and adverbials and prepositions, on the other, is that conjunctions normally do not occur at the ends of sentences; we would not say,

^{2}Hĕ $+$ wênt $+$ ^{3}ánd^1↘

but we would say,

^{2}Hĕ $+$ wênt $+$ ^{3}ĭn^1↘

or

. . . ^{2}thĕ $+$ ^{2}cár^2→^{2}hĕ $+$ ^{3}wént $+$ ĭn^1↘

Moreover, when a preposition does not stand at the end of a sentence, it is usually followed by a nominal; if the nominal following the preposition is a pronoun, the pronoun must be in its object form or second possessive form if those forms are overtly marked (*to him, with ours*). In contrast, there is no such limitation on the forms which follow a conjunction. If they constitute a subject-predicate combination, as they often do, that combination as a whole need not be nominal; and if the conjunction is one of those which connect single words, the following word may belong to any class and have any of its possible inflectional forms.

Examples will clarify these statements. In the following sentences, the italicized words are prepositions:

1. *By* the use *of* examples, he made his statements clear.
2. *To* me, his story sounded odd.
3. He found some mistakes *in* mine.
4. *From* what he said, I knew he was suspicious.

All the prepositions are followed by nominals, some of which are words (*examples, me, mine*), and some of which are larger forms (*the use, what he said*). These larger forms, when we consider them as units, must be placed in the nominal class, even though they contain forms which are *not* nominals (*the, said*); for we can replace the larger forms by single nouns, and we can put the larger forms into some of our nominal testing frames. It should be observed that *me* is a distinctive object form, that *mine* is a distinctive second possessive form, and that *what he said* is a subject-predicate combination (a clause).

In the following contrasting sentences, the italicized words are not prepositions but conjunctions:

1. He *and* I made our statements clear *and* convincing.
2. He fired his gun, *but* he fired too soon.

Here the three conjunctions, unlike the prepositions, are not all followed by nominals, but by a nominal (the pronoun *I*), an adjectival (the participle *convincing*), and a clause (*he fired too soon*) which belongs to none of our positional classes—that is, we would only make nonsense if we replaced *he fired too soon* by a single noun like *haste* or *failure*. Finally, the pronoun *I* is in its subject form. After a conjunction, a pronoun *can* have its object form (*She answered him and me*), and it *can* have its second possessive form (*The bills were ours and yours*); but the choice among subject, object, and possessive forms is not determined by the simple fact that a conjunction precedes.

KINDS OF CONJUNCTIONS. Among the forms which frequently or always occupy conjunctional positions are (1) *and, but* (often a preposition), *or, nor, for* (often a preposition); (2) *after* (often a preposition), *although, because, before* (often a preposition), *if, since* (often a preposition), *when;* (3) *either . . . or, neither . . . nor, both . . . and.* The traditional classes which these three groups represent are the *coordinating* conjunctions, the *subordinating* conjunctions, and the *correlative* conjunctions; and although other groupings are possible, these three will serve our turn. Correlative conjunctions are used in pairs, both members of which are usually followed by grammatically equivalent words or larger forms (*both the stars and the planets; neither can nor will; either stupid or lazy*). Subordinating conjunctions typically incorporate whole clauses into larger sentence structures; the clauses so incorporated often have considerable freedom of position, standing initially or medially or finally. For example:

> *When the rain stopped,* the Yankees and the Indians finished the second game of their double-header.
>
> The Yankees and the Indians, *when the rain stopped,* finished the second game of their double-header.
>
> The Yankees and the Indians finished the second game of their double-header *when the rain stopped.*

A clause introduced by a coordinating conjunction cannot be shifted about in this way. We can say,

$$^{2}Thĕ + {}^{3}râin + {}^{2}stópped^{2} \nearrow {}^{2}ănd + thĕy + fînĭshed + thĕ + sêcŏnd + {}^{3}gáme^{1} \searrow$$

but we cannot say

$$^{2}ănd + thĕy + fînĭshed + thĕ + sêcŏnd + {}^{3}gáme^{2} \rightarrow {}^{2}thĕ + {}^{3}râin + {}^{1}stópped^{1} \searrow$$

Exercise thirteen. Which of the following sentences end with prepositions, and which with adverbials?

1. $^{2}Thât's + thĕ + {}^{2}mán^{2} \rightarrow {}^{2}yŏu + {}^{3}spóke + tò^{1} \searrow$
2. $^{3}Vandăls^{2} \rightarrow {}^{2}blêw + thĕ + hôuse + {}^{3}úp^{1} \searrow$
3. $^{2}Whàt + ăre + yŏu + {}^{3}lóokĭng + àt^{1} \searrow$
4. $^{2}Thĕ + trêe + fêll + {}^{3}dówn^{1} \searrow$
5. $^{2}Thĕ + {}^{3}nûrse + {}^{2}cáme^{2} \nearrow {}^{3}tóo^{1} \searrow$

Exercise fourteen. In the following sentences, underline the prepositions once and the conjunctions twice.

1. Everybody understood but him.
2. Everybody understood, but he pretended not to.
3. For some time, the building had been vacant; for nobody wanted to live in a haunted house.
4. After what he said, they had no choice.
5. Before I was sixteen, I had to come in before ten.
6. Their accident has occurred since ours.

RELATIVES. Closely related to the subordinating conjunctions is a small class of forms which traditionally are called *relative pronouns,* although only one of them, *who (whose, whom),* will be called a pronoun in this book. The most important members of this class, which we will call simply the relatives, are *who* (*whose, whom*), *which,* and *that.* They occur in positions like the following:

The student *who* asked the question felt silly.

The question *which/that* he asked was stupid.

If we change the verbs in the first sentence to the present tense, we may note an important correlation of forms among the relative, a preceding nominal (the *antecedent* of the relative), and the following verb:

The *student who asks* the question feels silly.

The *students who ask* the question feel silly.

Thus, although the relatives, like the subordinating conjunctions, incorporate whole clauses into larger sentence structures, the relatives are distinguished from the conjunctions partly by this kind of agreement in number among the antecedent, the relative, and a following verb. The distinction appears very clearly when we compare sentences like the following:

The students *who ask* the question feel silly.

The students, *when he asks* the question, feel silly.

The students, *when they ask* the question, feel silly.

The relative *who,* in the first sentence, is itself the subject with which the verb *ask* agrees in number; in the second and third sentences, *when* has no correlation with the number of *asks* or *ask.*

RELATIVES AND THE OTHER NOMINALS. Since the relatives, unlike the subordinating conjunctions, can be subjects, and since they can also fill other structural positions often filled by nominals, we will treat the relatives as a nominal subclass. It is a particularly useful subclass, because it provides a means of making other subdivisions among the nominals. Just as nominals can be subdivided in one way by their correlation with *he, she,* or *it,* so they can be subdivided in another way by their correlation with *who, which,* or *that.* For instance, nominals like *man* and *boy* appear with *he, woman* and *girl* with *she,* and all four with the relatives *who* and *that* but not with *which.* Nominals like *book, chair, lecture,* and *picture* appear with *it* and with the relatives *which* and *that* but not with *who.*

The relative *that* is distinguished by its appearance with all these groups of nominals and by the position which it fills, like "zero" as a relative, with respect to prepositions. When the relative is *which* or a form of *who,* the preposition may immediately precede it, or the preposition may stand at the end of the subject-predicate combination which the relative introduces:

The nurse *to whom* he gave the message said nothing.

The nurse *whom* he gave the message *to* said nothing.

When the relative is *that* or "zero," the preposition *must* stand at the end of the subject-predicate combination:

The nurse *that* he gave the message *to* said nothing.

The nurse [zero] he gave the message *to* said nothing.

"Zero" as a relative is not normally a subject in standard English.

Several forms in *-ever* (*whoever, whichever, whatever*) often belong to the relative subclass of nominals, too; but their positions and classification need not detain us long. Most notably, they introduce clauses which may sometimes stand initially in larger structures and for which either adverbials or nominals may be substituted.

Whoever answers the door, deliver my message.

Anyhow, deliver my message.

Give the message to *whoever opens the door.*

Give the message to *him.*

INTERROGATIVES AND THEIR KINDS. When the words *who* and *which* stand initially in sentences, they are not relatives but belong to another small positional class, which we will label *interrogatives.* It is a rather complicated little group, traditionally divided into interrogative pronouns, interrogative adjectives, and interrogative adverbs, partly on the basis of occurrence in frames like the following:

(1) ²Whô + caûsed + thĕ + ³díffĭcùltў¹↘

²Whât + caûsed + thĕ + ³díffĭcùltў¹↘

²Whât + dìd + yŏu + ³sée¹↘

(2) ²Whîch + ²mán²→²seêmed + ³góod¹↘

²Whîch + ²mán²→²dìd + yŏu + ³sée¹↘

²Whât + ²státemĕnt²→²caûsed + thĕ + ³díffĭcùltў¹↘

(3) ²Whên (where, why, how) + dìd ĭt + ³háppĕn¹↘

Several remarks are suggested by these examples. The interrogatives of the first group, like *who* and *what,* may be considered as another special subset of nominals, since they act as subjects and objects. As subjects, they may appear either with a simple present or past tense (e.g., *caused*) or with a sequence of verbals like *has seen* or *is seeing,* but as objects they appear almost exclusively with the verbal sequences. A similar difference in the verbals appears with the interrogatives of the second group. These sometimes come close to fitting the frame which we have used to define the determiners (e.g., *Which man seemed good?*); but since interrogatives such as *which* and *what* do not occur, like many of the determiners, with weakest stress, and since interrogatives regularly occur in positions where determiners do *not* occur, as in *Which man did you see?* with its distinctive verbal sequence, we are justified in classing the interrogatives of this group as a kind of adjectivals but not as determiners. The interrogatives of the third group, which we will consider adverbials, do not appear as subjects or objects and are regularly correlated with verbal sequences, not simple pasts or presents. At this point, it need hardly be said that in other positions a form like *when* is often not an interrogative but a subordinating conjunction:

> Interrogative: When did it happen?
> Conjunction: When it happened, I left.

INTENSIVES AND REFLEXIVES AS NOMINALS. Among our smaller positional classes, we have now established two, the relatives and Group 1 of the interrogatives, which we will treat as subgroups of nominals. We will also consider as nominals the forms in *-self* and *-selves* (traditionally, intensive and reflexive pronouns), which we have mentioned before (p. 77). These often stand after another nominal, with which they show an important correlation of forms. For example:

> The *man himself* was uninjured.
> The *women themselves* were frightened.

The correlation, it will be noted, is like that between the personal pronouns and other nominals, involving both gender (*masculine—he, himself; feminine—she, herself; neuter—it, itself*), number (*the man himself, the women themselves*), and person (*I myself, you yourself, he himself*). The same correlation applies not only in the *intensive* uses of the *-self/ -selves* forms, which we have just illustrated, but in their *reflexive* uses as well:

> The *man* cut *himself.*
> The *women* screamed *themselves* hoarse.
> The *man* talked to *himself.*
> The *women* talked to *themselves* and everybody else.

Exercise fifteen. In the following sentences, point out the relatives, their antecedents, and the verbs of which the relatives are subjects or objects. Which verbs agree in number with the relatives?

1. The points which he argues are unimportant.
2. He argues points which are unimportant.
3. Nobody could win the cases he loses.
4. Is the man who invents a new machine a hero?

5. Are the machines that he invents of any value?
6. The heroes whom one country reveres are villains that are despised in other lands.

Exercise sixteen. Which of the following nouns would you refer to by *he,* which by *she,* which by *it?* Could you refer to any of these nouns by more than one of the pronouns *he, she,* or *it?* With which of the nouns would you use *who* or *that* as a relative, and with which would you use *that* or *which?* Here are the nouns: *clock, dog, house, child, room, armor, ship, window, bear, father.*

Exercise seventeen. In each of the following sentences, replace "zero" as a relative first with *that* and then with *whom* or *which.* If different word orders are possible in the sentences with *whom* or *which,* make a sentence for each of the possible orders.
1. The box he left the money in was missing.
2. The orator he meant was Cicero.
3. Smithers left his books to a library he had founded.
4. The town the boat docked at next was Glennville.
5. The judge said the questions the lawyer had asked were irrelevant.

Exercise eighteen. Classify the interrogatives in the following sentences as Group 1 ("interrogative pronouns"), Group 2 ("interrogative adjectives"), or Group 3 ("interrogative adverbs"). In which of the sentences could a simple present or past tense be used? In which of the sentences are the interrogatives the subjects or parts of the subjects?
1. Who has killed Cock Robin?
2. Why did he do it?
3. What vegetables are you cooking for dinner?
4. How has the team looked in practice?
5. Which kind of advertising has pleased the public most?
6. Which did you mean—pine or oak?
7. Where does the poet find an audience today?
8. What difference does it make?
9. When did any dictator willingly resign?
10. What was troubling the chairman?

Exercise nineteen. Classify the *-self/-selves* forms in the following sentences first as intensives or reflexives and then by gender, number, and person. For example, in *The man cut himself, himself* is reflexive, third person, singular, masculine. Some of the forms will not show gender, and some may be either singular or plural.
1. You yourself were never good at mathematics.
2. He liked the game itself, but not the practice.
3. We Americans often deceive ourselves.
4. The cardinal thought the duchess herself was guilty.

5. The soldiers told themselves that peace was near.
6. You girls should keep yourselves busy.
7. "I myself was honest once," the salesman said.
8. Napoleon himself must sometimes have doubted himself.
9. The selfish mother neglects her children and lives for herself alone.
10. The platitude itself is sometimes useful.

VERBAL PHRASES AND AUXILIARIES. Among the verbals, we must likewise set up at least one small but very important subclass, which usually is known as the class of *auxiliaries*. To establish this subclass clearly, we will have to illustrate most of the types of verbal phrases, those sequences of verb forms which, as sequences, fill the blanks in our testing frames for verbals. The auxiliaries and the phrases in which they appear are a basic feature of English.

1. The first such pattern consists of *have / has / had* plus any past participle, as in the sentence, *The boys have made a mess*. The sequences like *have made* or *has made* are often called *perfect tense* or *present perfect tense*, and those like *had made* are called *past perfect* or *pluperfect;* but we must carefully *avoid* calling any of the verbal phrases *tenses*. Tense, as we have defined it, is a matter of the forms and endings of single words; *plays* is present tense, and *played* is past. If we give the name *tense* to verbal phrases, we are confusing classification according to endings with classification according to position in sentences. English has two tenses and only two.

2. The second pattern consists of *am / is / are / was / were* plus any *present* participle, as in the sentence, *The firm is losing money*. Such verbal constructions are often called *progressive*. They differ from the first pattern in two ways: the first uses the forms of *have,* the second the forms of *be;* the first uses the *past* participle of any verb, the second the *present* participle.

3. The third pattern consists of *am / is / are / was / were* plus the past participle of any verb which can take a direct object (any *transitive* verb), as in the sentence, *His son was spanked*. Such constructions are often said to be in the *passive voice*. Pattern 3 differs from Patterns 1 and 2 in that it cannot be formed with *every* past participle; we cannot say *His house was been* or *His house was dwelt*.

4. Pattern 4 consists of *have / has / had,* plus *been,* plus the past participle of any transitive verb, as in the sentence, *His son had been spanked*. These constructions, too, are called passive. They are limited, like

Pattern 3, to the inclusion of the past participles of transitive verbs only, but they differ from all the first three patterns in having *been* in the second of the three positions in the phrase.

5. *Have / has / had,* plus *been,* plus any *present* participle, as in the sentence, *The ladies of the Missionary Society have been making fudge.* This fifth pattern differs from the fourth in two ways: Pattern 5 ends with a present participle, not a past participle as in Pattern 4; and this participle is not limited, as in Pattern 4, to transitive verbs. An *intransitive* verb, one which does *not* take an object, appears in the sentence, *The ladies had been chattering.* Like Pattern 2, Pattern 5 is often called progressive.

6. *Am / is / are / was / were,* plus *being,* plus the past participle of any transitive verb, as in the sentence, *A house was being built on the corner.* This pattern differs from all the others in having the word *being* in its second position. It is sometimes called the progressive passive.

Summing up the distinctions among the six patterns, we see that we have classified them by the following criteria: (a) the use of the forms of *have* or the forms of *be* in the initial position in the verbal phrase; (b) the use of a participle of *any* verb or of a transitive verb only, in the final position; (c) in final position, the use of a past participle or a present participle; (d) the presence of only two positions in the phrase, as in Patterns 1–3, or of three positions, as in Patterns 4–6; (e) the use of *been* or *being* in the second position of three-place sequences. As we said before, we will treat every word in any of these six patterns as a verbal, and we will call the patterns as wholes verbal phrases.

VERBAL PHRASES WITH INFINITIVES. So far, none of the patterns which we have distinguished includes any *infinitives* or *infinitive phrases.* The infinitive of a verb, as we have said, is the simple name or base form of that verb, in some of its uses; thus *be, do, have, kick, make,* and *put* may be used as infinitives. For most verbs, *infinitive phrases* are also possible after the models of the first five verbal patterns: *(to) have kicked, (to) be kicking, (to) be kicked, (to) have been kicked, (to) have been kicking.* Infinitives and infinitive phrases enter into important verbal phrases other than the six which we have already described.

a. The verbals *will, would, shall, should, may, might, can, could,* and *must* may precede any infinitive or infinitive phrase, as in the sentence,

I would have been kicked if I had said that. In these verbal patterns, the infinitive without *to* (the *unmarked* infinitive) is used.

b. The verbal *ought* may precede any *marked* infinitive or infinitive phrase, as in the sentence, *The women ought to have made the judge.* The word *to* is here the *mark* or *sign* of the infinitive.

c. The verbals *do, does,* and *did,* under primary stress, may precede any unmarked infinitive but not the five infinitive phrases, as in the sentence, $^2H\grave{e}$ $^+$ $^4d\acute{o}es$ $^+$ $st\hat{u}d\ddot{y}^1$\ A verbal pattern of this sort is often called *emphatic,* but the emphasis results from the patterns of stress and intonation, not from the use of the forms of *do.* The forms of *do* with an unmarked infinitive are also frequently used in questions and in negative statements; for example, *Does he study?* and *He does not study.* But the forms of *do* are not used with an unmarked *stressed* infinitive in affirmative statements; there is no sentence, $^2H\grave{e}$ $^+$ $d\breve{o}es$ $^+$ $^3st\acute{u}d\ddot{y}^1$\

AUXILIARIES DEFINED. Our list and description, though incomplete, now include most of the important English patterns of verb forms. All of the positions which make up these patterns are verbal positions, so that all the forms which appear in them, except *to,* are verbals. Only some of these verbals, however, belong in our class of auxiliaries, which we may most easily define by exclusion: in any of the nine verbal patterns 1–6 and a–c, all the verbals except the last are auxiliaries. A list of the principal auxiliaries therefore includes, in some or all of their uses, the forms *have, has, had* (past tense); *be, am, is, are, was, were, been, being; will, would; shall, should; may, might; can, could; must; ought; do, does, did.*

Except for *being, may, might, ought,* sometimes the forms of *do,* and perhaps one or two others, the auxiliaries are characterized by the possibility of appearance under weakest stress, as can be heard if the examples which we have given are read aloud. The auxiliaries, moreover, occupy distinctive positions in questions (*Have you replied? Must he go?*); they are used as substitutes for larger verbal forms (*They are being hurt, and so are we*); and under one of the three stronger stresses, many of them occur in close transition with *n't* "not," as in the sentences *I haven't gone, They weren't singing, They wouldn't have answered.*

We can use these characteristics to rule out of our auxiliary group the forms of such verbals as *get* and *keep.* We say,

$^2H\grave{e}$ $^+$ $g\hat{o}t$ $^+$ $^3k\acute{i}lled^1$\

and

$^2Th\breve{e}$ $^+$ $^2c\acute{a}r^2$→$^2k\hat{e}pt$ $^+$ $^3m\acute{o}v\breve{i}ng^1$\

but in such sentences verbs like *got* and *kept* usually have a stronger stress than an auxiliary like *was* in the sentences,

$$^2\text{Hè} + \text{wăs} + {}^3\text{kílled}^1\searrow$$

and

$$^2\text{Thĕ} + {}^2\text{cár}^{2\rightarrow2}\text{wăs} + {}^3\text{móvĭng}^1\searrow$$

There is, besides, no *gotn't* and no *keptn't;* in questions, genuine auxiliaries must be used with *get* and *keep* (*Did he get killed? Has he kept working?*); and *get* and *keep* are not used as substitutes. The importance of such criteria for the auxiliaries is that without them, the group would become an unmanageable catchall, like the traditional pronouns; for we would have to include in it such verbals as *begin, continue, get, keep, stop,* etc., in sentences like *The car began moving / continued moving / got moving / kept moving / stopped moving / wanted moving.*

Exercise twenty. Across the top of a sheet of paper, write the first of the verbal patterns which we have just listed: "*have / has / had* plus any past participle." On the same sheet, list twenty common verbs. Make a sentence in which each verb appears in the stated pattern. Do the same for patterns 2–6.

Exercise twenty-one. For as many as possible of the first twenty verbs which you listed in Exercise twenty, list the (marked) infinitive and the five infinitive phrases. For some one of the twenty verbs, form all the verbal phrases (patterns a–c) in which infinitive phrases or the infinitive alone appears; use each verbal phrase in a sentence.

ADVERBIALS OF DEGREE. One last group of forms will complete our outline of the "parts of speech." It is a subgroup of adverbials which we may label *adverbials of degree,* and its members occur before adjectivals and adverbials in frames like the following:

$$^2\text{Thĕ} + {}^2\text{gáme}^{2\rightarrow2}\text{wàsn'}t + \underline{\quad\wedge\quad} + {}^3\text{góod}^1\searrow$$
$$^2\text{Hè} + {}^2\text{wént}^{2\rightarrow2} + \underline{\quad\wedge\quad} + {}^3\text{quícklў}^1\searrow$$
$$^2\text{Thĕ} + {}^2\text{gáme}^{2\rightarrow2}\text{hăd} + \text{beèn} + \underline{\quad\wedge\quad} + {}^3\text{béttĕr}^1\searrow$$

Representative adverbials of degree, as discovered by the use of these frames, include forms like *extremely, more, much, quite, surely, too,* and *very.* We should perhaps repeat once more the now familiar cautions that our frames are unchanged if we substitute other nominals, verbals, adjectivals, adverbials, or determiners for the particular ones which we have chosen here, that many forms which are adverbials of degree when they appear in these frames, appear also in other positions and therefore in different positional classes, and that no contradiction is involved when we make *much* and *more* adjectives by one definition (they are compared words) and adverbials by another.

Exercise twenty-two. Which of the italicized forms in the following sentences are adverbials of degree?
1. You're the *very* man we're looking for.
2. She answered, *too.*
3. The day was extremely cold.
4. *Quite* eagerly, the monkey drank the beer.
5. *More* students mean *more* teachers.
6. The *awful* stranger looked *awful* strange.
7. *Surely* you don't think he drives *too* fast.
8. "Tom Jones" is *much* longer than "Joseph Andrews."
9. *Much* study is a weariness to the flesh.
10. *Very* gracefully, she bowed and turned away.

Summary

Forced to abandon the traditional definitions of the parts of speech by their inconsistency and the resultant difficulty of applying them, we have framed our own definitions in two different ways.

First, we have recognized five classes of *words* distinguished by the endings with which they appear: nouns, verbs, pronouns, adjectives, and adverbs. A noun is a word which is inflected to mark the contrasts between singular and plural numbers and between the common and possessive cases; that is, a noun is any word belonging to a series like *man, man's, men, men's.* Our pronouns include *only* the traditional personal pronouns and *who*—words which have distinctive object forms or two possessive forms which are not related one to the other as singular to plural. A verb is a word which is inflected for tense and whose forms will fit into a series like *sing, sings, sang, sung, singing.* An adjective is a compared word. An adverb is an uncompared word which consists of the positive degree of an adjective plus the form *-ly.*

Second, we have defined a different set of classes on the basis of the positions which words, phrases, and clauses occupy in sentences. Using testing frames, we distinguished four main positional classes—nominals, verbals, adjectivals, and adverbials—and eight smaller positional classes—determiners, prepositions, conjunctions, relatives, interrogatives, intensive-reflexives, auxiliaries, and adverbials of degree. Relatives, interrogatives of type 1, and intensive-reflexives are subclasses of nominals;

determiners and interrogatives of type 2 are subclasses of adjectivals; auxiliaries are a subclass of verbals; and interrogatives of the third type and adverbials of degree (of course) are subclasses of adverbials. Prepositions and conjunctions are independent of the four main positional classes. All twelve positional classes must be kept carefully distinct from the five classes which we established by their endings. Though an adjective, for example, will usually be an adjectival, as in the sentence,

The *poor* boy became President,

it may sometimes belong to a different positional class, like the nominal in the following sentence:

The *poor* can afford no vacations.

To force this distinction, we have used the ending -*al* in the names of our largest position*al* classes.

❧ Bibliography

FRANCIS, W. NELSON, *The Structure of American English*. New York: The Ronald Press Company, 1958. Ch. v, "Grammar—Part I: The Parts of Speech," pp. 222–290.

FRIES, CHARLES CARPENTER, *The Structure of English*. New York: Harcourt, Brace and Company, 1952. Ch. v, "Parts of Speech," pp. 65–86.

GLEASON, H. A., JR., *An Introduction to Descriptive Linguistics*. New York: Henry Holt and Company, 1955. Ch. viii, "Outline of English Morphology," pp. 92–110; Ch. x, "Syntax," pp. 128–142.

HILL, ARCHIBALD A., *Introduction to Linguistic Structures*. New York: Harcourt, Brace and Company, 1958. Ch. ix, "Inflection," pp. 138–165; Ch. x, "Form Classes Marked by Derivational Morphemes," pp. 166–172.

HOCKETT, CHARLES F., *A Course in Modern Linguistics*. New York: The Macmillan Company, 1958. "Grammatical Systems," pp. 147–267.

ROBERTS, PAUL, *Patterns of English*. New York: Harcourt, Brace and Company, 1956. "Part One: The Four Form Classes," pp. 1–24; "Part Two: Three Important Structure Groups," pp. 25–55; "Part Ten: Review," pp. 286–297.

TRAGER, GEORGE L., and HENRY LEE SMITH, JR., *An Outline of English Structure*. Norman, Okla.: Battenburg Press, 1951. Part II, "Morphemics," pp. 52–80.

ZANDVOORT, R. W., *A Handbook of English Grammar*. London: Longmans, Green and Co., 1957. Part I, "Verbs," pp. 1–89; Part II, "Nouns," pp. 90–127; Part III, "Pronouns," pp. 128–186; Part IV, "Adjectives and Adverbs," pp. 187–194.

Note: The preceding chapter owes most to Fries and to Trager and Smith. Its most distinctive feature is its establishment, not of one, but of two sets of parts of speech. For this method, Trager and Smith provided the suggestion. Zandvoort's erudite work makes an excellent contrast for the recent American books; it is quite traditional but rich in precise detail.

CHAPTER THREE # Nominal Sequences

In Chapter One, we outlined the system of English sounds. In Chapter Two, we defined the word, established four word classes in terms of inflectional endings and one in terms of a derivational ending, and finally established twelve different but related positional classes which include both words and forms larger than words (phrases and clauses). We have thus prepared ourselves to go a step further and consider not just sounds, or words, or classes of words, but these larger forms which can be systematically substituted for the single-word members of our various positional classes. That is, we are now ready to pursue the study of phrases and subordinate clauses.

❖ Nominal phrases

Since nominals and verbals are our two most important positional classes, we will first consider certain *nominal* phrases, sequences which include more than one base and which can replace single-word nominals in some or all of their positions, but which do not constitute a subject-predicate combination. Using nouns as the words most likely to behave as typical nominals, we may illustrate some important nominal positions by the following sentences:

1. *Money* talks.
   The day broke.
2. His god, *money*, talked too loud.
   His father, *the coach*, talked too loud.
3. His work in *school* was unsatisfactory.
   His work in *the school* was unsatisfactory.
4. He loved *money*.
   He disliked *the school*.
5. He gave *students* much difficulty.
   He gave *the students* much difficulty.
6. His teammates chose him *captain*.
   His training made him *a leader*.
7. John is *captain* for this game.
   This is *the center* of the campus.

In all these positions, various phrases can replace the single words, as we have suggested by including in each pair of sentences one nominal without a determiner and one nominal with a determiner. We may note, for further illustration, some of the phrases which can replace the nominal *dogs* in the sentence *Dogs are vicious animals:*

The dogs are vicious animals.
Big dogs are vicious animals.
The big dogs are vicious animals.
Annoyed by punishment, the dogs are vicious animals.
The dogs in the kennel are vicious animals.
The dogs which are in the kennel are vicious animals.
²Thĕ + ³dógs + thêre²→²ăre + vĭciŏus + ³ănĭmăls¹↘

Dogs trained for hunting criminals are vicious animals.

For an elementary description like ours, the most important of all these expansions are the first three, which exemplify the very common group of nominal phrases consisting of nouns preceded by determiners, or by adjectivals other than determiners, or by both. We will use the determiner as the basis for organizing our discussion of such phrases.

❧ Determiners in nominal phrases

Of course, as we said in Chapter Two, not all nouns regularly occur with determiners. Nouns denoting things which can be counted as separate units regularly do take both *a* (*an*) and *the* in the singular, and sometimes take *the* in the plural: we say *a house, the house,* and *the houses.* Nouns denoting masses which can be divided or united but not numbered as aggregates of separate units may take *the* in the singular (*the flesh*); they have no plural. On the other hand, both nouns like *flesh* and the plural of nouns like *house* also occur without *the,* and nouns like *flesh* never take *a* or *an.* Nevertheless, the determiners provide a center for a helpful outline: all the nominal phrases which we are first to consider fit into the pattern

	Predeterminer	Determiner	Postdeterminer	Noun,

which is represented by the phrase

	all	the	good	men.

❧ Order of modifiers before nouns

Some of the facts about this pattern have been stated in Chapter Two. There it was pointed out that most postdeterminers are adjectivals, that they can stand under second stress before a following nominal which has strongest stress, and that their relative order is essentially fixed. What is needed now is a more detailed statement of this order. The position under second stress immediately before the final noun is the only position in which the traditional "noun adjuncts," "nouns used as adjectives," can appear:

^{2}thĕ $+$ stône $+$ ^{3}wáll^1↘

^{2}ä $+$ brîck $+$ ^{3}búildĭng^1↘

Adjectivals which traditionally are called *descriptive* precede the noun adjunct and may in turn be preceded by adverbials of degree:

a *stone* wall

a *fine* stone wall

a *very* fine stone wall

The traditional *limiting* adjectivals occupy the fourth position before the final nominal:

the *two* very fine stone walls

If now we wish to add a possessive form of a noun to our sequence, we can do one of two things. First, we can substitute the possessive of some nouns for the determiner, with a change of stress (*John's two very fine stone walls*); and, second, we can place the possessive of other nouns after the determiner (*the mason's two very fine stone walls*), in which case the determiner is taken with the possessive and we can go on to construct a second series of adjectivals between them (*the industrious old mason's two very fine stone walls*). The predeterminers, finally, are rather various but limited in number. Examples are *many / such / what a man; all / both the men; almost / nearly all the men; not quite all the men;* etc.

The order which we have described, therefore, may be stated more fully as (1) predeterminer, (2) determiner, (3) limiting adjectival, (4) adverbial of degree, (5) descriptive adjectival, (6) "noun adjunct," (7) nominal (here a noun). With the proper intonation patterns, the whole sequence can be preceded by descriptive adjectivals, including both adjectives and participles, both phrases and single words. Thus, in rather formal English, we can speak and write such sentences as these:

^{3}Bêautĭfŭl $+$ bŭt $+$ ^{2}dúmb^2↗^{2}thĕ $+$ ^{2}gírls^2→^{2}flûnked $+$ ^{3}óut^1↘

^{2}Ĕx^{3}haûstĕd $+$ bỳ $+$ thĕ $+$ òr^{2}déal^2↗^{2}thĕ $+$ prîsŏnĕr $+$ ^{3}fáintĕd^1↘

Exercise one. The sentence *Teachers are strange people* is grammatically equivalent to *Dogs are vicious animals.* Expand the nominal *teachers* as we expanded the nominal *dogs* in our illustration. Thus your first expansion will be *The teachers are strange people.*

Exercise two. Which of the following nouns are *count-nouns,* like *house,* and which are *mass-nouns,* like *flesh?* Can any of them be used in both ways? If so, with what difference in meaning?

1. noun	3. water	5. cotton	7. nail	9. tree
2. dirt	4. iron	6. lamp	8. oil	10. pork

Exercise three. Make up ten sentences to illustrate the order which we have described as (1) predeterminer, (2) determiner, (3) limiting adjectival, (4) adverbial of degree, (5) descriptive adjectival, (6) "noun adjunct," (7) nominal (here a noun).

❧ Modifiers after nouns

What we have said so far in this chapter might be described, in traditional terms, as a statement of the position of modifiers before nouns. As the examples on p. 115 suggest, however, there are other nominal phrases in which the single-word nominal for which the whole sequence may sometimes be substituted does not stand finally in the sequence. A very common example is the type

Nominal	Preposition	Nominal
men	at	work.

Traditionally, we would say that prepositional phrases follow the nouns they modify. *At work* is said to modify the noun *men* and hence to be used adjectivally partly because the whole phrase, *men at work,* can be substituted for one of its parts, *men,* and partly because the position after a nominal is sometimes occupied by undoubted adjectivals (*God almighty, the worst book imaginable, something awful*). The same position may also be filled by participles, marked infinitives, clauses introduced by relatives, and clauses introduced by subordinating conjunctions:

1. Participle: the players *reporting* (were all veterans)
2. Marked infinitive: a time *to laugh*
3. Clause introduced by relative: the tree *that fell*
4. Clause introduced by subordinating conjunction: the morning *after the news arrived*

Two comments are necessary on these four examples. First, Example 3 illustrates the traditional statement that "relative clauses follow the nouns they modify"—a statement, incidentally, which illustrates itself. Second, in the analysis of such examples and the classification of their parts, discussion must proceed systematically if confusion is to be avoided. The fourth example may be considered at some length in this connection.

❧ What goes with what

The whole construction *the morning after the news arrived* is classified as
nominal because it can consistently occupy positions which single nouns
consistently occupy:

Day	breaks.
The day	breaks.
The day	is fine.
The morning	was fine.
The morning after the news arrived	was fine.

As we have pointed out, however, the classification of a whole construction is not necessarily the same as the classification of its parts. Though
the morning after the news arrived is a nominal when we consider it as
a unit, only the first of its two parts, (1) *the morning* and (2) *after the
news arrived,* is itself a nominal. *The morning* is nominal because it occurs in nominal positions like those we have just illustrated; but *after
the news arrived* may be called adjectival for the same reasons that allowed us to call *at work* adjectival in *men at work.*

Continuing the analysis, we note further that *after,* although it occurs
in an adjectival sequence, is a subordinating conjunction, while *the news
arrived* may be broken into two parts, of which the first, *the news,* is
nominal and the second, *arrived,* is verbal. In short, the members of our
positional classes combine systematically in larger sequences which may
also be classified as nominal, verbal, adjectival, and so on; but the multiple classifications are not contradictory, since a whole sequence may very
well be substitutable in positions where some or all of its members could
not occur, and since its members, on the other hand, may fill positions
from which the sequence would be barred.

❧ Apposition

One other very important sequence which can substitute, in some positions, for a single nominal needs discussion in this chapter; it is the sequence containing two nominals, one of which is usually said to be in
apposition with the other. Examples are plentiful:

^{2}Thĕ + ^{3}bóok$^{2\rightarrow2}$ă + lârge + ^{3}fólĭò^1 ↗^{2}wăs + vèrў + ^{3}héavў^1 ↘

^{2}Thĕ + ^{3}fármĕr$^{2\rightarrow2}$ă + ^{3}lâzў + ^{1}mán^1 ↗^{2}wăs + ^{3}póor^1 ↘

^{2}Ã + ^{3}lâzў + ^{1}gróup^1 ↗^{2}thĕ + fârmĕrs + wĕre + ^{3}póor^1 ↘

^{2}Thĕ + ^{3}órchĭd$^{2\rightarrow2}$thàt + fîne + ^{3}ládў + ămòng + flôwĕrs^1 ↗

^{2}wăs + ^{3}lóvelў^1 ↘

The nominals which would here be called *appositives* are *folio, man, group,* and *lady;* the phrases in which they occur, like *a large folio,* are *appositive phrases;* and the entire sequences *the . . . folio, the . . . man, a . . . farmers,* and *the . . . flowers* fill positions which might be filled simply by *the book, the farmer, the farmers,* and *the orchid.* One or both of the two nominals in sequences of this kind is usually a noun; the same personal pronoun would usually be substituted for both the nominals; and the appositive usually stands second in the sequence. Thus *book* and *folio, farmer* and *man* are all nouns; the substitute for *book* and *folio* is *it,* while *he* substitutes for *man* and *farmer;* and *book* and *farmer* precede their appositives, *folio* and *man.* It should be noted, however, that in the third sentence the appositive *group* occupies the first position, where it is followed by a terminal, and that the substitutes for *orchid* and *lady,* in the (literary) fourth sentence, would be different (*orchid—it; lady—she*).

Exercise four. From the sentence *Something happened,* make five new sentences by following these instructions:
a. Insert a prepositional phrase after *something.*
b. Insert an adjective after *something.*
c. Insert a participle after *something.*
d. Insert a marked infinitive after *something.*
e. Insert a relative clause after *something.*

Exercise five. To which of our four main positional classes (nominals, verbals, adjectivals, and adverbials) would you assign the underlined phrases and clauses in the following sentences? Note that you are asked to classify the phrases and clauses as wholes; a phrase need not be nominal because it contains a noun, or adjectival because it contains an adjective.
1. A big striped cat was swimming in the goldfish bowl.
2. A big striped cat was swimming in the goldfish bowl.
3. A big striped cat was swimming in the goldfish bowl.
4. A big striped cat was swimming in the goldfish bowl.
5. A big striped cat was swimming in the goldfish bowl.
6. A big striped cat was swimming in the goldfish bowl.
7. Sixty-four dollars, the sum he owed the tailor, seemed a lot of money.
8. Sixty-four dollars, the sum he owed the tailor, seemed a lot of money.
9. Sixty-four dollars, the sum he owed the tailor, seemed a lot of money.
10. Sixty-four dollars, the sum he owed the tailor, seemed a lot of money.

Exercise six. In the following sentences, underline the nouns which are used as appositives.

1. Tom married Sophia, the squire's daughter.
2. The lion's behavior made the trainer, a stern disciplinarian, very angry.
3. A dubious project at best, the toll roads had to be abandoned.
4. He gave the Swede, a laborer, ten dollars as his pay for the week.
5. William the Conqueror was a great soldier and a great ruler.

Note: The bibliography for Chapters Three through Six is provided at the end of Chapter Six, since the different organization of different grammars makes limited reference unwieldy.

CHAPTER FOUR Verbal Sequences

Introduction

In Chapter Two, we outlined the main types of verbal phrases, sequences of verbal forms which can occupy some of the same positions as single verbals. We limited the outline, however, to sequences consisting of verbals and did not consider the larger sequences which can also be substituted in some positions for single verbals and which include words from other positional classes. Now we must extend the discussion, as Chapter Three should already have suggested, to include these larger sequences. When we have done so, we will have described the two main parts of the English sentence, whose chief pattern is

Nominal	Verbal
Birds	sing.

Just as a nominal phrase may sometimes substitute for a single nominal, so a sequence of words (a verbal phrase) may sometimes substitute for a single verbal; we may replace *sing,* in the sentence just given, with a variety of phrases:

Birds	sing sweetly.
Birds	sing songs.
Birds	sing sweet songs.

To avoid confusion, we must repeat that by *verbal phrase* we mean a sequence of words which, in certain positions, can replace a single verbal. By this definition, *sing sweet songs,* in our third sentence, is a verbal phrase, although one of its parts, *sweet songs,* is a nominal phrase. Our treatment of verbal phrases must therefore include remarks not only on adverbials (like *sweetly* in *sing sweetly*) but on a number of familiar constructions such as direct objects, indirect objects, and the like.

Verbal phrases including adverbials

In Chapter Two, we described the adverbial as the positional class which includes no forms in nominal, verbal, or adjectival positions but only adverbs and forms typically replaceable by adverbs or by such uninflected words as *then, there, thus;* one position, we noted, in which adverbs commonly occur is under strongest stress after a nominal at the end of a sentence. Words fitting this description are underlined in the following sentences:

He went quickly.
He went in.
He went fast.

❧ Adverbials that are not adverbs

We need not talk at length about the detailed limitations of position for adverbials—limitations which native speakers "automatically" observe and which we remarked on briefly in Chapter Two; but several other important matters do require attention. We should first repeat the observation that not all adverbials are adverbs; both nouns and adjectives may occupy certain adverbial positions, as in the sentences

He works nights

and

He talks loud.

Sentences like the second of these two will give us no trouble if we simply remember that there is nothing incorrect about them; *He talks loud* and *He went fast* and *He drove slow* are perfectly normal utterances, for which there is no need to substitute *He drove slowly* or the like. The possibility of such substitution merely justifies the statement that *slow,* an adjective, is an adverbial in *He drove slow.* (Of course, in some other adverbial positions, *slowly* alone occurs, and not *slow: He walked slowly down the street, He slowly walked down the street.*)

It may be a little harder to decide when a noun is used not as a nominal but as an adverbial. One good test is substitution. If the noun can be replaced by a personal pronoun, it is a nominal, as in the sentence

He lêft hóme,

for which, with a change in the stress pattern, we can substitute

He léft ĭt.

If the noun cannot be replaced by a personal pronoun but *can* be replaced by an adverbial like *then, there,* or *thus,* the noun too is an adverbial, as in the sentence

He works nights.

(He works then.)

If we put both a nominal and an adverbial after a verb like *left,* then the nominal comes first:

He left home yesterday,

not

He left yesterday home.

We might remark in passing that at the beginning of a sentence the relative order of adverbial and nominal is just the opposite. There the adverbial usually precedes:

Yesterday the dean was late.

That way [thus] that way [it] will be forgotten.
If we put the adverbial in second position at the beginning of a sentence,
we would usually have to set it off by terminals:

^{2}Thĕ + ^{3}déan$^{2\rightarrow1}$thìs + ^{1}mórnĭng^1 ⟋^{2}wăs + ^{3}láte^1 ↘

↜ Adverbial phrases and clauses

Like single nouns and adjectives, certain sequences can also appear in adverbial positions in the larger sequences which we have chosen to call verbal phrases. We can construct series of sentences to illustrate these possible substitutions:

He left.
He left quickly.
He left yesterday.
He left at that time.
He left when he pleased.

The sequences in question are the phrase *at that time* and the clause *when
he pleased. At* is a preposition, followed as usual by a nominal sequence,
and *when* is a subordinating conjunction, which is usually followed by an
instance of the basic sentence pattern Nominal-Verbal. The occurrence of
these sequences in these positions reminds us that prepositional phrases
and subordinate clauses may be used adverbially.

A striking difference may here be noted between the comparative freedom of position of clauses introduced by relatives and of most clauses introduced by subordinating conjunctions. In the sentence

The class which met at eight was unlucky,

the clause *which met at eight* can occupy no other position; but in the
sentence

The teacher could be very pleasant when she pleased,

when she pleased could also stand first or after *teacher.* A similar observation applies to the prepositional phrases in the following sentences:

The teacher *of mathematics* could be very pleasant.
The teacher, *at times,* could be very pleasant.
At times the teacher could be very pleasant.
The teacher could be very pleasant *at times.*

The difference is parallel to that between the relatively fixed position of
an adjectival like *good* (*a good book*) and the more various positions of
an adverbial like *quickly* (both *replied quickly* and *quickly replied*).
Though both *of mathematics* and *at times* are traditionally (and rightly)

called prepositional phrases because they are introduced by prepositions, positionally *of mathematics* is adjectival and *at times* is adverbial.

❧ Adverbials and prepositions

Our third and last main topic in this section has already been suggested by our remarks in Chapter Two about the distinction between adverbials and prepositions—a distinction which sometimes depends on stress patterns. The following sets of sentences should be carefully compared:

(1) ²Ì + spôke + tŏ + thĕ + ³téachĕr¹↘   (²Ì + ³spóke + tò hĭm¹↘)
    ²Ì + bûrnt + ùp + thĕ + ³hóuse¹↘   (_ _ _ _ _ _ _ _ _ _ _ _ _ _)

(2) _ _ _ _ _ _ _ _ _ _ _ _ _ _ _ _ _ _ _   (_ _ _ _ _ _ _ _ _ _ _ _ _ _)
    ²Ì + bûrnt + thĕ + hôuse + ³úp¹↘   (²Ì + bûrnt ĭt + ³úp¹↘)

(3) ²Thĕ + têachĕr + Ì + ³spóke + tò²→²rĕ³plíed¹↘
    ²Thĕ + hôuse + Ì + bûrnt + ³úp²→²wăs + ³míne¹↘

(4) ²Thĕ + têachĕr + tŏ + whòm + Ì + ³spóke²→²rĕ³plíed¹↘

_ _

Although our examples by no means represent the full complexity of the situation, into which a good many dialectal differences probably enter, still it is clear that *to* in *speak to* and *up* in *burn up* belong to different positional classes. When they occur in comparable positions, as in (1) and (3), *up* always has stronger stress than *to,* and each word appears in one sequence where the other is not used. We do not say *I spoke the teacher to* or *the house up which I burnt.* As an uninflected word which appears under strongest stress after a nominal at the end of a sentence, *up* is an adverbial; but *to,* with its third or weakest stress and its different set of positions, is a typical preposition. The same features which distinguish these two words in the sequences *speak to* and *burn up* characterize other pairs, such as *think of* vs. *bring down, look at* vs. *carry off, run from* vs. *make over,* etc.

Exercise one. In the following sentences, the italicized items are classified as adverbials. Give reasons for that classification in each sentence.
1. The child waved the flag *proudly.*
2. The rabbit ran *as hard as he could.*
3. *Last night* the wind blew the signboard *over.*
4. He sings in the choir *on Sunday,* but *Mondays* he gets drunk.
5. He's always acting *tough.*

Exercise two. As we have said, phrases consisting of a preposition and a following nominal are called *prepositional* phrases not because of their position or function but because they are introduced by prepositions; they may also be classified, according to their positions, as nominal, adjectival, and adverbial. Give a positional classification of the prepositional phrases in the following sentences. When you classify a phrase as adverbial, shift it in turn to every other position which it can occupy in its sentence.

1. The attendance was quite large in the mornings.
2. From London to Edinburgh is only a few hundred miles.
3. In the future he must read the history of Abyssinia.
4. The girl across the river was going with the boy from town.
5. The janitor kept a mop behind the door.
6. Daniel Boone cut down the tree.

Verbal phrases including objects

⌇ Kinds of objects

Among the sequences which can sometimes replace single verbals, there are some, as we said at the beginning of this chapter, which contain nominals or nominal phrases. Such nominals or nominal phrases include those which are traditionally called objects: direct objects, indirect objects, and object complements. Here are some examples:

1. Direct object: He made *pictures.*
2. Indirect object: The nurse gave the *patients* (indirect object) their *pills* (direct object).
3. Object complement: Stupid people thought the *criminal* (direct object) a *martyr* (object complement).

The direct object, it is said, names the direct and immediate goal or receiver of the action; the indirect object names the person or thing which is less directly acted on or to which something is given or said or shown; and the object complement completes the assertion and refers to the same person or thing as the direct object.

VALIDITY OF THE DISTINCTIONS. Many linguists do not accept these distinctions, partly because the traditional definitions are semantic definitions of the type which linguists usually avoid. To say that an indirect object and a direct object refer to different things but that a direct object and an object complement refer to the same thing is to obscure the linguist's basic problem: What forms convey these different meanings? Some linguists think the different meanings are determined by the meanings of the individual nominals and verbals in the sentence rather than by its grammatical structure. (In the sentence *The tailor made the boy a suit,* we say that *boy* is an indirect object and *suit* is a direct object because we know that tailors make suits for boys. If tailors were magicians and transformed boys into suits, we might just as logically call *boy* a direct object and *suit* an object complement.) These linguists therefore refuse to distinguish the sequence direct object plus object complement from the sequence indirect object plus direct. They say instead that English transitive verbs take either one or two objects, but not three, and that when two objects occur together in one sentence, they may be labeled simply as *first object* and *second object*.

Occasionally, however, sentences with three objects do occur. A well-known American linguist and professor of English was once heard to remark in a political conversation, "We've elected us Ike president, and now we're stuck with him." Many native speakers have no difficulty understanding and explaining a similar sentence: *"Elect me Stevenson president next year,"* said Truman, *"and I'll be happy."* Both sentences contain three objects in a fixed order. Indirect objects come first (*us, me*), then direct objects (*Ike, Stevenson*), and then object complements (*president, president;* the phrase *next year* in the second sentence is adverbial). We could not describe such a pattern in terms of first and second objects only.

The suggestion has also been made that we have difficulty in classifying objects not because the three traditional terms are too many but because they are not enough. In some sentences, we can apply the traditional terms accurately and adequately; but for the objects in sentences like *He made the boy a leader,* where two interpretations are left open, we have no names which do not force an impossible decision. The sentence can mean either that someone gave the boy qualities of leadership or that someone prepared a piece of fishing tackle for him; and there is nothing in the sentence itself to tell us which meaning the speaker intends. It might be useful to have special names for objects like *boy* and *leader* in sentences where they may or may not refer to the same thing. Then we could talk about indirect and direct objects in sentences where we knew we had them, like *She built John the ruler,* meaning that she made a measuring-stick for him; we could talk about direct objects and object complements in other clear sentences, like *She thought John the ruler,* meaning that she thought he governed; and we could use our new names in sentences like *He made the boy a leader.*

POSITION OF OBJECTS. In this book, we will try simply to clarify the traditional terms as fully as possible, and we may begin by noting one feature which is common to all objects: an object regularly follows its verbal unless the object is either an interrogative or a nominal preceded by an interrogative. In these latter cases, the order is different:

> He made pictures.
> What did he make?
> What pictures did he make?
> What pictures he made!

The change in order, it should be observed, is accompanied in questions by a change in the verbal.

TRANSITIVE VERBS. Another characteristic of objects is that they do not occur after all verbs but only after those which are called *transitive*. Although the list of transitive verbs is very long, some verbs are definitely excluded from it. Thus we can say,

> He has lied about his studies,

with the preposition *about* between the verbal and the nominal; but we cannot say,

> He has lied his studies.

To lie is not a transitive verb.

A much more common intransitive verb is the verb *to be,* which is followed often enough by nominals but not by objects. Evidence for this statement is the fact that the personal pronoun which we can substitute for a single direct object must always be the object form and usually has weakest stress; after *to be,* on the other hand, though we frequently have the object form, at least sometimes in some dialects the subject form appears. Moreover, whichever form occurs after *to be* will usually have strongest stress or second stress. For instance:

> 1. He made pictures.
> ^{2}Hè + ^{3}máde + thĕm^1↘
> 2. This is your teacher.
> ^{3}Thís + ĭs + shê^2↘
> ^{2}Ìt's + ^{3}mé^1↘
> ^{2}Ìt + ĭs + ^{3}í^1↘

RELATIVE ORDER OF OBJECTS. Like postverbal position, however, occurrence only with transitive verbs is useless for distinguishing one kind of object from another, since it is common to all three kinds. There is no problem when there is only one object, and there is no problem in the rare sentences where there are three: a single object is always direct, and in a sequence of three objects the order is always (1) indirect object, (2) direct object, (3) object complement. But a sentence with two objects does present a problem. One of the two is always direct, and the direct object follows an indirect and precedes an object complement; but the direct object has still to be identified. The classification of the other object will then follow immediately from its position.

CLASSIFICATION BY PRECEDING VERBALS. One clearly formal clue to the identity of the direct object is the preceding verbal, for different transitive verbs take different kinds of objects. *To deceive* is transitive and takes a single object (*She deceived him*); *to give* is transitive and takes either a single object (*They gave a dollar*) or an indirect plus direct (*They gave him a dollar*); *to designate* is transitive and takes either a single object (*The court designated the place*) or a direct object plus an object complement (*The president designated him ambassador*); etc. Just as we know that any single object is direct, we can be fairly sure that a second object after verbs like *give* and a first object after verbs like *designate* are also direct.

Verbs like *make* are not limited so narrowly. *Make* may have a single object or either of the two pairs of objects:

> The tailor made a suit.
> The tailor made the boy a suit.
> The fine clothes made the boy a dandy.

Such objects naturally cannot be classified according to the preceding verbal, but three further distinctions, in none of which the verbal is involved, may be suggested. They are all generally applicable.

CLASSIFICATION BY PERSONAL SUBSTITUTES. First, as we indicated in Chapter Two, we can divide English nouns into several *substitution classes* according to the personal pronouns which may be substituted for them; and having made this division, we can add that an indirect object and a direct object may have different personal substitutes, whereas a direct object and an object complement will usually belong to the same substitution class. Since we almost always have or can get a context of accompanying sentences for a problematic one, we can apply this test by looking in the accompanying sentences for the relevant personal pronouns. Suppose, for instance, that the given sentence is one of those we have already discussed, *He made the boy a leader*. We first note the substitution class of *boy* and of *leader;* that is, we note what personal pronouns can be substituted for *boy* and *leader* generally, not just in this particular sentence, where we cannot replace *leader* with a pronoun unless we make other changes as well. We refer to *boy* by *he,* to *leader* (one who leads) by *he* or *she*, to *leader* (a piece of fishing tackle) by *it*. If now we find in an accompanying sentence that *he* is used to refer to *leader*, we know that *leader* means "one who leads" and belongs to the same substitution class as *boy*. In this case we conclude that *leader* in *He made the boy a leader* is probably an object complement, since it belongs to the same substitution class as the other object, *boy*. We would draw the other conclusion and call *leader* a direct object if we found that *leader* was replaced by *it* in an accompanying sentence. The use of *it* would define *leader* as "fishing tackle" and would place the word in a *different* substitution class from that of *boy:* we do not normally call a boy *it* or a piece of wire or nylon *he*.

CLASSIFICATION BY NUMBER. A second distinction helps to provide for sentences like *He made the boys leaders*. Here both *boys* and *leaders* are words for which the personal substitute is *they*, so that substitution does not decide the nature of the two objects unless we change them to the singular (*the boy* and *a leader; he* and *it*, or *he* and *he*). For this reason we add the statement that although indirect objects and direct objects will often be of different numbers, direct objects and object complements will usually be of the same number, either both singular or both plural; in a sentence containing a direct object and an object complement, we usually cannot change the number of just one of the two objects without disturbing the structure. In *He made the boys leaders*, we can decide whether or not *leaders* is an object complement simply by changing it from the plural to the singular (*a leader*). If the structure is unchanged by this alteration, *leaders* is a direct object; otherwise it is an object complement.

CLASSIFICATION BY TRANSLATION. Our last device for classifying objects is translation, which provides for a given sentence a formally distinctive set of equivalent sentences; different sequences of objects require different translations. One familiar translation test involves the use of *to* or *for*, since a sentence containing an indirect object will usually have an equivalent sentence with one of these prepositions, while there are no equivalents with *to*, and often none with *for*, for sentences with direct objects and object complements. So, if we start with the sentences *He taught that villain a lesson* and *He bought his wife a mink coat*, we can construct the equivalents *He taught a lesson to that villain* and *He bought a mink coat for his wife*. In the equivalent sentences, the original indirect objects, here *villain* and *wife*, become the objects of *to* or *for* in prepositional phrases which most commonly follow the direct objects. The sequence direct object plus object complement does not allow this introduction of *to* or *for* into a sentence like *The mayor appointed a newcomer chief constable.*

Frequently, another translation test is also possible. For most sentences containing a direct object of an active verbal, there are equivalent sentences in which the verbal is passive. Thus for the sentence *I cut my foot,* there is the equivalent *My foot was cut. Foot,* the direct object of the active *cut,* becomes the subject of the passive *was cut.* For the sentence *The referee assigned each player a number,* where *player* is the indirect object and the direct object is *number,* there are two equivalents, not just one: both *Each player was assigned a number* and *A number was assigned each player.* In the first of the two equivalents, *Each player was assigned a number,* the indirect object of the original sentence, *player,* becomes the subject, while the direct object, *number,* is retained after the passive verbal. In the second equivalent, *A number was assigned each player, number* is shifted and *player* is retained after the verbal. Only *one* of these two equivalents is possible for sentences which contain a direct object and an object complement, not a direct and an indirect object. We can translate a sentence like *They considered an innocent bystander a criminal,* where *criminal* is object complement and *bystander* is direct object, into the equivalent sentence, *An innocent bystander was considered a criminal;* but we cannot make the translation *A criminal was considered an innocent bystander.* This last sentence has a very different meaning.

It follows from such examples that we might identify as a direct object any single object of an active verbal, the second of two objects in an active sentence for which there are two passive equivalents, and the first of two objects in an active sentence for which there is only one passive equivalent. This amounts to saying that *foot* in *I cut my foot* is recognized as a direct object because it is the only object in the sentence, that *number* in *The referee assigned each player a number* is recognized as a direct object because the sentence has two passive translations, and that *bystander* in *They considered an innocent bystander a criminal* is so recognized because for this sentence only one passive translation can be made.

SUMMARY. In summary, we have attempted neither the reduction of the three traditional kinds of object to two nor the description of more kinds of object than three. Instead, we have attempted to clarify the traditional terms. English transitive verbs, we have said, occasionally take three objects but usually take either one or two. Unless an object is an interrogative or a nominal preceded by an interrogative, it follows the verbal. Per-

sonal pronouns used as objects are commonly in their object form, and
personal pronouns used as *single* objects are regularly unstressed. A single
object is always direct; in a sequence of three objects the order is always
(1) indirect object, (2) direct object, (3) object complement; and the
sequence indirect object plus direct object may be distinguished from the
sequence direct object plus object complement in five ways. These are
(1) by definitions in terms of meaning, (2) by considering the nature of
the verbal preceding the objects, (3) by considering the personal pronouns
which can be generally substituted for the words used as objects, (4) by
considering the number of the objects and (if necessary) observing the
effect of a change in the number of one of them, (5) by translation of the
original sentence into its equivalent with *to* or *for* or into its equivalent
passive sentence or sentences.

Exercise one. Point out the objects in the following sentences.
  1. What answer did he give you?
  2. The examination left the student a total wreck.
  3. The moderator appointed an elderly ³wómăn²→⁴sécrĕtàrў¹↘.
  4. The jockey dealt the horse a hard blow with his whip.
  5. The mechanic worked himself to death.
  6. They told us only what we already knew.
  7. What does that make me?
  8. The edict called the general a traitor.
  9. The keeper fed the lion three pounds of steak.
10. How much steak can a professor feed his family?

Exercise two. Study the following sentences, each of which contains two
objects.
  1. The master made him a prefect.
  2. An uncle offered the young man a car.
  3. The librarian sent the patron a letter.
  4. His answers branded him a fool.
  5. The guest brought his hostess a box of candy.
Now change the verbals in the respective sentences to *was made, was offered, was sent, was branded,* and *was brought.* In which of the sentences
may both of the original objects become subjects of the changed verbals,
and in which of the sentences may only the first object become subject?

Exercise three. List ten *factitive* verbs; that is, ten verbs like *designate,*
which take direct objects and object complements.

Exercise four. Try to classify the objects in the fifteen sentences in Exercises one and two as direct, indirect, or object complements. Give reasons for your classifications.

Verbal phrases including predicate nominatives

⌁ Predicate nominative and direct object

To describe all the sequences which can substitute for single verbals would make this book too long, but even a brief discussion would be incomplete without some remarks on sequences including *predicate nominatives,* especially since the predicate nominative usually follows the verbal, like the direct object from which it must be distinguished. The label *predicate nominative* need not, of course, disturb us. Beyond the fact that it is traditional, its origin or the reasons for its use are unimportant here; and it may be replaced by any other term, such as subject complement, which may seem preferable.

A SEMANTIC DISTINCTION. It is easy to state an approximate distinction in meaning between the direct object and the predicate nominative: the predicate nominative refers to the same thing as the subject, while the direct object, unless it is a form in *-self/-selves,* does not. We cannot be satisfied, however, with this distinction, partly because, as we have said repeatedly, definitions in terms of meaning obscure the formal signals which communicate that meaning. We must center our attention on the forms.

EQUATIONAL VERBS. One of the distinctions which we need has already been used in the attempt to separate the different kinds of objects. Direct objects occur after transitive verbs; predicate nominatives after a special list of intransitive verbs like *be, become,* and *seem,* which we may call *equational.* In the sentences

The student caught a monkey

and

The student was a monkey,

the transitivity of *caught* makes a great difference.

SUBSTITUTES AND STRESS. Another distinction already familiar to us lies in the personal pronouns which substitute for direct objects and predicate nominatives. As we have said, only the object form of a personal pronoun may substitute for a single direct object, but at least sometimes in some dialects, a predicate nominative may be replaced by the subject form:

1. The victim disliked the teacher.

The victim disliked him (/^{2}dìs^{3}láɪktɪ̆m^1\/).

2. The victim was the teacher.
The victim was he (^{2}wɔ̆z $+$ ^{3}hí:^{1}↘).

The rarity of sentences like this last indicates that predicate nominatives are much more likely to be nouns than personal pronouns, although personal pronouns as direct objects are very common. Except in answering the telephone, we have little occasion to use sentences like *This is he,* and there may be many speakers who would naturally use the object forms of the pronouns after any verb. But we can still use pronominal substitution to distinguish predicate nominatives from direct objects. Whether we say *The victim was he* or *The victim was him,* we will normally put strongest or second stress on the pronoun; but a direct object like the *him* of *The victim disliked him* is regularly unstressed. The stress will provide the distinction if the form of the pronoun itself does not.

FINAL DISTINCTIONS. With two final comments, we may conclude this section. It is usually true (not always) that a predicate nominative will be in the same number as the subject and that both will belong to the same substitution class. In other words, if the subject is singular, the predicate nominative will usually be singular; if the personal substitute for the subject is *he,* the substitute for the predicate nominative will usually be *he;* etc. These statements are not true of direct objects. In the sentence

The stenographers dislike the electric typewriter,

stenographers (the subject) is plural, but *typewriter* (the direct object) is singular. In the sentence

His wife bought a new hat,

the substitute for *wife* is *she,* but the substitute for *hat* is *it.* In contrast, both subject and predicate nominative are singular, and both have *it* as their substitute, in the sentence

The new hat was the cause of the argument.

↻ The predicate adjectival

Our second and last comment introduces another traditional grammatical term, *predicate adjective,* which we will replace, following our established method, by *predicate adjectival.* An example of the predicate adjectival appears in the sentence

The steak was *expensive.*

Expensive, we note, follows an equational verb, is not preceded by a determiner or followed by a nominal, and can be replaced by any number of adjectives (*good, bad, tough,* etc.). These observations provide the needed definition.

Exercise one. Review the definitions of transitive, intransitive, factitive, and equational verbs. Classify the verbals in the following sentences accordingly.

1. Until midnight, the dance had seemed dull.
2. The soloist had been singing wretchedly.
3. Matilda's embroidery won first prize at the county fair.
4. The dealer regularly gave himself three aces.
5. This singular ability made him a rich man.
6. When the cold front passed, squalls damaged a number of small boats.
7. If I don't die first, that woman will kill me.
8. Squirt's classmates elected him president of Blue Nose, the senior honor society.
9. When Toby joined the Boy Scouts, he immediately became helpful, friendly, courteous, and kind.
10. How he did it nobody will ever know.

Exercise two. In the following sentences, point out the predicate nominatives and the direct objects. Where substitution seems easy and natural, replace each object and each predicate nominative with a personal pronoun.

1. The tenderfoot bought a twelve-gallon hat.
2. In that way, he showed his dislike for big-talking Texans.
3. It was the same pitcher who lost the first game.
4. This is Mrs. Houston.
5. The landlady disliked Mrs. Houston.
6. At adolescence, children first learn the pleasures of snobbery.
7. To his neighbors, he seemed a queer duck, because he actually liked books.
8. The sportsman enjoyed good hunting that day: he stalked and wounded a tethered calf.
9. This is the best of all possible worlds.
10. I never saw any purple cows.

Summary

If we use the terms *nominal* and *verbal* to mean both single-word nominals and verbals, and sequences which can substitute for them in certain positions, then a favorite English sentence pattern is

Nominal	Verbal
Birds	sing.
The pretty birds	sing sweet songs.

Defined in this way, a verbal can include within itself adverbials, adverbial phrases, nominals, nominal phrases, adjectivals, adjectival phrases, and subordinate clauses.

Adverbials fall into a number of different positional subclasses. Certain adverbial positions can be occupied by nouns and adjectives. In a sentence like

He studies his lessons nights,

the adverbial *nights* follows the nominal *lessons* and would be replaced by the adverbial *then* as a substitute, not by a personal pronoun. Both position and stress distinguish an adverbial like the *up* of *burn up* from a preposition like the *to* of *speak to*.

Among the nominals which may be included in verbal phrases are those which are traditionally grouped together as objects: direct object, indirect object, and object complement. Although all three objects regularly follow verbals, the objects may be distinguished by their relative positions, by the preceding verbals, by the personal substitutes for the objects, by the number of the objects (singular or plural), and by translations into equivalent sentences.

Unlike objects, which follow transitive verbs, predicate nominatives occur after a special list of intransitive verbs which we may call equational. Personal substitutes for predicate nominatives normally have primary or secondary stress and in some dialects may have their subject form. Generally, predicate nominatives are linked to subjects both by substitution class and by number. For an adjectival following an equational verb, the name *predicate adjectival* may be used.

CHAPTER FIVE Subjects
and
Predicates

Introduction

In the last two chapters, we moved from a consideration of single words and their classification to the consideration of nominal and verbal sequences—sequences of words which in certain positions can replace single-word nominals or single-word verbals. In discussing some of these sequences, we had occasion to describe a number of patterns which have borne such traditional labels as *appositives, direct objects, indirect objects, object complements, predicate nominatives,* and *predicate adjectives* (our *predicate adjectivals*). We are ready, in this chapter, to consider two more of the familiar terms: *subject* and *predicate.* We will begin by defining these terms and indicating both the variety of items to which they may refer and certain items which are excluded from them. A second section will be devoted to the relative order of subjects and predicates. Finally, in a concluding section, we will present formulas which will sum up, in abstract form, a number of our principal observations concerning some main constructions in English grammar.

Definitions

As we have said, a favorite English sentence pattern is

        Nominal   Verbal,

in which the terms *nominal* and *verbal* represent either single-word nominals and verbals, or nominal sequences and verbal sequences, which are linked together, whenever it is possible, by agreement in number:

Birds	sing.
The bird	sings sweetly.
The birds and the bees	frolic and play.

❧ The familiar terms

In these sentences, the nominal *birds* and the nominal phrases *the bird* and *the birds and the bees* would traditionally be called the *complete subjects;* the nominals *birds, bird, birds,* and *bees* would be called the simple subjects; and the complete subject *the birds and the bees* would also be labeled *compound.* The verbal *sing* and the verbal phrases *sings sweetly* and *frolic and play* would traditionally be called the *complete predicates;* the verbals *sing, sings, frolic,* and *play* would be called the *simple predicates;* and the complete predicate *frolic and play* would again be also labeled *compound.* Each sentence shows agreement in number between subject and predicate, and each subject may be separated from its predicate by a terminal, here represented by a wide space.

↻ Simple predicate

Our examples suggest rather easy definitions for simple, complete, and compound predicates. A simple predicate is a single verbal or one of the sequences of verbal forms (a special set of verbal phrases) which we described in Chapter Two; except in imperative sentences like *Close the door,* in which there is no subject, a simple predicate is linked by agreement in number, when agreement is possible, to some nominal or nominal sequence as its subject. In the following sentences, the simple predicates are italicized:

Prices *were* lower in 1939.
A good book *finds* many readers.
The birds *had taken* cover.
Give me time.

↻ Compound predicate

A compound predicate includes two or more simple predicates, linked up by intonation patterns (pitches and terminals), or by coordinating or correlative conjunctions, or by both:

$$^2\text{Hè} + {}^2\text{cáme}^2 \nearrow {}^2\text{sáw}^2 \nearrow {}^3\text{cónquěred}^1 \searrow$$
$$^2\text{Hè} + \text{câme} + \text{ănd} + \text{sâw} + \text{ănd} + {}^3\text{cónquěred}^1 \searrow$$
$$^2\text{Hè} + {}^2\text{cáme}^2 \nearrow {}^2\text{sáw}^2 \nearrow {}^2\text{ănd} + {}^3\text{cónquěred}^1 \searrow$$

↻ Complete predicate

A complete predicate, which is often separated from its subject by a terminal, includes one or more simple predicates and all the elements which go with them to constitute the verbal part in a single nominal-verbal sentence pattern; an imperative sentence without a subject consists only of a complete predicate. The elements accompanying a simple predicate may be, of course, any of those which we have mentioned: adverbials, objects, predicate nominatives, predicate adjectivals, etc. A slant line separates the complete predicates from their complete subjects in the following sentences:

Time / passed.
Guests / came and went.
The sky / darkened ominously.
The populace / had bread and circuses.

A sudden cry / caused him great alarm.

The first storm of winter / made the road an impassable bog.

The candidate / was a victim of his own enthusiasm.

His opponent / had been more prudent and less provocative.

It is obvious that in the first of these examples the single verbal *passed* is both simple and complete predicate.

Exercise one. Point out the simple predicates and the complete predicates in the following sentences. A subordinate clause used as a nominal will first be included in or excluded from the complete predicate of the whole sentence, as the case may be; its own simple and complete predicate will then be pointed out. For example, in the sentence, *The fisherman said that he had had good luck,* the clause *that he had had good luck* is nominal, the object of the verb *said;* hence it is part of the complete predicate. Its own complete predicate is *had had good luck;* its simple predicate is *had had.* Adjectival clauses may be treated in the same way. Adverbial clauses are not exemplified in the sentences, since it is often impossible to decide objectively whether they are sentence modifiers or parts of the complete predicate.

1. The wasp buzzed angrily about his head.
2. The smoke from the factories had blackened the lungs of the workmen who breathed it. (Here *who breathed it* is an adjectival clause, a part of the complete predicate. What are its own complete and simple predicates?)
3. The man who was struck by the bursting hose was reported to have died.
4. The speed of his service, which had failed him the day before, showed that he had regained his form.
5. The visitor never knew whether he should reply.
6. The young cedars which the farmer had transplanted from the swamps were being killed by the hot, dry weather. (As a direct object, *which* is part of the complete predicate in its own clause. Is the clause part of the complete predicate of the whole sentence?)
7. The alarm clock reminded him that his vacation was over.
8. That the ice age would return was his constant fear. (*That . . . return* is the complete subject of the whole sentence. What is the complete predicate of this nominal clause?)
9. The manners of the young have grown constantly worse.
10. The modern hunter is an unheroic figure who kills for pleasure and respects no law.

⌁ Complete subject

Simple and complete subjects likewise may sometimes be identical. A complete subject, which is often separated from its predicate by a terminal, includes one or more simple subjects and all the elements which go with them to constitute the nominal part in a single nominal-verbal sentence pattern. When the complete subject is a single-word nominal, it must, of course, be identical with the simple subject:

> *Birds* sing.
> *John* sings.
> *Fishing* is his favorite sport.
> *He* sells sea shells.

Simple and complete subjects are also identical when the complete subject is a nominal sequence for which no one of its own parts can be substituted without changing the meaning of the original grammatical structure. This is the case, for example, when the complete subject is a prepositional phrase, a marked infinitive, or a nominal-verbal sequence introduced by an interrogative or by a subordinating conjunction (a nominal clause):

> *In the morning* would be too late.
> *To study* exhausted the gridiron hero.
> *What he meant* was unmistakable.
> *That he desecrated the chapel* disturbed no one.

↬ Forms used as simple subjects

In many sentences, however, the simple subject is only a part of the complete subject. Often the simple subject is a noun, which may be accompanied by predeterminers, determiners, postdeterminers, and postposed adjectivals or adjectival sequences:

> All the pretty *girls* in the senior class who could read and
> write / decided to help him.

Adjectives, participles, pronouns, and uninflected words also may be used as simple subjects:

> The *good* / die young.
> Those *few* / will be enough.
> The *injured* / were taken to the hospital.
> All *mine* / are ready.
> The *chaos* / was complete.

Sometimes the complete subject includes both the simple subject and one or more appositives:

> The teacher [simple subject], a surly fellow [appositive],
> disapproved.

An adverbial standing at the beginning of a sentence may also have to be distinguished from the simple subject:

> That afternoon [adverbial phrase] they [both simple and complete subject] take calisthenics.

Unlike appositives to the simple subject, an initial adverbial, it should be noted, is not a part of the *complete* subject.

↱ Identifying the simple subject

Despite these complexities, the simple subject is not hard to isolate. It is always a nominal or nominal sequence, and if possible the verb agrees with it in number. A noun used as the subject will generally be in the common case, and a personal pronoun will generally appear in its distinctive subject form if it has one, although second possessives may sometimes stand as simple subjects, too:

> *Mine* is not a happy life.

A possessive form of a noun may be a simple subject only if it does not stand in the position of determiner or postdeterminer with respect to a following nominal:

> The *man's* [postdeterminer] new car [simple subject] was a total wreck.
>
> The *man's* [simple subject] was a total wreck.

The statement that the verb agrees in number with the simple subject needs some elaboration. The simple subject is often best identified by such agreement, as in the following sentences:

> A father [sg.] with three children [pl.] was [sg.] drafted last month.
>
> His debts [pl.] were [pl.] his only worry [sg.].

When the complete subject is compound, however—that is, when it includes two or more simple subjects joined by coordinating or correlative conjunctions, or by intonation patterns, or by both—then the number of the verb is usually determined by the inner structure of the complete compound subject. For example, if the conjunction linking the simple subjects is *and*, the verb is usually plural; if the conjunctions are *either* . . . *or* and the simple subjects are singular, the verb is usually singular; if the conjunctions are *neither* . . . *nor*, usage varies even though both simple subjects may be singular; etc. Thus:

> John *and* Tom *are* there.
>
> *Either John or Tom is* there.
>
> *Neither* the *price nor* the *time was* [sometimes *were*] acceptable.

Again, the simple subject and the verb sometimes do not agree, and sometimes the verbal is an uninflected word with which agreement is impossible, as in the following examples:

> There's only *you* [verb: third person singular; subject: second person singular or plural].

> The instructor *ought* to instruct, and the students *ought* to study [*ought* is uninflected].

In such cases, we must depend on other criteria than agreement for the identification of the simple subject. The facts of order which we will present in the next section are helpful clues, and a process of elimination can also be used: the items which we have already labeled as adverbials, appositives, objects, predicate nominatives, etc., will obviously not be classed as subjects.

Exercise two. In the following sentences, simple and complete subjects are identical. Classify them as single-word nominals, prepositional phrases, marked infinitives, or nominal clauses.

1. To write had ceased to amuse him.
2. What children will say is unpredictable.
3. From Dallas to Fort Worth is no great distance.
4. Socrates endured the shrewishness of Xantippe.
5. You may encounter an unlovely modern shrew.

Exercise three. In the following sentences, point out the simple subjects, the appositives to simple subjects, and the initial adverbial phrases. Classify the simple subjects as nouns, pronouns, adjectives, participles, or uninflected words.

1. His boat, a small skiff, threatened to capsize.
2. One day last summer, it actually did tip over.
3. The sweet and the bitter must be accepted together.
4. Farming is no life for a lazy man.
5. Hepatitis has apparently been spread by blood transfusions.
6. Yesterday, yours were very bad-tempered children.
7. The big dog, a boxer which had a great reputation as a fighter, was completely routed by a tiny cat.
8. The man in the moon is carrying a bundle of thorns.
9. If the judge's life is hard, the policeman's is even harder.
10. That night his dear mother slipped arsenic in his drink.

❦ Sentence adverbials

There are, finally, a number of sentence elements which cannot be very well included in either complete subject or complete predicate and in which, therefore, the simple subject will not be found. We will close this

section with a brief account of these elements, most of which we will call
sentence adverbials.

Various kinds of sentence adverbials can be recognized, and they differ
considerably in the closeness of their attachment to the rest of the sentence, so that in borderline cases it may be hard to say whether the element in question is a sentence adverbial or a part of the basic nominal-
verbal sentence pattern. For example, a good many native speakers would
feel that in the following sentence, the adverbial phrase *quickly and
clearly* may be treated as part of the complete predicate:

$$\text{²Hè + ânswĕred + thĕ + ³quéstĭons²}^{\rightarrow}\text{²quîcklў + ănd}$$
$$\text{+ ³cléarlў¹}\searrow$$

A terminal, however, does set off *quickly and clearly;* and if we shift the
phrase to the beginning of the sentence, it is very hard to say whether it
is part of the subject, part of the predicate, or part of neither:

$$\text{³Quîcklў + ănd + ²cléarlў²}\nearrow\text{²hè + ânswĕred + thĕ}$$
$$\text{+ ³quéstĭons¹}\searrow$$

Probably the best procedure, in such doubtful instances, is to state
the classes of words which compose the element in question, to state its
position with respect to the rest of the sentence, to describe the accompanying intonation patterns, and then to leave open the question whether
the element is or is not a sentence adverbial. In our illustrative sentence,
we would simply say that *quickly and clearly* consists of two adverbials
joined by a coordinating conjunction, that the sequence stands under the
intonation pattern $/^{32}\nearrow/$, and that it precedes the basic nominal-verbal
sequence. The alternative would be to accept the phrase as part of the
complete predicate, in spite of its position and in spite of the terminal
which sets it off.

⌁ Types of sentence adverbials

There remain a number of patterns which can definitely be classed as
sentence-adverbial. One obvious group of sentence adverbials are the so-
called "interjections"—words like *gosh, drat,* and others less quaint and
less polite. These usually precede or follow the basic nominal-verbal sequence, from which they are normally set off by terminals, and often
they are further marked by a rise in pitch to the fourth and highest level
and by unusual loudness:

$$\text{⁴Gósh²}\searrow\text{²Ì’ve + fŏrgôttĕn + mў + ³wállĕt¹}\searrow$$

A second list of words which are sentence adverbials in many of their uses would include *yes, no,* and the words which can be substituted for *yes* and *no,* like *yeah* and *nope,* or *certainly* in a sentence such as the following:

$$\text{²Cértăinlỹ² ↗²Ì'm + lêăvǐng + tŏ³mórrŏw¹ ↘}$$

A third set would include a number of words (and larger forms) which are frequently used in making transitions: *still, however, nevertheless, therefore,* etc., as in the sentences:

$$\text{³Stíll²→²Ì + ǐn³sístěd¹ ↘}$$
$$\text{²Nèvěr + thě + ³léss²→²Ì + ǐn³sístěd¹ ↘}$$

ABSOLUTE CONSTRUCTIONS. Not all sentence adverbials, then, consist of single words. We will also class as sentence adverbials the sequences which we may distinguish as <u>absolute constructions, confirmatory clauses,</u> and <u>interjected clauses.</u> Absolute constructions, though rare in English speech, do occur rather frequently in written English. Sometimes they consist of two words or phrases belonging to the same class and connected by the conjunction *or:*

> *Plan or no plan,* the work had to be done.
> *Sink or swim,* he would make the effort.

Another common pattern is a nominal plus certain adjectivals or adjectival phrases:

> *The paper typed,* she had no other work to do.
> *The lecture at an end,* the audience dispersed.

It should be noted that an absolute construction may be removed from its sentence without making the basic nominal-verbal pattern incomplete, that the main verbal in the sentence need not agree in number with any word in the absolute construction, and that the absolute construction usually stands before the rest of the sentence, with a terminal between.

CONFIRMATORY CLAUSES. Confirmatory clauses are more common than absolute constructions, at least in speech. Typical examples appear in the sentences:

> Australia is a continent, *isn't it?*
> Texas isn't a continent, *is it?*

Isn't it and *is it* are themselves clauses, with subjects and predicates of their own; but with respect to the whole sentences, they may be classed as sentence adverbials. Such confirmatory clauses stand somewhere after the main verbal in the sentence. They often consist of an auxiliary, which may appear in close transition with the contraction *n't,* followed immediately by *there* or by a personal pronoun in the subject form:

The White Sox really clobbered them, *didn't they?*

There's a man at the door, *isn't there?*

INTERJECTED CLAUSES. Like the other sentence adverbials, interjected clauses are normally set off by terminals, but they are distinguished by the fact that often they are on the lowest of the four pitch levels, pitch /¹/. They follow the pattern which can be seen in *I believe, John thinks, she hopes, said the farmer,* and the like:

$$\text{²Thĕ} + \text{trâvĕlĭng} + \text{³sálesmăn}^{2 \rightarrow 1}\text{shè} + \text{¹hópes}^1 \nearrow ^2\text{wĭll}$$
$$+ \text{rĕ³túrn}^1 \searrow$$

That is, interjected clauses usually contain as their own simple subject either a noun or a personal pronoun, and as their simple predicate or part of their simple predicate a verb from a list which includes *believe, hope, say, think,* and a number of others. Interjected clauses stand medially or finally in an utterance, not initially. Note the differences in word order, stress patterns, and intonation patterns between

$$\text{²Thĕ} + \text{³méetĭng}^{2 \rightarrow 2}\text{îs} + \text{ăt} + \text{tên} + \text{ŏ'} + \text{³clóck}^{2 \rightarrow 1}\text{Î}$$
$$+ \text{bĕ¹líeve}^1 \searrow$$

and

$$\text{²Î} + \text{bĕlîeve} + \text{thĕ} + \text{³méetĭng}^{2 \rightarrow 2}\text{îs} + \text{ăt} + \text{tên} + \text{ŏ'} + \text{³clóck}^1 \searrow$$

❧ Vocatives

Vocatives (forms used in direct address) are the last in our list of elements which are parts neither of the complete subject nor of the complete predicate. The typical vocative is not an adverbial but a nominal, very commonly a proper noun; it is not preceded by an article (*a, an, the*), though sometimes other adjectivals do precede it; and it is set off by a terminal from the rest of the sentence, whose usual agreement of subject with predicate it does not affect. Unlike the absolute construction, vocatives occur freely in initial, medial, and final position. For example:

Philip, the canoe is leaking.

The canoe, Philip, is leaking.

The canoe is leaking, Philip.

❧ Summary

In summary, both sentence adverbials and vocatives are sentence modifiers which are not parts of the complete predicates and not parts of the complete subjects. They are usually set off by terminals, they do not affect the agreement of subjects and predicates outside themselves, and they may be removed from their sentences without making the basic nominal-verbal patterns incomplete. Other characteristics include the classes and forms of words which compose the sentence modifiers, the order of these words with relation to one another and to the rest of their sentences, and the accompanying stress and intonation patterns.

Exercise four. Point out the sentence adverbials in the following sentences, and classify them as absolute constructions, confirmatory clauses, and interjected clauses. Tell how you recognize and classify the various forms.
1. Rain or shine, the work went on.
2. The danger being past, he forgot his new-found piety.
3. The low dark clouds, the driver thought, threatened a heavy snow.
4. The schoolmistress could answer her own questions, couldn't she?
5. The examination, we hope, will be easier.

Order

❧ The order S   P

Many if not most of the sentences which we have used as illustrations so far in this book have been simple sentences; that is, they have contained only one basic nominal-verbal sequence and so have consisted of only one clause. The nominal element and the verbal element, moreover, have usually stood in that order. In other words, in most of our examples the complete subject (S) has preceded the complete predicate (P):

S   P

The simple sentence, as a kind of expandable model for the other sentence types, is the basic sentence for our purposes in this grammar; within the simple sentence, moreover, the order S   P is basic, for if we understand this pattern thoroughly, we will usually be able to deal with sentences which have other orders. The formulas for the most important of these other orders are

and
$$\left\{ \begin{array}{ccc} P & S & \\ P_1 & S & P_2, \end{array} \right\}$$

in which P_1 stands for that part of the complete predicate which precedes the complete subject and P_2 stands for the part which follows the complete subject. Assuming that the order S   P has already been sufficiently explained, we will ignore the more complicated orders which are possible and limit our discussion to the patterns P   S and P_1 S P_2.

⌁ The order P   S

Examples of the order P   S are sentences like these:

P	S
There seem to be	no matches.
Is there	time?
Who are	they?
Did	he?
Here comes	the train.
There goes	my girl.

We cannot give a full analysis and description of the various kinds of P   S sentence here. They are too numerous and varied. A partial description, however, of the sentences containing the "expletive" *there* will be helpful, since it will show that in many different kinds of sentences, the same familiar kinds of evidence will guide our analyses.

⌁ The expletive *there*

We may begin by noting that <u>intonation, stress, and order enable</u> us to distinguish the expletive *there* from *there,* the adverbial of place.

Expletive: ³Ônce ⁺ ŭpòn ⁺ ă ⁺ ²tíme² ↗²thère ⁺ wăs ⁺ ă ⁺ ³kíng¹ ↘

Adverbial of place: ²Thêre ⁺ gôes ⁺ mў ⁺ ³gírl¹ ↘

For one thing, *there* as an expletive takes weaker stress than *there* as an adverbial of place. Even when the expletive and the adverbial of place occur together in the same sentence, they are easily distinguished; for the adverbial of place stands first and is normally both fully stressed and set off by a terminal:

³Thére² →²thĕre's ⁺ nò ⁺ ²tíme² →²tò ⁺ ³pláy¹ ↘

With this difference in stress, there are often associated differences in the vowels and consonants, despite the identical spellings. So *there* as an adverbial of place will have such shapes as /ðɛər/, /ðæər/, or /ðæə/, according to the dialect involved; while the expletive will be "reduced" to shapes like /ðər/ or even /ðɟ/.

We should also note the kinds of subjects and predicates which most often occur in sentences containing the expletive *there*. The simple subjects are usually nouns, and not personal pronouns:

There's a *reason* for such remarks.

Indefinite determiners of the simple subject, like *a, an, no,* and *some,* are more common than definite determiners like *the, this* and *that:*

> There were *no* seats to be had.

Finally, the most common verb in sentences of this type is *to be,* which usually agrees in number, in both present and past tenses, with the following subject:

> There *are* three main types.

The following sentences are therefore somewhat exceptional:

> Personal pronoun as simple subject: There's only *you.*
>
> Simple subject with definite determiner: (Who can I invite to my party?) Well, there's always *the* milkman.
>
> Verb other than *to be:* There *came* a great spider.

Exercise one. Collect or compose ten sentences with the P   S order. Pool your examples with those of a fellow student. Of the twenty sentences in the joint collection, how many are questions? How many begin with an adverbial like *here* or *there?* Are auxiliaries common among the verbs in the twenty sentences? Are personal pronouns more common than subjects belonging to other word classes?

Exercise two. Compose five sentences containing *there* as an adverbial of place and five containing *there* as an expletive. Compare the adverbial and the expletive in your ten sentences in terms of intonation, stress, order, and phonemic shape.

❧ The order P_1 S P_2

We may illustrate the order P_1 S P_2 with six examples:

Is	the driver	sick?
Was	she	disgusted!
What color are	they	now?
There stands	Jackson	like a stone wall.
Do	the players	smoke much?
Don't	you	say that!

Translating the formula P_1 S P_2, we may say at once that in all these sentences and in all others represented by this formula, some part of the complete predicate precedes the complete subject, and some part of the complete predicate follows the complete subject. Three subtypes may be distinguished among such sentences.

TYPE V   s. In one subtype, the simple predicate precedes the complete subject, which is then followed by some other part or parts of the complete predicate. The most commonly occurring verbs in this subtype are *be* and *have:*

Is	it	certain that he can come?	
Has	he	any money?	
What time is	it	now?	
Have there been	any fires	lately?	

Other verbs than *be* and *have* occur when certain adverbials stand in the initial position:

Here comes	the train	now.	
Off went	Oily	to tell the dean.	

TYPE S   V. A second subtype may be noted when, in the sentence *Here comes the train now,* we replace *the train* by *it.* Unlike the noun *train,* the pronoun *it* must precede the verb:

Here	it	comes now.

In this second subtype, it will be apparent, the simple predicate follows the complete subject; but the complete subject is preceded by some other part of the complete predicate. In other words, if we use the letter V for the simple predicate, the second subtype of the order P_1 S P_2 has the partial order S V, while the first subtype of the order P_1 S P_2 has the partial order V S. Examples of the second subtype are rather varied:

This morning	the bus	was late.	
Quickly	we	went away.	
How long	we	had to wait!	
Never	you	mind!	
Right	you	are.	
What a hero	that soldier	has been!	
That	I	can't say.	

THE FRAMED SUBJECT. In the third and last subtype of the order P_1 S P_2, an auxiliary precedes the complete subject, and the accompanying verb form or verb forms follow the complete subject. This arrangement, in which the complete subject is framed by the two parts of the simple predicate, is very common:

Does	your roommate	talk too much?	
Is	the class in European history	still meeting here?	
Are	things	looking better now?	
Must	we	say more?	
Is	the gymnasium	being built this summer?	
May	he	never say die!	

Where	does		the	girl	who	drives	that	converti-

Where   does   the   girl   who   drives   that   converti-
ble   live?
Never did   I   see such a sight!
There's   a train   coming.
Was there   a train   coming?

⌖ Summary

With these examples we may conclude our analysis of primarily simple sentences according to the relative order of their subjects and predicates. The three most common orders, as we have said, are S   P, P   S, and P₁   S   P₂; but whatever the order, our procedure in finding and separating the complete subjects and complete predicates may be much the same. After removing the sentence adverbials, which are parts of neither subject nor predicate, we find the simple predicate—a single verbal or one of the sequences of verbal forms which we described in Chapter Two. We then find the simple subject, using as our clues the restriction of the simple subject to nominals or nominal sequences, the agreement in number of simple subject and simple predicate, the form of the simple subject or of its possible pronominal substitutes, and the facts of order which we have presented. Among these facts of order, the most important are the relative positions of simple subject and simple predicate, and the positions, relative to that of the simple subject, of adverbials, appositives, predeterminers, determiners, postdeterminers, and postposed adjectivals or adjectival sequences. In the complete subject, we include the simple subject or simple subjects with any accompanying predeterminers, determiners, preposed or postposed adjectivals or adjectival sequences, appositives, and connectives. The complete predicate is then all that remains of the sentence; that is, it is the simple predicate or simple predicates with any accompanying adverbials or adverbial sequences, objects, predicate nominatives, predicate adjectivals, or connectives.

⌖ Illustration

This procedure may be illustrated in the analysis of the following sentence:

²Wĭn + ŏr + ³lóse²→²thĕ + teâms + frŏm + Tĭdelànds
+ ³Cóllĕge²→²ăre + àlwàys + gôod + ³spórts¹↘

Win or lose is a sentence adverbial, an absolute construction consisting of two verbals joined by the conjunction *or;* it is set off from the rest of the sentence by a terminal and is not a part of the subject or the predicate.

The simple predicate is *are,* the only verbal outside the absolute construction; and since *are* is plural, its simple subject must be the plural noun *teams.* This identification of the simple subject is confirmed in various ways. For *the teams,* the pronoun *they,* a subject form, might be substituted (*they are always good sports*); the determiner *the* precedes *teams;* the prepositional phrase *from Tidelands College,* an adjectival sequence, is as usual postposed; and *teams* with its determiner and following prepositional phrase all precede *are.* Noting further that there is a terminal before *are,* we can now say that the complete subject is *the teams from Tidelands College;* and the complete predicate must therefore be *are always good sports.*

Exercise three. We have distinguished three subtypes of sentences having the order P_1 S P_2; what are they? Assign the following sentences to their proper subtypes.

1. Down went the flags to start the race.
2. How dull the chairman always managed to be!
3. Did he ever make a sensible speech?
4. Have you the time to answer all those silly questions?
5. Long may it wave!
6. Slowly the former champion picked himself up.
7. When do the apples get ripe around here?
8. Were they right to put rum in the preacher's eggnog?
9. What fun a psychiatrist would have with these sentences!
10. Will the sales tax really be repealed in two years?

Exercise four. The following questions are designed to illustrate the steps in analyzing a sentence into complete subject and complete predicate.

1. How can you identify the sentence adverbial in the following sentence? *Whatever the reason, the old portrait of his grandparents which was being hung in the hall did not quite give him the expected pleasure.*
2. After the sentence adverbial has been removed, what verbs remain in the sentence?
3. Which verb form is clearly in an adjectival position and hence not the simple predicate of any clause?
4. Of the two remaining verbals, which stands in a relative clause?
5. What, then, is the simple predicate of the main clause?
6. How can *grandparents, which,* and *hall* be eliminated as possible subjects of this simple predicate?
7. After the sentence adverbial has been removed and *grandparents, which,* and *hall* have been eliminated, what single-word nominal remains before the simple predicate of the main clause?
8. List the preposed and postposed adjectivals which accompany the simple subject of the main clause.

9. What is the complete predicate of the main clause?
10. What are the complete subject and complete predicate of the relative clause?

Exercise five. In the sentences *Time passes, Truth hurts,* and *Faith remains,* the first words are of course both simple and complete subjects, and the second words are both simple and complete predicates. Expand each simple subject in as many ways as you easily can. For example, you can add determiners, postdeterminers, predeterminers, prepositional phrases, or relative clauses. In each expansion, state the simple and complete subjects (they will not be identical). Similarly expand the simple predicates, and state the simple and complete predicates of the expansions. To the predicates with which you begin, you might add adverbials, objects, predicate nominatives, or predicate adjectivals.

Formulas

Our purpose in this section is to represent, by means of symbols for certain positional classes, some nominal positions typical of those which we traditionally label as subjects, appositives, direct objects, indirect objects, object complements, and predicate nominatives. Since nouns typically fill these positions, our formulas will represent primarily the main uses of nouns. To make the representation more nearly complete, we will add one formula for the noun adjunct and another for nouns in adverbial positions.

❧ Value and limitations

Both the value and the limitations of our formulas need careful explanation. Their value lies in the fact that they are a generalized representation of thousands of sentences which may be constructed on them: by substituting particular words of the classes indicated by our symbols, we will be able to turn our abstract formulas into concrete sentences. The sentences so constructed on a single formula will mean many different things, because we can fill each position with many different words of the class which the formula indicates; but to all of the many different sentences, a certain element of meaning will be common. That common meaning will be carried not by the individual words, which we can vary freely, but by the grammatical structure symbolized in the formula—a structure which remains unchanged so long as we follow the formula in making our substitutions. In short, the formulas help to give us a conscious, organized knowledge of the most abstract and general patterns of our language. It is these patterns which are the essentials of English grammar; it is these patterns which shape our thought and control its expression; yet it is just these patterns which native speakers most easily overlook.

The main limitation of the formulas is that they are not complete. They represent only a fragment—though an important fragment—of the structure of English, and any native speaker regularly uses many patterns which the formulas do not account for. They are neither general enough nor systematic enough to show us the grammatical form of all or even most of the things we say; but if we do not ask too much of the formulas, they can still be extremely useful to us. They can give us a glimpse of the nature of language in general and of English in particular which it would be hard to get so clearly in any other fashion.

❧ Symbols

For the sake of simplicity, the formulas will be limited to four positional classes of words: determiners, nominals, adverbials, and verbals. All the verbals will be verbs, and all the other words, except the determiners, will be nouns. In seven of the formulas, the nouns will occupy only nominal positions. These limitations will enable us to use only three symbols for large classes of words:

> D—determiner
> N—noun
> V—verb.

In similar ways, our accessory symbols can also be held to a minimum. All nouns will be in the common case form and will be either singular or plural unless a subscript *sg* (Nsg) particularly indicates a singular. If two nouns both take the same personal substitutes, a subscript *x* will be used (N_x . . . N_x), and a subscript *th* will indicate that a noun can be replaced by an adverbial substitute like *then, there, thus.* Verbs from the list which can take a direct object and an object complement (*choose, designate, elect, make,* etc.) will have a subscript *fac* (V_{fac}; *fac* stands for *factitive*); equational verbs will be symbolized V_{eq}; all other verbs are transitive but not factitive. Arrows connecting *N*'s and *V*'s will indicate agreement or potential agreement in number. As for intonation, only the terminals are marked. Unless a particular exception is made, the sequence of pitches /²³²/ is assumed before /→/, and the sequence /²³¹/ is assumed before /↘/. The last word before a terminal will have pitch /³/ and strongest stress; otherwise, determiners have third stress or weakest stress, and nouns and verbs have second stress. Open transition is assumed between words. The formulas are printed, two to a page, on the right-hand pages (157 ff.). On the left-hand pages, facing the formulas, is a table of the symbols used.

❧ Using the formulas

Though literally thousands of sentences can be constructed on these formulas, their application, as we have emphasized, is limited. The present sentence, for example, fits none of them. On the other hand, substitution will show that a good many more complicated sentences can be reduced to these formulas, which can therefore be used as guides to the analysis of sentences which they do not directly represent. Since Formulas 1 and 3 are identical, symbolizing both the simple subject and the direct object, they will make good illustrations. Our earlier discussions and our exercises should have made clear that numerous elements can be added to sentences built on these formulas without changing their essential construction. If we allow possible changes in stress patterns and intonation patterns, we can insert adjectivals before both the subject and the direct object:

> The *neglected* farmers feed the *ungrateful* world.

The addition of the adjectivals *neglected* and *ungrateful* does not change the status of *farmers* as simple subject or of *world* as direct object. Their status still remains unchanged if we change the verbal to a verbal phrase and add an adverbial:

> The neglected farmers *have always fed* the ungrateful world.

Again, we can add adjectival phrases or clauses after the nominals:

> The hunter wounded the bear.
> The *stupid* hunter wounded the *vicious* bear.
> The stupid hunter *had superficially wounded* the vicious bear.
> The stupid hunter *from the city* had superficially wounded the vicious bear, *which charged him savagely.*

After all these expansions, *hunter* is still the simple subject of the main clause, and *bear* is still the direct object.

Similar expansions are possible for all the other formulas, simply because, as we have repeatedly seen, whole phrases and clauses can be systematically substituted for single words in certain positions. It will be recalled that our chapters on nominal and verbal sequences were entirely devoted to this process of expansion by substitution. At least for the native speaker of English, then, who already knows the language and can intuitively control the allowable substitutions, the analysis of a few typical, uncomplicated sentences provides a key to the analysis of many more

Table of symbols

D	determiner
N	noun
$\mathbf{N_{sg}}$	noun in the singular
$\mathbf{N_x \ldots N_x}$	nouns having the same personal substitutes
$\mathbf{N_{th}}$	noun replaceable in its formula by an adverbial substitute like *then, there, thus*
V	transitive but not factitive verb
$\mathbf{V_{fac}}$	factitive verb
$\mathbf{V_{eq}}$	equational verb
N V ↑___↑	noun and verb agreeing in number (if agreement is possible)
→	The terminal /→/, preceded by /232/
↘	The terminal /↘/, preceded by /231/

All nouns are in the common case.

Before terminals, all nouns and all verbs have pitch /3/ and strongest stress; elsewhere they have second stress.

All determiners have third stress or weakest stress.

Open transition is assumed between words.

1.

D $\quad$ N$^{\rightarrow}$ $\quad$ V $\quad$ D $\quad$ N$_\searrow$

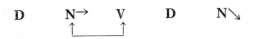

The first noun is the *simple subject*.
Sentences built on this formula include the following:

²Thĕ + ³fármĕrs²→²fêêd + thĕ + ³wórld¹$_\searrow$
²Thĕ + ³húntĕr²→²wôundĕd + thĕ + ³béar¹$_\searrow$
²Thĕ + ³tráctŏr²→²lêvĕls + thĕ + ³gróund¹$_\searrow$

2.

D $\quad$ N$_x^{\rightarrow}$ $\quad$ D $\quad$ N$_x^{\rightarrow}$ $\quad$ V $\quad$ D $\quad$ N$_\searrow$

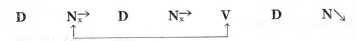

The second noun is an *appositive* to the first.
Examples follow:

²Thĕ + ³drívĕr²→²ă + Că³nádĭăn²→²nêêds + thĕ + ³cár¹$_\searrow$
²Hĭs + ³dóg²→²ă + ³bóxĕr²→²jûmped + thĕ + ³fénce¹$_\searrow$
²Mў + ³fáthĕr²→²thĕ + ³dóctŏr²→²wânts + ă + ³chánge¹$_\searrow$

Table of symbols

D	determiner
N	noun
$\mathbf{N_{sg}}$	noun in the singular
$\mathbf{N_x} \ldots \mathbf{N_x}$	nouns having the same personal substitutes
$\mathbf{N_{th}}$	noun replaceable in its formula by an adverbial substitute like *then, there, thus*
V.	transitive but not factitive verb
$\mathbf{V_{fac}}$	factitive verb
$\mathbf{V_{eq}}$	equational verb
N V	noun and verb agreeing in number (if agreement is possible)
$\rightarrow$	The terminal $/\!\!\rightarrow\!/$, preceded by $/^{232}/$
$\searrow$	The terminal $/\searrow/$, preceded by $/^{231}/$

All nouns are in the common case.

Before terminals, all nouns and all verbs have pitch $/^3/$ and strongest stress; elsewhere they have second stress.

All determiners have third stress or weakest stress.

Open transition is assumed between words.

3.

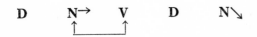

In this formula, which is identical with No. 1, the second noun is a *direct object*.

²Thĕ + ³wínd²→²ăffêcts + thĕ + ³spórt¹↘
²Thèir + ³spéed²→²dìscôurăgĕs + thèir + ŏp³pónĕnts¹↘
²Thĕ + cŏm³pútĕrs²→²mâke + nò + mĭs³tákes¹↘

4.

D   N→   V   D   N   D   N↘
     ↑_____↑

The second noun in the formula, which is the first noun after the verb, is an *indirect object*.

²Thĕ + ĕx³pósŭre²→²câused + thĕ + bôy + ăn + ³íllnĕss¹↘
²Hĭs + ³trávĕls²→²ăffôrd + thĕ + tôurĭst + nò + ³pléasŭre¹↘
²Thĕ + ³hérŏïne²→²têachĕs + thĕ + vĭllaïn + ă + ³léssŏn¹↘

Table of symbols

D	determiner
N	noun
N_{sg}	noun in the singular
$N_x \ldots N_x$	nouns having the same personal substitutes
N_{th}	noun replaceable in its formula by an adverbial substitute like *then, there, thus*
V	transitive but not factitive verb
V_{fac}	factitive verb
V_{eq}	equational verb
N ␣␣␣ V	noun and verb agreeing in number (if agreement is possible)
$\rightarrow$	The terminal $/\!\!\rightarrow\!\!/$, preceded by $/232/$
$\searrow$	The terminal $/\!\searrow\!/$, preceded by $/231/$

All nouns are in the common case.

Before terminals, all nouns and all verbs have pitch $/3/$ and strongest stress; elsewhere they have second stress.

All determiners have third stress or weakest stress.

Open transition is assumed between words.

5.

$$\mathbf{D} \qquad \mathbf{N}^{\rightarrow} \qquad \mathbf{V}_{fac} \qquad \mathbf{D} \qquad \mathbf{N}_x \qquad \mathbf{D} \qquad \mathbf{N}_x \searrow$$

The last noun is an *object complement*.

²Hìs + cŏm³pláints²$^{\rightarrow}$²mâke + thĕ + stûdĕnt + ă + ³bóre¹$\searrow$
²Thĕ + ³mémbĕrs²$^{\rightarrow}$²ĕlêctĕd + thĕ + sêcrĕtàrў + thèir + ³spókesmăn¹$\searrow$
²Thĕ + pŏ³líce²$^{\rightarrow}$²mâde + thĕ + pîck + pòckĕt + ă + ³prísŏnĕr¹$\searrow$

6.

$$\mathbf{D} \qquad \mathbf{N}_x^{\rightarrow} \qquad \hat{\mathbf{V}}_{eq} \qquad \mathbf{D} \qquad \mathbf{N}_x \searrow$$

The second noun is a *predicate nominative*.

²Hïs + ³stúdïes²$^{\rightarrow}$²àre + ă + ³próblĕm¹$\searrow$
²Yŏur + ³nérves²$^{\rightarrow}$²bĕcôme + ă + ³hándĭcàp¹$\searrow$
²Thĕ + ³gárdĕn²$^{\rightarrow}$²sêems + ă + ³fáilŭre¹$\searrow$

Table of symbols

D	determiner
N	noun
$\mathbf{N_{sg}}$	noun in the singular
$\mathbf{N_x} \ldots \mathbf{N_x}$	nouns having the same personal substitutes
$\mathbf{N_{th}}$	noun replaceable in its formula by an adverbial substitute like *then, there, thus*
V	transitive but not factitive verb
$\mathbf{V_{fac}}$	factitive verb
$\mathbf{V_{eq}}$	equational verb
N V	noun and verb agreeing in number (if agreement is possible)
→	The terminal /→/, preceded by /²³²/
↘	The terminal /↘/, preceded by /²³¹/

All nouns are in the common case.

Before terminals, all nouns and all verbs have pitch /³/ and strongest stress; elsewhere they have second stress.

All determiners have third stress or weakest stress.

Open transition is assumed between words.

7.

D   N$_{sg}$ N$^{\rightarrow}$ V   D   N$\searrow$

The first noun is a *noun adjunct*. As we have explained (p. 92), it is not an adjectival, since it fills a position typically occupied by nouns; but traditional grammars do often call a noun adjunct a "noun used as an adjective."

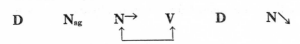

²Thĕ + brĭck + ³hóuse²$^{\rightarrow}$²côsts + ă + ³fórtŭne¹$\searrow$
²Thĕ + ôil + ³páintĭng²$^{\rightarrow}$²dĕlîghtĕd + thĕ + ³crítĭc¹$\searrow$
²Ă + stône + ³wáll²$^{\rightarrow}$²sŭrroûnds + thĕ + ³gárdĕn¹$\searrow$

8.

N$_{th}^{\rightarrow}$ D   N   V   D   N$\searrow$

The first noun is an *adverbial*.

³Mórnĭngs²$^{\rightarrow}$²thĕ + têachĕr + wrîtes + hĭs + ³léctŭres¹$\searrow$

In a common variation of this formula, a determiner precedes the first noun (which is then a nominal), and *then / thus / there* may be substituted for the initial determiner and the initial noun together:

D   N$^{\rightarrow}$ D   N   V   D   N$\searrow$
th

The first noun and its determiner constitute an *adverbial phrase*.

²Thìs + ³mórnĭng²$^{\rightarrow}$²thĕ + âdmĭrăl + ĭnspêcts + thĕ + ³státĭon¹$\searrow$
²Thàt + ³wíntĕr²$^{\rightarrow}$²thĕ + hûntĕr + bâgged + ă + ³déer¹$\searrow$

involved structures. For this reason, our formulas may be accepted as usefully summarizing a substantial part of the grammar of English sentences.

Exercise one. Read aloud the twenty-four sentences which illustrate our eight formulas. Be sure to use the indicated patterns of stress and intonation.

Exercise two. Construct three sentences of your own to illustrate each formula. Then write each formula on a blank note card, shuffle the cards, and practice illustrating each formula as it appears at random.

Exercise three. Shuffle the cards again. As each formula appears, construct at least three sentences which you can show to be expansions of it. Explain the nature of each expansion.

CHAPTER SIX

The Sentence and Its Kinds

Beginning with the sounds of English, we have worked our way to a point at which we can consider the largest of the grammarian's units, the sentence. In this chapter, we will attempt a definition of the sentence and a twofold classification of sentences—one classification according to their form and another according to their meaning. Both the definition and the classifications will be formulated with the purposes of a composition course in mind. For other purposes, a different definition and different classifications would be more valuable, but that fact need give us no concern. No single analysis of our language can serve all purposes.

Definition

⌁ The old stand-by

What is a sentence? The question has been asked and answered dozens of times and in dozens of different ways. Perhaps the most familiar definition is that a sentence is a group of words which expresses a complete thought. This definition has one main defect: it does not allow us to recognize a sentence when we hear one. It does not tell us what a complete thought is, and it does not tell us what signals in our speech indicate the completeness of a thought. For example, we may take the very typical English utterance,

$$^2\grave{\text{I}}\text{t} + {}^3\acute{\text{ı}}\text{s}^1 \searrow$$

We will all agree that this is a sentence, but the familiar definition is not the basis of our agreement. We could not possibly say whether or not the thought expressed is complete; in fact, we could not say what the thought is. Our agreement must rest on some other foundation than the familiar definition.

⌁ Definition by terminals

Since the familiar definition is unsatisfactory, we must try to frame a better one. If we use the materials of Chapter I, we will get a definition in terms of sounds. We have just indicated one possible intonation for our utterance:

$$^2\grave{\text{I}}\text{t} + {}^3\acute{\text{ı}}\text{s}^1 \searrow \qquad \text{"It is."}$$

We could also say, quite naturally,

$$^2\grave{\text{I}}\text{t} + {}^3\acute{\text{ı}}\text{s}^3 \nearrow \qquad \text{"It is?"}$$

Both the statement and the question are undoubtedly sentences, and when our attention is called to their intonations, we note that neither ends with the terminal /→/, but that the statement ends with the terminal which we write with the downward arrow and that the question ends with the terminal which we write with the upward arrow. Here is our clue to a possible definition of the sentence in terms of sound: any stretch of speech between silence and one of the two terminals /↘/ and /↗/, or any stretch between two such terminals, might be called a sentence.

Using this definition, we could divide any English utterance, simply and exactly, into definite parts which we might call sentences. The following utterance, for example, would contain two units, two "sentences":

$$^2\text{Whèn} + \text{thĕ} + {}^3\text{tîme} + {}^1\text{cáme}^1 \nearrow^2 \hat{\text{Ì}} + {}^3\text{léft}^1 \searrow$$

If we wished, we could carry our analysis further and subdivide our first terminally marked units by considering any "level-arrow" terminals and any open transitions within the initial units. For example, we have seen that the open transitions would sometimes correspond with the spaces between "words" in ordinary spelling, as they would in the utterance which we have just written; sometimes they would correspond with hyphens, as in *night-rate* (/^{3}náɪt + rè:t$^1 \searrow$/); sometimes they would fall within what are written as single "words," as in *trayful* (/^{3}tré: + fᴜl$^1 \searrow$/). Regardless of spelling, we could find our main units, our "sentences," by the terminals /↘/ and /↗/, and our smallest sub-units, our "words" (if we wished to call them such), by the open transitions. Moreover, we could sometimes correlate this classification with other, more familiar ones, as the following sentences will show:

1. Statement: ^{2}Yŏu + ^{3}stóp ĭt$^1 \searrow$ "You stop it."
2. Question: ^{2}Yŏu + ^{3}stóp ĭt$^3 \nearrow$ "You stop it?"
3. Command: ^{3}Yôu + ^{3}stóp ĭt$^1 \searrow$ "You stop it!"

Obviously, a classification in terms of sound, with its emphasis on pitches and terminals, stresses and transitions, would here help us to distinguish what are often called *declarative* sentences (statements), *interrogative* sentences (questions), and *imperative* sentences (commands).

↝ Its weakness

We would encounter, however, a number of difficulties with a classification of this sort. For one thing, open transition is not always easy to hear.

For another, the classification would not always fit in neatly with useful distinctions made in other ways. Not all statements have the same intonation pattern, for example, and a single intonation can sometimes be used on statements, or questions, or commands:

$$^2\text{Yŏu} + {}^3\text{stóp ĭt}^1 \searrow$$
$$^2\text{Whò} + {}^3\text{stópped ĭt}^1 \searrow$$
$$^2\text{Gô} + {}^3\text{stóp ĭt}^1 \searrow$$

Again, if terminals alone marked off our largest units, we would have to break up an utterance like the following one into four parts:

$$^3\text{Yéstĕrdày}^1 \nearrow {}^1\text{shĕ} + \text{bôught} + {}^2\text{béef}^2 \nearrow {}^1\text{pŏ} + {}^2\text{tátŏes}^2 \nearrow {}^2\text{ănd} + {}^3\text{léttŭce}^1 \searrow$$

When we had analyzed this utterance into the four units which the terminals indicate, our method would give us no way of putting the four parts together again into a larger whole; and yet, as speakers of English, we know that the four parts do somehow go together, and if we are students of composition we want to treat them together as a single sentence. To define the sentence *purely* in terms of sound would not, then, be very helpful to us; for although the terminal $/\searrow/$ rarely occurs within that kind of unit which we will call a sentence, the terminal $/\nearrow/$ does occur there, and $/\searrow/$ occurs at the ends both of our sentences and of other units. We must look further for a definition which will be of greater use.

❧ The subject-predicate test

If we frame a definition in terms primarily of grammatical units smaller than the sentences which they compose, we will still be able to say that every English sentence ends in a terminal which we write with an upward or a downward arrow; but we will not have to say that every upward or downward arrow marks the end of a sentence. We will have a means of classifying as nonsentences certain units which end in these terminals; and in particular we will have a means of passing over certain occurrences of the terminal $/\nearrow/$ within utterances which we would like, for the purposes of a composition course, to classify as sentences. To find this means of classification, we need only remember what we have all been taught and what we have assumed through much of our discussion: a sentence must contain a complete subject and a complete predicate. Our long example in the preceding paragraph, by this rule, is only one sentence and not four, for it contains only one subject-predicate combination. *Yesterday* cannot be a sentence, since that part of the utterance contains no verbal; and the rest of the utterance is basically identical in structure with a simple nominal-verbal sequence like *She did.*

↫ Sentence fragments

Most of us will not have much difficulty in using the subject-predicate test, but it is not in itself a complete definition; it needs both qualification and extension. The qualification is very important. We often say things, in perfectly normal speech, which do not contain a complete subject and a complete predicate. We might very well say, possibly in answer to a question,

$$^2\text{thĕ} + {}^3\text{chóir}^1 \searrow$$

just as we might say,

$$^2\text{thĕ} + {}^3\text{chóir}^2 {\rightarrow}{}^2\text{wĭll} + {}^3\text{síng} + \text{nôw}^1 \searrow$$

Both answers are correct English utterances, and both end in the terminal /$\searrow$/. Only the second, however, contains a complete subject, *the choir,* and a complete predicate, *will sing now.* We will therefore find it useful to say that only the second utterance is a complete sentence, while the first is a sentence fragment or a nonsentence. The label "sentence fragment" must not, of course, suggest that we never do (or never should) write or say anything which does not contain a subject and a predicate; and we must not forget that in limiting our discussion to complete sentences and neglecting the sentence fragment, we are deliberately choosing, for our own special purposes, to neglect a substantial part of the English language.

↫ Independent clauses

As the first extension of our subject-predicate test, we must add a third condition which a complete sentence has to satisfy. Every sentence, we have said, will end in one of the two terminals which we write with upward or downward arrows, and every sentence will contain at least one combination of complete subject with complete predicate. A third condition is that a sentence must contain at least one *independent* combination of subject and predicate—that is, one independent clause. We will define independence negatively. An independent clause, we will say, is neither confirmatory nor interjected; it does not help us to compose an expansion of any smaller unit, though it may be linked in various ways to other independent clauses; and for it we cannot substitute a single nominal, adjectival, or adverbial but only another unit like itself.

We have already dealt with interjected and confirmatory clauses, and a few examples will clarify this third condition. As we have seen, the subject of a sentence like

$$^2\text{thĕ} + {}^3\text{frúit}^{2\rightarrow2}\text{wăs} + \text{nòt} + {}^3\text{rípe}^1 \searrow$$

may be expanded not only by single words but by groups of words, like *in the orchard:*

$$^2\text{thĕ} + \text{frúit} + \text{ìn} + \text{thĕ} + {}^3\text{órchărd}^{2\rightarrow2}\text{wăs} + \text{nòt} + {}^3\text{rípe}^1 \searrow$$

Some of these groups of words may themselves contain subjects and predicates:

$$^2\text{thĕ} + \text{frúit} + \text{thăt} + \text{shĕ} + {}^3\text{bóught}^{2\rightarrow2}\text{wăs} + \text{nòt} + {}^3\text{rípe}^1 \searrow$$
$$^2\text{thĕ} + \text{frúit} + \text{shĕ} + {}^3\text{bóught}^{2\rightarrow2}\text{wăs} + \text{nòt} + {}^3\text{rípe}^1 \searrow$$

Within the word group (*that*) *she bought,* there is a nominal, *she,* and a verbal, *bought,* linked up as subject and predicate; but the sequence *the fruit* (*that*) *she bought* is an expansion of *the fruit,* and for the whole clause (*that*) *she bought* we can substitute a single word, like *purchased:*

$$^2\text{thĕ} + \text{frúit} + {}^3\text{púrchăsed}^{2\rightarrow2}\text{wăs} + \text{nòt} + {}^3\text{rípe}^1 \searrow$$

⟡ Dependent clauses

For most clauses connected to the rest of their sentences by subordinating conjunctions, relatives, or interrogatives (including "zero" members of these classes), it can thus be shown either (1) that the clauses help to compose expansions of smaller units, or (2) that the clauses are equivalent to single nominals, adjectivals, or adverbials, or (3) that both these conditions are met.

1. *The dog that bit him* was rabid.—*The dog* was rabid.
2. *That he left* is certain.—*It* is certain.
3. *The fruit* (*that*) *she bought* was not ripe.

We will call all clauses of this type *dependent,* and we will treat neither these nor interjected and confirmatory clauses as complete sentences; they are distinctly different from a combination like *He left,* which is not interjected or confirmatory, which is not an expansion of any smaller unit, and whose only equivalent is another expanded or unexpanded sequence of nominal and verbal, related as subject to predicate. Grammatical equivalents of *He left* are such things as *She leaves, She is leaving, The teacher is leaving,* not words like *purchased* or *it* or *then. He left* and its equivalents are therefore independent clauses and complete sentences.

❧ Expanding a sentence

A second extension of the subject-predicate test has already been so strongly implied that perhaps it might be left without explicit statement, but for clarity we should add that an utterance may be an incomplete sentence as well for what it contains as for what it does not contain. A single complete sentence remains complete and single if we add to it a dependent clause, connected to the independent clause in one of the ways which we have suggested:

> The fruit was not ripe.
> The fruit (*that*) *she bought* was not ripe.

A single complete sentence remains complete and single if we add a sentence adverbial:

> The work had to be done.
> *Plan or no plan,* the work had to be done.

We still have a single complete sentence even if we add one or more such sentences to another, connecting them, for example, by certain sequences of intonation patterns together with coordinating or correlative conjunctions, or by a combination of equivalent grammatical structures with certain sequences of intonation patterns, or in both these ways:

> (1) ^{2}thĕ $^+$ stôrm $^+$ ^{3}pássed^1 ↘
> ^{2}thĕ $^+$ stôrm $^+$ ^{3}pássed$^{2\rightarrow2}$ănd $^+$ wĕ $^+$ wênt $^+$ ^{3}ón^1 ↘

Here the connecting device is the use of the coordinating conjunction *and* and the substitution of the intonation pattern /$^{232}\rightarrow$/ for the pattern /^{231}↘/.

> (2) ^{2}hĕ $^+$ ^{3}cáme^1 ↘
> ^{2}hĕ $^+$ ^{3}cáme^3 ↗ ^{2}hĕ $^+$ ^{3}sáw^3 ↗ ^{2}hĕ $^+$ ^{3}cónquĕred^1 ↘

Here each clause consists of the personal pronoun *he,* a nominal, in subject position, and a single verbal, the past tense of a verb, in predicate position; the grammatical structure of all the clauses is equivalent. Moreover, the sequence of terminals (/↗/, /↗/, /↘/) indicates a single grammatical entity, which is not broken up as it would be if the terminal /↘/ followed the first or second clause.

> (3) ^{2}hĕ $^+$ ^{3}cáme^3 ↗ ^{2}hĕ $^+$ ^{3}sáw^3 ↗ ^{2}ănd $^+$ hĕ $^+$ ^{3}cónquĕred^1 ↘

Here the connection is established by the conjunction *and,* the intonation patterns, and the equivalent structures—all three.

❧ Unattached parts

There are evidently a number of ways of expanding a single complete sentence without destroying its completeness or its unity, but there is one kind of expansion which does make the sentence incomplete. A complete sentence cannot contain any subject without a predicate, any predicate without a subject, or any unattached *fragment* of a complete subject or a complete predicate. *I told him to go* is a sentence; but if we add *and if he had done it*, the result is a nonsentence:

$$\text{²Ĭ} + \text{tôld hĭm} + \text{tŏ} + \text{³gó²} \rightarrow \text{²ănd} + \text{ĭf} + \text{hĕ} + \text{hăd} + \text{³dóne ĭt¹} \searrow$$

If he had done it is an unattached adverbial clause which makes the originally complete sentence incomplete.

Finally, in concluding this section, we must now make one exception to our subject-predicate rule. Commands or imperatives, which our conventions of end punctuation in writing make it best to treat as complete sentences, do not always contain a subject. We can say either

$$\text{³stóp} + \text{thàt¹} \searrow$$

or

$$\text{³yóu} + \text{stóp} + \text{thàt¹} \searrow$$

without much change of meaning. In other words, before the verbal of an imperative sentence which does not contain a subject, we can often add as subject the nominal *you;* but whether or not a subject is present in utterances of this sort, we will consider them as complete sentences. One justification for doing so is that we often use coordinating conjunctions to link imperatives to independent subject-predicate clauses, and constructions so linked are syntactically equivalent.

Quit talking, or I'll spank you.

Go away, and I'll tell you later.

❧ Summary

Our attempt to define the sentence has now yielded moderately familiar results, partly because we have adjusted our definition to meet our particular needs. If we framed a definition by sound alone, our sentences would be stretches of speech between the two terminals which we write with upward and downward arrows, or between silence and one of these terminals; within these units, open transitions would enable us to mark further divisions which we might call words; but words and sentences defined in this way would not be particularly useful in the study of composition.

We have chosen, instead, to define the sentence, as we have defined the word, primarily in terms of the classes of elements that compose it. We identify the stretches of speech that lie between terminals, or sequences of these stretches, either as complete sentences or as sentence fragments. A complete sentence will always end in one of the terminals /↘/ and /↗/ (never /→/), and it may or may not contain occurrences of /↗/ or /→/ within itself; but it will also contain, in every case except that of the imperative, at least one independent combination of complete subject with complete predicate, expanded or unexpanded. To a complete sentence various elements may be added without destroying its completeness, and two or more complete sentences may be variously linked up in one; but no utterance is a complete sentence if it contains an unattached subject, an unattached predicate, or an unattached fragment of a subject or predicate. Whatever its intonation, a stretch of speech which does not satisfy these conditions will be treated in this book as a sentence fragment or nonsentence, though our method of description must not be taken as implying condemnation of the sentence fragment.

Exercise one. Study the following characteristics of the English sentence as we have attempted to define it.

1. A sentence ends in one of the terminals which we write with upward or downward arrows.
2. A sentence must contain at least one independent combination of complete subject with complete predicate (one independent clause). A clause is independent
   a. if it is neither confirmatory nor interjected;
   b. if it does not help to compose an expansion of any unit smaller than a clause;
   c. if for it we can substitute only another unit like itself, not a single nominal, adjectival, or adverbial.
3. A sentence cannot contain any subject without a predicate, any predicate without a subject, or any unattached *fragment* of a complete subject or a complete predicate.

Commands or imperatives are the one exception to the subject-predicate rule. They often contain no subject but consist of the simple name or base form of the verb, followed as usual by any objects, etc.

Exercise two. Read the following items aloud. Be particularly careful to use the indicated terminals.

1. ²a ³terminal²→²is part of an into ³nation pattern¹↘
2. ²when it ²rains²↗³it ¹pours¹↘
3. ²you're ³going¹↘

4. ^{2}you're ^{3}going^3↗
5. ^{2}if you're ^{3}going^2→^{2}you'd better take your ^{3}hat^1↘
6. ^{2}willy-^{3}nilly^2→^{2}he must answer the ^{3}questions^1↘
7. ^{2}the truck was ^{3}red^2→^{2}but it wasn't a ^{3}fire truck^1↘
8. ^{2}the truck was ^{3}red^1↘^{2}but it wasn't a ^{3}fire truck^1↘
9. ^{2}the ^{3}flowers^2→^{2}which were drooping in the ^{3}sun^2→^{2}looked less at-^{3}tractive^1↘
10. ^{2}I don't want ^{3}that dress^2↗^{2}but the one you picked last ^{3}night^1↘
11. ^{2}the ^{3}rain^2→^{1}he ^{1}said^1↗^{2}will spoil the ^{3}game^1↘
12. ^{2}English is ^{3}easy^2→^{3}isn't it^1↘
13. ^{3}no^2→^{1}she re^{1}plied^1↘
14. ^{2}never a dull ^{3}moment^1↘
15. ^{2}it rained ^{3}heavily^2→^{2}and since the ^{3}lakes^2→^{2}were already ^{3}full^1↘

Exercise three. In each of the items in Exercise two, point out all the complete subjects and complete predicates. Are there any items which contain no subject-predicate combination? Which of the clauses are dependent? Which of the clauses are interjected or confirmatory?

Exercise four. (a) According to our definition, how many sentences are there in Item 7? In Item 8? (b) According to our definition, how many independent clauses are there in Items 11, 12, and 13? (c) According to our definition, are Items 13, 14, and 15 complete sentences? Are any of the other items not complete sentences?

Classification

❧ Classification by clauses

In earlier chapters, we have suggested several different ways by which sentences might be classified. One way is by the order of subjects and predicates: S   P, P   S, P$_1$ S   P$_2$, etc. We will return to this particular method of classification at the end of the present section, but our discussion will be more smoothly connected if, at the moment, we build a set of sentence classes around the term *clause.* A clause, we said, is either a combination of a complete subject with a complete predicate or, less commonly, an imperative with any expansions; and the number of clauses within a single complete sentence, and the relationships among them, are the bases for the familiar classification of sentences as *simple, compound, complex,* and *compound-complex.*

SIMPLE SENTENCES. A *simple sentence* contains only *one independent clause.*

> Dogs bite.
> Dogs bite postmen.
> Vicious dogs bite postmen.
> Vicious dogs bite harmless postmen.
> The vicious dogs and cats bite the harmless postmen and tear their trousers.

None of these expansions of a minimal complete subject and a minimal complete predicate produces anything but a simple sentence, since none of them adds another clause. The last example should be noted with particular care. To the preceding sentence, it adds another simple subject, *cats,* and another simple predicate, *tear;* but the additions are so made that no second clause is produced. There is still only one *complete* subject and one *complete* predicate, although both have been made *compound.*

COMPOUND SENTENCES. If, however, we begin our series of examples with two simple sentences, slightly modify the intonation pattern on the first, and insert a coordinating conjunction between them, the resulting *sentence* has been made compound and is no longer simple:

> ²dôgs + ³bíte¹\²pôstmĕn + ³rún¹\
> ²dôgs + ³bíte²→²ănd + pôstmĕn + ³rún¹\

A *compound sentence* contains *two or more independent clauses.* The most common means of connection between the two clauses (though not, as we have shown, the only means) are certain intonation patterns, along with the coordinating or correlative conjunctions. For another example:

> ³hé + leâves¹\³Í + dô¹\
> ²eithĕr + ³hé + leâves¹↗²ŏr + ³Í + dô¹\

The contrast should be noted between the finality signaled by the terminal which we write with the downward arrow and the continuity suggested by the other two terminals, /→/ and /↗/. Except as a deliberate stylistic device, the downward arrow is not likely to occur before a coordinating conjunction introducing an independent clause.

COMPLEX SENTENCES AND RESTRICTION. A different way of connecting clauses produces complex and compound-complex sentences. Both the following sentences are simple:

> ²thĕ + ³óffĭcĕr²→²sâw + thĕ + ³dóg¹\²ĭt + hăd + bîttĕn + thĕ + ³póstmăn¹\

If we substitute *which* for *it* and change the intonation patterns, the result is a *complex sentence,* defined as containing *one independent clause and one or more dependent clauses:*

> ²thĕ + ³ôffĭcĕr²→²sâw + thĕ + dôg + whìch + hăd + bîttĕn + thĕ + ³póstmăn¹↘

The dependent clause *which had bitten the postman* would traditionally be labeled *restrictive; restrictive* would in turn be defined as "essential to the meaning of the sentence." Like the traditional definition of the sentence, this definition of a restrictive clause hardly tells us how we know one when we hear it. Certainly, in our example, the clause *which had bitten the postman* is essential to the meaning of the sentence, since it singles out, from the whole class of dogs, a single previously unidentified specimen; it tells us which particular dog the officer saw. The question here is how this meaning "identifier of previously unidentified specimen" is signaled, and the answer lies, in large part, in the intonation patterns. The contrast with the corresponding *nonrestrictive* clause (the "inessential, parenthetical" clause) will make the signal clear. Suppose we say,

> ²thĕ + ôffĭcĕr + sâw + thĕ + ³dóg²→²whìch + hăd + bîttĕn + thĕ + ³póstmăn¹↘

In this sentence, the clause *which had bitten the postman* does not identify a dog which was unknown before, but merely adds a distressing fact about a beast already identified. The same intonation patterns are used (/²³²→/ and /²³¹↘/), but the terminal between them (/→/), although it indicates the larger unity of the two clauses in a single sentence, nevertheless is now so placed that it gives each clause a certain separateness; the rise to pitch /³/ on *dog,* along with strongest stress, tells us that this animal is no stranger to us. On the other hand, if we leave the terminal /→/ after *officer* and use only pitch /²/ and second stress on *dog,* the two clauses are given a closer unity and our attention is not called to the familiarity of the animal but to his conduct toward the postman. Thus the presence or absence of a terminal after the nominal which precedes the relative and which is linked by agreement in number to the verb of the dependent clause—that is, the presence or absence of a terminal after the *antecedent* of the relative—will often tell us whether the dependent clause is restrictive or not.

TYPES OF DEPENDENT CLAUSES. Not all dependent clauses, as we have pointed out, are introduced by relatives. Often dependent clauses are introduced by interrogatives or subordinating conjunctions:

I asked him what [interrogative] he meant to do about it.
Then I told him that [subordinating conjunction] I didn't care.
He said [verbal, followed by a "zero" subordinating conjunction] he didn't care either.

Although relative clauses, moreover, are normally grammatical equivalents of adjectivals, we have seen that other dependent clauses may be adverbial or nominal.

Adverbial: *When the sun rose,* the shooting began.
Nominal: The stool pigeon reported *what he had heard.*

These differences are irrelevant to the classification of sentences as simple, compound, complex, or compound-complex; all five of the immediately preceding examples are complex sentences, despite the differences among their single dependent clauses.

COMPOUND-COMPLEX SENTENCES. Sentences of our fourth class, the *compound-complex,* contain *two or more independent clauses, and one or more dependent clauses.* To construct a compound-complex sentence, we may begin with three simple sentences:

$$^2\text{it's} + {}^3\text{spríng}^1 \searrow {}^2\text{bírds} + {}^3\text{síng}^1 \searrow {}^2\text{flôwĕrs} + {}^3\text{blóom}^1 \searrow$$

To unite the three sentences, we may make the first a dependent clause by introducing it with a subordinating conjunction, and connect the last two by placing a coordinating conjunction between them:

$$^2\text{whèn} + \text{ĭt's} + {}^3\text{spríng}^{2 \rightarrow}{}^2\text{bírds} + {}^3\text{síng}^{2 \rightarrow}{}^2\text{ănd} + \text{flôwĕrs} + {}^3\text{blóom}^1 \searrow$$

The illustration again shows the importance of intonation.

Exercise one. How many clauses does each of the following sentences contain? Which are independent, and which are dependent? Classify the sentences as simple, compound, complex, or compound-complex.

1. The tree by the window bears some kind of red fruit.
2. The smallest birds which I've seen there are kinglets.
3. The wind blew, the rain fell, and the roof leaked.
4. Although the tenant's wife died of pneumonia, the landlord raised the rent, and the community praised him for his enterprise.
5. Fielding maintained that a great man is a great scoundrel.
6. The corporation exhibited all of its products except a mechanical politician.
7. The garden was covered with weeds, but the melons were thriving.
8. When the motorcycle went into the curve, the back tire blew out, and the officer was gathered to his fathers.

9. It would have been very impolite to say that he got killed.
10. The adolescent hoodlum is not found in one country only.

❧ Classification by meaning

We have now completed the classification of sentences according to the number and interrelations of the clauses which they contain. This is basically a classification according to form. We have still to deal with the equally familiar classification of sentences, according to their meanings, into statements, questions, commands, and exclamations. These kinds of sentences are perhaps best distinguished in terms of the differing responses which they evoke. To a *statement,* the typical response may be described simply as "continuing attention." To a *question,* an oral response, an answer, is typically appropriate. To a *command,* the most common response is an action. An *exclamatory* sentence, a sentence "expressing strong feeling," may evoke any or all of the three responses—attention, an answer, or action.

❧ Relationship of meaning to form

Such approximate distinctions as these are of relatively little use in our grammar, which we have chosen to build on the forms which signal meanings rather than on the meanings themselves; and the situation is further complicated by the fact that the relationship between form and meaning, as we have seen, is not simple. There is no one formal pattern which marks all questions, no one formal pattern for all statements, exclamations, or commands. Just as a $/^{231}\searrow/$ intonation, for example, may be used in a question, a command, or a statement, so the sentence order P_1 S P_2 may occur in sentences which call for an answer, request an action, provoke attention, or do any of these three things by "expressing strong feeling." The following sentence is a question:

$$^2\grave{a}re + y\breve{o}u + {}^3g\acute{o}\breve{i}ng^1\searrow$$

The same intonation occurs so often with statements that we have limited ourselves almost entirely to it in this book:

$$^2yo\grave{u}'re + {}^3g\acute{o}\breve{i}ng^1\searrow$$

The sentence order P_1 S P_2 requests an action and therefore constitutes a command in

$$^2n\grave{o}w + {}^3y\hat{o}u + l\hat{o}\hat{o}k + {}^3h\acute{e}re^1\searrow$$

A different subtype of the order P_1 S P_2 constitutes an exclamation, expressing strong feeling, in

^{4}wâs $^+$ hè $^+$ dìs^{1}gústed^1↘

It follows, since we have built our grammar more on forms than on meanings, that our previous classifications have separated some sentences which are broadly similar in meaning, and united others whose meanings are different. This is not to say that completely identical forms will signal different meanings. Some formal patterns will be ambiguous, it is true, but in far the greater number of instances a difference in meaning will be signaled by a statable difference in form. The relative position of the subject and the verb, for example, distinguishes the following question and statement, although the intonations are the same:

^{2}ĭs $^+$ shĕ $^+$ ^{3}háppў^1↘
^{2}shè $^+$ ĭs $^+$ ^{3}háppў^1↘

WORD ORDER IN STATEMENTS. Generalizing, we may say that word order is the most important signal, though not the only signal, which distinguishes statements, questions, and commands. Of the features of word order, in turn, the most important is the relative position of simple subject and simple predicate. Thus, if we use the general term *complement* to mean any object, or a predicate nominative or adjectival, the favorite order in statements is simple subject, simple predicate, complement (if any):

> The rain [simple subject] soaked [simple predicate] the dry fields [complement].

WORD ORDER IN QUESTIONS. In questions, the facts of order are more complex, and we must distinguish between questions where the simple subject is an interrogative or is preceded by an interrogative as an adjectival part of the complete subject, and all other questions. If such an interrogative is present, then the order is simple subject, simple predicate:

> Who   is in the kitchen with Dinah?
> What   caused the fight?
> Which books   are needed?
> What scoundrel   stole my tobacco?

Other types of questions can be classified according to their verbals. If the only verbal is a form of *be* or an auxiliary, the order simple predicate, simple subject is commonly used.

> Is   he   a scholar?
> What are   these things?

         Will   you?

         Why must   we?

Sometimes the same order is used in questions where the verbal is a single form of *have* (not in auxiliary position):

         Has   he   any money?

More commonly in questions with *have,* an auxiliary precedes the simple subject, and the form of *have* follows the simple subject:

         Does   he   have any money?

         What must   he   have?

This last pattern is also the favorite in questions involving verbs other than those which we have specified earlier in the paragraph:

         Did   you   see anyone?

         Is   he   reading aloud?

         What can   the speaker   say to that?

    WORD ORDER IN COMMANDS. Commands are generally distinguished from statements and questions largely by the fact which we have already noticed, that in commands there often is no subject. The verbal in commands is the simple name form of the verb, without ending; and complements follow it, as usual:

         Stop your complaining.

         Be good.

If a subject *is* present in a command, the affirmative order is simple subject, simple predicate, complement:

         Everybody   get in there and pitch.

The negative order appears in

         Don't   you   say that,

where the auxiliary *do* (with *n't* in close transition) precedes the simple subject, and the rest of the simple predicate (with any complements) follows the simple subject.

    EXCLAMATIONS. Finally, for the exclamatory sentence, as the label is generally used, no such clear patterns can be described. It is true that there are some arrangements which clearly mark exclamations; we may contrast

         What a man   he   is!

with

         What man is   he?

Sometimes, again, intonation distinguishes an exclamatory sentence from a statement or a question:

    1. Statement: ²shè's + ³góne¹\

Exclamation: ^{2}shè's + ^{4}góne^{2}↘
or
^{2}shè's + ^{4}góne^{2}↗

2\. Question: ^{2}wère + yŏu + ^{3}ángrў^{1}↘
Exclamation: ^{4}wêre + yôu + ^{4}ángrў^{2}↘

Examples like the preceding, however, remind us that almost any selection and arrangement of forms can be spoken with an intonation or with some distortion or special qualification of normal speech, such as overloudness, which will make the utterance express strong feeling. Except for those few sentences, like *What a man he is,* whose patterns are always and only exclamatory, the class of sentences "expressing strong feeling" is another traditional vague catchall, and we may dismiss it with these brief remarks.

Exercise two. Turn the following affirmative statements into the corresponding negative statements. For example, the negative of *The rain soaked the dry fields* is *The rain didn't (did not) soak the dry fields.*

1. The sergeant was a very good-natured fellow.
2. The salesman covered a large territory.
3. The manufacturers use chromium for sucker bait.
4. The women have whined and complained more than usual.
5. The organ is playing now.

Exercise three. Turn both the affirmative statements and the negative statements of Exercise two into questions. For example, to the statement *The rain soaked the dry fields,* the corresponding question is *Did the rain soak the dry fields?* The negative question is *Didn't (did not) the rain soak the dry fields,* or *Did the rain not soak the dry fields?*

Exercise four. In the following questions, point out the simple and complete subjects and predicates, and state the relative order of simple subjects and predicates.

1. What were the symptoms of the disease?
2. Who put the overalls in the chowder?
3. How many men have run a four-minute mile?
4. Which rabbit did he pull out of the hat then?
5. What is your brother using instead of money?

Bibliography

Note: In the United States during the last twenty years, a number of attempts have been made to present more or less extensive outlines of English syntax which would meet the standards of modern descriptive linguistics. The present book is one of the more conservative and less ambitious of these attempts. Other works in the same general tradition, besides those of Francis, Fries, Hill, Roberts, and Trager-Smith which we have already listed (pp. 57, 111), include the following:

FRIES, CHARLES CARPENTER, *American English Grammar*. New York: Appleton-Century-Crofts, Inc., 1940.

LLOYD, DONALD J., and HARRY R. WARFEL, *American English in Its Cultural Setting*. New York: Alfred A. Knopf, Inc., 1956.

ROBERTS, PAUL, *Understanding English*. New York: Harper & Bros., 1958.

WHITEHALL, HAROLD, *Structural Essentials of English*. New York: Harcourt, Brace & Co., Inc., 1956.

In addition to Zandvoort's previously listed *Handbook* (p. 111), valuable one-volume treatments of English grammar by European scholars include:

JESPERSEN, OTTO, *Essentials of English Grammar*. New York: Henry Holt and Company, 1933.

PALMER, HAROLD E., and F. G. BLANDFORD, *A Grammar of Spoken English*. 2d ed. Cambridge, England: W. Heffer & Sons, Ltd., 1939.

Serious students will wish also to consult the big standard grammars, which remain permanently valuable, though some of them are now rather old-fashioned:

CURME, GEORGE OLIVER, *Parts of Speech and Accidence*. Boston: D. C. Heath and Company, 1935.

————, *Syntax*. Boston: D. C. Heath and Company, 1931.

JESPERSEN, OTTO, *A Modern English Grammar on Historical Principles*. 7 vols. Copenhagen: Einar Munksgaard, 1909–1949.

KRUISINGA, E., *A Handbook of Present-Day English*. 5th ed. 3 vols. Groningen: P. Noordhoff, 1931.

POUTSMA, H., *A Grammar of Late Modern English*. Groningen: P. Noordhoff. Part I, 2d ed., 1928–1929; Part II, 1926.

SWEET, HENRY, *A New English Grammar*. Oxford: Clarendon Press. Part I, 1891; Part II, 1898.

The most recent development in the study of English syntax has been the transformational analysis by the American linguist Noam Chomsky. Though Chomsky's work as yet is largely programmatic, it is of the first importance. No attempt has been made to introduce his methods or results into the present book, which was complete, in a trial version, as long ago as 1953; but future grammars will take account of such studies as these:

CHOMSKY, NOAM, review of B. F. Skinner, *Verbal Behavior*, in *Language*, 35.26–58 (1959).

————, *Syntactic Structures*. 's-Gravenhage: Mouton & Co., 1957. Reviewed by Robert B. Lees, with further bibliography, in *Language*, 33.375–408 (1957).

————, "A Transformational Approach to Syntax," paper read at the Texas Conference on English Syntax, 1958 (to be published, under the editorship of A. A. Hill, in the proceedings of that conference).

CHAPTER SEVEN

A Glossary of Grammatical Terms

❧ Comparing grammars

The history of English grammar and of the teaching of English will make it increasingly necessary, in the next few years, for most of us to be able to use grammars of more than one kind. The older and more conventional grammars, on which most educated Americans have been brought up, still dominate the field, but have been sharply criticized in our century. Greater knowledge of language and languages, and greater skill in describing languages, have made many linguists believe, as we have said, that these older grammars seriously misrepresent the facts of English speech and writing. New books are appearing which are not like the old books, and neither the new nor the old agree in all points among themselves; so that as teachers and students, if we want to think rationally about our language and to benefit fully from the labors of many different scholars, we must have some way of comparing different methods and different results in English grammar.

❧ Difficulties involved

Not all of us will have to make the same kinds of comparison or to face the same difficulties in making them. A student who thoroughly learns and understands one modern grammar of English should not have much trouble with another modern grammar, because the basic principles of the different books are likely to be much the same. Most of these books, for example, will define their parts of speech not by their meanings but by their positions in sentences, by their occurrence with prefixes and derivational suffixes, by their inflections, or by combinations of these criteria; and other grammatical classes than the parts of speech will likewise be defined in terms of form. Modern grammars share this method of formal definition, which allows us to define and use our classes more precisely and effectively than we were able to do in the old ways.

Moving from one system of grammar to another may be a problem, then, mainly for the student who has learned an old-fashioned grammar and now is learning a new one and for the student who is now learning a modern grammar but later must learn an old-fashioned one. What evidence there is on the subject suggests that the second student will have less difficulty than the first. If a student has once grasped the concept of a grammar as one of several possible descriptions of a language, and if he has once realized that grammatical definitions are means which the grammarian shapes to his own ends, he seems able to move rather easily from a formally based grammar to a grammar based on meaning. The real difficulty seems to lie in moving from the old-fashioned to the modern grammars; but that is precisely what most of those who seriously study English grammar have had to do or must do in the future. They must face the modern challenge to the grammar which they have studied from their schooldays—to grammar as a set of definitions in terms of meaning and a set of somewhat arbitrary *do's* and *don't's*.

ꝗ Nature and purposes of this glossary

Such students need all the help they can get, and this glossary is intended primarily for them. It provides, in simple form, many of the traditional definitions, to which it adds the nearest equivalents in the system of this book. It also separately defines those of our terms which lack traditional equivalents. Thus the glossary is at once a selective index to our sketch of the structure of English, a summary of important statements in that sketch, and a means of relating our statements to the corresponding parts of the grammars which may already be familiar to most students. Careful reading of the glossary should promote the ability to operate either the older or the newer grammatical systems and to move easily from one to the other.

ꝗ Using the glossary

Though the glossary is available for selective reference, it can best be studied systematically; for if we want to understand the nature and significance of a linguistic feature, or if we want to understand and judge a grammarian's description of that feature, we ought ideally to examine both the feature and its description in their context: the feature as a part of the whole system which is the language, the descriptive statement as a part of the whole picture which the grammarian has drawn of the language. Different statements of the same linguistic facts can often be translated one into the other; and what looks in isolation like a pointless contradiction of established doctrine may turn out, in its full context, to be a different and perhaps even a better way of saying a familiar thing.

The glossary may be studied systematically in more ways than one. In some situations, it might be used alone; or it might be read either before, during, or after the study of the six preceding chapters. The student can begin in the glossary, with the names of the traditional parts of speech or with the entry *Parts of speech* itself, and can let the definitions, references, and cross references introduce him to the content and method of the connected discussion. He may or may not then proceed to detailed study of the grammar proper. Alternatively, while the student is working through the preceding chapters, he can turn to the glossary for each new term he encounters and can see how it is related to terms he already knows from older grammars. Finally, and most obviously, the glossary can be used in review. However it is used, its form should not be allowed to suggest that the mere memorizing of grammatical definitions is an end in itself.

a

ABSOLUTE CONSTRUCTION. In traditional terms, an absolute construction is a kind of sentence adverb or sentence modifier. In the terms of this book, it is a kind of sentence adverbial, a construction which is not a part of either the complete subject or the complete predicate of its sentence. Usually an absolute construction precedes the rest of the sentence and is followed by a terminal, which the customary comma suggests in written English. The absolute construction contains no subject or predicate of its own but often consists (1) of two words or phrases belonging to the same class and connected by the conjunction *or* or (2) of a nominal plus one of certain kinds of adjectivals.

Lunch or no lunch, he had to finish his work.

The doors being closed, no more spectators could enter.

References: 145–46, 151.

ABSTRACT NOUN. An abstract noun is usually defined as the name of something like an idea or a quality, which we can think about but cannot perceive with our five senses as we can perceive material things like chairs and tables. Many nouns which are called abstract occur in the singular either with *a*, with *the*, or with neither (*a kindness, the kindness, kindness*). Their meaning often changes from singular to plural (*kindness, kindnesses*). See CONCRETE NOUN.

ACCIDENCE. The system of inflection in a language or the study and description of that system are often called accidence.

ACCUSATIVE CASE. See OBJECTIVE CASE.

ACTIVE VOICE. See VOICE.

ADJECTIVAL. In most grammars, the term *adjectival* is used to mean "of or pertaining to an adjective" and not as we have used it. We have defined an adjectival as a word or larger form which occupies a position that adjectives regularly occupy—for example, *good* in *the very good dog* or *chaotic* in *The situation was quite chaotic.* We have extended this basic definition in two ways: (1) to include *a, an, the,* and the other determiners as well as the interrogatives of type 2 (*what* man, *which* book); (2) to include certain phrases and dependent clauses which regularly serve to expand nominals. Thus, in the following sentences, the italicized constructions are adjectival:

The book *on the table* was a history *of England.*

The picture *which the reporter drew* was very gloomy.

See PARTS OF SPEECH.

References: 92–4, 98, 103–05, 109, 115–19, 124–26, 134–35.

ADJECTIVAL CLAUSE. An adjectival clause is a dependent clause which is used to expand a nominal. For example:

The captain was pleased by the letter.

The captain was pleased by the letter *that came today.*

Adjectival clauses are introduced by relatives or by subordinating conjunctions and are placed after the nominals which they expand; thus:

The morning was very bright.

The morning *when we arrived* was very bright.

Our definition is equivalent to the traditional statement that an adjective clause modifies a noun or pronoun.

References: 118–19, 140–41, 170, 177, 286–87.

ADJECTIVE. We have defined an adjective as a compared word—any word that fits into an inflectional series like *tall, taller, tallest.* This definition is narrower than the traditional statement that an adjective is a word that modifies a noun or pronoun; for the traditional adjective would include both compared words (our adjectives) and other words that occupy the same positions as compared words (many of our adjectivals). See PARTS OF SPEECH.

References: 79–81, 92–4, 115–17, 123, 134–35, 305–06.

ADVERB. An adverb is a word which consists, like *quickly,* of the positive degree of an adjective plus the derivational suffix *-ly* and which cannot be compared itself. Like our definition of the adjective, this definition of the adverb is narrower than the traditional one.

If the adverb is defined traditionally, as a word that modifies a verb, an adjective, or another adverb, then it will include many of our adverbials in addition to such words as *quickly*. Our adverb is our typical adverbial, but many of our adverbials are not adverbs. See PARTS OF SPEECH.

References: 60–2, 70, 79–81, 84, 94–6, 110, 305–06.

ADVERBIAL. Roughly, our adverbial is a word or larger form which occupies a position that our adverbs regularly occupy—for example, *slowly* in *He spoke slowly* or *thus* in *He answered thus*. More precisely, the positional class of adverbials includes no forms in nominal, verbal, or adjectival positions but only adverbs and forms typically replaceable by adverbs or by such uninflected words as *then, there, thus*. One position in which adverbials commonly occur is under strongest stress after a nominal at the end of a sentence:

He pushed the snowman *over*.

We have extended this basic definition in three chief ways: (1) to include *very* and other adverbials of degree; (2) to include interjections, absolute constructions, and other sentence adverbials; (3) to include certain phrases and subordinate clauses which regularly serve to expand verbals, adjectivals, and smaller adverbials. The italicized forms in the following sentences all satisfy our definition:

The wound healed *quickly*.
The bandages were *then* removed.
Five minutes after the knockout, the fighter came *to*.
The ballet seemed *quite* good.
No, we can't deliver it immediately.
That glutton lives *to eat*.
The moccasin is more dangerous *than you think*.
They wrecked the building as promptly *as they could*.

Most of these forms would be called adverbial, but not adverbials, in traditional grammars. Traditionally, *adverbial* is used to mean "pertaining to an adverb," but we have used it as the name of a distinct positional class. See PARTS OF SPEECH.

References: 94–9, 103, 109–10, 122–26, 143–48, 163, 303, 313.

ADVERBIAL CLAUSE. We have classified as adverbial three kinds of clauses, none of which is independent. (1) Confirmatory and interjected clauses have been classified as sentence adverbials:

The facts are clear, *aren't they?*

The facts, *he insists,* are clear.

(2) Also adverbial are certain dependent clauses which (a) are introduced by forms in *-ever* (*whoever, whichever, whatever, whenever,* etc.) and (b) can be replaced by single-word adverbials like *then, there, thus:*

Whenever it rains, this underpass is flooded.

(3) The most numerous and typical adverbial clauses are those introduced by subordinating conjunctions like *because, if, since, though,* and *when.* Such clauses are not nominals themselves and do not expand nominals. They often enjoy considerable freedom of position, like the single-word adverbials which may commonly replace them.

When he tried to explain, he stammered and stuttered.

He stammered and stuttered *when he tried to explain.*

The traditional name *adverb clauses* is most commonly given to clauses of this third kind, and they are often elaborately classified according to their meaning. Thus, it is said, an adversative or concessive clause makes or suggests an assertion which is opposed or contrary to the assertion made or suggested in the main clause:

Though he was brave, he was prudent.

Similarly, clauses which state reasons are said to be causal, and those which state conditions are labeled conditional:

The monkey died *because it ate too much.*

If you eat too much, you'll die too.

Other semantic labels for adverbial clauses include *clauses of degree, manner, place, purpose, result,* and *time.* The list is indefinitely but not very usefully expandable.

References: 100–01, 103, 124, 140, 170, 177, 287–88, 290–91.

ADVERBIAL OBJECTIVE. This term is sometimes applied to nouns in adverbial positions after verbals, as in the sentence:

He works *nights.* (Compare: He works *then.*)

If a nominal also follows the verbal, the adverbial comes last:

He studies his lessons *nights.*

Here, as usual, the noun used as direct object (*lessons*) follows the verb (*studies*) but precedes the noun used adverbially (*nights*).

References: 123–24, 136.

ADVERBIAL OF DEGREE. Adverbials of degree are a subclass of adverbials, such as *extremely, quite,* and *very,* which regularly stand under second or third stress before descriptive adjectivals or before certain other adverbials:

The evidence is *extremely* weak.

The sunset faded *quite* rapidly.

A *very* tired old man was trying to cross the street.

The name *adverbial of degree* indicates the common meaning of these forms. They place the quality signified by the following adjectival or adverbial on a scale of more or less, of higher or lower degree. In other grammars, they are sometimes known as adverbs of degree, intensives, or intensifiers.

References: 109–11, 116–17.

ADVERSATIVE CLAUSE. See ADVERBIAL CLAUSE.

AFFRICATE. We have defined an affricate as a continuant (a consonant which can be continued or prolonged) made by opening the closure for a stop so slowly that friction is heard at the widening aperture. *Chin* and *gin* begin with affricates.

References: 40, 43–4.

AGREEMENT. Certain parts of speech, when they are used together, regularly appear in matching pairs. For example, we might say:

This book itself, which is just as old, is very useful.

If now we change *book* to *books,* a whole series of other changes will follow:

These books *themselves,* which *are* just as old, *are* very useful.

Such formal correspondences are called agreement.

References: 73, 90, 102–06, 138, 142, 149, 176, 198–99.

ALVEOLAR. The alveolar ridge is the hard ridge behind the upper front teeth. An alveolar consonant is one in whose production the tongue tip touches or approaches this ridge.

References: 40, 42–4.

ALVEOLO-PALATAL or PALATO-ALVEOLAR. An *alveolo-palatal* consonant is one in whose production the blade and front of the tongue touch or approach the alveolar ridge and the hard palate.

Reference: 40.

ANALOGY. By the process of analogy, the basic structural patterns of a language may be extended to materials in which those patterns have not previously been established. For example, if we encounter the nonsense word *splan* in the sentence

That splan is broken,

we can readily produce the form *splans* to fill the blank in the sentence

    Those _____ are broken.

The process may be represented by the proportion *span : spans :: splan : x,* where *x* stands for the plural *splans.*

    Somewhat more loosely, the term *analogy* is applied to a technique of grammatical description by which the analysis of one construction is determined through comparison with the previous analysis of another, similar construction. Thus, since *he* is the subject of *went* in the sentence

    He went home,

some grammarians call *him* the subject of *go* in the sentence

    The teacher made him go home.

ANTECEDENT. Several important groups of forms, including the relatives (*who,* etc.), the intensive-reflexives (*myself,* etc.), the personal pronouns (*I, you, he,* etc.), and the words *this, that, these,* and *those* when they are nominals, are used in pairs or sets with other nominals, as in the following sentences:

    Although the *motion* was sensible, *it* was defeated.

The nominal to which such a form refers, or for which it is substituted, is called its antecedent; *motion* is the antecedent of *it.* Here are some other examples:

    The *man* (antecedent) *who* replied was ineffective.

    The *policeman* (antecedent) controlled *himself* well.

    I needed to know one *fact* (antecedent). *That* was the identity of the driver.

References: 102, 104–06, 176, 286–87, 314–15.

APPOSITION. For a single nominal, we can often substitute a sequence containing two nominals, one of which is usually said to be in apposition with the other:

    The speaker was not impressive.

    The speaker, a frail and nervous man, was not impressive.

In the second sentence, the noun *man* would be called an appositive; that is, it is put to or placed beside the noun *speaker.* One or both of the two nominals in sequences of this kind is usually a noun, as here, though either *may* be a one-word nominal of some other kind, or a phrase, or a clause:

    What he loved best in the world, fishing, was denied him.

For both the nominals, the same personal pronoun would usually be substituted, and the appositive usually stands second in the sequence.

A few other uses of the terms *apposition* and *appositive* should be noted. (1) Sometimes a distinction is drawn between close apposition and loose apposition. In close apposition, there is commonly no terminal between the two nominals, one of which is usually a proper noun (*Alfred the Great; my sister Florence*). To loose apposition, these restrictions do not apply. The contrast of loose with close is plain in the following example:

> Alfred the Great [close apposition], the most famous of Old English kings [loose apposition], was both soldier, statesman, and educator.

(2) Some grammarians give the name *appositive clause* to constructions like the following:

> The fact *that he ran* counted against him.
>
> The question *why he did it* was never answered.
>
> I disliked the suggestion *that I had tricked him.*

The examples show that appositive clauses are nominals, that they follow a special list of nouns like *fact, question,* and *suggestion,* that to many of these nouns, such as *suggestion* or *hope,* there are corresponding transitive verbs which take nominal clauses as their objects, and that the appositive clauses are most commonly introduced by interrogatives or by subordinating conjunctions.

(3) Some grammarians classify adjectival forms, according to their positions, as appositive, attributive, or predicative. In the first two of the following sentences, the adjectivals are in appositive position, in the third sentence in attributive position, and in the fourth sentence in predicative position:

> *Pale* and *wan,* the girl was a musician.
>
> The girl, *pale* and *wan,* was a musician.
>
> The *pale, wan* girl was a musician.
>
> The girl was *pale* and *wan.*

References: 119–20, 141, 157.

APPOSITIVE; APPOSITIVE ADJECTIVE; APPOSITIVE CLAUSE; APPOSITIVE PO-
SITION. See APPOSITION.

ARTICLE. *The* is often called the definite article; *a* (*an*) the indefinite article. In this book, we call them definite and indefinite determiners. See DETERMINER.

ATTRIBUTIVE ADJECTIVE. See APPOSITION.

AUXILIARY. In the verbal phrases described in this text (those sequences of verb forms which, as sequences, fill the blanks in our testing frames for verbals), all the verbals except the last are auxiliaries. A list of the principal auxiliaries therefore includes, in some or all of their uses, the forms *have, has, had; be, am, is, are, was, were, been, being; will, would; shall, should; may, might; can, could; must; ought; do, does, did.* Most of the auxiliaries are characterized by the possibility of appearance under weakest stress; and under one of the three stronger stresses, many of them occur in close transition with *n't* "not":

He *căn* go.

He *cân't* go.

The positions of the auxiliaries in questions and their use as substitutes for larger verbal forms are also distinctive:

Have you replied? *Must* he go?

They are being hurt, and so *are* we.

Our definition resembles the usual definition of auxiliaries as helping verbs, but with one main exception: we do not give the label *verb* to *must* and *ought,* since they are uninflected.

References: 74, 106–11, 145–46, 149–51, 179–80.

b

BACK VOWEL. A back vowel is one in whose production the tongue is bunched up to narrow the breath stream in the back of the mouth. Words like *boot, boat,* and *bought* contain back vowels.

References: 41, 46–9, 52–6.

BASE. Bases follow prefixes and precede suffixes and constitute the most numerous and the most obviously and concretely meaningful parts of English words. They are sometimes free forms (*kind*), but not always (the *-tain* of *contain*). In some grammars, the term *root* means almost the same thing as our term *base.*

References: 65–8, 72, 74–6, 78–9.

BILABIAL. A bilabial consonant is one in whose production the breath stream is stopped or impeded by the two lips. *Pin* and *bin* begin with bilabials.

References: 39–40, 42–4.

C

CASE. In English grammars, *case* is one of the terms used to label the different inflectional forms of a noun or a pronoun. Thus *man* and *men* are the common case forms of a noun, *man's* and *men's* the possessive or genitive case forms. The subject form of a pronoun is sometimes called nominative or subjective, or said to be in the nominative case; the object form is sometimes called accusative or objective. Most pronouns have two possessive case forms as well: *I, me, my, mine.* Since the different case forms do not occupy the same sets of positions in sentences, a difference in case usually marks a difference in the relationship of the noun or pronoun to the other words with which it is used.

Many of the older grammars extend the use of the term *case* considerably beyond the limits which our definition imposes. Attempting to describe English as if it were Latin, these books distinguish not only the inflectionally marked common and possessive (or genitive) cases of nouns and the inflectionally marked nominative (or subjective), genitive (or possessive), and accusative (or objective) cases of pronouns but certain other cases as well. For both nouns and pronouns, many old-fashioned grammars recognize *five* cases: nominative, genitive, dative, accusative, and vocative. For example:

John [vocative], did the man [nominative] give him [dative] Mary's [genitive] address [accusative]?

The Latinate analysis serves no good purpose. On the contrary, it once again confuses classification by inflection with classification by position in sentences; for neither nouns nor pronouns have distinctive forms for the positions which are labeled vocative and dative, and nouns have no distinctive forms for "accusative" positions as opposed to "nominative" positions. Thus, in our illustration, *Mary's* is uniquely marked, by its inflection, as a genitive; but *John* could be called vocative and *him* could be called dative only because of their positions. As subject or object, *John* would not have a different form from *John* as vocative, and *him* as direct object would not have a different form from *him* as indirect object.

Clarity is gained, and nothing whatever is lost, if no more cases are recognized than the inflectional system demands. Positions in sentences may then be separately labeled as we have labeled them. References: 68, 70–2, 76–80, 84–5, 87–8, 92–4, 99–100, 110.

CENTRAL VOWEL. In the production of a central vowel, the narrowing of the breath stream in the mouth is neither back nor front, but in between. The vowel of *but* is a central vowel.
References: 41, 46–9.

CLAUSE. A clause is either (1) a combination of a complete subject with a complete predicate or (2) an imperative with any complements or other expansions but without a subject.

    (1) I   told him   you   said so,
    (2) Close the door at once.

A clause may contain one or more sentence adverbials, which are not parts of its subject or of its predicate; but it cannot contain any subject without a predicate, any predicate (except an imperative) without a subject, or any unattached *fragment* of a complete subject or a complete predicate. Clauses are variously classified according to their possible substitutes, the sentence elements which they expand, and their relationships one to another; sentences may be classified by the kind and number of clauses they contain. See ADJECTIVAL CLAUSE, ADVERBIAL CLAUSE, COMPLEX SENTENCE, COMPOUND-COMPLEX SENTENCE, COMPOUND SENTENCE, CONFIRMATORY CLAUSE, COORDINATE CLAUSE, DEPENDENT CLAUSE, INDEPENDENT CLAUSE, INTERJECTED CLAUSE, NOMINAL CLAUSE, NONRESTRICTIVE CLAUSE, RELATIVE CLAUSE, RESTRICTIVE CLAUSE, SIMPLE SENTENCE.
References: 82, 99–103, 145–47, 169–70, 174–78, 273–306.

CLOSE APPOSITION. See APPOSITION.

CLOSE TRANSITION. See TRANSITION.

COGNATE OBJECT. Some verbs, including a number which are usually intransitive, may take derivationally related nouns as their objects (*to die a painful death, to dream a dream, to sing a song*). Such objects are sometimes called cognate objects.

COLLECTIVE NOUN. Nouns which refer to a group are often called collective nouns: the word *group* itself is an example.

    That *group* is rather snobbish.

Nouns of this sort are usually inflected like other nouns; but plural pronouns are sometimes used as substitutes for their singular forms, which may also stand as the subjects of plural verbs. For example:

    The *committee* are here now. *They* will vote soon.

The plural verb and pronoun, it is said, show that the group involved is thought of not as a unit but as a number of individuals.

COLLOQUIAL ENGLISH. Though *colloquial* is often used as a synonym for *vulgar, low,* or *incorrect,* better educated people and the makers of good dictionaries apply it to words and structures which fitly and frequently occur in ordinary conversation but do not so occur in formal speech or formal writing. *Dumb* meaning "stupid" is a colloquialism. See LEVELS OF USAGE.

References: 320–21, 330.

COMMAND. See IMPERATIVE MOOD, IMPERATIVE SENTENCE.

COMMON CASE. The forms of nouns that correspond to *man* and *men, boy* and *boys,* etc., are said to be in the common case, because they are used without distinction in all those positions where the possessive forms are not called for. See CASE.

References: 68, 70–2, 84–5, 88, 93–4, 110, 142.

COMMON GENDER. Nouns like *attendant, clerk,* and *driver,* which may be referred to either by *he* or by *she,* are sometimes said to be in the common gender.

COMMON NOUN. The names of classes or of members of classes are often called common nouns, since they may be applied to a whole group or to any of its members, not just to one particular member; we use the noun *dog* of a boxer or a beagle, a terrier or a dachshund, but we call our particular dog *Rover* or *Spot.* Common nouns like *dog* have singular and plural forms and are used with the articles; but proper nouns like *Spot* and *Rover* are most often used without an article and in the singular. See PROPER NOUN.

COMPARATIVE DEGREE. The forms of adjectives which end in *-er* are said to be in the comparative degree. Sometimes, though not in this book, the label *comparative degree* is also applied to phrases like *more conventional.* See COMPARISON.

COMPARISON. We have defined the adjective as a compared word—any word that fits into an inflectional series like *tall, taller, tallest.* To compare an adjective is to give this series of three forms to which it belongs; and the act of giving the forms, or the group of forms itself, is called the comparison of the adjective. The individual forms are known as the positive degree (*tall*), comparative degree (*taller*), and superlative degree (*tallest*). Adjectivals like *beautiful* cannot be compared by inflection; but since instead of the nonexistent *beautifuler* and *beautifulest* we do say *more* and *most beautiful,* the sequence *beautiful, more beautiful, most beautiful* is traditionally called periphrastic comparison. Similarly, because we say *more quickly* and *most quickly,* traditional grammars speak of the periphrastic comparison of adverbs. In this book, we have limited the term *adjective* to words like *tall, taller, tallest* and the term *comparison* to such inflectional sets or to the listing of such a set. To speak of periphrastic comparison and to treat *more beautiful* or *more quickly* as grammatically equivalent to *taller* is to confuse morphology with syntax, the analysis of words (*tall,* etc.) with the analysis of phrases (*more beautiful,* etc.).

References: 79–81, 110, 197.

COMPLEMENT. The general term *complement* may be used to mean any object of a verbal, or a predicate nominative or predicate adjectival. Usually, verbals precede their complements, as in the present sentence.

Reference: 179–80.

COMPLETE PREDICATE. A complete predicate, which is often separated from its subject by a terminal, includes one or more simple predicates and any elements which go with them to constitute the verbal part in a single nominal-verbal sentence pattern; an imperative sentence without a subject consists only of one or more complete predicates. For example:

Birds sing.

The bus driver quickly gave him his change and let him go.

Be sure to give lots of illustrations and repeat yourself often.

The elements accompanying a simple predicate may include:

Adverbials: The farmer looked *stupidly* around.

Objects: His mother had made *him a new space-suit.*

Predicate nominatives: I am *the state.*

Predicate adjectivals: The claim was *ridiculous.*

See PREDICATE.

References: 138–40, 147–64, 168–75, 181.

COMPLETE SUBJECT. A complete subject, which is often separated from its predicate by a terminal, includes one or more simple subjects and all the elements which go with them to constitute the nominal part in a single nominal-verbal sentence pattern. The simple subject and complete subject may sometimes be identical, but more commonly the simple subject is only a part of the complete subject.

This is usually the case when the simple subject is a noun, since nouns may be accompanied by predeterminers, determiners, postdeterminers, postposed adjectivals or adjectival sequences, or appositives. The noun *car* is the simple subject of the following sentence, whose complete subject extends from *the* through *limousine:*

The first wrecked car, a black limousine,   was burning.

If there is only one simple subject, the verb agrees with it in number (*car . . . was*); but when the complete subject contains two simple subjects or more, the number of the verb is usually determined by the inner structure of this compound complete subject.

Both the car *and* the bus   *were* damaged.

Either pencil *or* ink   *is* acceptable.

See SUBJECT.

References: 138–43, 147–64, 168–75, 181.

COMPLEX SENTENCE. A complex sentence is a sentence which contains one independent clause and one or more dependent clauses. (The preceding sentence is complex; the dependent clause is *which . . . clauses.*) See DEPENDENT CLAUSE, INDEPENDENT CLAUSE.

References: 175–78, 275–77.

COMPOUND-COMPLEX SENTENCE. A compound-complex sentence contains two or more independent clauses and one or more dependent clauses.

Because he had a bad knee, he could not play football; but he was an excellent swimmer.

Here the dependent clause is *because . . . knee;* the other two clauses are independent. See DEPENDENT CLAUSE, INDEPENDENT CLAUSE.

References: 175, 177–78.

COMPOUND PERSONAL PRONOUN. Forms like *myself, yourself, himself,* and *ourselves,* which consist of the object form or the first possessive of a personal pronoun plus *-self* or *-selves,* are sometimes called compound personal pronouns. In this book, they are called intensives and reflexives. See INTENSIVE-REFLEXIVE.

COMPOUND PREDICATE. A compound predicate includes two or more simple predicates linked up by intonation patterns (pitches and terminals), or by coordinating or correlative conjunctions, or by both:

²Shè + ²cóaxed² ↗²téased² ↗³thréatĕned¹ ↘

²Shĕ + cŏaxed + ănd + ³téased¹ ↘

²Shè + ²cóaxed² ↗²téased² ↗²ănd + ³thréatĕned¹ ↘

In the first sentence the simple predicates are linked up by intonation patterns, in the second by a coordinating conjunction, in the third both by intonation patterns and by the *and.* See PREDICATE. References: 138–40, 175.

COMPOUND SENTENCE. A compound sentence contains two or more independent clauses, but it contains no dependent clause. (In the preceding sentence, which is compound, there are two independent clauses. They are connected by *but,* which will be preceded in many readings by the terminal /↗/.) See DEPENDENT CLAUSE, INDEPENDENT CLAUSE.

References: 171, 175, 177–78, 275–77.

COMPOUND SUBJECT. A compound subject includes two or more simple subjects joined by coordinating or correlative conjunctions, or by intonation patterns, or by both. For example:

The crop, the poultry, the livestock were all destroyed.

Wagons and buggies have vanished from our roads.

Either one man or two boys were needed.

The old men, the women, and even the children answered the call.

In such sentences, the number of the verb is usually determined by the inner structure of the complete compound subject. When no conjunction is used, or when *and* or *both . . . and* is used, the verb is usually plural. When *either . . . or* or *neither . . . nor* is used, some speakers and writers make the verb agree with the nearer (or nearest) of the simple subjects—a practice which arouses no criticism, though it is not universal. See SUBJECT.

References: 138–39, 142, 175.

COMPOUND WORD. The definition of a word and the definition of a compound word are among the most difficult problems of English grammar. In this book, we have tried to leave them partially open, though we have chosen not to speak of compound words.

If we were dealing only with the writing system, we might say that a word consists of one or more letters preceded and followed by a space and that a compound word consists of two or more sequences of letters which elsewhere are written between spaces but which in the compound are either written solid or separated by a hyphen or hyphens. Though this rough description would answer some purposes, we would still have to allow for differences in practice, since some publishers print solid where others use hyphens or spaces; and we would encounter a number of more serious difficulties, such as the classification of the hyphenated elements in the following sentence:

The salesman offered six-, seven-, and eight-foot rugs.

In speech, the problem of definition is even harder. We have said that we will treat as a word any free form which consists of a single base, with or without accompanying prefixes or suffixes but with a superfix; but we have not ruled out the possibility that certain multibase forms might also be considered words. In this way, though we have limited *our* use of the label *word* to forms like *rug*, we have not denied that forms like *salesman* might usefully be called words as well. If we did call *salesman* a word, it would be a compound; for when we analyze it, we divide it first into *sales* and *man*, both of which are words themselves. A somewhat similar form is *Spánĭsh* + *stûdĕnt*, with the stress pattern /~ + ^~/, which we have called a compound nominal (not a compound word) to distinguish it from *Spánĭsh* + *stúdĕnt*, with the stress pattern /~ + ~/. We treat *Spanish* as nominal in *Spánĭsh* + *stúdĕnt* (a student of Spanish), but we call it adjectival in *Spânĭsh* + *stúdĕnt* (a student from Spain). Our label *compound nominal* does not commit us to the recognition of compound words, since a nominal may be either a word or a larger form. See BASE, PREFIX, SUFFIX, SUPERFIX.

Reference: 93.

CONCESSIVE CLAUSE. See ADVERBIAL CLAUSE.

CONCORD. See AGREEMENT.

CONCRETE NOUN. A concrete noun is usually defined as the name of a material thing which we can perceive with our senses, like a house or a train, not the name of an idea or a quality, like truth or goodness. Between some concrete nouns, like *house*, and some abstract nouns, like *truth*, there is a formal difference. We use *truth* in the singular either with *a*, or with *the*, or with no determiner at all; but normally the singular *house* must be accompanied by *a, the,* or some other determiner. The distinction does not apply, however, to all concrete nouns: we say *Beer is good* just as we say *Truth is noble.* For this and other reasons, many linguists do not divide nouns into abstract and concrete. See ABSTRACT NOUN.

CONDITIONAL CLAUSE. See ADVERBIAL CLAUSE.

CONFIRMATORY CLAUSE. Confirmatory clauses are a variety of sentence adverbials. They stand somewhere after the main verbal in the sentence and often consist of an auxiliary, which may appear in close transition with the contraction *n't,* followed immediately by *there* or by a personal pronoun in the subject form:
> The street is being paved, *isn't it?*
> There was nothing more to do, *was there?*

The name *confirmatory clause* means that these "tag questions," as they are sometimes called, ask for confirmation of the preceding statement.

References: 145–47, 169–70, 174.

CONJUGATION. The conjugation of a verb may mean the list of its inflectional forms or the giving of that list; so that the conjugation of *sing* may be the list *sing, sings, sang, sung, singing* or the recital of those forms. Since verbs may be placed in different classes according to their inflections, these classes are also known as conjugations. For example, some grammars say that *sing* belongs to the strong conjugation of English verbs, since its forms show changes in the vowel of the base, and that *play* belongs to the weak conjugation, since it takes the inflectional suffix *-ed.* (The metaphorical terms *strong* and *weak* are inherited from the German grammarians of the nineteenth century.)

Very often in traditional English grammars, the name *conjugation* is not limited to inflection but is further applied to various sets of verbal phrases. By this broader definition, the conjugation of *sing* would include not only inflected forms like *sings* and *sang* but also phrases like *will sing, has sung, had sung, will have sung.* Usually the number of phrases which are included in such a "conjugation" is determined by the number of forms of Latin verbs which Latin grammars conventionally list; the so-called "complete conjugation" of an English verb seldom includes all the verbal phrases in which the verb appears. See IRREGULAR VERBS.

CONJUNCTION. Traditionally, a conjunction is defined as a word that connects words, phrases, or clauses; and three subclasses of conjunctions are recognized: coordinating, subordinating, and correlative. In this book we distinguish the same three subclasses but provide our own definitions, emphasizing that conjunctions are defined in terms of position in sentences, not in terms of inflectional endings, and that they must not be confused with adverbials or with such other "connecting words" as prepositions, relatives, or interrogatives.

As their name indicates, the conjunctions *are* connectives. They are usually uninflected, often stand under third or weakest stress, and do not normaily occur at the ends of sentences. Among the forms which frequently or always occupy conjunctional positions are (1) the coordinating conjunctions *and, but* (often a preposition), *or, nor, for* (often a preposition); (2) the subordinating conjunctions *after* (often a preposition), *although, because, before* (often a preposition), *if, since* (often a preposition), *when;* and (3) the correlative conjunctions *either . . . or, neither . . . nor, both . . . and.*

A major difference between conjunctions and prepositions is that conjunctions usually do not occur, as prepositions often do, at the ends of sentences and that conjunctions need not be followed by nominal forms, as prepositions within sentences generally are. A major difference between the conjunctions on the one hand and (on the other) the relatives and those interrogatives which are used as nominals is precisely that those interrogatives and the relatives do occur in nominal positions, as the conjunctions do not; the conjunctions, moreover, are not inflected like such a relative and interrogative as *who,* do not have antecedents, do not stand in agreement with verbs or dictate the form of following verbal phrases, and do not "modify" nominals as interrogatives like *which* and *what* may do. Conjunctions will not often be confused with adverbials, since adverbials are typically replaceable, as conjunctions are not, by adverbs (with their suffix *-ly*) and by such uninflected words as *then, there, thus;* a further distinction is that adverbials, as a group, have much greater freedom of position than conjunctions, commonly appearing, for example, under strong stress at the ends of sentences.

There is more likelihood of confusion between conjunctions and the traditional "interrogative adverbs" and "conjunctive adverbs." The "conjunctive adverbs" are best treated as sentence adverbials. Unlike the conjunctions, they too enjoy considerable freedom of position and are very frequently set off by terminals. To illustrate:

I had given him full instructions, and [conjunction] he knew precisely what to do.

I had given him full instructions; therefore ["conjunctive adverb"] he knew precisely what to do.

. . . he therefore knew precisely what to do.

. . . he knew, therefore, precisely what to do.

. . . he knew precisely what to do, therefore.

Conjunctions and "conjunctive adverbs" may occur together, in various fixed patterns:

I had given him full instructions, and therefore he knew precisely what to do.

The positions of *and* and *therefore* could not be reversed.

Sometimes, however, the "interrogative adverbs" and subordinating conjunctions may occupy exactly the same positions, so that ambiguous sentences result, like *I told him when it happened.* This may mean either that I told him the time of its happening or that I told him *at* that time; in the first sense, *when* is an "interrogative adverb" and introduces a nominal clause, but in the second sense *when* is a subordinating conjunction and introduces an adverbial clause. The two *when's* may be distinguished by the facts that the position of the adverbial clause may be shifted and that the adverbial clause may be replaced by an adverb (*When it happened, I told him; I told him quickly*). The nominal clause would not normally be shifted and can be replaced by a nominal but not by an adverb (*I told him that*). See PARTS OF SPEECH.

References: 60–1, 98–102, 104, 110–11, 139, 142, 312–13.

CONJUNCTIVE ADVERB. The label *conjunctive adverb* is often given to a group of forms including *consequently, furthermore, however, indeed, moreover, nevertheless, therefore.* Other names for this group are *adverbial conjunction, illative conjunction, introductory adverb,* and *relative adverb.* We have treated these forms as sentence adverbials. See CONJUNCTION, SENTENCE ADVERBIAL.

CONNECTIVE. Connectives are obviously forms which connect. The term is often applied to the traditional conjunctions, prepositions, and conjunctive adverbs; but it is too vague to be of much use. See CONJUNCTION.

CONSONANT. Those sounds are most likely to be consonants in which the air either creates audible friction in the mouth or passes over one or both sides of the tongue, not over the center of the tongue; at some point the stream of air is disturbed or cut off. Consonants do not form the peaks of syllables. The English consonants are listed on pp. 42–44. Though speech and writing should not be confused, the term *consonant* is also used, in old-fashioned grammars, for the letters of the English alphabet other than *a, e, i, o,* and *u*. In this sense, *consonant-letter* would be a better name. See VOWEL.

References: 39–45, 56.

CONSTRUCTION. The term *construction* is generally used rather loosely in grammatical discussions, and we have not defined it in this book. Sometimes it is defined as a group of forms arranged in a grammatical unit or as the arrangement itself—the pattern—in which those forms appear. So the particular prepositional phrase *of forms* might be called a construction, and so might the general pattern of all prepositional phrases. By these definitions, constructions might vary in size from single words (*warmth*) to complete sentences (*He liked the warmth*). If the term is limited to groups or arrangements of forms for which a single word may be substituted, then our nominal sequences, verbal sequences, subjects, predicates, and many of our dependent clauses will be constructions; but independent clauses will not be constructions, since the only substitute for an independent clause is another independent clause.

CONTINUANT. We have used the word *continuant* to mean a consonant which can be continued or prolonged; /l/, /m/, /n/, and /r/ are among the English continuants.

References: 40, 43–4.

CONTRACTION. Some English words have both longer and shorter forms. Under certain conditions of stress and in the presence of certain other words, the shorter forms appear in constructions which are often called contractions. For example, many auxiliaries appear in contractions after personal pronouns or before *n't* (*I'll, you've, don't, mustn't*).

COORDINATE CLAUSE. Coordinate clauses are, literally, clauses of the same grammatical rank. The name is usually given to the independent clauses of a compound or compound-complex sentence. See INDEPENDENT CLAUSE.

COORDINATING CONJUNCTION. The chief coordinating conjunctions are *and, but, or, nor, for*. They must stand between the grammatically

equivalent words, phrases, or clauses which they connect. See CON-
JUNCTION.

References: 100–01, 139, 142, 171–72, 175.

COPULA. The special list of intransitive verbs like *be, become,* and *seem,*
which we have called equational, are also known as linking verbs,
because they join a subject to a predicate nominative or predicate
adjectival. An equational or linking verb, particularly the verb *to
be,* is sometimes called a copula or a copulative verb. *Copula* is a
Latin word meaning "link."

References: 133–36, 161.

CORRELATIVE CONJUNCTION. The chief correlative conjunctions are *either
. . . or, neither . . . nor, both . . . and.* They are used in pairs,
both members of which are usually followed by grammatically
equivalent words, phrases, or clauses. The correlative and coordinating conjunctions are thus alike in linking equivalent elements. See CONJUNCTION.

References: 100–01, 139, 142, 171, 175.

COUNT-NOUN. Nouns denoting things which can be counted as separate
units regularly take both *a (an)* and *the* in the singular, and sometimes take *the* in the plural (*a staple, the staple; the staples,
staples*). In the plural, they appear in frames like *two* _____,
many _____, *a large number of* _____. Some linguists call them
count-nouns. See MASS-NOUNS.

References: 98, 115, 117.

d

DANGLING MODIFIER. A dangling modifier is or contains a verb form in *-ing*
or an infinitive. The modifier is so placed that the nominal with
which it is taken cannot logically be made the subject of the corresponding finite verb or verbal phrase. In the following sentences,
the italicized forms would therefore be called dangling modifiers:

Concluding, his reasons were stated.

We saw the Grand Canyon *flying from San Francisco to
Dallas.*

In running the race, his heart was dilated.

> *To approach the airport safely,* the flight of the planes is regulated from the control tower.
>
> *Reasons* cannot logically be made the subject of *concluded;* the Grand Canyon does not fly; etc.

DECLARATIVE SENTENCE. See STATEMENT.

DECLENSION. The declension of a noun or pronoun may mean the list of its inflectional forms or the giving of that list; so that the declension of *man* may be the list *man, man's, men, men's,* or the recital of those forms. Since nouns and pronouns may be placed in different classes according to their inflections, these classes are also known as declensions. For example, some grammars say that *ox* belongs to the weak declension of English nouns, since it forms its plural in *-en.* (As they are applied to the conjugations of verbs and the declensions of nouns, the metaphorical terms *strong* and *weak* are inherited from the German grammarians of the nineteenth century.)

DEFINITE DETERMINER. See DETERMINER.

DEGREE. See COMPARISON.

DEMONSTRATIVE. The words *this, that, these,* and *those* are traditionally called demonstratives. They are called demonstrative pronouns in sentences like *That's what I told him,* and demonstrative adjectives in sentences like *He gave this answer.* In this book, we have included *this, that, these,* and *those* among the nouns, because of their inflections. Positionally, they are sometimes used as nominals ("demonstrative pronouns") and sometimes used as determiners ("demonstrative adjectives"). See PRONOUN.

Reference: 79.

DENTAL. A dental consonant is one in whose production the tip of the tongue approaches or touches the backs of the front teeth. For example, some speakers of English use a dental /t/.

References: 39–40, 42–4.

DEPENDENT CLAUSE. Dependent (or subordinate) clauses either (1) help to compose expansions of smaller grammatical units, or (2) are equivalent to single nominals, adjectivals, or adverbials, or (3) meet both these conditions.

(1) The press was broken.

The press *I normally use* was broken.

(2) He knew that.

He knew *who had done it.*

Afterwards, he was not very popular.

After he broke the dean's pipe, he was not very popular.

(3) The only book was printed in 1572.

The only book available was printed in 1572.

The only book *which is available* was printed in 1572.

As the examples show, dependent clauses are introduced by relatives, subordinating conjunctions, or interrogatives (including "zero" members of these classes) and may themselves be classified as nominal, adjectival, or adverbial.

References: 100–02, 117–19, 124, 140, 170–71, 174–78, 275–85.

DERIVATION; DERIVATIONAL SUFFIX. We have used *derivation* to refer to the process of adding prefixes or derivational suffixes to bases. Generally, derivational suffixes precede inflectional suffixes; derivational suffixes commonly (not always) change the class of the form to which they are added; and since there are more derivational than inflectional suffixes, a given derivational suffix usually occurs with fewer different bases than a given inflectional suffix. A useful rule of thumb is this: the final suffix of a word is derivational if that word can always be replaced by a word containing no suffix at all; but the final suffix of a word is inflectional if that word, in at least some environments, can be replaced only by other words containing suffixes. So the suffix *-th* in *depth* is derivational: it precedes the inflectional suffix *-s* in *depths;* it changes the adjective *deep* into a noun; it occurs with relatively few bases (*deep, long, warm, wide,* and a handful more); and *depth* never occurs in any environment where only words containing suffixes can occur. See INFLECTION.

References: 63–70, 72, 75, 79–81.

DESCRIPTIVE ADJECTIVAL; DESCRIPTIVE ADJECTIVE. In this book, the term *descriptive adjective* is not used, since the class to which it generally refers is a positional class and we have used *adjective* for an inflectional class. Our term is *descriptive adjectival.* It refers to that group of postdeterminers which precede noun adjuncts and may in turn be preceded by adverbials of degree—for example, *heavy* in the nominal phrase *an extremely heavy lead pipe.*

Reference: 116–17.

DESCRIPTIVE GENITIVE. See GENITIVE CASE.

DETERMINER. The words *a, an, the, your, our,* and *their* are always determiners and are in some ways typical of their class, a subclass of adjectivals. Regularly, they stand under third or weakest stress before a following nominal, as in the phrases *a storm, our dock*. We also include among the determiners a number of forms, both words and phrases, which are excluded from prenominal position by the presence of a word like *the;* if *the* stands before a nominal, none of these other forms appear, and if one of these other forms appears, *the* is excluded. In at least some of their uses, then, the following forms all qualify as determiners: *another, any, each, either, every, her, his, its, my, neither, no, one, some, that, those, this, these.* But we do not include among determiners the traditional "interrogative adjectives," like *which* in *Which town did it hit?* These interrogatives do not occur with minimal stress, and they show distinctive correlations with the forms of the following verbals (*Which storm hit the town? Which town did it hit?*). The determiners may be divided into two classes, (a) definite determiners, including *the, this, these, that, those,* and the first possessives of the personal pronouns, and (b) indefinite determiners, typified by *a (an)* and also including *any, each, either, every, neither, no,* etc. See PARTS OF SPEECH.

References: 83–5, 97, 103, 114–17, 146, 149, 154–64, 315.

DIPHTHONG. A diphthong is a succession of two vowels joined in a single syllable under a single stress by a continuous, smooth glide of the tongue from one vowel position to another. Not all analyses of the distinctive sounds of English recognize the existence of diphthongs; but we have recognized both short diphthongs, in which the first vowel is short, and long diphthongs, in which the first vowel is long. The long diphthongs are much less common than the short. References: 41, 45, 47–56.

DIRECT DISCOURSE. This term is used to mean direct quotation, the repeating by one speaker of another's precise words. Direct discourse is often marked by an interjected clause, as in the sentence, "*The game*," he said, "*is over*." Such clauses are set off from the rest of their sentences by terminals, commonly stand under pitch /¹/, usually occur in medial or final position, not initially, and may show inversion of subject and predicate. In writing, quotation marks enclose the quotation. See INDIRECT DISCOURSE.

DIRECT OBJECT. Traditionally, it is said that the direct object names the direct and immediate goal or receiver of the action of the verb. Abandoning this semantic definition, we have said that English transitive verbs occasionally take three objects but usually take either one or two. Unless an object is an interrogative or a nominal preceded by an interrogative, it normally follows the verbal. Personal pronouns used as objects are commonly in their object form, and personal pronouns used as *single* objects are regularly unstressed. A single object is always direct; in a sequence of three objects the order is always (1) indirect object, (2) direct object, (3) object complement; and the sequence indirect object plus direct object may be distinguished from the sequence direct object plus object complement in four ways besides the traditional semantic distinction. (1) After some verbs, such as *give,* two objects are normally indirect and direct; after other verbs, such as *designate,* two objects are normally direct and object complement; after still other verbs, such as *make,* either sequence appears. (2) The direct object and the object complement normally belong to the same substitution class, but an indirect object and a direct object often belong to different substitution classes. For example, in *He threw the batter a strike,* we take *batter* as indirect object and *strike* as direct partly because the regular substitute for *batter* is *he* while the regular substitute for *strike* is *it.* In *Some considered the son a better man than the father,* the fact that the substitute for both *son* and *man* is *he* supports the interpretation of *son* as direct object, *man* as object complement. (3) A direct object and an object complement are usually in the same number, but an indirect object and a direct object often differ in number. We could not substitute *sons* for *son* in *Some considered the son a better man,* but we *could* say *He threw the batter two strikes.* (4) To a sentence containing an indirect object and a direct object, there are two passive equivalents and one equivalent with *to* or *for;* to a sentence containing a direct object and an object complement, there is only one passive equivalent, no equivalent with *to,* and often none with *for.*

    (a) He left his son a fortune.

        His son was left a fortune.

        A fortune was left his son.

        He left a fortune to his son.

    (b) The nurse thought the man an intruder.

        The man was thought an intruder (by the nurse).

References: 126–36, 159.

DOUBLE COMPARISON. Traditionally, forms like *more better* and *most happiest* are called double comparatives and double superlatives, and the process of forming them is called double comparison. See COMPARISON.

DOUBLE NEGATIVE. Combinations like *n't* with *hardly* and *n't* with *no* are called double negatives in such sentences as these:

I can't hardly make this typewriter work.

Don't tell nobody.

Though educated speakers and writers avoid such constructions, the rather different pairing of negatives in phrases like *not impossible* is very common.

e

ELLIPSIS. This term is frequently used to mean the omission of a word or words which can be supplied from the context. A serious difficulty in using the concept is that native speakers very often do not agree on the omitted words. To the question *What did you say?* a perfectly normal answer would be *That I am ill;* but the answer might be expanded to *I said that I am ill* or to *What I said was that I am ill.* Unless there is a satisfactory way of saying what the words are which are omitted but "understood," good grammarians seldom or never appeal to ellipsis in describing English.

EMPHATIC DO. The strongly stressed form of *do* in sentences like ^{2}Ă + ^{2}séal^2→^{4}díd + bârk + àt + mĕ^1↘ is sometimes called the emphatic *do,* but any other auxiliary under the same pitch and stress would be equally emphatic.

References: 108, 315.

EQUATIONAL VERB. See COPULA.

EXCLAMATION; EXCLAMATORY SENTENCE. In some conventional grammars, there is a special part of speech, the exclamation or interjection, which is defined as expressing strong feeling or emphasis. Exclamatory sentences are similarly defined as strongly emotional or emphatic. Though there are a few arrangements which are always and only exclamatory (for example, *What a man he is!*), almost any form can be spoken with an intonation, a stress pattern, or some special distortion of normal speech which will make it express strong feeling. Hence the application of the terms *exclama-*

tion, exclamatory, and *interjection* is too vague and extensive for them to be of much use. See PARTS OF SPEECH.

References: 60–2, 144, 178–81.

EXPLETIVE. The word *expletive* means "a filler." *It* is sometimes called an expletive when it precedes a verbal which is followed by a "logical subject":

> It is his duty to resign.
> It is doubtful that he will do it.
> It's easy for you to criticize.

In these sentences, an equational verb is followed by a nominal or an adjectival in the position of a predicate adjectival or predicate nominative, and the following "logical subject" is either a nominal clause (*that he will do it*) or a form containing a marked infinitive (*to resign; for you to criticize*). There is a comparable use of *it* in object position:

> He found it hard to study.

There as an expletive, like *there* as an adverbial of place, often occurs in sentences where the subject follows the predicate or is framed by the two parts of the predicate:

> Expletive: There's no ice in the tray.
> Adverbial of place: There went Sputnik.

In such sentences, the expletive takes weaker stress than the adverbial of place; in many dialects, the two forms differ even in their vowels and consonants, despite the identical spellings. When both forms occur in the same sentence, the adverbial of place stands first and is normally both fully stressed and set off by a terminal:

> There, there's some reason to work.

In sentences with the expletive *there,* the simple subjects are usually nouns, not personal pronouns; indefinite determiners of the simple subject, like *no* and *some,* are more common than definite determiners like *this* and *that;* and *to be* is the most common verb.

References: 145–46, 148–49.

f

FACTITIVE VERB. We have used the term *factitive verb* for those transitive verbs, like *choose, designate, elect,* and *make,* which can take a direct object and an object complement. Other factitive verbs include *appoint, call, consider, find, imagine, judge, keep, label, name, prove,* and *think*.

References: 129, 132, 135, 161.

FINITE VERB. In English, a finite verb is a verb in the present or past tense. These forms are called finite ("limited") because some of them are limited with respect to person (*I am, he is*), number (*he is, they are*), etc.

FIRST POSSESSIVE. The personal pronouns have two possessives which are not related one to the other as singular to plural: *my, mine; your, yours; his, his; her, hers; its, its; our, ours; their, theirs.* The first members of these pairs are called first possessives. Their principal use is as determiners.

References: 76–7, 80.

FREE FORM. A free form is any form that in normal speech occurs alone, with silence before and after it.

Reference: 63–8.

FRICATIVE. We have defined a fricative as a continuant (a consonant which can be continued or prolonged) in whose articulation the obstruction to the breath creates audible friction. *Sin* and *shin* begin with fricatives.

References: 40, 43–4.

FRONT VOWEL. A front vowel is one in whose production the tongue is bunched up to narrow the breath stream in the front of the mouth. Words like *beat, bait,* and *bat* contain front vowels.

References: 41, 46, 52–6.

FUNCTION. The term *function* is so loosely and variously used in English grammars that in this book we have avoided it as unnecessary and confusing. Sometimes function is metaphorically explained as the work that a word or larger form does in the environment of some more inclusive linguistic unit. In this sense, the chief functions are said to be those of subject, verb, complement, modifier, and connective; sometimes an absolute function is also recognized for constructions which are not themselves included in any larger construction. More literally, the functions of a word may be defined as its capacity to fill certain positions in normal utterances. The concept of function, so defined, seems to add nothing to the concepts of morphological form and syntactic position. See MORPHOLOGY, SYNTAX.

FUNCTION WORD. Such smaller positional classes as determiners, prepositions, conjunctions, and the like are sometimes known as function words. These are small, closed classes whose membership is relatively fixed and slow to change. They show no such relations to classes defined by inflection as nominals show to nouns, verbals to verbs, etc. See PARTS OF SPEECH.

References: 74, 76–9, 96–111.

FUNCTIONAL CHANGE. When a word is used with more than one set of inflections or when it is used in such different syntactic positions that it is assigned now to one part of speech and now to another, it is said to undergo functional change. For example, *run* is inflected both as a noun (*one run, two runs*) and as a verb (*run, ran*), and it is used in both nominal and verbal positions (*He had to run hard to score the run*).

FUTURE PERFECT TENSE. Since we have defined tense inflectionally and have therefore limited the English tenses to the present and the past, we do not use the traditional term *future perfect tense,* which conventional English grammars borrow from Latin grammars and apply to verbal phrases like *shall / will have said, shall / will have been said, shall / will have been saying.* Such phrases are said to represent actions which will be completed between the present moment and some point of future time.

Reference: 107–08.

FUTURE TENSE. Traditionally, verbal phrases like *shall / will make, shall / will be made,* and *shall / will be making* are called *future tense.* See FUTURE PERFECT TENSE, TENSE.

Reference: 107–08.

g

GENDER. In English grammars, the term *gender* is traditionally used to refer to a grammatical distinction which corresponds roughly to the semantic distinction between males, females, and sexless things. The gender of an English noun is determined primarily by the personal pronoun which substitutes for it, whether *he* (masculine), *she* (feminine), or *it* (neuter). With nouns for which *he* or *she* is the usual substitute, *who* and *that* are used as relatives; with nouns which *it* replaces, *that* and *which* are usual.

References: 76–8, 102, 104–06, 215.

GENITIVE CASE. In English, the forms of nouns which correspond to *man's* and *men's,* the forms of personal pronouns which correspond to *my* and *mine,* and the one form *whose* are said to be in the genitive case. Since these forms sometimes express the idea of possession, the name *possessive* is often used instead of *genitive;* but the idea of possession need not be involved at all (*the instructor's consent; a men's store; the victim's assailant*). Indeed, the meanings of the genitive are so varied that elaborate classifications are frequently attempted: descriptive genitive (*a man's man*), genitive of measure (*a week's time*), genitive of origin (*Thurber's essays*), objective genitive (*the victim's assailant*), subjective genitive (*their attack*), etc. See CASE.

References: 60, 70–2, 76–7, 80, 84–5, 92, 110, 116, 142.

GENITIVE OF MEASURE; GENITIVE OF ORIGIN. See GENITIVE CASE.

GERUND. In the following sentences, the verb forms in *-ing* would conventionally be called gerunds:

Reading bored him.
Good reading was beyond him.
Reading well was beyond him.
Reading the book took time.

In the first and second sentences, *reading* is itself a nominal; in the third and fourth sentences, the phrases in which *reading* occurs are nominals. Hence it is often said that a gerund, in English, is a verb form in *-ing* when that form is used as a noun; but the statement is somewhat inaccurate. The typical substitutes for *reading* in our third and fourth sentences would not be nouns, but other verb forms in *-ing* and marked infinitives, so that although *reading* here stands in nominal phrases, it is not nominal itself but verbal.

GLIDE. A glide is often said to be a speech sound which seems to be produced not by any fixed position of the tongue and other speech organs, but by a movement of the organs from one position to or toward another position. In English, the most important glides are those from, to, or toward the approximate positions for the vowels of *pit, putt,* and *put.* They occur in the words *yet, bite, boa, wet, bout.*

References: 41, 44, 51.

GLOTTAL. We have applied the term *glottal* to consonants in whose production the breath stream is stopped or impeded at the glottis (the opening between the vocal cords). Some Americans would use a glottal stop for the middle consonant in *glottal* itself.

References: 38, 40, 44.

GRAMMATICAL GENDER. When a system of gender distinctions among masculine, feminine, and neuter does not roughly correspond to distinctions among males, females, and inanimates, the system is traditionally called grammatical gender. Grammatical gender is then opposed to natural gender, a system in which gender distinctions and sex distinctions do roughly correspond. Thus Latin is said to have grammatical gender, and English is said to have natural gender; but since languages are extremely various systems of conventions, it is probably unwise to use the term *natural* in this way. We can hardly say that one linguistic system is more natural than another. See GENDER.

GROUP GENITIVE. In English grammars, the term *group genitive* is often used to label constructions like the following: *the man with the hoe's mentality; the girl I met's parents.* In these constructions, an adjectival phrase or clause, like *with the hoe* or *I met,* follows a noun like *man* or *girl;* and the genitive ending is not placed after the noun itself but after the whole nominal of which the noun is one part. See GENITIVE CASE, NOMINAL, NOUN.

h

HIGH VOWEL. A high vowel is one in whose production the tongue is raised so high in the mouth that the breath stream is considerably narrowed. Words like *beet* and *boot* contain high vowels.

References: 41, 46–9, 52–6.

HISTORICAL PRESENT. A historical present is a present tense used to report past action. By its inflectional form, the verb may be recognized as present; its reference to past action may appear from the situation in which it is used, from the presence of other verbs which are in the past tense, from the presence of adverbials like *yesterday,* etc. For example:

Yesterday I was waiting in the hall for the elevator.

This fellow *comes* up to me and *says,* "Say, bud, can you tell me where the drinking fountain is?"

See PRESENT TENSE.

i

IDIOM. An idiom is sometimes defined as a construction peculiar to a given language; but either this definition makes all constructions idioms, since they are all uniquely determined by the structure of the languages of which they are parts, or the definition is inapplicable, since no one knows enough languages to say with any certainty what constructions are peculiar to some one particular language. The term *idiom* is also used to mean a construction which does not conform to some artificial, external standard of grammar or logic, or one which seems not to fit the central structural patterns of the language where it occurs. For example, the use of *sell* might be called an idiom in sentences like *The book hasn't sold very well.* Some grammarians simply dismiss a construction as an idiom if they cannot describe it.

IMMEDIATE CONSTITUENTS. Linguists often say that English sentences can be analyzed by dividing them into two parts and then by dividing each part successively into two more until no further division is possible. For example, the sentence *The train was late* might first be divided into the complete subject, *the train,* and the complete predicate, *was late.* The complete subject might in turn be divided into *the* and *train,* and the complete predicate into *was* and *late.* At each step in this kind of analysis, the smaller units into which a larger unit is divided are called its immediate constituents; the immediate constituents of *The train was late* might be given as *the train* and *was late.* Such an analysis by twos works very well on some sentences and sentence parts, but it quickly encounters difficulties, even with familiar sentences like *It's a shame the way he loafs* or *Actually, I don't have the least idea what he's talking about.* In addition, there is the problem of the pitch patterns and stress patterns (intonation patterns and superfixes), which must appear as constituents at some point but which many analyses of constituents quietly ignore. Since the analyses which have so far been proposed differ widely among themselves and are often quite arbitrary, it has seemed best to make no direct statement about immediate constituents in this book.

IMPERATIVE MOOD (IMPERATIVE MODE). The uninflected form, or name form, of a verb is said to be in the imperative mood (or mode) when it is used in sentences like *Start talking* or *Everybody work hard.* (The word *imperative* comes from a Latin word which means "pertaining to a command.") See INDICATIVE MOOD, MOOD, SUBJUNCTIVE MOOD.

References: 73, 90, 139, 167, 172–73, 178–81.

IMPERATIVE SENTENCE. By its meaning, an imperative sentence is traditionally defined as a sentence which makes a request or gives a command; another way of saying the same thing is that an imperative sentence is one to which the most common response is an action. Formally, the most striking feature of imperative sentences (commands) is that they often contain no subject:

Quit complaining.

Don't start complaining.

The verbal in imperative sentences is the simple name form of the verb, without ending; and complements follow it, as usual. If a subject *is* present, the affirmative order is simple subject, simple predicate, complement:

Everybody be quiet.

The negative order appears in

Don't you start complaining,

where the auxiliary *do* (/do:/, with *n't* in close transition) precedes the simple subject, and the rest of the simple predicate (with any complements) follows the simple subject. See IMPERATIVE MOOD, QUESTION, STATEMENT.

References: 139, 167–68, 172, 178–81.

INDEFINITE DETERMINER. See DETERMINER.

INDEFINITE PRONOUN. Traditionally, a large number of quite various words and phrases are called indefinite pronouns, because they "take the place of nouns" but do not refer to any person, place, or thing as definitely as *this* or *that* would do. The usual list includes *another; anybody, everybody, nobody, somebody; anyone, everyone, no one, someone; anything, everything, nothing, something; all, any, both, each, either, neither, none, one, other, several, some.* Since our inflectional class of pronouns includes only the personals and *who,* it does not include the traditional indefinites. Those indefinites which are inflected may be distributed among our other inflectional classes; *all* the indefinites, including those which are uninflected, may be classified according to their positions in sentences. They are usually nominals. See PARTS OF SPEECH, PRONOUN.

Reference: 78–9.

INDEPENDENT CLAUSE. An independent clause is often defined as a clause which can stand alone, a clause which by itself can make a sentence. We have defined independence negatively, saying (1) that an independent clause is neither confirmatory nor interjected, (2) that it does not help to compose an expansion of any smaller unit, though it may be linked in various ways to other independent clauses, and (3) that for it we cannot substitute a single nominal, adjectival, or adverbial, but only another unit like itself. The italicized clauses in the following sentences are therefore *not* independent:

(1) Their child's a girl, *isn't it?*
"Yes," *he said,* "the child's a girl."
(2) The child *which was born last night* is a girl.
(3) Some people are afraid to say *what they mean.*

The italicized clauses in the following sentences *are* independent:
Their child's a girl.
Some people are afraid, but *others speak their minds.*

Other names for independent clauses are *coordinate clauses, main clauses,* and *principal clauses.*

References: 169–73, 177–78, 275–85.

INDICATIVE MOOD (INDICATIVE MODE). Those verbal forms which ask questions or state facts are traditionally said to be indicative or in the indicative mood (mode). In English, the simple predicates in most clauses *are* indicative. The chief exceptions are imperatives and a small group of forms which are called subjunctive. See IMPERATIVE MOOD, MOOD, SUBJUNCTIVE MOOD.

INDIRECT DISCOURSE. The label *indirect discourse* is used for a nominal clause which (a) stands typically as a direct object after one of a special list of verbs like *ask, inform, report, say, tell* and (b) reports an earlier utterance, often with systematic changes in its pronouns, verbs, or word order. There is often no terminal or pitch change between the nominal clause and the verb of which it is the object, and the subject of that verb is usually in normal preverbal position. For example:

Reported utterance: I feel bad.

Indirect discourse: He says *he feels bad*.

Reported utterance: Do you feel bad?

Indirect discourse: He asked me *if I felt bad*.

Reported utterance: It's getting cold.

Indirect discourse: He tells me *that it's getting cold*.

Nominal clauses which report questions, as in our second example, are often called indirect questions; the reported questions are called direct. See DIRECT DISCOURSE, INDIRECT QUESTION.

INDIRECT OBJECT. Traditionally, it is said that while the direct object names the direct and immediate goal or receiver of the action of a verb, the indirect object names the person or thing which is less directly acted on or to which something is given or said or shown. Like other objects, an indirect object normally follows its verbal. Personal pronouns used as indirect objects are commonly unstressed and in their object form. Indirect objects never occur alone, but as the first object in a sequence either (a) of three objects or (b) of two objects when the second object is direct. Such two-object sequences normally occur after verbs like *give*. Unlike a direct object and an object complement, a direct object and an indirect object often belong to different substitution classes and often differ in number. To a sentence containing a direct and an indirect object, there are two passive equivalents and one equivalent with *to* or *for;* but in this book we do not call the object of *to* or *for* an indirect object. That is, we do not call *waiter* an indirect object in the sentence *The stranger gave a big tip to the waiter*. See DIRECT OBJECT.

References: 126–36, 159.

INDIRECT QUESTION. The term *indirect question* is sometimes used for nominal clauses which report a question or ask one indirectly. They are introduced by a special list of "question words," including *who, what, when, where, why,* and *how;* and typical examples occur as direct objects after verbs like *ask* (*He asked me what time it was*). See INDIRECT DISCOURSE.

INDIRECT QUOTATION. See INDIRECT DISCOURSE.

INFINITIVE. The infinitive of a verb is the simple name form, in some of its uses. It occurs both with and without *to*. The unmarked infinitive (the infinitive without *to*) is used in verbal phrases after *will, would, shall, should, may, might, can, could, must,* and *do* (*He will now reply*); with a preceding nominal to form the complement of certain verbs (*The medicine made the baby sleep*); after *let's* (*Let's move*); etc. The unmarked infinitive is always a verbal.

Similarly, within a *marked* infinitive like *to go,* the name form itself is verbal; but the whole construction may belong to any one of several positional classes. A marked infinitive may be used as a nominal or as a sentence adverbial or to expand a nominal, a verbal, or an adjectival:

> *To remain* there was *to die.*
> *To tell the truth,* the chapter puzzles me.
> Morning is the time *to work.*
> He struggled *to escape.*
> Green persimmons aren't good *to eat.*

In the last three sentences, some grammars would classify the marked infinitives as adjectival (*to work*) and as adverbial (*to escape, to eat*). Other important uses of the marked infinitive include the following: (1) after a "question word" in certain nominal phrases (*He knew what to say, but how to say it was a problem*); (2) with a preceding nominal to form the complement of certain verbs (*I meant him to hear it,* with the passive equivalent *He was meant to hear it*); (3) in a number of distinctive verbal phrases (*have to go, is going to go, is to go, ought to go, seems to go, used to go,* etc.); (4) in sentences with "expletive" *it* (*It's nice to be rich*). In a number of these uses, the marked infinitive may be replaced by a longer phrase in which the marked infinitive is preceded by *for* and a nominal (*for you to be rich,* etc.)
References: 73, 90, 107–09, 117, 119, 141, 143, 270–71.

INFINITIVE PHRASE. We have used the term *infinitive phrase* primarily to mean such sequences as (*to*) *have kicked,* (*to*) *be kicking,* (*to*) *be kicked,* (*to*) *have been kicked,* (*to*) *have been kicking.* Often the name is also given to an infinitive with any accompanying complements or adverbials (*to make a deal, to invest wisely*). See IN-FINITIVE.
Reference: 107–09.

INFLECTION; INFLECTIONAL SUFFIX. We have used *inflection* to mean the addition of inflectional suffixes to bases. Inflectional suffixes follow derivational suffixes and often close the constructions in which they occur; inflectional suffixes less commonly change the class of the forms to which they are added than derivational suffixes do; and since there are fewer inflectional than derivational suffixes, a given inflectional suffix usually occurs with more different bases than a given derivational suffix. A useful rule of thumb is this: The final suffix of a word is inflectional if that word, in at least some environments, can be replaced only by other words containing suffixes; but the final suffix of a word is derivational if that word can always be replaced by a word containing no suffix at all. So the suffix -/d/ in *beautified* (past tense) is inflectional: when it has been added to the derivational suffix -*fy* no other suffix can be added; the -/d/ does not change the verbal *beautify* to another class; this same -/d/ is added to thousands of other verbs; and *beautified* cannot be replaced by an uninflected word in the sentence *Last year he greatly beautified his grounds.* The English inflectional suffixes are illustrated by the following sets: *child, child's, children, children's; go, goes, went, gone, going; I, me, my, mine,* and *he, him, his, his; tall, taller, tallest.* See DERIVATION, DERIVATIONAL SUFFIX.

Reference: 63–81.

INTENSIFIER; INTENSIVE. See ADVERBIAL OF DEGREE.

INTENSIVE-REFLEXIVE. Forms like *myself, yourself, himself, herself, itself, ourselves, yourselves,* and *themselves* are traditionally called reflexive and intensive pronouns. We do not call them pronouns, since our pronouns are the inflectional class of words (forms containing only one base) which includes only the personals and *who.* Instead, we place these forms in a special subclass, the intensive-reflexives, of the positional class of nominals. They are said to be reflexive when they are used in sentences like *The saint denied himself* and intensive when they occur in positions like *His grandmother herself was only forty.* See PARTS OF SPEECH, PRONOUN.

References: 76–8, 104–06, 110.

INTERDENTAL. An interdental consonant is one in whose production the tip of the tongue is placed lightly between the front teeth. Many speakers of English use an interdental /θ/ in *thin.*

References: 39–40, 43–4.

INTERJECTED CLAUSE. Interjected clauses, which are normally set off by terminals, are distinguished by the fact that often they are on the

lowest of the four pitch levels, pitch $/^1/$. They usually contain as
their simple subject either a noun or a personal pronoun, and as
their simple predicate or part of their simple predicate a verb like
believe, hope, say, or *think.* Interjected clauses do not normally
begin sentences. For instance:

²Gôod + ³bóoks²→¹ì̀ + ¹thínk¹↗²àre + ă + nĕ³céssĭty̆¹↘

See DIRECT DISCOURSE.
References: 145–47, 169–70, 174.
INTERJECTION. See EXCLAMATION.
INTERROGATIVE. We have divided the positional class of interrogatives
into three groups, which traditionally would be labeled interrogative pronouns, interrogative adjectives, and interrogative adverbs.
1) *Who* tore my overalls?
To *what* do you attribute his success?
2) *What* animal made these tracks?
Which reason did the mayor give?
3) *When (where, why, how)* did you see him?
Group 1 of the interrogatives are a subset of nominals, appearing
as subjects either with simple present or past tenses or with verbal
phrases, but appearing as objects almost exclusively with verbal
phrases. A similar difference in verbals appears with the second
group of interrogatives, which we have classified as adjectivals but
not as determiners. The interrogatives of Group 3 may be considered adverbials, and regularly appear with verbal phrases, not
simple pasts or presents. See PARTS OF SPEECH, PRONOUN.
References: 76–8, 103–05, 110–11, 128, 141, 170, 176–77.
INTERROGATIVE ADJECTIVE; INTERROGATIVE ADVERB; INTERROGATIVE PRO-
NOUN. See INTERROGATIVE.
INTERROGATIVE SENTENCE. See QUESTION.
INTONATION; INTONATION PATTERN. The distinctive pitches and terminals
of English compose its intonation patterns. More specifically, an
intonation pattern consists of a sequence of two or more pitches,
followed by a terminal. The name *intonation* is often given to the
whole system which the pitches, terminals, and patterns together
constitute. See PITCH, TERMINAL.
References: 20–31, 139, 144–48, 155–81, 269–71, 307–11.
INTRANSITIVE VERB. Intransitive verbs are verbs like *appear, arrive, differ,*
glow, lie, which do not have objects. Some verbs which normally

have no object may occasionally be used with an object of a special kind; that is, many normally intransitive verbs are sometimes transitive (*to die,* but *to die a painful death; to doze,* but *to doze the afternoon away*). Other verbs appear freely either with an object or without (*to call,* or *to call the dog*). See COPULA, EQUATIONAL VERB, FACTITIVE VERB, TRANSITIVE VERB.

References: 107, 128, 133–36.

INVERSION. Inversion is the placement of the verb, or of some part of the verbal phrase, before its subject. Inversion is used in many questions, in statements with "expletive" *there,* sometimes in clauses introduced by certain adverbials, in some negative commands, etc.:

> *Is* your *uncle* at home?
> *Do salmon* spawn in this river?
> There *was* no *time* for an answer.
> Here *comes* a *taxi.*
> *Do*n't *you* call me names!

Almost always, the verb which precedes the subject is the tense-marked form.

References: 147–51, 179–81.

IRREGULAR VERB. The most common way of forming the past tense and past participle of an English verb is to add a suffix: /ɪd/, /ɨd/, or /əd/ if the verb ends in /d/ or /t/; otherwise /t/ if the verb ends in a voiceless consonant, and /d/ if the final sound is voiced. Such verbs are sometimes called regular, while verbs which form their past tense or past participle in some other way are called irregular. Among the irregular verbs, there are some which do not add a suffix containing /d/ or /t/ but which instead show a change in the vowel of the base (*ring, rang, rung*). This group is sometimes called strong, while the verbs which take the "*-ed* ending" are called weak. If the labels are used in these ways, then all regular verbs are weak, and all strong verbs are irregular; but some weak verbs, like *build,* are also irregular. See CONJUGATION.

Reference: 73–6.

j

JUNCTURE. See TERMINAL, TRANSITION.

1

LABIODENTAL. A labiodental consonant, like /f/ and /v/, is one in whose production the lower lip touches or approaches the edges of the upper front teeth.
References: 39–40, 43–4.

LATERAL. A lateral consonant, like /l/, is one in whose production a closure along the center line of the tongue allows the breath to escape only over one or both of the tongue's sides.
References: 40, 44.

LEVELS OF USAGE. Among speakers and writers of English, different social and occupational groups speak and write differently, and the individuals within a single group use more than one style. To these different styles and dialects, the metaphorical label *levels of usage* is often applied. Formal English, colloquial English, and illiterate English may thus be arranged in a descending series, as if illiterate people never spoke formally and as if the language of the lecture platform were somehow better than everyday talk. The implied statement of fact and judgment of value are commonly false and harmful. There are formal styles of illiterate English, and any style may be used either well or badly. The observance of an unreasoned taboo is no substitute for purposeful choice among different varieties of usage.
References: 320–23, 330.

LIMITING ADJECTIVAL. By this term, which corresponds to the traditional *limiting adjective,* we mean that positional subclass of adjectivals whose members follow determiners (*a, the,* etc.) but precede both descriptive adjectivals (like *fine, finer, finest*) and the intensifiers which may accompany descriptive adjectivals (*very fine*). Among the limiting adjectivals, which are themselves divided into smaller groups, are *few, many, other, same,* the numerals, etc. Most limiting adjectivals are not compared and are not accompanied by intensifiers. Semantically, they indicate quantity, position, or relation. Many grammars include the determiners among the limiting adjectivals, but in this book we have kept the two classes separate.
See ADJECTIVAL, ADJECTIVE, PARTS OF SPEECH.
Reference: 116–17.

LINKING VERB. See COPULA.

LONG VOWEL. We have classed as long vowels the vocalic parts of words like *beat, bait, boot, boat,* and a number of others. Sometimes the difference between our long and our short vowels is quite literally the difference between long and short—for example *calming* /ɑ:/ vs. *comic* /ɑ/ in some dialects. Sometimes, however, the difference between so-called long and short vowels is *not* primarily a difference in length; the two vowels differ in quality as well—for example, *pool* /u:/ vs. *pull* /ʊ/. Despite the difficulties, we still consider it wise to recognize a separate series of long vowels, which we treat as units, not as sequences. The writing of a colon to mark a vowel as long is a mere device of transcription and does not affect our unit interpretation.
References: 45, 50–6.

LOOSE APPOSITION. See APPOSITION.

LOW VOWEL. A low vowel is one in whose production the tongue is held low in the mouth, so that the breath stream is narrowed relatively little. Words like *bat* and *bought* contain low vowels.
References: 41, 46–9, 52–6.

m

MAIN CLAUSE. See INDEPENDENT CLAUSE.

MARKED INFINITIVE. A marked infinitive is the simple name form of a verb preceded by the word *to,* which in this use is sometimes called the mark or sign of the infinitive. See INFINITIVE.

MASS-NOUN. Nouns denoting masses which can be divided or united (but not numbered as aggregates of separate units) take *the* in the singular, if they take any determiner there at all, and have no plural; they never take *a* or *an* (*flesh, the flesh;* not *a flesh* or *fleshes*). Some linguists call them *mass-nouns.* It should be noted that certain nouns sometimes occur as mass-nouns but are also used as count-nouns (with *a* or in the plural):
> *Coffee* comes from Brazil.
> *The coffee* is in that bag.
> Let's have *a coffee.*
> I've had two *coffees* already.

The meaning of such a noun changes strikingly in its different
uses. See COUNT-NOUN.
References: 115, 117.

MID VOWEL. A mid vowel is one in whose production the tongue is neither
high nor low in the mouth, but in a middle position. Words like
bait, bet, but, and *boat* contain mid vowels.
References: 41, 46–9, 52–6.

MODAL AUXILIARY. Some auxiliaries are said to indicate the relation of one
verbal in the sentence to another or to show the speaker's attitude
toward the state of affairs which a verbal represents. In the sentence *I suggest that the window should be closed,* the auxiliary
should is used in a nominal clause, the object of *suggest.* In *It
might rain soon,* the auxiliary *might* represents the rain as at least
possible though not actual. Auxiliaries of this kind are sometimes
called modal auxiliaries. They include *can, could, may, might,
must, ought, shall, should, will, would,* in at least some uses of
these words. See AUXILIARY.
References: 74, 106–11, 145–46, 149–51, 179–80.

MODIFICATION; MODIFIER. Sometimes one of the two parts of a construction occurs in much the same positions that the whole construction
fills. For example, the one word *birds* occurs in most positions
where the phrase *the birds* occurs; for the longer phrase *the birds
in the trees* we can usually substitute the shorter phrase *the birds;*
etc. In constructions of this kind, the part which can replace the
whole is called the *head,* and the other part is said to modify the
head or to be its modifier. The relation between a head and a modifier is called modification. A little more loosely, it would be said
that in a construction like *the pretty houses on the corner that are
being rebuilt,* the word *houses* is the head, and the modifiers are
the words *the* and *pretty,* the phrase *on the corner,* and the clause
that are being rebuilt.

Unfortunately, there are several difficulties in the use of the
term *modification.* (1) If we define modification in terms of meaning and say that a modifier limits or describes the meaning of
another word or group of words, then we must talk about modification whenever the meaning of an ambiguous word is determined by
its context. For example, we sometimes use *rat* to mean a dirty
little animal with a long tail, and we sometimes use it to mean a

dirty, treacherous man. In the sentence *He's a rat,* we know that *rat* refers to a man because we normally would not call the little animal *he*. The semantic definition of modification therefore requires us to say that *he* modifies *rat;* but no grammarian would tolerate such an analysis. Users of the semantic definition are never consistent. (2) If we say, as we said in the preceding paragraph, that the part of a construction which accompanies the head is a modifier, we must say that objects modify verbs; for just as we say *Birds sing,* so we say *Birds sing songs,* where *sing* is clearly the head of the predicate, *sing songs*. Words which modify verbs are traditionally called adverbs, but no grammarian wants to make an adverb of a direct object like *songs*. Hence grammarians who define modification by using the idea of the head have also been inconsistent, because they do not call objects modifiers. (3) Finally, grammarians do not always agree in identifying the head of a construction and the modifiers of the head. In verbal phrases, for example, the auxiliary can be substituted for the whole phrase ("He *has been working.*" "Yes, he *has.*"); but grammarians who are accustomed to calling the final verb in the phrase the main verb would say that in this sentence the head is not *has* but *working*.

For these reasons, we have not undertaken any direct and extended analysis of modification in this book. See IMMEDIATE CONSTITUENTS.

Reference: 114–18.

MOOD (MODE). The term *mood,* or *mode,* refers to distinctions in verbal forms which indicate the relations between one verbal in the sentence and another or which show the speaker's attitude toward the state of affairs which a verbal represents. In English, there are three moods: indicative, subjunctive, and imperative. The distinctions among them are primarily inflectional; and although some grammarians give the name *subjunctive* to certain verbal phrases, like *would go, should say,* it is better not to confuse inflectional distinctions with positional distinctions in this manner. See IMPERATIVE MOOD, INDICATIVE MOOD, SUBJUNCTIVE MOOD.

MORPHEME. In this book terms have been chosen for limited practical purposes, and where such purposes would not be served, even the most basic terms of modern linguistics have been avoided. One such term is *morpheme*. It cannot be defined briefly, but a first very rough approximation to its meaning is that a morpheme is a minimum meaningful linguistic unit; that is, it is a bit of speech which has a meaning and which cannot be divided, without remainder, into smaller meaningful units. If we ignore the possibility that there are morphemes distinguished by stresses, transitions, pitches, and terminals, then *man* is one morpheme, *manly* two, *manlier* and *unmanly* three, and *unmanliness* four.

MORPHOLOGY. We have used *morphology* to mean the descriptive analysis of words. See SYNTAX.

n

NASAL. We have defined a nasal as a sound in whose production the nasal passage is open so that at least part of the breath passes out through the nose. In most dialects of English, no vowels are distinguished by nasality; but some of the consonants are nasal and others oral. In the production of the three nasal consonants (/m/, /n/, and /ŋ/ as in *ram, ran,* and *rang*), the breath passes out through the nose only.

References: 38–40, 43–4.

NATURAL GENDER. See GRAMMATICAL GENDER.

NOMINAL. A nominal is a word or larger form which occupies a position typically occupied by nouns. Such positions include those for subjects, appositives, objects, and predicate nominatives, as in the following sentences:

The *student* considered the *question.*

He gave *it* his undivided *attention.*

His real *ambition,* his one great *desire,* was *to write.*

Among the forms which sometimes occupy noun positions and thus are sometimes nominals are the common and possessive case forms of our nouns, the participles of verbs, all three forms of our adjectives, all forms of the personal pronouns except the first possessives, many other *traditional* pronouns, numerous uninflected words, a variety of phrases, and some clauses. Our adverbs and some forms of verbs do not appear as nominals.

To the term *nominal* as thus defined, the corresponding term in traditional grammars is *substantive*. See NOUN, PARTS OF SPEECH. References: 83–92, 101–06, 114–20, 126–43, 146, 153–64, 300–02.

NOMINAL CLAUSE. A nominal clause is a dependent clause which is "used as a noun"; that is, a dependent clause for which a one-word nominal or a nominal phrase may be substituted. In the following sentences, the nominal clauses are italicized:

That the boat would overturn was the great danger.

The leader told him *what he had to do.*

From *what I read,* I learned very little.

One trouble was *that the battery was dead.*

Somewhat loosely, certain other clauses are also called nominal, because their positions resemble those where nouns occur more than they resemble those where adjectives and adverbs occur.

I'm afraid *you have the wrong number.*

The belief *that comfort is all-important* is stupid.

It is impossible *that he should fail.*

Though we have thus adopted the traditional classification of dependent clauses as nominal, adjectival, and adverbial, its looseness sometimes makes it difficult to apply.

NOMINAL PHRASE (NOMINAL SEQUENCE). A nominal phrase is a group of words which can replace single-word nominals in some or all of their positions and which, though it may contain a clause, is not a clause itself. For example:

The big clock in the tower struck ten.

To read only what is easy is a bad policy.

Both the italicized phrases, in conventional terms, are "used as nouns."

References: 84, 100, 114–20, 126–27, 138–43, 300–02.

NOMINATIVE ABSOLUTE. See ABSOLUTE CONSTRUCTION.

NOMINATIVE CASE. The subject forms of *who* and the personal pronouns, when they are used in sentences, are conventionally said to be in the nominative case; and sometimes nouns too are said to be in the nominative when they occupy positions where subject forms of pronouns would be called for. In the preceding sentence, for example, the noun *forms* might traditionally be called nominative in both its occurrences, since its substitute would be *they* (*they are said to be . . . ; they would be called for . . .*). In this book, we would say simply that *forms* is in the common case, which occurs both as subject and as object. See CASE, COMMON CASE.

NONRESTRICTIVE CLAUSE. In its most common use, the term *nonrestrictive clause* is applied to an adjectival clause which does not identify a particular member or subclass of the larger class indicated by its antecedent but which simply adds further information about an already identified class or individual. That is, if a nonrestrictive clause were omitted from its sentence, its antecedent would still refer to the same individual or individuals. For example:

My father, who has only one eye, is still a good shot.

My father is still a good shot.

A restrictive clause, on the other hand, does identify a particular member or subclass of the larger class which its antecedent indicates; so that, if a restrictive clause were omitted, the antecedent would *not* refer to the same individual or group.

Students who have bad hearts should not run races.

Students should not run races.

The omission of the restrictive clause *who have bad hearts* makes its antecedent, *students*, refer to *all* students, not just the subclass of students who have bad hearts.

Among the formal distinctions which mark a clause as restrictive or nonrestrictive in its meaning, there are (1) the nature of the antecedent, (2) the relative which introduces the clause, (3) contrasts in accompanying intonation patterns.

(1) A restrictive clause is rarely attached to phrases like *my father, my mother, my maternal grandfather.* Like some proper nouns, these phrases usually refer to just one thing and hence are usually followed by nonrestrictive clauses.

(2) The relatives *that* and "zero" normally introduce restrictive clauses only; *who* and *which* introduce clauses of either type.

(3) The contrasting intonations of restrictive and nonrestrictive clauses have never been fully described, partly because not all dialects have the same contrasts; but some useful illustrations can be given. Sometimes, a restrictive clause is preceded by level pitch and the terminal /→/, while the pitch before the corresponding nonrestrictive clause is not level and the terminal is /↗/:

2The stupid 2magistrate2→2whom you saw last 3night2→. . .

2The stupid 3magistrate2↗2whom you saw last 3night2→. . .

At other times, a terminal will stand between the antecedent of a nonrestrictive clause and the following relative, while between the antecedent and the relative of a restrictive clause no terminal will occur (see p. 176). Most students can find these or similar distinctions in their speech.
Reference: 176.

NONSENTENCE. See SENTENCE.

NOUN. We have defined a noun as a word inflected like *man* or *boy*—any word that fits into an inflectional series which is built, like *man, man's, men, men's* or *boy, boy's, boys, boys'*, on either or both of the contrasts between singular and plural numbers and between common and possessive or genitive cases, and on no other contrasts. This definition is narrower than the traditional statement that a noun is the name of a person, place, or thing; for the traditional noun would include both words inflected for plural, for possessive, or for both, and other words that occupy the same positions as these inflected words. That is, the traditional noun would include many of our nominals as well as our nouns. See NOMINAL, PARTS OF SPEECH.
References: 68–73, 77–89, 98, 114–20, 153–64.

NOUN ADJUNCT. A noun adjunct is traditionally defined as "a noun used as an adjective," a noun which modifies a following noun. In the terms of this book, a noun adjunct is a kind of nominal. Typically, it is a noun in the singular number and the common case which stands under second stress before an immediately following noun head (²thĕ + glâss + ³hóuse¹↘).
References: 92, 115–16, 163.

NOUN CLAUSE. See NOMINAL CLAUSE.

NUMBER. Roughly, the distinction between singular and plural numbers marks the difference between one and more than one; *man* is singular, and *men* is plural. If a noun is singular, it can often take derivational endings which cannot be added to its plural (*boyish*, not *boysish*). *This* and *that* occur before singular nouns, which are also used as the subjects of singular verbs; but *these* and *those* stand before plural nouns, the subjects of plural verbs. Finally, for a singular noun the personal substitute is *he, she,* or *it,* not *they,* which substitutes for plurals.
References: 68–79, 104–06, 110, 115, 130, 134, 138–43.

O

OBJECT. The term *object* is a general name for the direct object, the indirect object, the object complement, and the object of a preposition. See these entries.

OBJECT COMPLEMENT. Traditionally, it is said that the object complement completes the assertion and refers to the same person or thing as the direct object. Like other objects, an object complement normally follows its verbal. Personal pronouns do not often occur as object complements. Object complements never occur alone but as the last object in a sequence either (a) of three objects or (b) of two objects when the first object is direct. Such two-object sequences normally occur after verbs like *designate.* Unlike an indirect object and a direct object, a direct object and an object complement usually belong to the same substitution class and are usually in the same number. To a sentence containing a direct object and an object complement, there is only one passive equivalent, no equivalent with *to,* and often none with *for.* See DIRECT OBJECT, FACTITIVE VERB.
References: 126–36, 161.

OBJECTIVE CASE. The object forms of *who* and the personal pronouns, when they are used in sentences, are conventionally said to be in the objective case (less commonly, in the accusative case). Sometimes nouns too are said to be in the objective case when they occupy positions where object forms of pronouns would be called for. For example, in the clause *when they are used in sentences,* the case of the noun *sentences* might traditionally be called objective, since its substitute would be *them.* We would say that *sentences* is in the common case, which occurs both as subject and as object. See CASE, COMMON CASE.

OBJECTIVE GENITIVE. See GENITIVE CASE.

OBJECT OF A PREPOSITION. Typical prepositions are *at, by, for, from, in, of, on, to,* and *with.* Unless a preposition stands at the end of a sentence, it is usually followed by a nominal for which the object form of a pronoun would be the normal substitute; this nominal is the object of the preposition.

The man with the *pilot* was the navigator.
The man with *him* was the navigator.

When the preposition stands at the end of the sentence, its object is some preceding nominal:

That's the house *that* I was born in.

Who did you give it to?

Whom did you give it to?

References: 84, 98–101, 117, 125–26.

OBLIQUE CASE. Any case of a noun or a pronoun except the common case or the nominative case may be called an oblique case. See CASE, COMMON CASE, NOMINATIVE CASE.

OPEN TRANSITION. See TRANSITION.

ORAL SOUND. An oral sound is one in whose production the nasal passage is closed, so that the breath passes out through the mouth. In most dialects of English, all vowels are oral, and most consonants; but the three consonants /m/, /n/, and /ŋ/ are nasal.

Reference: 38–40.

P

PALATAL. A palatal consonant is one in whose production the front of the tongue approaches or touches the hard palate. The initial consonants in *geese* and *key* are palatal.

References: 40, 42–4.

PALATO-ALVEOLAR. See ALVEOLO-PALATAL.

PARADIGM. A set of forms representing the inflection of a part of speech is a paradigm; for example, *man, man's, men, men's* or *sing, sings, sang, sung, singing*. See INFLECTION, PARTS OF SPEECH.

PARTICIPLE. Verbs are inflected like *sing* (*sings, sang, sung, singing*) and *play* (*plays, played, played, playing*). Verb forms like *sung* and the second *played* are called past participles; verb forms like *singing* and *playing* are called present participles. Participles occur in nominal, verbal, and adjectival positions. A present participle in a nominal position is sometimes called a *gerund* (*His singing annoyed me*). Both present and past participles occur, as verbals, in verbal phrases (*has sung, had played, are singing, were playing*, etc.). As adjectivals, participles often occur either before or after noun heads (*The injured players included the captain; The players injured included the captain*).

References: 73–6, 84, 90–1, 106–07, 116–19, 141, 143.

PARTS OF SPEECH. Traditionally, eight parts of speech are recognized: noun, pronoun, verb, adverb, adjective, preposition, conjunction, and interjection. The traditional definitions of these classes are sometimes in terms of meaning, sometimes in terms of function or use; they state neither use nor meaning clearly; and they largely neglect the forms which *signal* meanings. For such reasons as these, linguists in America today have either abandoned or extensively modified the traditional system.

In modern descriptions of English, parts of speech are defined in terms of distribution; that is, the class to which a form belongs is determined by the places in which it occurs. Since the distribution of a form may be stated on three levels, parts of speech may be established in three ways. (1) A form may be classified according to the inflectional endings which it takes. *Child* belongs to one class because it is inflected *child, child's, children, children's;* and *sing* belongs to another class because it is inflected *sing, sings, sang, sung, singing.* (2) A form may be classified according to its possible prefixes or derivational suffixes. *Child* belongs to one class because it occurs before *-ish* in *childish,* but *sing* does not belong to this class because there is no word *singish.* (3) A form may be classified according to its position in constructions larger than words. *Sing* belongs to one class because we say *He will sing,* but *child* does not belong to this class because we do not say *He will child.* Classes of the first type are called inflectional classes, classes of the second type derivational classes, and classes of the third type syntactic or positional classes. Together, inflectional and derivational classes, since their members are usually words, are called morphological classes and are opposed to the syntactic or positional classes, which include both words and larger forms.

A fourth kind of distributional classification is also possible. In the preceding paragraph, we have distinguished between *child* and *sing* in three separate ways—by inflection, by derivation, and by syntax; a fourth way would be to state distinctions on more than one level at a time. For example, we might define a class of words by saying that its members have two characteristics: they are inflected for plural and for possessive, and they occur before the suffix *-ish.* Then *child* would belong to this class, because both *children, child's,* and *childish* occur; but *fish* would not belong to this class because, although we do say *(two)* *fishes* and *(the)* *fish's* *(tail)*, we do not say *(It sounds)* *fishish*.

One main distinction among modern grammarians lies in their willingness or unwillingness to establish such mixed classes. A grammarian who uses mixed classes may define the noun by saying that nouns are inflected for plural and for possessive, that they take derivational suffixes like *-ish* and *-ize* *(characterize)*, and that they occur in frames like *The* (   ) *was good;* if a particular noun does not have all these characteristics, at least it occurs in the given syntactic frames. A grammarian who does not employ mixed classes may also define the noun by saying that nouns are inflected for plural and for possessive; but he will use the syntactic frame for defining a different class, the nominal. The first grammarian will have a smaller number of classes with more complicated definitions; the second will have a larger number of classes with simpler definitions; but if both have done their work well, their statements should ultimately come to much the same thing.

In this book, we have generally kept the levels of our analysis separate and have not established mixed classes (the main exception is our adverb). Our parts of speech are the following:

> I. Morphological classes
> > A. Inflectional classes
> > > 1. Noun 2. Verb 3. Pronoun 4. Adjective
> > B. Mixed class, inflectional and derivational: Adverb
>
> II. Syntactic classes
> > A. Main syntactic classes
> > > 1. Nominal 2. Verbal 3. Adjectival 4. Adverbial
> > B. Minor syntactic classes

1. Determiners	5. Interrogatives
2. Prepositions	6. Intensive-reflexives
3. Conjunctions	7. Auxiliaries
4. Relatives	8. Adverbials of degree

More logically, we should say that we have only two independent minor syntactic classes, the prepositions and the conjunctions. The other minor syntactic classes are subclasses of the main ones. Relatives, interrogatives of type 1 (not separately listed in the table), and intensive-reflexives are subclasses of nominals. Determiners and interrogatives of type 2 are subclasses of adjectivals. Auxiliaries are a subclass of verbals. Interrogatives of the third type and adverbials of degree (of course) are subclasses of adverbials.

The members of our morphological classes would also be nouns, verbs, pronouns, adjectives, or adverbs in a traditional grammar; but not all the members of the traditional classes with these names would belong to our morphological classes. For example, *chaos* is not a noun in our system, *must* and *ought* are not verbs, and *beautiful* is not an adjective, because none of these words is inflected; our only pronouns are the personals and *who;* and our only adverbs are certain uncompared words which end in *-ly*.

It is more difficult to equate our syntactic classes with the traditional parts of speech, since our syntactic classes include both words, phrases, and clauses. In so far as the members of our main syntactic classes are words, our nominals would typically be traditional nouns, our verbals verbs, our adjectivals adjectives, and our adverbials adverbs. Among the minor positional classes, our determiners might fall into various traditional parts of speech (articles, possessive adjectives, etc.). Our prepositions and conjunctions would be prepositions and conjunctions; our relatives, relative pronouns. Our interrogatives would split up into interrogative pronouns, interrogative adjectives, and interrogative adverbs. The intensive-reflexives would be intensive and reflexive pronouns; the auxiliaries, auxiliary verbs; and (finally) the adverbials of degree would be adverbs.

Reference: 60–111.

PASSIVE VOICE. See VOICE.

PAST PARTICIPLE. See PARTICIPLE.

PAST PERFECT TENSE. Traditionally, verbal phrases like *had named, had been named,* and *had been naming* are called past perfect tense. They are said to represent actions which were already complete before some point in past time. See FUTURE PERFECT TENSE, TENSE. Reference: 106.

PAST TENSE. Of the inflectional forms of verbs, those which correspond to *sang* and to the first *played* in the series *play, plays, played, played, playing* are in the past tense (*He sang loudly while I played the piano*). Generally, past-tense forms refer to past time. See TENSE.

References: 73–6, 90.

PERFECT TENSE. Traditionally, verbal phrases like *has waited, has been given,* and *has been stopping* are called perfect tense. They are said to represent actions which began in the past and have continued to the present, actions whose results persist in the present, etc. See FUTURE PERFECT TENSE, TENSE.

Reference: 106.

PERSON. Person is the general name for those formal grammatical distinctions which mark the difference between the speaker (first person), the spoken to (second person), and anyone or anything else (third person). Among the pronouns, *I* and *we* are first person; *you* is second person; and *he, she, it,* and *they* are third person. There are some corresponding distinctions in verb forms (*I am, you are, he is; I sing, he sings;* etc.).

References: 73–7, 104, 142–43.

PERSONAL PRONOUN. The English personal pronouns include the following forms: *I, me, my, mine; you, you, your, yours; he, him, his, his; she, her, her, hers; it, it, its, its; we, us, our, ours; you, you, your, yours; they, them, their, theirs.* These pronouns distinguish the speaker, the spoken to, and anyone or anything else. See PARTS OF SPEECH, PRONOUN.

References: 76–7, 84, 87–8, 104–05, 128–30, 133–35, 142.

PHONEME. In this book terms have been chosen for limited practical purposes, and where such purposes would not be served, even the most basic terms of modern linguistics have been avoided. One such term is *phoneme.* It cannot be defined briefly, but a first very rough approximation to its meaning is that a phoneme is a minimum structural unit in the sound system of a language. A phoneme as such does not have any meaning, but since differences between phonemes distinguish one morpheme from another, a difference between phonemes often signals a difference in meanings. For example, the difference between /b/ and /f/ distinguishes *bat* from *fat.* Such comparisons between forms are among the basic techniques for discovering the phonemes of a language. See MORPHEME.

PHRASE. We have used the term *phrase* to mean a free grammatical unit which contains two or more bases and so does not fit our use of the term *word,* but which does not consist of a subject-predicate combination and so is not a clause. According to their distribution, most phrases can be classified as nominal, verbal, adjectival, or adverbial: the typical one-word substitute for a nominal phrase is a noun; for a verbal phrase, a verb; etc. In the following sentence, the subject is a nominal phrase, and the predicate is a verbal phrase:

The man with the hoe   stared gloomily at his feet.

Within both subject and predicate, prepositional phrases are included (*with the hoe; at his feet*). We have labeled phrases like *with the hoe* as adjectival prepositional phrases and those like *at his feet* as adverbial prepositional phrases. Their classification as adjectival or adverbial depends on their position, but their classification as prepositional follows from the fact that they begin with prepositions. Such double classification of phrases, first according to their position and second according to one of their own parts, is useful when two conditions are met: (1) forms belonging to a single class, like prepositions, occur in many phrases, and (2) these phrases themselves fall into a number of different positional classes.

References: 82–4, 114.

PITCH. If one sound is higher or lower than another on a musical scale, the sounds are said to differ in pitch. We have recognized four relative but significantly different pitch levels in English and have numbered them from /^{1}/, the lowest pitch, through /^{4}/, the highest. Pitch /^{2}/, a little higher than pitch /^{1}/, is often a beginning pitch in American English and is a kind of base line for normal conversation; words pronounced on this level are normally not brought into any special prominence. Pitch /^{3}/, a normal high pitch, often does make words prominent; and the very high pitch /^{4}/ is likely to get them greater attention still. See INTONATION, TERMINAL.

References: 22–31, 33, 37, 56.

PLUPERFECT TENSE. See PAST PERFECT TENSE.

PLURAL NUMBER. See NUMBER.

POSITIVE DEGREE. See COMPARISON.

POSSESSIVE ADJECTIVE. The forms *my, your, his, her, its, our,* and *their,* when they are used as determiners, are sometimes called possessive adjectives. We have treated them as a subclass of adjectivals. See

ADJECTIVAL, ADJECTIVE, DETERMINER, PERSONAL PRONOUN, PRO-
NOUN.

POSSESSIVE CASE; POSSESSIVE GENITIVE. See GENITIVE CASE.

POSSESSIVE PRONOUN. The forms *mine, yours, his, hers, its, ours,* and
theirs, when they are used as nominals, are sometimes called possessive pronouns. Syntactically, we have classed them as nominals;
inflectionally, as pronouns. See NOMINAL, PERSONAL PRONOUN,
PRONOUN.

POSTDETERMINER. To describe the positions of "modifiers before nouns,"
we have distinguished predeterminers, which precede the determiner in such phrases, and postdeterminers, which follow the determiner:

> *all* [predeterminer] *the* [determiner] *good* [postdeterminer]
> *men.*

Most postdeterminers are adjectivals; they can stand under second stress before a following nominal which has strongest stress;
and they appear in an essentially fixed order: (1) limiting adjectival, (2) adverbial of degree, (3) descriptive adjectival, (4) noun
adjunct.

Reference: 115–17.

PREDETERMINER. Predeterminers, a small group of forms drawn from
various positional classes, have this in common, that they stand
before the determiner in the sequence (1) predeterminer, (2) determiner, (3) postdeterminer, (4) noun (*many a weary mile;
both the strong walkers; not quite all the exciting races*). See POST-
DETERMINER.

Reference: 115–17.

PREDICATE. Traditionally, it is often said that the predicate is that part of
a sentence or clause which makes the statement or asks the question about the subject. A distinction is also commonly drawn between simple predicates, compound predicates, and complete predicates. In this book, we have kept the traditional terms but have
given our own definitions.

A simple predicate is a single verbal or one of a special set of
verbal phrases—sequences of verbal forms, like *has answered, are
dancing, was added,* etc. Except in imperative sentences like *Make
the arrangements,* in which there is no subject, a simple predicate
is linked by agreement in number, when agreement is possible, to
some nominal or nominal sequence as its subject. When agree-

ment is not possible, as in the past tense of all verbs except *to be,* word order is the main clue to the identity of the simple predicate, which is nearly always (1) a verb in the present or past tense, (2) a verbal phrase beginning with a verb in the present or past, or (3) an imperative.

A compound predicate includes two or more simple predicates, linked up by intonation patterns, or by coordinating or correlative conjunctions, or by both (*They fought, bled, and died for Stan-field U*).

A complete predicate, which is often separated from its subject by a terminal, includes one or more simple predicates and all the elements which go with them to constitute the verbal part in a single nominal-verbal sentence pattern; an imperative sentence without a subject consists only of one or more complete predicates. The elements accompanying a simple predicate may include adverbials, objects, predicate nominatives, predicate adjectivals, etc. References: 122–64, 168–73, 296–97, 302–06.

PREDICATE ADJECTIVAL; PREDICATE ADJECTIVE. Distinguishing as usual between syntactic and morphological classes, we have used the term *predicate adjectival* instead of the familiar *predicate adjective.* A predicate adjectival follows an equational verb (a linking verb), is not preceded by a determiner or followed by a nominal as its head, and can typically be replaced by adjectives (compared words). *Difficult* is a predicate adjectival in *The revision was difficult.*

Reference: 134–36.

PREDICATE NOMINATIVE; PREDICATE NOUN. Traditionally, these labels mean the same thing; but since not all forms to which the labels are given are nouns, we have used only the label *predicate nominative.* Other terms which are sometimes used are *predicate complement* and *subject* (or *subjective*) *complement.*

A predicate nominative is a nominal which follows an equational verb (a linking verb). At least sometimes in some dialects, a predicate nominative may be replaced by the subject form of a personal pronoun. Whatever the form of a personal pronoun which replaces a predicate nominative, the pronoun will normally take either strongest stress or second stress (primary or secondary stress). Usually, a predicate nominative will be in the same number as the subject of its clause, and both will belong to the same substitution class; both, indeed, refer to the same thing. For example:

The culprit was a *housemaid*.

The culprit was *she*.

References: 133–36, 161.

PREFIX. In English, a prefix is one of a long list of forms like *con-, dis-, ex-, in-, pre-, re-,* and *un-*. Although prefixes are numerous, their number is still much less than the number of bases. Prefixes occur before bases or other prefixes, not alone (as free forms) or directly before suffixes. When two prefixes occur in sequence, they stand in a fixed order; and any given prefix can precede only certain bases —not just any prefix can be used with any base. See BASE, SUFFIX. Reference: 63–8.

PREPOSITION. A preposition is a form, usually uninflected, which regularly occurs with third or weakest stress in positions regularly filled by *at, by, for,* etc. See CONJUNCTION, OBJECT OF A PREPOSITION, PARTS OF SPEECH, PREPOSITIONAL PHRASE. References: 98–103, 117, 124–26.

PREPOSITIONAL PHRASE. A prepositional phrase is a phrase consisting of a preposition followed by a single nominal, or a nominal sequence, as its object. For the nominal, the object form of a personal pronoun can be substituted. As units, prepositional phrases may stand in adjectival, adverbial, or even nominal positions:

Adjectival: The books *at hand* were *of no value*.

Adverbial: *In emergencies,* he acted *with real courage*.

Nominal: *Over the fence* is out.

Of the three types, the adverbial prepositional phrase is the most freely movable. See OBJECT OF A PREPOSITION, PHRASE. References: 84, 117, 119, 124–26, 141, 143, 286–87.

PRESENT PARTICIPLE. See PARTICIPLE.

PRESENT PERFECT TENSE. See PERFECT TENSE.

PRESENT TENSE. Of the inflectional forms of verbs, those which correspond to *sings, plays,* and (sometimes) *sing* and *play* are in the present tense (*I suggest that he sing, since he plays badly*). The present tense does not always refer to present time, the moment of speaking; it may refer to past, present, or future.

Yesterday, this fellow *comes* to me with a silly story.

Now he *thinks* I'm a sucker.

Tomorrow, he *goes* on television with his yarns.

See TENSE.

References: 73–6, 90.

PRETERIT TENSE. The past tense is sometimes called the preterit (preterite) or the preterit tense. See PAST TENSE.

PRINCIPAL CLAUSE. See INDEPENDENT CLAUSE.

PRINCIPAL PARTS OF VERBS. The uninflected name form of a verb, its past tense, and its past participle are often called its principal parts, because its complete conjugation can be given if these forms are known.

PRINCIPAL VERB. The name *principal verb* is sometimes given to the infinitive or participle occupying the final position in a sequence of verbal forms which, as a sequence, can fill some of the same positions as single verbals. For example:

If you would *talk* less, you could *learn* more.

By this time, your work should have been *finished*.

See AUXILIARY, INFINITIVE, PARTICIPLE, VERB, VERBAL, VERBAL PHRASE.

PROGRESSIVE. Verbal phrases like *is typing, was typing, has been typing, had been typing, is being typed, was being typed,* etc., are often called progressive, on the grounds that they represent actions as continuing or in progress. The progressive forms always contain a present participle preceded by some form of *to be.*

Reference: 106–07.

PRONOMINAL ADJECTIVE. Forms like *my, your, his, whose, which, this, that, few, some,* and *either* are traditionally called pronominal adjectives when they are used in sentences like the following:

Your prejudice is showing.

Which prejudice do you mean?

That suggestion was not intended.

Either suggestion was enough to anger your audience.

These forms, it is said, share the characteristics of the (traditional) adjective and the (traditional) pronoun. *His,* for example, in *his intention* is said to be pronominal because in connected speech it would have an antecedent and because it belongs to the series *he, his, his, him; his* is said to be adjectival because it modifies *intention.* Roughly, then, a pronominal adjective is a traditional pronoun which stands in an adjectival position. We have not used the term *pronominal adjective* in this book but have distributed the forms which traditionally are so called among our morphologic and syntactic classes: pronoun, determiner, interrogative, demonstrative, etc. See ADJECTIVAL, ADJECTIVE, DEMONSTRATIVE, DETERMINER, INTERROGATIVE, LIMITING ADJECTIVAL, PARTS OF SPEECH, PRONOUN.

PRONOUN. A pronoun is traditionally defined as a word which stands for a noun, takes the place of a noun, or is used instead of a noun; but the definition is unsatisfactory, partly because it is not easily applicable to undoubted pronouns like *I, you,* and the relative *who,* and partly because many forms to which the definition *is* applicable differ sharply in their other characteristics. We have given the label *pronoun* only to the personals and *who,* which show either or both of two features: (1) distinct subject and object forms; (2) two possessives, not related one to the other as singular to plural.

Among the subclasses of the traditional pronouns are (1) the forms in *-self* and *-selves,* the so-called intensive and reflexive pronouns, which we have placed in a separate subclass of nominals, the intensive-reflexives; (2) the relative pronouns, notably *who, which,* and *that,* which we group together in a syntactic class of relatives but not of relative pronouns; (3) the interrogative pronouns, notably *who, which,* and *what,* which we have placed in a syntactic class of interrogatives; (4) the traditional reciprocal pronouns, *each other* and *one another,* which we would treat as nominal phrases of limited distribution; (5) the demonstrative pronouns, *this, that, these,* and *those,* which we classify as nouns according to their inflection and as either determiners or nominals according to their positions in sentences; and (6) a large, mixed group of so-called indefinite pronouns, including *all, any, both, each, either, neither, none, one, other, several,* and *some.* See PARTS OF SPEECH.

References: 76–80, 84–5, 101–06, 141, 143.

PROPER ADJECTIVE. Adjectival forms which are derived from proper nouns are traditionally called proper adjectives: *American* (from *America*), *Miltonic* (from *Milton*), *Spanish* (from *Spain*). Since such forms are not inflected, we do not call them adjectives but classify them by their positions in sentences, which are usually adjectival or nominal. See ADJECTIVAL, ADJECTIVE, PARTS OF SPEECH.

PROPER NAME; PROPER NOUN. A proper noun is often defined as the name of a unique individual object: *Maine, Podunk, Shakespeare*. We have implied a definition of proper nouns as nouns which never take a determiner; but if that definition is used, then phrases like *the Amazon River, The Hague, the High Street,* and *the Hilton Hotel* will not be proper nouns. In the first place, these *are* phrases, whereas we have limited our nouns to single words; and second, from these phrases the determiner is never omitted. See COMMON NOUN.
References: 84, 87–8, 116, 146.

q

QUESTION. By its meaning, a question is sometimes defined as a sentence which asks for information; another way of saying the same thing is that a question (an interrogative sentence) is a sentence to which the most common response is a reply—a reply whose form cannot be narrowly predicted from the form of the question. So defined, questions have no one formal pattern but are most commonly marked by word order, particularly the placing of the verbal or part of the verbal before the simple subject, by an interrogative, or by a final rise in pitch. When an interrogative is or precedes the simple subject of a question, the simple subject precedes the simple predicate:
> What hit me?
> Which animals have escaped?

When an interrogative is part of the predicate, then the simple predicate, or a part of the simple predicate, precedes the simple subject:
> Who is he?
> Which way did they go?

When no interrogative is present, the placing of all or part of the simple predicate before the simple subject is usually enough in itself to mark a question:
> Is the road closed?
> Have you the time to talk with me?
> Did Drake go ashore near San Francisco?

Sometimes intonation alone distinguishes questions from statements:

²Yòu're ⁺ ³góĭng¹.↘

²Yòu're ⁺ ³góĭng³?↗

See IMPERATIVE SENTENCE, STATEMENT.

References: 23–9, 103–05, 108–09, 149, 166–68, 178–81.

r

RECIPROCAL PRONOUN. The phrases *each other* and *one another* are traditionally known as reciprocal pronouns when they are used as objects of verbals or prepositions and have as their antecedents subjects which would require plural verbals:

The boy and the girl made faces at *each other*.

The refugees comforted *one another*.

See PRONOUN.

Reference: 78–9.

REFLEXIVE; REFLEXIVE PRONOUN. See INTENSIVE-REFLEXIVE.

REGULAR VERB. See IRREGULAR VERB.

RELATIVE; RELATIVE PRONOUN. *Who, which, that,* and certain other forms are traditionally called relative pronouns in sentences like these:

The salesman *who* waited on him was very friendly.

The cigars *which/that* he sold were excellent.

In this book, *who, which,* and *that* all belong to the positional or syntactic class of *relatives,* but only *who* (*whose, whom*) is called a pronoun. Like subordinating conjunctions, the relatives incorporate whole clauses into larger sentence structures; but a relative is always a part either of the subject or of the predicate of its own clause, it commonly has an antecedent, and when it is used as a subject it requires a verb of the same number as its antecedent. Relatives are a subclass of nominals. See PARTS OF SPEECH, PRONOUN.

References: 76–8, 101–03, 110, 117, 119, 170.

RELATIVE CLAUSE. A relative clause is a subordinate clause introduced by a relative. If the relative has an antecedent, the antecedent precedes the relative clause.

References: 117, 119, 124, 170, 176, 286–87.

RESTRICTIVE CLAUSE. See NONRESTRICTIVE CLAUSE.

RETAINED OBJECT. To sentences containing a direct and an indirect object, there are normally two passive equivalents, in each of which one of the objects becomes the subject and the other object is retained after the passive verbal. To sentences containing a direct object and an object complement, there is one such equivalent, in which the direct object becomes the subject. The objects after the passive verbals are called retained objects. For example:

Active sentence: He gave the boy a car.

Passive equivalents: The boy was given a *car*.

A car was given the *boy*.

See DIRECT OBJECT, INDIRECT OBJECT, OBJECT COMPLEMENT.

Reference: 131–32.

RETROFLEX. We have applied the term *retroflex* to a common kind of /r/, in whose production the tip of the tongue is turned back toward the roof of the mouth.

References: 40, 44.

ROUND VOWEL. A round (or rounded) vowel is one in whose production the lips are not at rest or spread but rounded and protruded. *Boot* and *boat* contain rounded vowels.

References: 41, 46–9, 52–6.

S

SECOND POSSESSIVE. The following forms of the personal pronouns are known as second possessives: *mine, yours, his, hers, its, ours,* and *theirs.* They are commonly used in nominal positions (*The best remark was yours*).

References: 76–7, 80, 84–5, 98–100, 110, 142.

SENTENCE. A *sentence* is traditionally defined as a group of words which expresses a complete thought; but the definition is useless, since it does not tell us what complete thoughts may be or what forms express them. Since no useful definition can be framed to include all and only the things which are often called sentences, we have provided a definition which will be useful to writers and readers of expository prose. We identify the stretches of speech that lie between terminals, or sequences of these stretches, either as complete sentences or as sentence fragments (nonsentences). A complete sentence will always end in one of the terminals /↗/ and /↘/

(never /→/), and it may or may not contain occurrences of /↗/ or /→/ within itself; but it will also contain, in every case except that of the subjectless imperative, at least one independent combination of complete subject with complete predicate, expanded or unexpanded. To a complete sentence various elements may be added without destroying its completeness; two or more sentences which in isolation would themselves be complete may be variously linked up in one complete sentence; but no utterance is a complete sentence if it contains an unattached subject, an unattached predicate (except an imperative without subject), or an unattached fragment of a subject or predicate. Whatever its intonation, a stretch of speech which does not satisfy these conditions is treated in this book as a sentence fragment or nonsentence, though our method of description must not be taken as implying condemnation of the sentence fragment.

References: 166–82, 273–306, 311–20.

SENTENCE ADVERBIAL. A sentence adverbial is a sentence element which does not destroy the completeness of the sentence but which cannot be included in either the complete subject or the complete predicate. Common types of sentence adverbial include absolute constructions, confirmatory clauses, interjected clauses, the so-called interjections, *yes* and *no* and their substitutes, and transitional forms like *still, however, nevertheless,* and *therefore* ("conjunctive adverbs").

References: 140, 143–47, 151, 169–71, 174.

SENTENCE FRAGMENT. See SENTENCE.

SEQUENCE OF TENSES. In some sentences, the tense of one verbal or the form of one verbal phrase demands that another verbal or verbal phrase be of a particular tense or form. Semantically speaking, the verbal forms which place the different actions in time must appear in certain fixed patterns. A general term for these patterns is the *sequence of tenses.* For example, in the sentence *When he comes I leave,* a proper sequence of tenses is *comes . . . leave;* the present tense *leave* could not be replaced by the past tense *left.*

SHORT VOWEL. We have classed as short vowels the vocalic parts of words like *pit, pet, pat, pot, but, put,* etc. When a short vowel and the corresponding long vowel occur in the same or similar environments (*i.e.,* with the same or similar sounds before and after them), the difference between the two vowels is sometimes quite literally a difference in length (duration in time). Sometimes, however, the difference between the vowels which we have called short and long is *not* primarily a difference in length. Despite the difficulties, we still consider it wise to recognize separate series of short and long vowels, all of which we treat as single sounds (units). Readers who wish to do so may consider the labels *short* and *long* as *mere* labels, like *x* and *y* or *1* and *2*. See LONG VOWEL.

Reference: 45–56.

SIMPLE PREDICATE. A simple predicate is a single verbal or one of a special set of verbal phrases—sequences of verbal forms like *has answered, are dancing, was added,* etc. Except in imperative sentences like *Make the arrangements,* in which there is no subject, a simple predicate is linked by agreement in number, when agreement is possible, to some nominal or nominal sequence as its subject. When agreement is not possible, as in the past tense of all verbs except *to be,* word order is the main clue to the identity of the simple predicate, which is nearly always (1) a verb in the present or past tense, (2) a verbal phrase beginning with a verb in the present or past, or (3) an imperative. See PREDICATE.

References: 138–40, 147–64, 179–81.

SIMPLE SENTENCE. A simple sentence contains only one independent clause and no dependent clauses. (Both sentences in this entry are simple sentences.)

References: 147, 175, 177–78.

SIMPLE SUBJECT. A simple subject is a nominal or nominal sequence placed in a fixed position with respect to an accompanying verb. A personal pronoun which replaces a nominal in subject position will generally appear in its distinctive subject form if it has one. The number of a verb which accompanies a simple subject as its simple predicate is usually determined either by the number of that simple subject or, if the complete subject is compound, by the compound subject's inner structure. A process of elimination may also help to identify the simple subject: it is always a nominal but neither an appositive, a complement, nor a part of a sentence adverbial. See SUBJECT.

References: 138–43, 147–64, 179–81.

SINGULAR NUMBER. See NUMBER.

SPLIT INFINITIVE. A construction in which an adverbial stands between *to* and a following infinitive is called a split infinitive. For example:

To deliberately split an infinitive is necessary here.
See INFINITIVE.

STANDARD ENGLISH. Although the term *standard English* is variously applied, the most serviceable definition is that the standard English of an area or a nation includes all those varieties of English which are actually used in the conduct of the important affairs of that area or nation. By this definition, the varieties of standard English are rather numerous, including the English of formal public address, the English of cultivated expository prose, the English of legal documents, the English of serious conversation among leading citizens, etc. See COLLOQUIAL ENGLISH, LEVELS OF USAGE.

STATEMENT. By its meaning, a statement is a sentence, neither exclamatory, imperative, nor interrogative, which expresses an assertion; another way of saying the same thing is that a statement (a declarative sentence) is a sentence to which the most common response is continuing attention. Although there is no one formal pattern for all statements, they are not commonly introduced by interrogatives; they frequently end in a falling pitch; the simple predicates of their main clauses nearly always are or include verbs in the present or the past tense; and the usual word order is simple subject, simple predicate, complement (if any). See IMPERATIVE SENTENCE, QUESTION.
References: 23–9, 108, 166–68, 178–81.

STEM. We have used the word *stem* to refer to forms like *annoyance, artist, artistic,* etc., which contain a base and one or more derivational suffixes but no inflectional suffixes.
References: 72, 75, 80.

STOP. A stop is a consonant in whose production the breath stream is quite cut off by a complete closure at some point from the glottis to the lips. The consonants /p/, /t/, /k/, /b/, /d/, and /g/ are all stops. We do not treat the nasals as stops, however, since in their production the breath is allowed to escape freely through the nose.
References: 40, 42–4.

STRESS. We have defined stress as relative prominence and have recognized four contrasting degrees of it in English speech. Strongest or primary stress is written with an acute accent /´/, second or secondary stress with a circumflex accent /^/, third or tertiary stress with a grave accent /ˋ/, and weakest or minimal stress with

a breve /˘/. All four stresses occur in many phrases: *tḗlĕphòne gîrl, wíndshìeld wîpĕr, jáck-ìn-thĕ-pûlpĭt, péanùt búttĕr.*
References: 22–3, 31–4, 93–9, 125, 133–34, 148, 307–11.

STRONG VERB. See IRREGULAR VERB.

SUBJECT. Traditionally, it is often said that the subject of a sentence tells what the sentence is about; the subject names the thing about which the predicate makes a statement or asks a question. A distinction is also commonly drawn between simple subjects, compound subjects, and complete subjects. In this book, we have kept the traditional terms but have given our own definitions.

A simple subject is a nominal or nominal sequence placed in a fixed position with respect to an accompanying verb. A personal pronoun which replaces a nominal in subject position will generally appear in its distinctive subject form if it has one. The number of a verb which accompanies a simple subject as its simple predicate is usually determined either by the number of that simple subject or, if the complete subject is compound, by the compound subject's inner structure. A process of elimination may also help to identify the simple subject: it is always a nominal but neither an appositive, a complement, nor a part of a sentence adverbial.

A compound subject includes two or more simple subjects joined by coordinating or correlative conjunctions, or by intonation patterns, or by both.

A complete subject, which is often separated from its predicate by a terminal, includes one or more simple subjects and all the elements which go with them to constitute the nominal part in a single nominal-verbal sentence pattern. The simple subject and complete subject may sometimes be identical, but more commonly the simple subject is only a part of the complete subject. This is usually the case when the simple subject is a noun. Only a complete subject may be compound.

References: 76–80, 103, 133–34, 138–64, 168–73, 296–302.

SUBJECT COMPLEMENT. See PREDICATE NOMINATIVE.

SUBJECTIVE CASE. See NOMINATIVE CASE.

SUBJECTIVE GENITIVE. See GENITIVE CASE.

SUBJUNCTIVE MOOD (SUBJUNCTIVE MODE). Most English verbs have only one distinctive subjunctive form, the third person singular, present tense, without the -s of the indicative. The verb *to be* has two subjunctive forms, *be* throughout the present tense and *were* throughout the past. The subjunctive forms are used mainly as simple predicates in nominal clauses after verbs like *ask, demand, move, suggest:*

I suggest that the committee *go* into executive session.

I demand that he *be* removed from office.

Subjunctive forms are also used in some adverbial clauses which express an unreal condition:

If I *were* you, I wouldn't be so sure of myself.

See IMPERATIVE MOOD, INDICATIVE MOOD, MOOD.

Reference: 73–6.

SUBORDINATE CLAUSE. See DEPENDENT CLAUSE.

SUBORDINATING CONJUNCTION. A subordinating conjunction introduces subordinate (or dependent) clauses, which may be used as adjectivals, adverbials, or nominals:

Adjectival clause: The discussion *before the meeting began* was more profitable.

Adverbial clause: *Before the meeting began,* there was a profitable discussion.

Nominal clause: The porter says *that the bag is lost.*

Adverbial clauses are often rather freely movable. See CONJUNCTION, PARTS OF SPEECH.

References: 100–04, 117–18, 124, 141, 170, 176–77.

SUBSTANTIVE. See NOMINAL.

SUBSTITUTION. In this grammar, we have based our classifications on distribution; that is, we have determined the class to which a form belongs by stating the positions in which the form occurs. In such a grammar, substitution must be a basic device, and we have repeatedly asked what forms can be substituted one for the other in a given position. We have discovered some forms, especially pronouns and relatives, which can be substituted, in some positions, for any member of a larger class or subclass. For example, *he* can be substituted for any one of a whole subclass of singular nouns (*boy, farmer, man, sailor, soldier*), *she* for any member of another subclass of singular nouns (*aunt, girl, mother, niece, woman*), *they* for any plural noun, etc. Forms of this kind, which replace any form belonging to some larger set, are called substitutes. They can be used, as we have used them, to define and subdivide the classes which they replace. And it is not only nouns and nominals which have substitutes. Substitutes are used as well for other classes, like the verbs. Often the first form in a verbal phrase can replace the whole predicate which contains the phrase, and a form of *do* can replace a predicate whose verbal is one word:

The other driver *must really have been speeding,* and so *must* you.

"The baritone *sings very well.*" "Yes, he *does.*"

References: 70, 80–136, 155–64.

SUFFIX. In English, a suffix is one of a long list of forms like *-al, -ed, -er, -ize, -ness.* Although suffixes are numerous, their number is still much less than the number of bases. Suffixes occur after bases or other suffixes, not alone (as free forms) or directly after prefixes. When two suffixes occur in sequence, they stand in a fixed order; and although some suffixes can follow any of a very large class of bases, not just any suffix can be used with any base. See DERIVATION, INFLECTION.

Reference: 63–81.

SUPERFIX. We have used *superfix* to mean a stress pattern, which consists of one or more stresses with or without an open transition. A superfix is an essential part of every English word.

References: 63–8, 93–9, 125, 133–34, 146–48, 155–64, 307–11.

SUPERLATIVE DEGREE. See COMPARISON.

SYNTAX. We have used *syntax* to mean the descriptive analysis of linguistic forms which are larger than words. See MORPHOLOGY.

t

TENSE. *Tense* is traditionally the general name for those distinctions in the forms of verbs and verbals which place the actions of the verbs and verbals in time. Since the familiar Latin grammars recognize six tenses for Latin, English grammarians have given the same six names to the English verbals which translate the Latin forms: *present tense, past tense, future tense, (present) perfect tense, past perfect tense, future perfect tense.* Only the present and the past, however, are marked by inflection in English; and to avoid the confusion of words with phrases, we have not used the other four labels and have not given the name *tense* to verbal phrases like *will sing, has sung, had sung, will have sung,* etc.

References: 73–6, 106, 110.

TERMINAL. In describing English intonation, we have recognized three terminals, which mark the ends of major syntactic units. We write the three terminals with three arrows. (1) The terminal /↗/ is a slight rise above the level of the last pitch in its intonation pattern. (2) The terminal /↘/ often follows a falling pitch but itself involves no further fall to a distinctively lower pitch level; it is marked, instead, by the fading away of the voice into silence. (3) The terminal /→/ involves neither a rise in pitch nor a fading of the voice into silence. At this terminal, the loudness of speech is often reduced, and the speed slowed down as it is before the other terminals as well; but the pitch remains unchanged until the next intonation pattern begins. This third terminal does not occur, like the other two, at the ends of sentences. Other names for all three terminals are *terminal juncture* and *terminal contour*.

References: 22–31, 139–40, 144–47, 166–68, 175–76, 308–11.

TRANSITION. We have used the terms *open transition* and *close transition* for what are often called open and close juncture; another name for open transition or open juncture is *plus juncture,* since this transition is usually written with a plus sign (/+/). Transition is the way we get from one sound to another when we talk, and open transition often marks the boundary between two words or between two meaningful parts of a single word. It is recognized by its effects on the preceding and following vowels and consonants. Where no such effects are heard, the transition is close, and the vowels and consonants are written side by side, with no space and no plus sign between them.

References: 31, 34–7, 56, 167.

TRANSITIVE VERB. A transitive verb is a verb which has an object. Some verbs, like *place,* are always or nearly always transitive; others, like *make,* usually have an object but are not rare without one (*Let's make for home*); still others, like *call,* appear freely in either pattern. See COPULA, EQUATIONAL VERB, FACTITIVE VERB, INTRANSITIVE VERB.

References: 106–07, 128–29, 133–35.

TRIPHTHONG. If it happens that sequences of three vowels are joined in a single syllable under a single stress by a continuous, smooth glide of the tongue, these sequences may be called triphthongs. In some dialects, the word *our* seems on occasion to contain a triphthong.

References: 41, 50, 52.

U

UNROUND VOWEL. An unround (or unrounded) vowel is one in whose production the lips are not rounded and protruded but either spread or at rest. *Beat* and *bait* contain unrounded vowels.
References: 41, 46–9, 52–6.

V

VELAR. The velum is the soft palate, the boneless, soft, back part of the roof of the mouth. A velar consonant is one in whose production the back of the tongue touches or approaches the velum. The initial consonant in *cool* is velar.
References: 40, 42–4.

VERB. We have defined a verb as any word belonging to an inflectional series which marks the difference between present and past tense and whose members will fit into a pattern like *sing, sings, sang, sung, singing* or *play, plays, played, played, playing*. Though this definition excludes *must* and *ought,* it precisely delimits almost the same class which is vaguely suggested by the traditional definition ("a verb is a word which expresses action, being, or condition"). It should be noted, however, that our verbs include words only and not phrases. See PARTS OF SPEECH.
References: 73–6, 89–92, 103–11, 128–29, 133–36, 153–64.

VERBAL. We have defined a verbal as a word or phrase which occupies a position typically occupied by verbs. The name form of a verb and its present and past tenses are always verbal. A sequence of verb forms which as a sequence can replace a simple verb in the present or past tense is a verbal phrase; and every word in it, including *must* and *ought* but not *to,* is a verbal as well. Thus the participles, like *sung, singing, played, playing,* are sometimes verbals; but they may also be adjectivals or nominals. For example:

Participle as verbal: He's *walking* away.
Participle as adjectival: He's a *walking* encyclopedia.
Participle as nominal: *Walking* is not much exercise.

Our use of the term *verbal* is therefore quite different from its traditional use, which applies the term to the participles, to the so-called gerund, and to some infinitives.

References: 89–92, 103–11, 119, 122–40.

VERBAL PHRASE; VERB PHRASE. We have defined a verbal phrase as a sequence of words which, in certain positions, can replace a single verbal. By this definition, verbal phrases can contain phrases of other types within themselves: in the sentence *He has asked a good question,* the words *has asked a good question* are a verbal phrase, which contains the nominal phrase *a good question.* More narrowly, the term *verbal phrase* can be limited to those sequences of verbal forms which can occupy some of the same positions as single verbals. By this more restricted definition, a verbal phrase begins with *must, ought,* or a verb form in the present or past tense and ends with an infinitive or a participle.

References: 103–09, 119, 122–40, 220.

VOCATIVE. A vocative, a form used in direct address, is a part neither of the complete subject nor of the complete predicate of its sentence. The typical vocative is a nominal, very commonly a proper noun; it is not preceded by an article, though sometimes adjectivals other than articles do precede it; and it is set off by a terminal from the rest of the sentence. Vocatives occur freely in initial, medial, and final position:

> Why did you call him out, *Blind Tom?*
> Your bill, *madam,* is past due.
> My *lord,* pray distinguish your napkin from your handkerchief.

Reference: 146.

VOICE. Traditionally, a verb or a verbal phrase is said to be in the active voice if it represents its subject as acting, and in the passive voice if it represents its subject as acted upon. Clauses and sentences are also called active if their simple predicates are active, and passive if their simple predicates are passive. Since distinctions of voice are not marked by inflection in English, the term *passive* may be applied only to verbal phrases; and some grammarians would not speak of voice in English at all, since to do so does invite the confusion of phrases with single words.

References: 106–07, 131–32, 302–03, 306.

VOICED; VOICELESS. A voiced sound is one in whose production the vocal cords vibrate and make a musical tone; a voiceless sound is one in

whose production the cords do not vibrate, so that there is no
musical tone but only noise. In English, all the vowels are usually
voiced, but some consonants are voiced and others voiceless.
References: 38–40, 42–4, 71, 73, 75.

VOICE QUALIFIER. This term has sometimes been applied to certain socially
important qualities or components of speech, like shouting, whispering, singing, whining, and chuckling, which do not fit into the
basic structure of vowels, consonants, stresses, pitches, etc., but
seem to be superimposed upon that basic structure. For example,
we can shout a sentence or we can whisper it; the shouting or whispering will extend over the whole sentence; but basically the sentence will remain the same.
Reference: 22–3.

VOWEL. Those sounds are most likely to be vowels in which the breath
stream passes over the center of the tongue without audible friction in the mouth; the air is not disturbed or cut off at any point.
Vowels most commonly form the peaks of syllables. The most
common American English vowels are listed on pp. 45–56. Though
speech and writing should not be confused, the term *vowel* is also
used, in old-fashioned grammars, for the letters *a, e, i, o,* and *u*.
In this sense, *vowel-letter* would be a better name. See CONSONANT.
References: 40–2, 45–56.

W

WEAK VERB. See IRREGULAR VERB.

WORD. See COMPOUND WORD.

WORD ORDER. It has sometimes been said that the basic grammatical de-
vices of English are inflections, function words, and word order.
The most important of the three is word order. See FUNCTION
WORD, INFLECTION.

Z

ZERO. Sometimes the description of a language can be simplified by the
recognition of zero forms. If we want to say that all English nouns
that have plurals form them by adding some variety of the plural

ending to the proper base, then we must recognize a zero ending for words like *sheep* (*The sheep are in the meadow*); if we want to say that all relative clauses are introduced by relatives, we must recognize a zero relative in sentences like *The violin you played is a better instrument.* Grammarians disagree concerning the wisdom and technique of establishing zero forms, and we have used them very sparingly in this book.

References: 71–2, 102–03, 105, 177.

CHAPTER EIGHT Applied
Grammar:
Some Notes on English Prose Style

Throughout this book, we have recognized that the English language can be described in more ways than one and that the grammarian's purposes will affect his choice of methods. Of the possible uses for a grammar, we have kept a very practical one in mind: the application of grammatical knowledge in the writing of exposition and argument. Our definition of the sentence, for example, was deliberately shaped to suit this purpose. Our remaining task is to suggest at least one way in which such application can be made, and so we have chosen, in this final chapter, to make some elementary remarks on English prose style.

An example

We all know the usual English translation of the report which Caesar made about a victory in battle: "I came, I saw, I conquered." It is a good translation; and since we need a simple example to begin our discussion, we will use it to suggest some of the things that the word *style* can mean.

↩ Speech or writing?

Our first question must be whether we are talking about marks on paper or about human speech. It is possible to talk sensibly about either, or about the relations between the two; but sensible talk is *not* possible if we try to talk about both at once without distinguishing one from the other. If we try to talk about speech, moreover, we immediately face another difficulty: the same marks on paper would not prompt all of us to make the same speech sounds.

I came, I saw, I conquered.

The writer of this book, if he were given these marks to read, would read them thus:

$$^2\text{àɪ} + {}^2\text{ké:m}^2 \nearrow {}^2\text{àɪ} + {}^2\text{sɔ́:}^2 \nearrow {}^2\text{àɪ} + {}^3\text{kɑ́ŋkɜd}^1 \searrow$$

Few of his colleagues would read the marks in just this way; for example, most of them would "pronounce the r" in *conquered* ($/^3\text{kɑ́ŋkɜrd}^1 \searrow/$) in a way which they consider quite natural and colorless but which the writer would use only for comic or satirical effects. Plainly we must not only decide whether to talk about speech or about writing; a decision to talk wholly or partly about speech will force us also to decide *whose* speech.

❧ One content in two forms

Postponing this group of questions about speech and writing for a while, we may tentatively proceed to consider the utterance which we have transcribed:

$$^2\text{àɪ} + {}^2\text{ké:m}^2 \nearrow {}^{12}\text{àɪ} + {}^2\text{sɔ́:}^2 \nearrow {}^{12}\text{àɪ} + {}^3\text{kɑ́ŋkɜ̆d}^1 \searrow$$

What does it mean? Presumably something like this—that the general arrived on the scene of battle, observed the situation, and won the victory. We now have two statements, the original utterance and our paraphrase of it, that mean much the same thing; or, if anyone should find our paraphrase inaccurate, we at least have the recognition that we can usefully ask what a statement means and expect an answer in other words than those of the statement itself. In short, we can say the same thing in different ways.

❧ Style as manner

This conclusion, though it seems painfully obvious, is very useful and important. It allows us to suggest what will ultimately be our definition of style, and it reminds us that we can ask stylistic questions both about the content of our utterances and about our expression of that content. Style, that is, will be for us the manner of saying what is said, but we will recognize that there is style in thought as well as style in language; and if sometimes we must separate matter and manner in our studies, we must always be able to put them together again. All that we shall say about style is implicit in these few remarks.

CONTENT. Turning again to our transcribed utterance, we note that its matter represents a very careful choice of detail. From a communiqué reporting victory in battle, the battle itself has been left out, as if victory were the easiest and most natural thing in the world for the omnipotent Me who had only to arrive and survey the field in order to win it. The battle has been left out, and the armies have been left out: *I* came, *I* saw; and a successful climax to the action is made to appear as inevitable as the rhetorically effective climax in the reporting of it.

EXPRESSION. The manner of the utterance is as essential to its effect as the carefully chosen details which are its matter. There are three clauses, *I came, I saw,* and *I conquered;* and though they are exactly parallel grammatically, the contrast between the dissyllabic verb in the third clause and the monosyllabic verbs in the first and second fits the climax in the matter of the report. Each clause, again, is as bare as possible, the unexpanded combination of a nominal (three times repeated) and a verbal; while between the clauses, intonation patterns provide the connections which conjunctions might have helped provide. The tight concision of the whole is enhanced by the arrangement of the stresses and by the alliteration in /ké:m/ and /káŋkɔ̌d/.

ᛣ Importance of style

Before going on, now, to develop one by one the topics which these introductory paragraphs have hinted at, we may say a word to the skeptic who doubts the wisdom of giving two paragraphs to a single sentence. It is easy to pretend that style does not matter, that it neither helps nor hinders communication or that it takes care of itself if the writer takes care that he has something to say. The pretense is easy, but it is only pretense, and experience destroys it. To show the importance of style, we may simply compare our paraphrase and the utterance with which we began:

> I came, I saw, I conquered.
> I arrived on the scene of battle, I observed the situation, I won the victory.

The paraphrase is as accurate as we can make it, but though the two statements are almost indistinguishable in their meaning, they are altogether different in their total effects. When we say the same thing in different ways, the total effects of what we say will depend to a considerable extent on how we say it; and the best style is often hard to find.

Definition

Recognizing that there is style in thought as well as style in language, we have yet suggested that style for us will be the manner of saying what is said. In this section, we must expand our definition and point out some of the things which it implies.

ᛣ Separability of matter and manner

The first implication, of course, is that matter and manner are separable, that what we say and the way we say it are different things. We make this assumption every day. We make it when we write or read a translation, a paraphrase, or a summary; when, in deductive logic, we say that one proposition is equivalent to another; or when we ask a friend what a third person has said and accept, as our answer, an indirect quotation. Indeed, if we did not assume that matter and manner are separable, language and communication would be impossible; for a man could explain himself only by repeating the words he said before, and if we did not understand him after the repetition, nothing more could be done. Our understanding of a lecture, for example, would end when we could no longer remember the precise manner of its delivery, and could be demonstrated or communicated only if we were perfect mimics. Such absurd consequences would follow directly from the denial that what we say and how we say it are different things.

❧ Style in thought

If style is the manner of saying what is said, then it follows that style is possible only because there *are* more ways of saying a thing than one. In one sense we can say that the same thing has been said in different ways when the same conclusion has been established on different premises or when different modes of persuasion have moved an audience to take the same action or entertain the same belief. It is in this sense of the word *manner* that we can talk about different styles of thought. We could say, for instance, that two men have different styles of thought if one prefers to argue deductively, from first principles, and the other reasons inductively, from empirical observations; or we could find different rhetorical styles in a closely reasoned appeal to the intellect and a gaudy play for the feelings of an audience. Style in this sense is less a matter of expression than of content, as when we spoke of the choice of detail in Caesar's arrogantly calm *I came, I saw, I conquered.*

❧ Style as linguistic choice

Style in this sense, however, is not our prime concern in this book. We want to talk mainly about style in its other connotation, style in language. Style in language is possible because all of us, fortunately, command more than one kind of English and because, even within a *single* kind of English, there are synonymous expressions from which we may make our choice. Illustrations are plentiful. Since few Americans spend all their lives in a single area and since no area is safe from the verbal barrage laid down by our talkative compatriots, we all recognize different regional dialects and have at least some facility in their use or abuse; and since the flexibility of our class structure allows us to move rather freely among the classes which we pretend not to recognize, we quietly make it our business to learn the lingo of more than one group. Regionally, the average American can at least give a bad imitation of Brooklynese or the "Southern drawl"; and socially, he is much too canny to talk to his preacher and his teacher, his boss and his barkeeper in just the same way.

Even the mythical unfortunate who might be confined to a single regional and social dialect would still face the linguistic choices which make style in language possible. Within each dialect, the same thing can be said in ways which differ in sounds, in inflections, in syntax, or in choice of words. Thus some Chicagoans can pronounce *park* as either /párk/ or /páərk/; as the plural of *index,* the writer of this book can use either *indexes* or *indices;* our teachers may have allowed us to say either "A big crowd of people *was* there" or "A big crowd of people *were* there"; and some of us have probably heard discussions of "synonyms at three levels," like *rise—mount—ascend* or *time—age—epoch.* We constantly choose among the lexical and grammatical variants which our dialects make available to us.

EFFECTS OF SUCH CHOICE. Why do we bother to make a choice among synonymous expressions, among different ways of saying the same thing? That we do bother to choose is plain, and for a very good reason: different ways of saying the same thing may produce effects which are even more strikingly different. For example, both /párk/ and /páərk/ can refer to the same expanse of lawn, covered with shrubs, trees, and couples lying on newspapers; they can point to the same thing. That is not to say that the total effects of the use of these two forms will also be identical. To the quaint people who dislike or pretend to dislike the "Midwestern *r,*" both might be objectionable when compared to an elegant /pá:k/; but of the two, /párk/ might be the more painful. Or, if this example seems far fetched, we need only remember the consternation which *I ain't got none* would cause in circles where *I haven't any* is expected, or the anguish which a four-letter word would cause to people who never blink an eye at its scientific synonym. Unless we know how to say the same thing in different ways, some of our efforts at communication are bound to fail; we will lose influence and make enemies.

NECESSITY OF COMPARISONS. It should be plain, by this point, that style in language is itself synonymous with linguistic choice; and choice implies rejection. Here our concept of style has important consequences for our method of studying it. We must recognize that if we want to talk about a man's style, we must know both how he said things and how he *might* have said them but chose not to; and we must also recognize that no one can *cultivate* his style unless he somehow knows enough about the resources of his language to choose those which he needs. A teacher, for example, considering a student's papers, might suggest to him that he was hurting his style by writing too many choppy sentences. The remark would have no point if *all* English sentences were choppy; and the student could do nothing to improve his work unless he was familiar, or could become familiar, with more fluent writing. Both critically and creatively, the study of style is basically comparative.

The necessary comparisons cannot be made, in any economical or systematic way, without a set of terms and distinctions by which to analyze, describe, and prescribe stylistic choices. If we are going to talk about choppy sentences and fluent sentences as features of contrasting styles, or if we are to profit from instructions to choose the one and avoid the other, we must first know what makes a sentence and what makes a sentence either fluent or choppy. That is, we must have a grammar; and a little reflection on the problems of word choice will show that we must also have a dictionary or its equivalent. The mere possession of grammars and dictionaries will not make us creative stylists or competent analysts of style; linguistic choice is not the whole of style; but the normally intelligent student, although he will concentrate during most of his school years on the content of his writing, may well give a little direct attention to its manner; and among his most valuable resources will be a grammar, a dictionary, and a shelfful of good books for models.

Exercise one. Study the following groups of sentences. Do the members of each group mean the same thing? Whenever your answer is no, try to state the differences in meaning precisely. Can you add other synonymous sentences to any of the groups?

1. The farmer plowed three acres.
   Three acres were plowed by the farmer.
2. Europeans sometimes consider Americans naïve.
   Americans are sometimes considered naïve by Europeans.
3. The Lions Club gave the winner a saddle.
   The winner was given a saddle by the Lions Club.
   A saddle was given the winner by the Lions Club.
4. In the quiet pools, trout will be rising.
   In the quiet pools, there will be trout rising.
   Trout will be rising in the quiet pools.

5. It is impossible to deny this simple fact.
   To deny this simple fact is impossible.
6. Mr. Trumbull, who was a good businessman, owned several large estates.
   Mr. Trumbull, a good businessman, owned several large estates.
7. We had always thought him to be an honest man.
   We had always thought that he was an honest man.
8. Chess is a more interesting game than checkers.
   Checkers is not so interesting a game as chess.
9. He got up slowly and closed the front door.
   Getting up slowly, he closed the front door.
10. Although the play had not been close, he complained loudly.
    The play had not been close, but he complained loudly.
11. It was raining hard. The country roads were impassable.
    It was raining hard, and the country roads were impassable.
12. Henry was vexed by Jane's inability to answer.
    Henry was vexed because Jane could not answer.
    Henry was vexed because Jane was unable to answer.
    That Jane could not answer vexed Henry.
13. The child always spoke to his parents with respect.
    The child always spoke to his parents respectfully.
14. "I'm a stranger here myself," the constable said.
    The constable said he was a stranger here himself.
15. My hobby is to make model planes.
    Making model planes is my hobby.

A few remarks on speech and writing

The relation between speech and writing is anything but simple, and we intend by the title of this section to suggest that our discussion will be selective and elementary. A mere glance at the keyboard of a typewriter will raise questions which we will not answer here. What, one might ask, are the connections between our uses of capital letters and the various features of our speech? How are the letters *etc.* related to the spoken words /²ăn⁺³só:⁺fòərθ¹↘/? When we see the symbols " ", ½, %, &, @, or ?, with what linguistic forms do we respond, and why? To solve such problems would take a good deal of knowledge about speech and a good deal about writing.

✧ Importance of writing

Writing systems, indeed, deserve more study than some students of language have been willing to give them, and a student of literary style certainly cannot concern himself with speech alone. Undoubtedly, many printed books make at least some of their appeals directly through the eye, without the mediation of the ear; the typographical practices of E. E. Cummings are an obvious illustration. Again, average readers are usually not conscious of any sound track accompanying their silent reading; we insult a man if we say of him that he can't read without moving his lips. Even a poet, who generally wants his verses to be read aloud, can direct that reading only by the marks which he instructs his publisher to make on the pages of his book. Such instances show how silly it would be, in a chapter about writing, to ignore writing.

❧ Speech our ultimate subject

The fact remains, as we said at the beginning of our grammar, that men spoke long before they wrote and that writing is still essentially a secondary representation of speech. More precisely, we might say that writing, essentially a secondary representation of speech, has been and is used to record only certain *kinds* of speech, not anything and everything that men say. Men have seldom bothered to write down their casual conversation, but our libraries hold great masses of the kinds of prose which we expect in serious exposition and argument. The use of writing, in turn, has had its effect on the discourses which are normally written, so that we do not and should not now converse as we write, or write as we converse. There are special "writing styles," special *kinds* of discourse, which it is part of our business to master; yet we will not distort the materials of our study if we decide that our *ultimate* subject, in discussing style, is speech. To justify this statement, we have only to remember that nearly everyone who has written about style has talked about sound and rhythm; and to convince a skeptic, we have only to write a sentence on a piece of paper and ask him what we have written. He will invariably read the sentence aloud, not recite the sequence of marks which we have made.

We will be talking, then, less about marks on paper than about human speech, and when any particular passage is under discussion, our remarks will chiefly apply to the best reading of it which the author of this book can give. In most instances, that reading will have much in common with other careful readings of the same passage, so that the comments made will be generally applicable; but in the last analysis our specimens will be one man's attempt at oral interpretation of other men's marks on paper. As far as literary style is concerned, we might even think of the writer's job as learning the conventions of certain kinds of discourse and learning the graphic means to direct a reader's reproduction of that discourse.

❧ Plain talk vs. speech for writing

Two basic facts to remember as we go about this job are that the reader of presumably serious prose does not expect to be presented with unconsidered chitchat and that the writer of any kind of discourse, so long as he uses the conventional orthography, cannot present his reader with a full representation of that discourse—he cannot write everything he says. The writer must find means to escape the resultant embarrassments and ambiguities.

A few quotations will clarify the statement that educated people do not and should not write as they casually talk. Here are two fragments of a telephone conversation which was recently recorded in an American academic community (the speaker is obviously a person of some education):

1. "he suggested that we go down and get Mrs. R———— and tell her who we are and that he sent us and try the fourteen-inch typewriters and see if our stencils would work with such type and if we can use them to get them right away because they have those in stock and we won't have to wait"

2. "we're short and we want to get rid of those rentals but they are expecting within two weeks or so to be receiving —ah—to start receiving their orders on eleven-inch machines with pica type and of course pica type has always been best for our stencils but I rather think there might be a chance that we can work with elite type" [1]

As oral communication, these utterances were apparently successful. The responses of the other party to the conversation were also recorded, and they consist largely of "yes" and "I see." Nor is there any reason to feel that the speaker was somehow debasing the English language. He was talking as we all talk, perhaps somewhat better than most of us; but for our present purpose, that is just the point. He was talking as educated people *talk,* not as they are expected to *write,* and so his remarks, when they are written down, strike us at once as awkward, incoherent, perhaps "illiterate." They show, indeed, some of the characteristics which we regularly associate with "Vulgar English," notably the very long and formless "sentences" loosely connected by repeated *and.* The suggestion again is obvious that much of our difficulty in learning to write results

[1] From *The Structure of English* by Charles Carpenter Fries, copyright, 1952, by Harcourt, Brace and Company, Inc.

from differences between oral and written styles; the elements and ex-pectations involved in oral and written discourse are not altogether the same.

The differences, although they are relatively small in comparison with the shared elements, nonetheless appear in every aspect of our language, perhaps most obviously in the construction of sentences and the choice of words. The writer of the immediately preceding sentence would never speak it in plain talk. In conversation he would not be likely to put an adverbial clause, like *although . . . elements,* between the simple sub-ject, *differences,* and the simple predicate, *appear;* he would not tack on the concluding adverbial phrase, *perhaps . . . words;* and he would not choose phrases like *nonetheless* and *perhaps most obviously.* The kind of speech of which our writing is a secondary representation typically differs, in such ways as these, from the speech of daily life; convention dictates different selections from the resources of our language when we write a book and when we talk to our family.

❧ Things we cannot write

The situation is complicated by the second fact which we have mentioned. Whatever kind of speech we try to record in writing, ordinary spelling does not allow us to write everything we say, and special devices of writing styles have had to be developed as substitutes for (or reminders of) the missing speech features. This statement is more than the common-place remark that when we write we cannot depend on our gestures or on the situation of things around us to make our meaning clear. We have also to get along without our "tone of voice," particularly without stress, pitch, and terminals. The immediate result is that we frequently lack detailed control of the reading of our work by others. For example, there are often a number of different intonations which native speakers are likely to use when they read a given sentence. Thus, in the second sentence of this paragraph, we may read *to write everything we say* in different ways; for example,

$$^2\text{tŏ} + \text{wrîte} + {}^3\text{everẏthìng} + \text{wĕ} + \text{sây}^2 \nearrow$$
$$^2\text{tŏ} + \text{wrîte} + \text{êverẏthìng} + \text{wĕ} + {}^3\text{sáy}^2 \rightarrow$$

❧ Some devices of writing

If we think it important that our reader should choose just one from these and the other readings which are possible, we must write into this sentence or into surrounding sentences the clues which may direct the reader's choice. We must try to make it clear either that we are contrasting *everything* we say with just *part* of what we say, in which case high pitch and loudest stress will fall on *everything*, or that we are contrasting what we *say* with what we can *write*, in which case *say* will get high pitch and loudest stress. Italics, as in this paragraph, are one possible clue; but they are an elementary device, and only one of many.

With at least some of the devices other than punctuation we are all familiar (learning to punctuate may itself be one of our problems). When we say that the context prevents ambiguity in a passage which might be misunderstood in isolation, we are saying that in surrounding passages the writer has managed to include enough information for us to interpret the difficult passage by inference. This is what happens when, in reading a newspaper, we see a headline like

PROFESSOR RAKES LEAVES

AFTER COLLEGE COMMENCEMENT [2]

In talk, the patterns of stress and pitch would tell us immediately whether Professor Rakes was leaving or whether some professor was raking leaves. As we read, we have to find our interpretation by looking at other parts of the story.

FULLNESS OF EXPRESSION. One of the devices of writing styles is therefore a greater fullness of expression. Either we add an extra clue to the sentence which might be ambiguous without it, or we provide the clues in other sentences and trust the reader to make the proper inference. If he is perverse or stupid or we are careless, the results may be ludicrous. A great newspaper once gave some of its readers a cheap laugh by reporting that a petty criminal had "pleaded guilty to stealing two Chinese reproduction boxes."

MANIPULATION OF WORD ORDER. "Greater fullness of expression" is a general term which applies to many specific devices of writing styles. Another feature of literary language is the manipulation of word order. As an example, we may cite the split infinitive, which is sometimes almost forced on writers because English spelling does not represent intonation. In talk, intonation would make the following sentences perfectly clear:

1. Such writers have not failed heartily to abet the leaders.
2. Her ill-fitting clothes failed altogether to conceal her figure.

---

[2] Robert C. Pooley, *Teaching English Grammar* (New York: Appleton-Century-Crofts, Inc., 1957), p. 67.

3. The gentlemen were determined deliberately to spread subtle propaganda.
4. Who makes it a business regularly to follow their activities?
5. Do you intend seriously to review such garbage?[3]

Hearing the second of these sentences, we would know immediately whether the young lady's embarrassment was slight or grave. A terminal after *failed* would make the situation no great matter, but a terminal after *altogether* would mean that the disaster was complete. The other sentences would be similarly clarified by intonation, but when they are written, the intonation is not shown and the writer must recast them. One possible revision is to split the infinitives, replacing the ambiguous *altogether to conceal,* for example, by *to altogether conceal,* which is unmistakable. The familiar taboo might be weakened if it were generally realized that split infinitives are sometimes a stylistic device to remedy the deficiencies of our writing system.

❧ Summary

Because of the insights into such problems which are afforded by an approach to writing through speech, we have tried, in this book, to say more than elementary grammars usually do say about the realities of living language. Even in the grammar, however, we have tried to enforce the realization that oral and written discourse are different and that these differences must be respected. If this were not the case, such a definition of the sentence as we have given might not be easily defensible. In the present section, again, we have insisted that although writing is an essentially secondary representation of speech, it is an often indirect and always incomplete representation of *special kinds* of speech; that the conventions of writing must be separately learned *after* one has learned the conventions of speech; and that consciousness of some of the relations between the two sets of conventions is an advantage in manipulating either set. Such choice and manipulation, we have said, is what we mean by style in language.

Exercise one. Here is a longer excerpt from the recorded conversation which we used as an example a few pages back. In it, a report is being made about the purchase of some typewriters. Translate the report into

---

[3] Examples adapted from Stuart Robertson and Frederic G. Cassidy, *The Development of Modern English* (New York: Prentice-Hall, Inc., 1954), p. 302.

the form it might have taken in a well-written impersonal letter—that is, translate it into one possible writing style. Punctuation must be added, and, in addition to changes in such grammatical matters as sentence structure and reference of pronouns, you will probably want to rearrange the order of the given details.

I wanted to tell you one more thing I've been talking with Mr. D_____ in the purchasing department about our typewriters . . . that order went in March seventh however it seems that we are about eighth on the list . . . we were up about three but it seems that for that type of typewriter we're about eighth that's for a fourteen-inch carriage with pica type . . . now he told me that R_____'s have in stock the fourteen-inch carriage typewriters with elite type . . . and elite type varies sometimes it's quite small and sometimes it's almost as large as pica . . . he suggested that we go down and get Mrs. R_____ and tell her who we are and that he sent us and try the fourteen-inch typewriters and see if our stencils would work with such type . . . and if we can use them to get them right away because they have those in stock and we won't have to wait . . . we're short one typewriter right now as far as having adequate facilities for the staff is concerned . . . we're short and we want to get rid of those rentals . . . but they are expecting within two weeks or so to be receiving—ah— to start receiving their orders on eleven-inch machines with pica type . . . and of course pica type has always been best for our stencils . . . but I rather think there might be a chance that we can work with elite type.[4]

Exercise two. None of the following sentences would be ambiguous in speech, but in writing they might be misleading, at least for a moment. Revise them, or punctuate them, so that they will be immediately clear. They are given with no punctuation at all.

1. when you use one you have to be careful but two are always perfectly safe
2. if she didn't have any money cars or fine clothes would be out of her reach
3. before everyone knew what was happening but the censors
4. a bursting shell injured the captain and the lieutenant took over
5. when the lights flashed on the board looked like a christmas tree
6. before eating the raccoons wash their food
7. the club wants more desirable members
8. under james brown's comets have won most of their games
9. our theory develops further notions already widely accepted
10. the ordinance rezoned as commercial and residential portions of the outlying areas
11. valuable as the statements of these witnesses are the accounts of others must be carefully considered
12. the teacher mrs brown is quite innocent [Vocative, or appositive?]

[4] From *The Structure of English* by Charles Carpenter Fries, copyright, 1952, by Harcourt, Brace and Company, Inc.

13. the man who was talking loudly replied
14. they came back from their vacation in the mountains on the railroad
15. students who fail often can't read well
16. the professor visited the man involved with his wife
17. he only paid you a dollar
18. if he doesn't pass within a month he'll be on probation
19. the man who was riding got thrown when the horse stumbled and broke his arm
20. we insisted that he should look for the watch was valuable

Some structural elements of style: sentences and clauses

A definition of style as choice and rejection would not be very helpful if it were not accompanied by some statement of the range of choices which are open to the writer. Actually, since we intend to talk mainly about style in language, such a statement has already been provided by our grammar; the grammarian names and describes some of the tools which the stylist uses. The use of the available tools, however, is precisely the problem in writing, where the grammarian's description of the language is not an end in itself; and so we shall go on now to consider the structure of our language not merely as a structure but as a system which each of us must use for his own purposes. The elements of our language must now be viewed as elements of style.

❧ Structure vs. vocabulary

Two important distinctions, both of which have already been suggested, must be reëmphasized at once. The first is the distinction between the structure of a language and its vocabulary, and the best way to reinforce this distinction is to return for a moment to the definitions of our positional classes, like nominal and verbal. A nominal, we said, is a form which occupies certain positions in our utterances, typically the positions that nouns occupy. If we are given the formula for a certain kind of sentence, and if that formula contains nominal positions, we can use the formula to construct hundreds of particular sentences just by putting nominals—any nominals—into the proper slots. For example, if we have the formula

$$D \quad N\!\rightarrow \quad V \quad D \quad N\!\searrow$$

we can construct sentences like the following:

The cat caught the bird.
The bird caught the cat.
The cop caught the robber.
The robber caught the cop.
The polymorphism discombobulates the neophyte.

The structure of all these sentences is the same. It is those grammatical properties which are common to them all, and it is represented by the formula. So long as the *classes* which we have called nominal and verbal remain in English, the grammatical structure of our language will not be changed even though the individual forms *cat, bird, cop, robber, catch,* and *discombobulate* disappear entirely.

The vocabulary, on the other hand, *would* be changed by the loss of these or any similar individual items, for the vocabulary consists of the particular forms whose common properties are the linguistic structure. By a rough analogy, the vocabulary might be compared to individual men and women, and the structure of the language to human nature. As individuals, Tom, Dick, and Harry may be of great importance, and when they die, the sum total of living men is certainly changed; for their grieving families, no one else will ever be quite like them. Textbooks of anatomy, physiology, and psychology, however, need not be rewritten at their demise. Tom, Jr., will resemble his father in many ways, and human nature will survive them both.

The student of style, therefore, must concern himself at least as much with structure as with vocabulary. The topics of his discussion will be not only words but sentences, clauses, phrases, the classes of forms that compose these larger units, and the sounds that underlie them all. When he talks about sound and rhythm, he will remember that the marks on the paper before him, although we loosely call some of them "words," are not the sounds themselves or adequate representations of the sounds; and even when he talks about words, as he certainly must, he will remember that words are not used in isolation and that they take much of their character from their environments. Style in language is choice of structural patterns as well as choice of words.

❧ Form and meaning once more

The second distinction which we must reëmphasize is the distinction between form and meaning, between words and either things or our thought *about* things. Grammatical classes, we must remember, are established on the basis of linguistic form, not on the basis of semantic content.

Sometimes, to be sure, formal classes coincide rather closely with semantic classes. For example, in modern English most plural nouns obviously share the meaning "more than one." This meaning is not present in all plurals, however: the noun *oats,* which is plural, refers to one kind of grain, while the noun *rice,* which is singular, refers to another; the singular *shirt* refers to a garment with two appendages for the upper half of the body, but a similar garment for the lower half has the plural name *trousers.*

Often the coincidence of formal with semantic classes is much less than it is where English plural nouns are concerned. Thus, only confusion can result from the old definition of *subject* as the name for the doer of the action or for what the sentence is about. A sentence is about its objects as well as about its subject; and typically, in passive sentences, the subject does not name the doer of the action. Our courts are eminently right when they consign to an asylum those people who insistently ignore the distinction between words and things.

⟨ Coordination and subordination

It is a particularly important distinction when we talk about stylistic choice among sentence structures, where one of our principal topics will be the relations between independent and dependent clauses. The terms *independent* and *dependent* are formal in their reference, not semantic. Too often this fact is forgotten, and we are advised to put our main ideas into our main clauses (which are also called independent, principal, or coordinate) and our subordinate ideas into subordinate clauses (which are also called dependent). Coordinate clauses, we may be told, express coordinate ideas, so that compound sentences, consisting of two or more such clauses, give equal emphasis to equal thoughts but weaken unity and coherence. Between the clauses of a compound sentence, which are said to be related just as separate sentences are related, there would be, then, no logical advance; two ideas, or two expressions of the same idea, would simply be placed side by side. With complex sentences, the case is said to be different. Since subordinate clauses, we are told, express subordinate ideas, complex sentences rank our thoughts in the order of their importance. The primary thought receives primary emphasis, and so complex sentences are called more unified and coherent than compound sentences.[5]

[5] This discussion of coordination and subordination is largely from my essay "Coordination (Faulty) and Subordination (Upside-Down)" in the journal *College Composition and Communication,* VII (December 1956), pp. 181–187.

The best that can be said for this widespread belief is that it is too simple to be true, and a more severe criticism might be that the doctrine rests
on a series of bad puns in which the same labels are carelessly applied to
words, thoughts, and things. Subordinate clauses are *grammatically* subordinate; that is, they are used like single nominals, adjectivals, or adverbials, often to expand smaller constructions. Just as we can say, for
example,

The man is my uncle,

so we can expand the nominal construction *the man* with a subordinate or
dependent clause and say,

The man *whom you met* is my uncle.

In this grammatical sense, *whom you met* is subordinate, precisely as we
might say that *big* is subordinate to *man* in the sentence,

The big man is my uncle.

Logically and psychologically, however, it is perfectly possible that in a
given situation the primary fact, the fact that mattered most to speaker
and hearer, would be the fact symbolized by *whom you met;* and if this
were the case there might still be no reason at all to put that fact into a
main clause. The things that matter most to us are often very effectively
reported in dependent clauses.

Similarly, coordinate clauses are *grammatically* coordinate; they are
subject-predicate combinations whose only *grammatical* equivalents are
similar combinations. It does *not* follow that the thoughts expressed in
coordinate clauses are or should be coordinate thoughts, ideas of equal
rank, or that the same real state of affairs always is symbolized or always
should be symbolized by the same pattern of clauses. A moment's reflection is enough to show that a grammatically complex sentence may be
precisely equivalent in meaning to a grammatically compound sentence.
So if we say,

Either it's not raining, or the streets are wet,

we have uttered a compound sentence, but the sentence may be exactly
translated,

If it's raining, the streets are wet.

The second sentence is complex, and the example shows that the same relation in nature may be spoken of in variously related clauses.

The two following examples are likewise virtually indistinguishable in
meaning but quite different in grammatical structure:

Since I wouldn't have anything to say, I won't write you.

$^2\hat{\text{I}}$ + wôn't + ^{3}write + yŏu^2→$^2\hat{\text{I}}$ + wôuldñ't + hàve + ânÿthìng + tŏ + ^{3}sáy^1↘

In the first of these two utterances, a complex sentence, the causal relation is expressed by the conjunction *since;* in the second utterance, a compound sentence, there is no conjunction, but the intonation patterns and the order of the clauses make the idea of causality equally clear. It would be absurd to say that because its two independent clauses are not clearly related, the second sentence lacks unity or coherence.

Finally, we may cite a sentence which we ourselves have just used: "The best that can be said for this widespread belief is that it is too simple to be true, and a more severe criticism might be that the doctrine rests on a series of bad puns in which the same labels are carelessly applied to words, thoughts, and things." The sentence is compound-complex, with two independent clauses and four dependent ones, but the main ideas are not in the main clauses, except in so far as the main clauses contain all the others. On the contrary, the main clauses are used primarily to make the transition from the statement of a doctrine to the criticism of it, and the criticism itself is stated in the nominal clauses *that it is too simple to be true* and *that the doctrine rests on a series of bad puns.* The sentence would not be improved by reversing this arrangement.

❡ Use and abuse of fragments

What, then, to proceed to positive statements, may we say about the sentence as an element of style? The first is obvious. One of the features of the writing styles which are considered appropriate for serious exposition and argument is that the complete sentence is favored and the sentence fragment generally avoided. In conversation, that is not the case; dialogues like the following are perfectly common:

"Who won the ball game?"
"The home team!"
"What was the score?"
"Nine to eight."
"Gee, that's a help. Gives 'em a chance for the pennant."
"You bet it does. See you at the ball park tomorrow."

There are also forms of serious literature, both poetry and prose, in which the sentence fragment is effectively used without disappointing any established expectations; and in these forms, as in plain talk, there can be no objection to the sentence fragment. In exposition and argument, however, the fragment is not only generally avoided but generally should be, not because it is bad in itself, but because its use would violate a recognized convention and so defeat the writer's purpose. Where complete sentences are expected, the fragment should be used only for special effects.

❧ Choices among sentence structures

If the writer's choice is generally restricted to complete sentences, he still has plenty of room to maneuver. (1) Within his sentences, he may or may not include sentence adverbials, and the sentences themselves may be simple, compound, complex, or compound-complex—a choice which will usually determine whether the sentences are long or short. (2) In all but the simple sentence, there is also considerable freedom in the placing of clauses and in the relations among them. As we said in the grammar, adverbial clauses in particular may be rather freely moved about, and this and other possibilities in the selection and order of the clause types give the writer a further choice. He can so order the formal elements of his sentences that the semantic content is not clear and fully shaped until the sentence end (the *periodic* sentence), or he can state his main idea earlier and keep the sentence end for qualifications and additions (the *loose* sentence). (3) Still other possibilities, of course, are open to him. Most notably, he may choose to vary the structure of his sentences and clauses, so that no two of a considerable number are just alike, or he may build a series of parallel or matching structures, often in such a way that matching forms point up likenesses and differences in content. Varieties of the latter device are given such names as *balance, parallelism,* and *antithesis.*

❧ (1) Clausal structures

We have already made it plain that the uses of independent and dependent clauses cannot be reduced to a simple formula. Obviously, elaborate patterns of subordination, like the use of many sentence adverbials, are somewhat literary and harder to follow than shorter and less involved constructions; yet complex subordination may at times be more useful than simplicity for the avoidance of monotony, the creation of desired sound effects, or the expression of the writer's thought, and some modes of subordination are much less literary than others. Zero conjunctions, for example, or zero relatives (especially when the relative clause ends with a preposition) can often be so used that even rather complex subordination will not seem unpleasantly bookish. Again, since style is choice and since any device depends for its effect on its similarity and dissimilarity to other means of expression, neither coordination nor subordination would have any stylistic value if the other did not exist. A statement like the common one, that short, simple sentences make effective introductions, transitions, and conclusions, would be meaningless but for the implied contrast with sentences having more than one clause.

One cannot hope, then, for comforting rules in black and white; and perhaps the best general advice that can be given, in the matter of subordination and coordination, is the not very helpful injunction to use them both in such a way that the natural or logical relations in one's material will be clear. The possibilities are much too complicated to be dealt with by mechanically putting main ideas in main clauses and subordinate ideas in subordinate clauses. Take, for instance, the following sentence:

> The barometer's falling, and those clouds have wind in them, and we'd better put into harbor at once.

The sentence is bad, but not because it contains three independent clauses; and it can be rewritten in different ways, any of which will be satisfactory so long as the relation of premise and conclusion, situation and consequence, is made clear. One rewriting changes the one sentence into two and makes the relation clear by easy inference:

> The barometer's falling, and those clouds have wind in them. We'd better put into harbor at once.

Two other rewritings make the relation explicit, but in different patterns of coordination and subordination:

> We'd better put into harbor at once; for the barometer's falling, and those clouds have wind in them.
>
> Since the barometer's falling and those clouds have wind in them, we'd better put into harbor at once.

Unless the sentence were placed in a determining context, there would be little to choose among the three rewritings.

STRINGY SENTENCES AND CHOPPY SENTENCES. Our bad example is what is often called a "stringy" sentence or an *and-so* sentence. If the conjunctions were removed, the resulting short sentences would commonly be condemned as "choppy":

> The barometer's falling. Those clouds have wind in them. We'd better put into harbor at once.

To be sure, a series of short sentences, most of them simple, can some-

times be used to good effect, as William Faulkner uses them in a passage
from his famous story "The Bear":

> Then the two weeks were up. They prepared to break camp.
> The boy begged to remain and his cousin let him. He moved
> into the little hut with Sam Fathers. Each morning he
> watched Sam lower the pail of water into the crib. By the end
> of that week the dog was down.[6]

Although the passage cannot be recommended for undiscriminating imitation, it is effective in its context; and the rewriting of its choppy sentences would only weaken them:

> When the two weeks were up and they prepared to break
> camp, the boy begged to remain. Having won his cousin's
> consent, he moved into the little hut with Sam Fathers, where
> each morning he watched Sam lower the pail of water into the
> crib. By the end of that week the dog was down.

The passage from Faulkner, however, is exceptional, and not to be compared with the monotonous, jerky series of disconnected simple sentences
which a beginner writes in ignorance or carelessness. The unfortunate effect which choppy sentences often have can be seen from a rewriting of
the first sentences in the Gettysburg Address. Lincoln wrote:

> Fourscore and seven years ago our fathers brought forth on
> this continent a new nation, conceived in liberty, and dedi-
> cated to the proposition that all men are created equal. Now
> we are engaged in a great civil war, testing whether that na-
> tion, or any nation so conceived and so dedicated, can long
> endure. We are met on a great battlefield of that war.

The first two sentences are complex, the third is simple; and the two complex sentences contrast even more strongly with the simple third because
of the repeated participial constructions which end them. The first sentence, moreover, deals with the birth of the nation, the second with the
present war, the third with the immediate occasion. The rewriting flattens
out the grammatical contrast and obscures the logical divisions of the
content:

> Fourscore and seven years ago our fathers brought forth on
> this continent a new nation. It was conceived in liberty. It was
> dedicated to the proposition that all men are created equal.
> Now we are engaged in a great civil war. We are testing

---

[6] From "The Bear" by William Faulkner, in *The Faulkner Reader* (New York:
Random House, Inc., 1954). Copyright, 1942, by William Faulkner.

whether that nation, or any nation so conceived and so dedicated, can long endure. We are met on a great battlefield of that war.

OVERLAPPING SUBORDINATION. Equally bad effects can be produced by awkwardly involved subordination, which can also obscure the logical or natural relations in a writer's material. A famous comic example of "overlapping subordination" is familiar to everyone who knows about the cow in "The House That Jack Built"—"that horned brute morose that tossed the dog that worried the cat that killed the rat that ate the malt that lay in the house that Jack built." Most of the time, these strings of subordinate clauses are more confusing than amusing; Lincoln would have caused more consternation at Gettysburg than Pickett did if he had spoken as follows:

> Fourscore and seven years after our fathers brought forth on this continent a new nation, conceived in liberty and dedicated to the proposition that all men are created equal, we are engaged in a great civil war, by which we are testing whether that nation, or any nation so conceived and so dedicated, can long endure, and on one of whose great battlefields we are met.

The lesson to be drawn from such an impudent monstrosity is not to avoid the complex sentence, or the simple sentence, or the compound sentence, or any other sentence but the bad sentence. Both independent and dependent clauses and all types of sentences should be used as the occasion demands, but with an ear for rhythm and with decent consideration for the reader's ease, convenience, and powers of attention. Most of all, they should be used to make sense.

Exercise one. On p. 274, we attempted to clarify the distinction between vocabulary and linguistic structure by an analogy: as human beings are to human nature, so words are to linguistic structure; "the vocabulary consists of the particular forms whose common properties are the linguistic structure." In no more than three paragraphs, attempt a statement of the same distinction, using an analogy of your own. For example, you might compare the use of language to a child's game with colored blocks. Each block (each word) has its own size, shape, and color; but the rules of the game allow the blocks to be arranged only in certain patterns and sequences (the linguistic structure).

Exercise two. The following sentences would be generally condemned for faulty subordination, especially for "upside-down subordination," or the placing of the "main thought" in a subordinate clause. Study the comments on the sentences, and rewrite them more effectively.

1. When my father was a young man, Lincoln was assassinated. (Most people would admit that the main idea here is in the main clause, but in most contexts the sentence would be bad. It dates the familiar and important—the death of Lincoln—by reference to the unfamiliar and less important—my father's youth; and it suggests that my father's youth was somehow directly connected, perhaps causally connected, with the assassination. In your rewriting, make the main clause into the subordinate clause.)

2. The shortstop dropped an easy fly, when the game was lost. (An obvious causal relation is suggested, but the structure of the sentence obscures it. In your rewriting, make the main clause into the subordinate clause.)

3. As I grew wiser, the years passed. (Again the obvious causal relation is obscured.)

4. After Joe went to Europe, the war began. (Put the "main thought" into the subordinate clause. Why?)

5. He had almost reached Gainesville when he saw the tornado that struck the town and killed two hundred people. (The first two clauses, *he . . . tornado,* state that two things happened about the same time; the third clause, *that . . . people,* has nothing to do with this temporal relation. The fault will remain if the first clause is subordinated and the second made independent. Make the third clause a separate sentence.)

Exercise three. The following are typical "stringy" sentences. Rewrite them according to the instructions given.

1. My back porch was rotten, and I complained to the landlord, and he talks a lot about improving the neighborhood, but he refused to make the repairs. (Subordinate the first clause, making it the object of *complained.* Use *although* to introduce the clause *he . . . neighborhood,* and omit *but.* Punctuate your revision as two sentences.)

2. Professor Pate is only an English teacher, and he drives a Cadillac, and I don't see how he does it. (Two of the three main clauses make statements which are not normally true of the same person. Either [a] coordinate these two clauses, using *but* as the conjunction, or [b] introduce the first of them by *though.* Make the remaining independent clause a separate sentence. Does [a] produce a meaning notably different from that produced by [b]?)

3. The student applied for admission early in the summer, and we had a vacancy, and so the student was admitted without delay. (More than one revision is possible. The first two clauses can be introduced by *since;* the first clause can be made a separate sentence while the second is introduced by *since;* etc. Note that *he* should be substituted for the second occurrence of *the student.*)

4. The clerk was surprised, and I repeated my story, and she still didn't

believe it. (Is it possible to say which clause contains the "main thought"? How would you rewrite the sentence to make the clerk's surprise the cause of the repetition? What seems to be the logical relation between the repetition and the clerk's disbelief? How would you express that relation?)

5. It began to rain, and the boys went in the house, and pretty soon the sun came out again. (Which of the three clauses might best be introduced by *when?* Which might best be made a separate sentence?)

Exercise four. Study the following passages.

1. I do not remember that I ever thought about being educated at all. I thought of getting through school. This, as I recall it, was a business of passing examinations and meeting requirements, all of which were meaningless to me but presumably had some meaning to those who had me in their power. I have no doubt that the Latin and Greek I studied did me good. All I can say is that I was not aware of it at the time. Nor did I have any idea of the particular kind of good it was intended to do me. Since I had got the habit of reading at home, I was perfectly willing to read anything anybody gave me. Apart from a few plays of Shakespeare nobody gave me anything good to read until I was a sophomore in college. Then I was allowed to examine the grammar and philology of the *Apology* of Socrates in a Greek course. And since I had had an unusual amount of German, I was permitted to study *Faust.*

My father once happened to remark to me that he had never liked mathematics. Since I admired my father very much, it became a point of honor with me not to like mathematics either. I finally squeezed through Solid Geometry. But when, at the age of sixteen, I entered Oberlin College, I found that the authorities felt that one hard course was all anybody ought to be asked to carry. You could take either mathematics or Greek. Of course if you took Greek you were allowed to drop Latin. I did not hesitate a moment. Languages were pie for me. It would have been unfilial to take mathematics. I took Greek, and have never seen a mathematics book since. I have been permitted to glory in the possession of an unmathematical mind.

My scientific attainments were of the same order. I had a course in physics in prep school. Every Oberlin student had to take one course in science, because every Oberlin student had to take one course in everything—in everything, that is, except Greek and mathematics. After I had blown up all the retorts in the chemistry laboratory doing the Marsh test for arsenic, the chemistry teacher was glad to give me a passing grade and let me go.

My philosophical attainments were such as may be derived from a ten weeks' course in the History of Philosophy. I do not remember anything about the course except that the book was green and that it contained pictures of Plato and Aristotle. I learned later that the pictures were wholly imaginary representations of these writers. I have some reason to believe that the contents of the book bore the same relation to their doctrines.

So I arrived at the age of eighteen and the end of my sophomore year. My formal education had given me no understanding of science, mathematics, or philosophy. It had added almost nothing to my knowledge of literature. I had some facility with languages, but today I cannot read Greek or Latin except by guesswork. What is perhaps more important, I had no idea what I was doing or why. My father was a minister and a professor. The sons of ministers and the sons of professors were supposed to go to college. College was a lot of courses. You toiled your way through those which were required and for the rest wandered around taking those that seemed most entertaining. The days of the week and the hours of the day at which courses were offered were perhaps the most important factor in determining the student's course of study.[7]

2. . . . I believe in personal relationships. Starting from them, I get a little order into the contemporary chaos. One must be fond of people and trust them if one is not to make a mess of life, and it is therefore essential that they should not let one down. They often do. The moral of which is that I must, myself, be as reliable as possible, and this I try to be. But reliability is not a matter of contract—that is the main difference between the world of personal relationships and the world of business relationships. It is a matter for the heart, which signs no documents. In other words, reliability is impossible unless there is a natural warmth. Most men possess this warmth, though they often have bad luck and get chilled. Most of them, even when they are politicians, *want* to keep faith. And one can, at all events, show one's own little light here, one's own poor little trembling flame, with the knowledge that it is not the only light that is shining in the darkness, and not the only one which the darkness does not comprehend. Personal relations are despised today. They are regarded as bourgeois luxuries, as products of a time of fair weather which is now past, and we are urged to get rid of them, and to dedicate ourselves to some movement or cause instead. I hate the idea of causes, and if I had to choose between betraying my country and betraying my friend, I hope I should have the guts to betray my country. Such a choice may scandalise the modern reader, and he may stretch out his patriotic hand to the telephone at once and ring up the police. It would not have shocked Dante, though. Dante places Brutus and Cassius in the lowest circle of Hell because they had chosen to betray their friend Julius Caesar rather than their country Rome. Probably one will not be asked to make such an agonizing choice. Still, there lies at the back of every creed something terrible and hard for which the worshipper may one day be required to suffer, and there is even a terror and a hardness in this creed of personal relationships,

urbane and mild though it sounds. Love and loyalty to an individual can run counter to the claims of the State. When they do—down with the State, say I, which means that the State would down me.[8]

In the clear and lively first passage, ideas are strung together like bright beads. The style seems direct and uninvolved but not commonplace, not fancy but not casual; and at least in this short passage, it does not become monotonous. How does the clause structure of the sentences help give this impression of smart simplicity? In particular, are the sentences long or short? Are they mainly simple and complex, or are compound and compound-complex sentences also freely used? Are periods (and presumably the terminal $/\searrow/$) ever used to separate what might have been two independent clauses within a single sentence? Do any of the short complex sentences turn out, on examination, to be more involved than they looked at first? Note that clause structure is only one element in the style of the passage; other features, for example, include the striking rarity of adjectives and the simplicity of the semicolloquial vocabulary.

The second passage is just as full of life as the first, more various and subtle without loss of clear conviction, not so smart and shiny but more deeply satisfying. To this impression, style in thought contributes more than style in language, and (as we have insisted) style in language is much more than the clause structure of sentences. Yet clause structure, in this passage, is not negligible. Are very short, grammatically simple sentences used for any particular purpose? Are any sentence fragments punctuated as complete sentences? If so, can you suggest any reason for their use? Are compound and compound-complex sentences used more or less freely than in the first passage? Does the length of the sentences vary more or less widely than in the first passage?

❧ (2) Order of sentence elements

Within the different sentence types, the *order* of the clauses may or may not have any great importance for the content. The following sentences are indistinguishable in their meaning, and the choice among them would have to be made on other grounds:

> When the explosion was heard, the crowd in the street took shelter in the courthouse.

> The crowd in the street, when the explosion was heard, took shelter in the courthouse.

> The crowd in the street took shelter in the courthouse when the explosion was heard.

[8] From "What I Believe," copyright, 1939, by E. M. Forster. Reprinted from *Two Cheers for Democracy* by E. M. Forster by permission of Harcourt, Brace and Company, Inc. By permission also of Edward Arnold, Ltd.

That meaning is not involved does not mean that no choice is to be made. The sentences produce different effects, if only because the second, in which the subordinate clause splits the main subject-predicate combination, is more remote from casual speech than the other two. Very frequently, moreover, a change in the position of a clause will cause a change, sometimes a catastrophic change, in the meaning of a sentence. Here is a simple example, if any is needed:

> When he was in Chicago, he learned that he could be happy.
> He learned that he could be happy when he was in Chicago.
> He learned that when he was in Chicago he could be happy.

Sentences of this sort, where the problem of order is almost entirely a problem of the intended meaning, do not much concern us in a discussion of style in language; but we *are* concerned with the whole range of sentences in which decisions about the order of clauses affect meaning less exclusively.

PLACING OF NOMINAL AND ADJECTIVAL CLAUSES. In the placing of nominal clauses, we have some choice, but no great deal. Sentences with nominal clauses for their subjects, for example, can be translated by sentences introduced by *it is:*

> That cigarettes are harmful to the lungs is undeniable.
> It is undeniable that cigarettes are harmful to the lungs.

Similarly, nominal clauses used as objects may precede both the subject and the verbal of the main clause, or they may follow the verbal:

> Where it is I don't know.
> I don't know where it is.

The relatively fixed orders, however, of English subjects, predicates, and complements do not leave much room for stylistic manipulation of the position of nominal clauses; and adjectival clauses are even less freely movable, since they regularly follow their nominals:

> The fight was won in the seventh round.
> The fight that brought him the championship was won in the seventh round.

Here the adjectival clause *that brought him the championship* is typically fixed in its position after the nominal *fight*.

Indeed, the only important stylistic question which arises in the placing of adjectival clauses is not whether they shall follow their nominals, but whether or not they shall follow their nominals immediately, as in the first of the following pair of sentences:

The book which I valued most of all is lost.

The book is lost which I valued most of all.

Occasionally, when an element which separates a nominal and its following adjectival clause contains a nominal within itself, there may be difficulty in identifying the antecedent of the relative. If the two nominals belong to different substitution classes, the identity of the antecedent will be clear:

There are not many men in the dormitories who have their own furniture.

In this sentence, *men* and not *dormitories* is the antecedent of *who,* since the relative with *dormitories* would be *which* or *that.* Again, if the two nominals differ in number, the verb in the relative clause may point to one or the other as its antecedent:

He was given the one room in all the dormitories which was least suitable for quiet study.

Here the singular number of *room* and *was* rules out *dormitories* as a possible antecedent of *which.* When such signs are lacking, however, the sentence will be ambiguous:

The room in the dormitory which I like best was already taken.

Both *room* and *dormitory* occur with *which;* and *room, dormitory,* and *was* are all singular. The difficulty in removing the ambiguity is that a prepositional phrase like *in the dormitory* and a relative clause such as *which I like best* must both follow their nominals. Stylistic choice comes into play in the necessary recasting of the whole sentence, which might be given any one of several forms:

The dormitory room which I like best was already taken.

The room which I like best in the dormitory was already taken.

My favorite room in the dormitory was already taken.

In the dormitory the room which I like best was already taken.

However the sentence may be revised, *dormitory* cannot be allowed to stand between *room* and *which.*

PLACING OF ADVERBIAL CLAUSES. Although there is not much freedom of choice in the placing of nominal and adjectival clauses, the adverbial clause, as we have seen, is rather freely movable. In general, it can stand initially, medially, or finally with respect to its main clause:

> When he saw what it was, the man was angry; the woman was frightened.
>
> The man, when he saw what it was, was angry; the woman was frightened.
>
> The man was angry when he saw what it was; the woman was frightened.

Complete statement of the more detailed limitations on the position of adverbial clauses would be long and difficult. They can stand after complete subjects but are not so common after pronoun subjects as they are after other nominal subjects. Though we might say,

> He, as you know, is a charlatan,

we would hardly do so unless we wanted to slow the pace of the sentence and to emphasize *he*. Adverbial clauses can also stand after the verbal, but they rarely interrupt the sequences of verbal forms which we described in the grammar (pp. 106–108). The following sentence would be rather awkward:

> Mr. Bradbottle had, when he received the message, been disappointed.

Adverbial clauses, finally, can stand after any complement, but not always without a sense of strain. In real speech, we would avoid ugly made-up examples like

> I told him, after I had warned him, this.

We would probably not even make up bad examples in which adverbial clauses were placed in certain other positions. So, if we should put one between a determiner and the following nominal or between a preposition and the following nominal, the result would simply not be English:

> You will like the when you meet him instructor.
>
> He lived in when he was a young man Chicago.

Nobody talks or writes like that.

Not only clauses, of course, can occupy more than one position. Whole sentences can obviously stand in various sequences, and we have seen in the grammar that certain sentence elements smaller than clauses can also be ranged in various orders. Of the stylistic consequences of these facts, two are particularly notable. The first is that we can choose, in arranging the content of our discourse, between climax, anticlimax, and less calculated orders which are neither. This choice, which has more to do with thought than with language, operates on all levels of organization, from the constituents of single sentences up to the chapters of a book. The second consequence is that we can choose, on the level of the sentence, between the loose and periodic arrangements, which we have defined partly in semantic and partly in formal terms.

CLIMAX AND ANTICLIMAX. Since climax and anticlimax are primarily patterns of thought, we will say little about them. Like all other elements of style, they have stylistic significance, only because they are not compulsory; they contrast with one another and with the more casual patterns which we are likely to use in ordinary conversation. Climax is less restricted in its uses than anticlimax. Anticlimax is humorous or satirical, a good means of knocking the stuffing out of a stuffed shirt:

> He picked up his bat, strode to the plate, and frowned savagely at the pitcher. Then he struck out.
>
> No other man has known so many of the great thinkers of the age: Dewey, Russell, Einstein, Casey Stengel.
>
> This institution has what it takes to be a great university: its endowment is rich, its library is magnificent, its faculty is distinguished—and its tackles are All-Americans.

Climax, on the other hand, may be very funny, or it may be very serious. It occurs in a wide variety of styles, but always as a means to emphasis, intensity, the heightening of whatever impression is desired:

> I came, I saw, I conquered.
>
> And for the support of this Declaration, with a firm reliance on the Protection of Divine Providence, we mutually pledge to each other our Lives, our Fortunes, and our sacred Honor.
>
> For four long years the stalwart farmers of the great state of Georgia have manfully endured a series of disasters: frost and heat, drought and flood, high costs, low prices, and a Republican administration.

Neither climax nor anticlimax should be much used in writing that is intended to seem quite easy and unstudied.

THE PERIODIC SENTENCE. The periodic sentence is also more common in writing styles than in everyday talk, and has been so for a long time. Two eighteenth-century examples will clearly show the difference between the more literary periodic sentence and the more colloquial loose sentence. A traveler in Scotland, describing some inconveniences of his accommodations there, wrote in a letter:

> When we were taken upstairs, a dirty fellow bounced out of the bed on which one of us was to lie.

Later, Samuel Johnson made a book about his journey and described the same incident in a very different style:

Out of one of the beds on which we were to repose started up, at our entrance, a man black as a Cyclops from the forge. Between these two sentences, there are notable differences in the choice of words: *bounced out* in the first has become *started up* in the second, and the *dirty fellow* has been fitted out with a simile (*a man black as a Cyclops from the forge*). For our immediate purpose, however, the more relevant differences are the differences in word order. In the first sentence, the subject of the main clause precedes the verbal (*a dirty fellow bounced*); in the second, the verbal, *started up*, precedes the subject, *man*. The bed has also been moved around so that the prepositional phrase and adjectival clause which end the first sentence now stand initially. The second sentence thus ends with the complete subject of its main clause. The rearrangement has changed the loose sentence, with its main idea stated fairly early and qualified later, into a periodic sentence, whose full meaning is kept up in the air as long as possible.

To judge this revision as good or bad would presuppose a study of the context of each sentence, but a few general comments on the periodic arrangement are still possible. As we have said, it is more common in writing styles than in plain talk. Its frequent use in conversation, therefore, would be as misguided as the old advice that we should always talk in complete sentences; but the literary quality of a device is no argument against its use in literature. Since a periodic sentence is an excellent means of emphasizing a fact or an idea, it can serve very well to highlight an important statement, like the topic sentence of a paragraph or the punch line of a concluding summary. It can also be very tiresome or distracting if it is used too freely or if it stands out too sharply from its context.

Exercise one. Revise each of the following sentences in several different ways, but be sure that each revision makes the sentence unambiguous.
1. The cause of the accident that he described was this.
2. The children of preachers whom I have taught have been very likable.
3. The money in the bank that you'll inherit will never support your family.
4. Jones writes essays about books that please everyone.
5. She paid a price for a dress that shocked me.
Could the ambiguity in any of these sentences be removed by the marking of intonation?

Exercise two. In each of the following sentences, identify the adverbial clauses. Move each adverbial clause around to occupy as many different positions as it can. Comment on the effect of each shift.

1. After the armistice was signed, poison gas was outlawed as a brutal and inhuman weapon.
2. When he heard this news, my father said that the weapon was only too human.
3. Because he was willing to take unfair advantages, he was a great success in student politics.
4. He was, if I am to describe him properly, a liar and a coward and a thief.
5. Although American readers are chiefly interested in comic books, they would resent a suggestion that they have less brains than earwax.

Exercise three. Rewrite the following sentences to make them periodic.

1. They gave him a hundred-dollar raise after he had taught for twenty-five years, had served on innumerable committees, and had published more than any of his colleagues.
2. I have only contempt for such statements and for the attitudes that prompt them.
3. The good constable staggered out of the tavern, waving a half-filled bottle and shouting a bawdy song.
4. That novel is poor, nasty, brutish, and short, like man's life in the state of nature.
5. The juvenile hoodlum, who is the protagonist of dozens of novels and the subject of countless lectures and dissertations, is the real folk hero of the western world.

❧ (3) Balance, parallelism, and antithesis

We will complete our remarks on sentences and clauses as structural elements of style by making some remarks on balance, parallelism, and antithesis. By parallelism we shall mean similarity of grammatical structures; by balance we shall mean similarity of grammatical structures expressing similar ideas; and by antithesis we shall mean similarity of grammatical structures expressing opposed ideas. The similarity and opposition of ideas which distinguish balance from antithesis are of course created by the words that compose the grammatical structures; for since the structures are by definition similar, a basic likeness of structural ideas must underlie both the opposition of antithesis and the similarity of balance.

The simplest forms of balance and parallelism, as we have defined them, can hardly be avoided by speakers of English. All coordinate constructions are parallel, and the language provides special markers of parallelism in forms like *both . . . and, either . . . or,* and *neither . . . nor.* With the inevitable, however, we are no more concerned in a discussion of style as linguistic choice than we are with the simple blunders which are commonly labeled as unnecessary shifts or faulty parallelism.

Our subjects are the balance and antithesis which speakers and writers deliberately create.

THEIR ELEMENTS AND EXTENT. The elements of balance and antithesis may be sentences, clauses, or parts of clauses (including, naturally, stress patterns and intonation patterns), and the grammatical parallelism involved may be so slight that it pairs only two words or so extensive that each form in one of the balanced or antithetical constructions has its grammatical equivalent in the other. In certain kinds of verse, the parallelism between sentences can approach completeness, as in the following lines by Alexander Pope:

> Steel could the labour of the gods destroy,
> And strike to dust th' imperial towers of Troy;
> Steel could the works of mortal pride confound
> And hew triumphal arches to the ground.

The interest of the example lies not only in the relatively precise balance of the first couplet against the second but also in the punctuation. If we ask how many sentences the four lines contain, we will get one answer in terms of speech and another in terms of marks on paper. A sentence ends, according to the definition in our grammar, with the word *Troy;* but if we judge by punctuation, there is only one sentence, ending with the period after *ground.* Like the parallelism between the couplets, the semicolon after the first and the period after the second help to indicate a semantic unity; but grammatically each couplet is a separate sentence. In other words, it is impossible to establish an exact correspondence between punctuation and linguistic form. Punctuation belongs to writing and can be learned only by the study of writing, so that the verses we have quoted reinforce our earlier statement: nobody ever learned to write without reading.

Exact parallelism is not so common in most prose as it is in the kind of verse which we have quoted, but even in prose some fairly elaborate specimens can be found, as in the following stylistic discussion:

> They [certain prefaces] have not the formality of a settled style, in which the first half of the sentence betrays the other. The clauses are never balanced, nor the periods modelled; every word seems to drop by chance, though it falls into its proper place. Nothing is cold or languid; the whole is airy, animated, and vigorous; what is little, is gay; what is great is splendid.

CHANGING TASTE. To most modern readers, this sort of thing is a little too much. The passage is certainly clear and emphatic, and the writer's skill in expressing his balanced or opposed ideas in parallel forms gives some pleasure in itself; but the vigor of these sentences is certainly not an airy vigor, and no word seems to drop by chance, though all are properly placed.

Many writers today, if they make two sentences elaborately parallel, are likely to qualify the effect by some means, perhaps by a contrast between the elaboration of the grammar and the colloquial tone of the vocabulary or between the high-flown expression and the humble content. Here is a paragraph from a recent description of a drive through New England:

> Stay with me on 62 and it will take you into Concord. As I say, it was a delicious evening. The snake had come forth to die in a bloody S on the highway, the wheel upon its head, its bowels flat now and exposed. The turtle had come up too to cross the road and die in the attempt, its hard shell smashed under the rubber blow, its intestinal yearning (for the other side of the road) forever squashed. There was a sign by the wayside which announced that the road had a "cotton surface." You wouldn't know what that is, but neither, for that matter, did I. There is a cryptic ingredient in many of our modern improvements—we are awed and pleased without knowing quite what we are enjoying. It is something to be traveling on a road with a cotton surface.[9]

The sentences about the snake and the turtle are closely parallel, but the writer is half teasing. Though he has serious things to say, he will not say them stuffily.

MODERATION. The danger of stuffiness may be less when the parallelism does not extend so far as sentences but is limited to clauses or their parts. Nothing is stuffier than self-admiration in a political discussion, yet one modern writer has managed to give two cheers for democracy without sounding like a commissar or a congressman. The following paragraph is not one of his most distinguished, but it does illustrate some quieter uses of balance and antithesis rather well:

> I believe in aristocracy, though—if that is the right word, and if a democrat may use it. Not an aristocracy of power, based upon rank and influence, but an aristocracy of the sensitive,

[9] From "Walden" by E. B. White, in *One Man's Meat* (New York: Harper & Brothers, 1942). Copyright, 1939, by E. B. White.

the considerate and the plucky. Its members are to be found in all nations and classes, and all through the ages, and there is a secret understanding between them when they meet. They represent the true human tradition, the one permanent victory of our queer race over cruelty and chaos. Thousands of them perish in obscurity, a few are great names. They are sensitive for others as well as for themselves, they are considerate without being fussy, their pluck is not swankiness but the power to endure, and they can take a joke.[10]

The last four clauses show the possibility of using balance and antithesis without monotony. They are all parallel in meaning, since they all state qualities of the "aristocracy," and the subject of three of them is *they;* but in the third clause of the four, the subject is not *they* but one of *their* qualities. Again, the fourth clause breaks the pattern of internal opposition which has been established in the first three, where qualities which the aristocrats do have are set off against qualities which they lack. Even the individual oppositions between virtues and their corresponding vices are expressed in grammatical forms which vary from clause to clause: *for others, for themselves; considerate, fussy; swankiness, the power to endure.*

SUMMARY. To speak of a contrast between virtues and vices is, of course, to speak of matter as well as manner. Although grammatical parallelism can be discussed in purely formal terms, the definitions themselves of balance and antithesis involve both content and expression, and our remarks on these devices have plainly not been limited to style in language. Indeed, in so far as balance and antithesis depend on the choice of particular words as well as the choice of particular structures, our remarks have not even been limited to structural elements of style. This is as it should be. Matter and manner *are* separable; structure *can* remain while words come and go; but the items that fit into grammatical structures are meaningful individual forms, and we choose both the single forms and the larger structures primarily to express meanings. "Style, that is, will be for us the manner of saying what is said, but we will recognize that there is style in thought as well as style in language; and if sometimes we must separate matter and manner in our studies, we must always be able to put them together again."

---

[10] From "What I Believe," copyright, 1939, by E. M. Forster. Reprinted from *Two Cheers for Democracy* by E. M. Forster by permission of Harcourt, Brace and Company, Inc. By permission also of Edward Arnold, Ltd.

Exercise one. Study the uses of balance, parallelism, and antithesis in the following excerpts.

1. Is not a Patron, my Lord, one who looks with unconcern on a man struggling for life in the water, and, when he has reached ground, encumbers him with help? The notice which you have been pleased to take of my labours, had it been early, had it been kind; but it has been delayed till I am indifferent, and cannot enjoy it; till I am solitary, and cannot impart it; till I am known, and do not want it. I hope it is no very cynical asperity not to confess obligations where no benefit has been received, or to be unwilling that the Publick should consider me as owing that to a Patron, which Providence has enabled me to do for myself.

2. My paramount object in this struggle is to save the Union, and is not either to save or destroy slavery. If I could save the Union without freeing any slave, I would do it; and if I could do it by freeing all the slaves, I would do it; and if I could save it by freeing some and leaving others alone, I would also do that.

3. There is no faith, and no stoicism, and no philosophy, that a mortal man can possibly evoke, which will stand the final test in a real impassioned onset of Life and Passion upon him. Faith and philosophy are air, but events are brass.

4. I decline to accept the end of man. It is easy enough to say that man is immortal simply because he will endure: that when the last ding-dong of doom has clanged and faded from the last worthless rock hanging tideless in the last red and dying evening, that even then there will still be one more sound: that of his puny inexhaustible voice, still talking. I refuse to accept this. I believe that man will not merely endure: he will prevail. He is immortal, not because he alone among creatures has an inexhaustible voice, but because he has a soul, a spirit capable of compassion and sacrifice and endurance. The poet's, the writer's, duty is to write about these things. It is his privilege to help man endure by lifting his heart, by reminding him of the courage and honor and hope and pride and compassion and pity and sacrifice which have been the glory of his past. The poet's voice need not merely be the record of man, it can be one of the props, the pillars to help him endure and prevail.[11]

Some structural elements of style: the parts of clauses

A discussion of the parts of clauses as elements of style is easily organized. The essential parts of a clause, we have said, are a subject and a

[11] From "Speech of Acceptance Upon the Award of the Nobel Prize for Literature" by William Faulkner, in *The Faulkner Reader* (New York: Random House, Inc., 1954).

predicate. The subject will be a nominal, the predicate a verbal, and both may be expanded or unexpanded. The topics of our stylistic discussion will therefore be the relative order of subject, predicate, and their parts; the nature of the simple subject; the nature of the simple predicate; and the nature and extent of the expansion of both.

❧ Varying the order of subjects and predicates

The basic patterns of English word order have been described or exemplified in the grammar. Precisely because these patterns are familiar, any departure from them is likely to produce some special effect; and because the familiar patterns are themselves rather varied, they also afford some opportunity for stylistic choice. The order subject-verbal-complement, for example, is so common in statements that departures from it draw special attention. Fifty years ago, Henry Adams wrote the following sentence to state his puzzlement about the dynamo and the relation between electric power and boiling steam:

> No more relation could he discover between the steam and the electric current than between the Cross and the cathedral.

In the topic sentence of a paragraph describing his attempt to think his way through the difficulty, the same old man continued:

> Here opened another totally new education, which promised to be by far the most hazardous of all.

The reversal of the normal order of subject, verbal, and complement, as in the first sentence, or of subject and verbal, as in the second, calls attention to itself and so to the meanings which the linguistic forms express; yet the warning which we have suggested is almost too obvious to be valuable. Even in writing styles, tinkering with the commoner orders of subject, verbal, and complement strikes a good many readers as an extreme and somewhat crude device, which must have some special reason. Thus the second sentence which we have quoted is at least better than some of its possible revisions, like putting *opened* at the end, where it would come in very awkwardly after the long relative clause:

> Here another totally new education, which promised to be by far the most hazardous of all, opened.

Again, the emphasis on the novelty of the experience would be lost if the sentence were made to read:

> Another totally new education opened here, which promised to be by far the most hazardous of all.

The fact remains that the prose of which our two sentences are examples is distinctly dated.

Less extreme departures from the common orders of subjects, predicates, and their parts are quite common. Sometimes they are less a stylistic device than an almost essential means to clarity, as when they are used to let the reader know what parts of a sentence go together. In the following sentence, the adverbial *delicately* separates *fingering* and its object *row* in a somewhat unusual way; but final position for *delicately* is the only other position that would clearly link *fingering* and *delicately* together:

He began fingering delicately a row of glistening dials.[12]

Final position is ruled out by the demands of rhythm and perhaps by the writer's wish to end his sentence strongly—the two causes which apparently account for the position of *was* in our next example:

Walter Mitty began to wonder what the other thing was his wife had told him to get.[13]

❧ Beginning and ending sentences

As a matter of fact, the advice is frequently given to begin and end sentences with strong or important constructions and to put such forms as interjected sentences and adverbials of transition in medial position. This is sometimes the practice of competent writers:

The refrain makes the commentary more explicit, more visibly dramatic, and renders quite plain, *as Hart Crane intimated,* the subjective character of the imagery throughout.[14]

The advice cannot be given as a general rule, however, since it is hard to say precisely what a "strong" construction is and since constant departures from the basic patterns of word order can very easily make prose seem stilted and unnatural. Probably it is better to say that particular care for the beginnings and ends of sentences is one way to cultivate a good style but that no one of the multiple demands on the writer can be given exclusive consideration. Whatever a strong construction may be, a subject would surely be an instance; yet a long series of sentences beginning with the subject of a main clause can be extremely tiresome. A more likely rule for general application would be that *aimless* choice among established patterns of order or *aimless* departures from them are always

---

[12] James Thurber, *My World and Welcome to It* (New York: Harcourt, Brace and Company, Inc., 1942), p. 75.
[13] Thurber, *op. cit.,* p. 76.
[14] Allen Tate, "Narcissus as Narcissus," *Virginia Quarterly Review,* Winter, 1938.

bad. The writer should know the possibilities of his language and keep his wits about him as he asks the final question of each device: Does it work?

Exercise one. Rewrite the following sentences so that the clauses all show the subject-verbal-complement order. How is the effect of each sentence changed by the rewriting?

1. Except for one thing, I know all there is to know about you, and a singularly dreary, dolorous and distasteful store of information it is, too.[15]
2. Among the interesting plants observed by the Maguire expedition were trees, some of them five feet in diameter and seventy-five feet high.[16]
3. Crime in the United States has reached alarming proportions, and most alarming is the fact that so many of the criminals are young people.[17]
4. Not until the jury got to the 18 lesser awards did a West Coast artist finally score.[18]
5. Only in France and Italy can there be seen at close range in the Western world the fantastic, influential buildup that Russia has shrewdly given herself as the international champion of peace.[19]
6. So innocent was she, and ignorant of academic snobbery, that she did not even realize that Mrs. Dean was now her determined foe.
7. Near them stood a dark stranger, who moved nearer still as their furtive talk went on.
8. Not only would the festival be continued next year, but it might well spread to Europe.[20]
9. In a twinkling, the fire severed telephone cables laid along the tunnel walls. Half of the city's long-distance circuits leading to the West and South were out. Gone were press-association wires, lines of three broadcasting companies, two coaxial TV cables.[21]
10. Small though the country is, it has two academies at which the art of hotelkeeping is taught.[22]

Exercise two. Would any of the following sentences be improved by beginning or ending them differently? If so, rewrite them.

1. Shallow-running lures are used, almost exclusively, during the spring and fall months while the fish are in shallow water.
2. He would have done very well in college if he had only tried, in my opinion.

[15] Thurber, *op. cit.*, p. 83.
[16] *The New Yorker*, June 4, 1955, p. 24.
[17] *Reader's Digest*, June 1955, p. 25.
[18] *Time*, July 18, 1955, p. 73.
[19] *The New Yorker*, June 4, 1955, p. 103.
[20] *Time*, July 25, 1955, p. 65.
[21] *Reader's Digest*, July 1955, p. 160.
[22] *The New Yorker*, August 13, 1955, p. 29.

3. However, if we are to give an accurate definition, we must consider the word in its present use.
4. Nobody has ever known who the man who put the overalls in Mrs. Murphy's chowder was.
5. Behind him the soldier left the one girl in the world whom he had ever loved.
6. That the behavior of most teen-agers would disgrace a self-respecting anthropoid is not insignificant perhaps.
7. The problem is not difficult of meeting and learning to live with new friends.
8. With his own hands he made the elegant little mechanical toys that the children liked best for them.
9. Every college student has, at one time or another, suffered from home-sickness.
10. Libel laws are more effective now though.

❧ Choice of forms for subjects

As we saw in the grammar, a good many different forms can be used as simple subjects or indeed in any of the nominal positions. Another source of variety in style is this choice among nouns, pronouns, adjectives, in-finitives, participles, uninflected words, phrases, or clauses; and under most of these heads, further choices are possible. For example, there are important distinctions, in English, between the familiar nouns which we use in everyday life from our very childhood and the bookish nouns which we pick up as we get educated. To the first group belong nouns like *cook, face, house, law,* and *love;* to the second belong such very different nouns as *delicacy, appendix, residence, legislation,* and *libido.*

"GOOD ANGLO-SAXON." The differences between the two groups cannot be explained by saying that the first are native English words ("good Anglo-Saxon") and the second are foreign-learned words. As a matter of fact, *cook, face,* and *law* all came into English from foreign languages, though to native speakers they seem about as English as any words could be. They seem English because very few of us know anything much about the history of our language before we ourselves entered the community of English-speaking people; but all of us do have a rich personal experience of words and their behavior. From this experience, we know that *law* and *love* carry with them the associations that they have acquired in a dif-ferent set of contexts from those of *legislation* and *libido;* we know that *love* belongs to one kind of word family (*love, lovely, loveliness,* etc.) and *legislation* to another (*legislate, legislation, legislator, legislature*).

We can draw on these contrasting associations and contrasting patterns of word formation when we set out to improve our style.

CONSISTENCY. There is, however, some danger in the very richness of our stylistic resources. If we are not likely to have much trouble with little things like the variant plurals of some of our bookish words (*indexes, indices; funguses, fungi*), we *are* liable to be confused by the variety of forms which can fill the nominal positions in English sentences, and the result is the faulty parallelism which we have discussed elsewhere:

> I advocate *the abolition of investigating committees* and *that persons slandered by personal opinions be granted the right to sue the slanderer*.[23]

We can put a noun, like *abolition*, in a nominal position, or we can put a clause there (*that . . . slanderer*); but when we are faced with two or three such choices together, we ought not to change our minds at will, particularly if we indicate, by a coordinating conjunction, that the items in our series are of the same kind.

EXPANDED AND OVEREXPANDED NOMINALS. The preceding example illustrates another kind of choice that we must make in forming the subjects of our sentences or in filling other nominal positions: the choice of elements by which the nominal constructions may be expanded. In the example, the noun *abolition* is accompanied by a determiner and a prepositional phrase, and the noun *persons* is followed by the participial phrase *slandered by personal opinions*. These phrases follow their nouns, as usual; the determiner *the* and the adjectival *personal* precede theirs; and we are thus reminded that predeterminers, determiners, and post-determiners precede their nominals, which in turn are followed by adjectival clauses, most adjectival phrases, and most appositives. All these possibilities give the writer ample opportunity to control and vary his style.

He should remember, as he makes his choices, that certain expansions of his nominals are likely to clog the movement of his prose, to make it seem fussy and overelaborate, and to hinder the reader's comprehension. In some of the styles which have been made popular by cheap journalism, the number of clauses is held to a minimum, but the few subjects and predicates that do occur are greatly expanded, often by adjectivals. The result is a lush, flabby, overstuffed prose. Here are some casually chosen specimens:

> The quick arrests of a rapist and a murderer recently were the
> result of observant cabbies spotting suspects described to

---

[23] *Chicago Sun-Times,* September 18, 1955.

them over their radios a few minutes after the crimes were committed.[24]

(This is a complex sentence with only two predicates, the equational verb *were* and the passive *were committed*. Note the expansion of the predicate nominative in the main clause.)

It is a perfect illusion of the African wild, achieved by cunningly engineered moats to separate the lions from their prey and the whole fabulous scene from the strollers watching it.[25]

(This is a simple sentence. Except for the first two words, the whole thing is one sprawling nominal. Without participles, such fabulous expansion would probably be impossible.)

Outside the hotel squatted the usual little group of swarthy, turbaned men surrounded by disturbing bags, ready with their bulb-shaped oboe-toned pipes to charm their swaying cobras, or eager to put on a battle between a snake and one of the red-eyed, badger-gray mongooses which clung about them like cats.[26]

(Again, a bulb-shaped, disturbing bag of a simple sentence is devoted almost wholly to the gaudy expansion of a single nominal.)

A hybrid population, "spreading rapidly over a new continent," created "a political and social climate favorable to invention and innovation, to the growth of individual enterprise, to the willingness to take risks and invest capital." [27]

Further criticism of these sentences is unnecessary. Besides their tired diction, they all share one fault: overexpanded nominals. The life and movement of a sentence are in its subject-predicate combinations, and if there are too few of these to shift the bulk of the nominals, the sentence does not move. In most exposition, at least, and in most argument, that is a fault.

Exercise three. Of the following ten words, which seem to you the most homely and familiar?

1. abide	3. act	5. adder	7. age	9. air
2. allay	4. amaze	6. angel	8. bane	10. bang

Which, would you guess, came into English from foreign languages? Check your guess by a good dictionary.

[24] *Reader's Digest*, July 1955, p. 80.
[25] *Reader's Digest*, July 1955, p. 133.
[26] *Reader's Digest*, August 1955, p. 174.
[27] *Reader's Digest*, August 1955, p. 72.

Exercise four. Using derivational suffixes, list as many words as you can which contain the noun *fear*. Similarly, list as many words as you can which contain the noun *fate*. Are there any suffixes which occur with both nouns? Are there any which occur with one but not the other? Does the primary stress shift its position in the words of either list? In which list do you find the longest series of suffixes within any one word?

Exercise five. Rewrite the first sentence which was quoted in the next to last paragraph. Among other changes, make *rapist* and *murderer* the subjects of *were arrested,* turn *the result of* into *because,* and change *spotting* to *spotted* (past tense). Then attempt your own similar rewritings of the following sentences. Be sure to increase the number of clauses even if you have to make two sentences of one.

1. A great party-boy and a confirmed habitué of the shadier bright spots, Gus Gooch was still the Amerindian League's most valuable player in 1955, leading the circuit in hits, runs, and runs batted in, stealing sixteen bases, and convulsing delighted crowds with the wildest antics since the days of Gomez.
2. Scorned by the slick-paper devotees of the fast buck, misunderstood by the increasingly shabby and pedantic professional custodians of the humanistic tradition, and humiliated by his inevitable dependence on the uncertain patronage of eccentric dowagers, the serious literary artist in Chicago is a frustrated and lonely man, with little but pride in his work and consciousness of his worth to sustain him in the unending struggle against Midwestern philistines.
3. Tall, spare, and somber, the conscious representative of the finest Philadelphia traditions, Havermore's ace historian took with him into the Deep South a settled determination to replace training by education, competence by understanding, and knowledge by wisdom, as well as a small but devoted and effective following of teachers and students, the vanguard of his crusade for the New Conservatism in education.

❧ Choice of forms for predicates

To call either the simple subject or the simple predicate the heart of an English sentence is impossible. Both are essential to any sentence or any clause. The choice, however, of the verbals that constitute a simple predicate is among the most important that the writer must make, since it controls the development of the rest of the sentence. The same constructions are not possible after transitive and intransitive verbals, factitive verbals and equational verbals, verbals in the so-called active voice and verbals in the so-called passive voice.

ACTIVE AND PASSIVE. The most important of these distinctions stylistically is that between the active and the passive, between forms like *bites* and forms like *is bitten*. Often a sentence is briefer and less complicated if the active is used than it would be if the verbal were made passive. *The dog bit the man* is shorter and simpler than *The man was bitten by the dog*. A further argument for the familiar instructions to "worship the active voice" is that the instructions really mean to choose active forms of transitive verbals and so to build sentences on the pattern subject-verbal-object, roughly actor-action-goal. In contrast, sentences with passive verbals will have the pattern subject-verbal, goal-action; and sentences with equational verbals are likely to identify two things (*That dog is the culprit*) or to specify a quality of something (*Man is mortal*). To choose the active voice is thus in many cases to express direct action directly.

That is all very well provided the direct expression of direct action serves the writer's purpose, but once more the familiar rule of thumb is subject to several qualifications. Frequently we have no reason to say who is doing something; we need only to say that something is being done. For example, if a house is being built on the next corner and if that is the fact we are interested in, we will say *A house is being built,* because to say *Someone is building a house* will suggest unnecessary questions about the builder. English, moreover, has only a limited number of ways to say that something is done by people in general, not by anybody in particular, and some of these ways are not generally acceptable in writing styles. *One grows oranges in Florida* is impossible for most of us; *they grow oranges in Florida* may not suit a formal context; but *Oranges are grown in Florida* gets us off the hook. Finally, in any given sentence we must consider what goes before and what comes after. Our choice between two sentences like *The Duke of Wellington defeated Napoleon* and *Napoleon was defeated by the Duke of Wellington* will then be governed by the ease or difficulty of the transition which each makes possible.

CHOICES AMONG ADVERBIALS. When once we have chosen our verbal, we have also chosen the kind or kinds of expansion of which the simple predicate is capable. A factitive verbal will take two objects, an equational verbal will take a predicate nominative or predicate adjectival, a verbal in the passive will sometimes take no complement at all, etc. The choice of a verbal does not, however, determine the kind or the number of adverbial forms that we can use. We can use adverbial clauses, adverbial phrases, or one-word adverbials; we can use many or few of them; and we can place them in various positions. Since we have already made some remarks on most of these topics, we will here discuss only three small matters, all of them connected with the differences between speaking styles and writing styles.

CONTRACTIONS. The first is the matter of contractions, like *can't* and *don't*, which we will discuss here because so many of them involve special forms of the adverbial *not*. For example, when we put the verb *do* /dú:/ and the adverbial *not* /nát/ together under a single stress, we use a special form of each word; the /u:/ of /dú:/ becomes /o:/, the /a/ of /nát/ drops out, and we have /dó:nt/. The same sort of thing frequently happens in phrases which contain auxiliaries: *I'm going, you've gone, he'll go, we won't come back*. Not to use these contractions in plain talk would make us ridiculous, and to some extent they are conventionally used in the less formal writing styles; but a series of contractions can give as much discomfort to a reader who expects formality as the uncontracted forms would give to one's partner in conversation. Except for special effects, then, we should abide by the established customs.

ONLY. A second small matter which rouses disproportionately strong feelings is the placing of a few adverbials like *only*. They should be placed, we are often told, near or next to the forms with which they are logically to be taken, and some people will often pretend that they cannot understand sentences in which *only* and its fellow adverbials are not so placed. Genuine misunderstanding is of course very rare in writing and almost nonexistent in talk; our purist friends are quick to tell us that we have not said what we really mean, as they never could do unless our real meaning was perfectly clear. In writing, the context guides the reader, and in talk the stress patterns and intonation patterns guide the listener. Hearing the sentence

^{2}Hè + ^{3}ónlÿ^2→^{2}wânts + fîve + ^{3}dóllărs^1\

we would think it a little strange, but we would all know its meaning: "Nobody but him wants five dollars." Looking at the sentence as it is written in ordinary spelling, without indications of pitch and stress, we might conceivably have to choose among several meanings: (1) "Nobody but him wants five dollars"; (2) "He wants no more than five dollars"; (3) "The only thing he does to five dollars is to want it; he doesn't *have* it"; etc. All the same, our choice in most contexts would be automatic. We would choose the second meaning unless the context plainly indicated one of the other two.

Ambiguity due to the position of *only* and similar adverbials is therefore no great danger, though it is certainly possible and should generally be avoided in exposition and argument. Native speakers would hardly need to bother their heads about the problem if it were not for one fact: purists do bother about it, and a careful writer will not offend even a purist unnecessarily. With a certain cynicism, then, and in the full realization that petty word-catching has little or nothing to do with the cultivation of a good style, we would probably do well, when we notice an *only*, to put it near the word it "modifies."

"FLAT ADVERBS." The third and last problem that needs attention here is a reflection of the difficulties that we had when we set out, in our grammar, to define the adjective and the adverb, the adjectival and the adverbial. The relations among those classes are rather complicated. Some words which end in *-ly* are adjectives and not adverbs and are typically used as adjectivals (*cleanly* /klénlĭ/, *deadly*), other words in *-ly* are adjectives but are often used as adverbials (*kindly*), some adjectives without *-ly* are also used as adverbials (*fast*), and sometimes an adjective and its corresponding adverb can be used interchangeably in an adverbial position (*slow, slowly*). It is not surprising that different speakers handle these complications differently and that some speakers are troubled by the differences.

As usual, the points at issue are too small to justify the debate which has gone on around them. Shall we say *He talks loud* or *He talks loudly*, *He drove slow* or *He drove slowly?* And are the forms that we use when we talk acceptable in writing, or do writing styles demand one thing and talk another? We have already given a partial answer in the grammar. In talk, there can be no possible objection in sentences like these to the adverbials without *-ly*, which many excellent native speakers actually prefer as more natural and less prissy; and certainly in the less formal styles, the writer who carefully replaced *loud* by *loudly* may also seem timid or pedantic. *Loud* is not unexampled even in formal writing. We should repeat, however, that the forms with and without *-ly* are interchangeable only in certain positions. For instance, although we say *He drove slow*, we would not say *Slow he drove away* or *He drove slow away*, and *He drove away slowly* is not at all stuffy. The forms with *-ly* are probably the better choice for such positions in all writing styles; and in sentences like *He talks loud*, formality might justify (though it would not dictate) the substitution of *loudly*.

Exercise six. Review the definitions of the terms *transitive, intransitive, factitive, equational, active,* and *passive.* Make up sentences to illustrate each definition.

Exercise seven. In the first five of the sentences below, the underlined passive forms are effective; in the second five, they are not. Why?

1. Our fathers worked hard to get the kind of education which <u>has been given</u> free to us.
2. He <u>was caught</u> in the trap that he himself had set.
3. His next pass <u>was intercepted</u>.
4. When he <u>was asked</u> to retire, he forgot all about his age and refused to do it.
5. Most of the houses <u>are built</u> on the eastern slopes of hills, so that they <u>will be protected</u> from the afternoon sun.

1. On the third finger of her left hand, three diamond rings <u>were</u> always worn.
2. Venizelos tossed the ball to Korzybski, by whom Maturin <u>was thrown</u> out at the plate.
3. Although registration <u>is made</u> hopelessly inefficient by the new rules, no one questions them, since they were devised by the dean.
4. I <u>was congratulated</u> by all my friends, but they secretly wished that I had died in the cradle.
5. They <u>are</u> not <u>blamed</u> by me.

Exercise eight. Rewrite any of the following sentences which you think are made ineffective by the use of contractions, the placing of *only* and similar adverbials, or the use of adjectives in adverbial positions. Assume a moderately formal context of exposition or argument.

1. In those days, animals were only killed for sacrifices.
2. He always bowed very low when he spoke to the manager's wife.
3. In the simpler agrarian societies, those who don't work don't eat.
4. The women never precisely understood why the men liked camping.
5. In writing their introduction, the editors didn't sufficiently consider the principles and methods which Bartleby had recommended.
6. A good style can only be developed by constant reading of good books.
7. Most Americans believe that they must talk very loud to make the stupid foreigner understand.
8. Three students spelled five of the ten words wrong.
9. In that department, students must take special pains with their term papers, since they aren't required to write a thesis.
10. When his horse threw him, he was only embarrassed, not hurt.

Other structural elements of style

Having dealt, after a fashion, with sentences, clauses, and the parts of clauses, we must now go on to consider both the smallest units which enter into the structure of our language and certain larger units that students of language cannot tell us much about—units larger than the sentence. We must talk first, that is, about sounds and sound effects; and we must then conclude our discussion of the structural elements in linguistic style by examining some of the methods of sentence connection.

❧ Sounds and sound effects

Concerning sound and sound effects, there is an ancient tradition of description and prescription in which sense and nonsense are elaborately intermingled; but we will give here only the briefest of notes on a subject which after all is of relatively slight importance for exposition and argument. It would do us no good to catalogue some dozens of tricky sound patterns and give them Greek or Latin names, and it would do us actual harm to talk about the symbolic values of individual sounds, the shapes and colors of vowels, the ten most beautiful words in the language, the coo of /u:/ in *croon* and the roll of /o:/ in *tone*. Such talk is not an infallible sign of charlatanism, but it comes close to being one.

SUPERFIXES AND INTONATION PATTERNS. A few practical suggestions still can and should be made. The primary elements by which sound effects are produced are of course the sounds we described in the first chapter of our grammar, *not* marks on paper; and as we suggested by our very first example (*I came, I saw, I conquered*) and as we should all know from our experience of English poetry, stress patterns and intonation patterns are particularly important. To be sure, we want our prose to be prose. Nobody wants to keep stumbling over bits of unintended verse, because to do so leads his mind astray and makes him conscious that the careless writer had let his own mind quietly go to sleep. On the other hand, even in prose the controlled repetition of stress patterns and intonation patterns can be effective. Here is part of the very moving conclusion of a modern story:

> Snow was general all over Ireland. It was falling on every part of the dark central plain, on the treeless hills, falling softly upon the Bog of Allen and, farther westward, softly falling into the dark mutinous Shannon waves. It was falling, too, upon every part of the lonely churchyard on the hill where Michael Furey lay buried. It lay thickly drifted on the crooked crosses and headstones, on the spears of the little gate, on the barren thorns.[28]

[28] From "The Dead" by James Joyce, included in *The Portable James Joyce,* copyright 1946, 1947, by The Viking Press, Inc. Reprinted by permission of The Vi-

If we scanned the three final prepositional phrases, using the symbol ˈ for a metrically stressed syllable and the symbol – for a metrically unstressed syllable, we would discover the following pattern:

on the crooked crosses and headstones

on the spears of the little gate

on the barren thorns

Each phrase, we note, begins with two metrically unstressed syllables followed by a metrically stressed syllable; the first two phrases have three metrically stressed syllables, the last phrase only two; and no two metrically stressed syllables come together without a metrically unstressed syllable between them. The phrases, finally, are marked off by terminals, of which the last would certainly be /‿\/.

THE SPACING OF TERMINALS. Since *full* metrical regularity is an undesirable intrusion into prose, sound effects there can be considered as examples not only of controlled repetition but of controlled variation, and the last example suggests one of the techniques of varying. By varying the length of sentences, clauses, and important parts of clauses, we vary also the length of the stretches between terminals, especially between successive occurrences of the terminal /‿\/, with its connotations of finality. In this way, sound can sometimes be made to combine with sense in the marking off of paragraphs by something less superficial than a mere indentation on the page. Note that each of the three paragraphs which are quoted just below begins with a relatively short sentence or a short phrase —a sentence or phrase which is shorter than the one that precedes or follows it. These short units would each be closed, in almost any reading, by the terminal /‿\/, and quite possibly there would be no second occurrence of this terminal until the end of the following longer sentence. In the third paragraph, however, with its very short opening phrase, the sentences or phrases that would close with /‿\/ are much shorter than the long sentences in the first and second paragraphs. The result is a keener irony in the jibe at soldiers.

> The desire for fame is rooted in the hearts of men. It is one of the most powerful of all human desires, and perhaps for that very reason, and because it is so deep and secret, it is the desire that men are most unwilling to admit, particularly those who feel most sharply its keen and piercing spur.

king Press, Inc., New York. By permission also of Jonathan Cape, Ltd., London, and the Executors of the James Joyce Estate.

The politician, for example, would never have us think that it is love of office, the desire for the notorious elevation of public place, that drives him on. No, the thing that governs him is his pure devotion to the common weal, his selfless and high-souled statesmanship, his love of his fellow man, and his burning idealism to turn out the rascal who usurps the office and betrays the public trust which he himself, as he assures us, would so gloriously and so devotedly maintain.

So, too, the soldier. It is never love of glory that inspires him to his profession. It is never love of battle, love of war, love of all the resounding titles and the proud emoluments of the heroic conqueror. Oh, no. It is devotion to duty that makes him a soldier. There is no personal motive in it. He is inspired simply by the selfless ardor of his patriotic abnegation. He regrets that he has but one life to give for his country.[29]

PACE. Of the patterns of stress and pitch, therefore, those that occur before instances of the terminal $/\searrow/$ are certainly not the least important; but none of the patterns are negligible, since they largely determine the rhythms of English prose, as of English verse. If terminals are widely spaced and if the stronger stresses do not immediately succeed one another, the pace is likely to be quick; but the movement is clogged if the stronger stresses are not separated by weaks or if terminals are placed close together. In the following sentences, it is quite hard to read the underlined bits quickly:

He has learnt to prefer real longlived things.[30]
Is it something . . . for use to me today here?
Their manners, speech, dress, friendships . . . are unrhymed poetry.
Of all nations the United States with veins full of poetical stuff most needs poets.
Out of him speaks the spirit of peace, large, rich, thrifty.

The next lot of examples, on the other hand, move faster:

Some of them were professional conformists who found it simply impossible to violate the established code.

---

[29] From Thomas Wolfe, *You Can't Go Home Again* (New York: Harper & Brothers, 1940). By permission of Harper & Brothers.

[30] Walt Whitman, Preface to *Leaves of Grass*. The next four examples are from the same source.

> Great masses of people appear to be unable to abstain from it.
> He had a genius for committing imbecilities comparable to
> that possessed by Herman.
> He sometimes called it "the credibility of the commonplace."
> As the essential situation in the East is the tension that we
> have already observed, our policy must be an attempt at a
> series of interventions.

A HORRIBLE EXAMPLE. Neither batch of sentences, slower or faster, has been cited for any other quality than its relative speed; but since we began this discussion of sound effects with an admirably rhythmic passage, we will balance that fine example with an abominable one. It would take some effort to produce an uglier sentence than the following:

> Then may we attain to a poetry worthy the immortal soul of
> man, and which, while absorbing materials, and, in their own
> sense, the shows of Nature, will, above all, have, both directly
> and indirectly, a freeing, fluidizing, expanding, religious char-
> acter, exulting with science, fructifying the moral elements,
> and stimulating aspirations, and meditations on the un-
> known.[31]

The ugliness of this particular sentence is due largely to its complete failure in rhythm, though *fluidizing* deserves some credit, too. Other kinds of ugliness may be unwarily produced by careless handling of vowels and consonants. Among the most common blunders are the use of rare sequences, like the consonant clusters in *glimpsed streams;* aimless alliteration; and aimless rhymes or jingles (including the aimless repetition of the same word, especially under stress or in similar grammatical positions). The word *aimless* has been deliberately repeated. Both alliteration and the repetition of a word can be used to good effect, but they are seldom pleasing when the writer has merely stumbled into them by accident.

A PRECAUTION. He is not likely to stumble if he takes the elementary precaution of reading his prose aloud or of having it read to him by a competent friend. For most expository and argumentative writing, it is enough that the speech-sounds should not force themselves on our attention or that, if we do notice them, we find their arrangement purposeful. Reading an essay aloud will warn us if it does not meet these elementary requirements, and *hearing* it read may do more. If our meaning does not

[31] Walt Whitman, *Democratic Vistas.*

come through in someone else's reading, or if our competent reader falters and has to go back, we can be sure that we have blundered in something more serious than euphony and rhythm.

Exercise one. Review the chapter on the sounds of English in the grammar. Then read the following speech aloud several times, until you feel confident that your reading is as good as you can make it.

My Friends: No one, not in my situation, can appreciate my feeling of sadness at this parting. To this place, and the kindness of these people, I owe everything. Here I have lived a quarter of a century, and have passed from a young to an old man. Here my children have been born, and one is buried. I now leave, not knowing when or whether ever I may return, with a task before me greater than that which rested upon Washington. Without the assistance of that Divine Being who ever attended him, I cannot succeed. With that assistance, I cannot fail. Trusting in Him who can go with me, and remain with you, and be everywhere for good, let us confidently hope that all will yet be well. To His care commending you, as I hope in your prayers you will commend me, I bid you an affectionate farewell.[32]

1. Mark the terminals that occur in your reading. What terminal regularly occurs at the ends of sentences?
2. Read again the sentence, "With that assistance, I cannot fail." In your reading how do you indicate the contrast between the words *with that assistance* and the words *without the assistance* in the preceding sentence?
3. In the next sentence, how do you indicate the contrast between *go with me* and *remain with you?*
4. How many terminals are there in your reading of the final sentence?
5. In the first sentence of the speech, do you find the repetition of /s/ and /š/ objectionable?
6. In the second and fourth sentences (*To . . . everything; Here . . . buried*), do you notice any significant alliteration?
7. Point out the important instances, throughout the speech, in which words are effectively repeated.
8. The speech is obviously quiet, thoughtful, and sad. Do the sounds as such help to give this impression, or is it due solely to the content?

ᕗ Sentence connection and larger units

To talk about methods of sentence connection is obviously to talk about units larger than the sentence; and to talk about such larger units is to suggest problems of content and organization that we have not discussed

---

[32] Abraham Lincoln, "Farewell Address at Springfield, Illinois."

in this book. In these areas, the grammarian can by no means tell us all we need to know. Not only is the sentence his largest unit. Within that unit he deals mainly with forms, not meanings; but the connections among sentences are connections in meaning as well as in form. By the use of transitions, with their references to earlier and later parts of the same discourse, a writer or speaker indicates both the relations among the individual states of affairs that he reports and his judgments concerning those states of affairs. The grammarian, by an extension of his normal methods, can deal with the transitional *forms*, which fall under the heading of style in language; he can show that here again, form and meaning are separable, since different transitional forms can express the same relations and judgments; but he *cannot* deal with the relations and judgments themselves, which belong to style in thought. In this section, therefore, we will deliberately modify the method which we have previously used and will talk about style in thought as well as style in language. Since we will see later that one of the criteria for judging style in language is precisely its harmony with content and organization, it is only proper that our discussion of stylistic detail should ultimately be linked with other more general considerations.

In English, the most important transitional devices include the conjunctions, certain sentence adverbials (words, phrases, and clauses), the pronouns and some other nominals, some of the determiners and auxiliaries (in uses which may require statements about accompanying intonation patterns and stress patterns), some uses of likeness and difference in sentence structure, and some uses of synonyms or of verbal repetition.

SOME USES OF CONJUNCTIONS. The conjunctions show clearly how such devices refer to earlier and later parts of the discourse, how they indicate the relations among individual states of affairs, and how they convey the writer's judgments. Take, for example, the following brief sentence:

There were two out, but Ruth was at bat.

A full paraphrase might be much longer:

There were two out, and with two out there is normally no very good chance that a side will get another hit. Ruth was at bat, and with him batting there *was* a good chance of a hit. These features of the situation were in contrast.

Here are some other examples:

Sentence: He's ill, but he intends to make the campaign.

or

Although he's ill, he intends to make the campaign.

Paraphrase: He's ill. He intends to make the campaign. It
is unusual that both these statements should be
true.

Sentence: I told him to come in, for I saw that he was tired.

or

Because I saw that he was tired, I told him to
come in.

Paraphrase: (a) I saw that he was tired, and (b) I told
him to come in; and (a) was the cause of (b).

DEGREE OF EXPLICITNESS. These examples not only remind us of our
earlier statement that the real problem of coordination and subordination
is to clarify the relations in one's material; they also suggest that a writer
can create very different stylistic effects by making his transitions more
or less explicit. Explicit transitions such as we have illustrated direct attention to certain relations and indicate the writer's judgments, so that
the material is ordered and judged at the same time that it is presented.
The reader's task is thus made easier, but the very fact that less is demanded of him may make him feel that the material has been only super-
ficially analyzed or that he himself has been treated with irritating con-
descension.

Less obvious transitions leave the reader more to do. If it takes a little
time and thought to discover the relation among successive statements, the
reader who eventually understands may congratulate both himself and
the writer on their wit and subtlety and may feel that such clever fellows
really get to the bottom of things. The writing may seem more spontaneous
and more rewarding, the material closer to the confused variety of direct
experience. There is a danger, however, in these bare, suggestive, carefully
careless ways of handling transitions. A reader will tolerate them only if
he is convinced that the reward is worth the effort, and he will dismiss as
a conceited ass the writer who says nothing in a cryptic way. Most of us
will find enough difficulties in communication without inventing others.

PLACING ADVERBIALS TO MARK TRANSITIONS. Some of the difficulties we
may encounter are likely to be on a considerably lower level than our discussion so far has suggested. Probably we will not have much trouble with
the sentence adverbials that mark transitions. They are a mixed lot, including such forms as the following, in at least some of their uses: *first,
second, however, moreover, for example, as follows, since this is so, as we
shall see.* If we do have any trouble with these adverbials, it will be in placing them. Often it is said that a form like *however* should not stand at the

beginning or end of a sentence, and perhaps medial position is more common in formal writing; but end position is by no means unknown, even in casually elegant styles. *His house is in the village though* certainly need not be translated into *His residence, however, is in the village.*

REFERENCE OF PRONOUNS. Beginning writers frequently do have trouble with the pronouns and other nominals as means of transition. They have trouble with the relation between a pronoun or other nominal and the word the pronoun or other nominal refers to; and since they have had little practice in manipulating the resources of the literary language, they overdo the use of *this* and *that.* The first of these difficulties can easily be exaggerated. So long as the writer's meaning is perfectly clear, there is no reason why a pronoun or a nominal like *this* or *that* must refer to some one particular word in a preceding sentence; the reference may be to a larger form, like a clause, or even to no form at all but to the general *idea* of a sentence. Such uses as the following are regular in all kinds of good prose:

> Three decades ago, Dr. Westlake, Julius Flickerbaugh the lawyer, Merriman Peedy the Congregational pastor and himself had been the arbiters. That was as it should be . . .[33]

It is possible, however, to cause real confusion by careless reference. For example:

> It is possible, however, to cause real confusion by careless reference, and this must by all means be avoided.

> I have read the advertisement of Old Reeky's Dental Cream, but I don't like it.

There is no excuse for this really troublesome ambiguity.

THE "THIS" HABIT. The excessive use of *this* and *that* to mark transitions is among the commonest of all the signs of stylistic unconsciousness in writing, partly because transitional *this* and *that* are so freely and innocently used in plain talk. In the two typical paragraphs that follow, a student has used *this* or *these* in four out of six sentences:

> The major part of orientation is the friendships one makes when new students are placed in the new and different surroundings. These friendships usually help a student take the tremendous break between high school life and college life. With these newly-made friends the student will become ac-

---

[33] Sinclair Lewis, *Main Street* (New York: Harcourt, Brace and Company, Inc., 1920), p. 48.

quainted with the programs sponsored by campus religious organizations, athletic organizations, fraternities and other campus clubs and organizations.

In the University of Utopia, the main part of the Orientation Period is occupied by the administration of Placement Tests. These examinations show what fields the student is proficient in and what program must be completed for the Bachelor's degree. This part of orientation week is very tedious.

It would be ridiculous to discuss the style of a passage which manages to pack so much clumsiness into so small a space, but a first shove toward the awareness that style is possible might be a warning against the *this* habit.

OTHER MEANS OF TRANSITION. A second shove might be the repetition of the statement that the English language provides numerous other ways of getting from sentence to sentence. In addition to *this* and *that* as nominals and as determiners, we use the determiners *a* and *the*.

Once upon a time, there was *a* king who lived in a castle with his queen and three princesses. *The* king was very old, and *the* princesses were very beautiful.

The is here used like a weakened *this*, to indicate, in the second sentence, that the king and the princesses have already been identified. Somewhat similarly, we can use the auxiliary *do*, with a high pitch and loudest stress, to indicate that a contrasting statement on the same subject has already been made:

"What's the reason for John's low grades?"

"I don't think he studies very hard."

"Oh, but he *does* study, too; he studies all the time."

We ourselves used this method of transition to introduce the second paragraph before the present one:

Beginning writers frequently do have trouble with the pronouns and other nominals as means of transition.

On page 312, we used *the* in the phrase "the transitional *forms*" because we had already spoken of transitions as connections both in form and meaning.

OVERDOING IT. We cannot, then, dismiss the determiners, the auxiliaries, and the patterns of pitch and stress on the grounds that they are useful signs of transition only in talk; they have their very definite uses in writing styles as well. A more distinctly literary device is the question-answer pattern, in which the writer plays stooge to himself as we did on page 277 of this chapter:

> What, then, to proceed to positive statements, may we say about the sentence as an element of style? The first is obvious.

A hard-boiled criticism of these two sentences would be that they are a sign of too *much* care for clear transitions; the pitcher is spending too much time in his windup. The sentence adverbial *then* looks backward, the infinitive phrase *to proceed to positive statements* looks forward but also suggests that negative statements have been made before, the determiner *the* in the phrase *the sentence as an element of style* indicates that this topic is not newly introduced, and the literary question-and-answer device prepares for the first positive statement in the next sentence. The writer has left the reader nothing to do but go where he is told.

LIKENESSES AND DIFFERENCES IN SENTENCE STRUCTURE. The last structural means of transition which we will mention is the use of likeness and difference in sentence structure, including variation in the length of sentences. As we have said before, it is the contrast with longer sentences which makes the short, simple sentence effective as an introduction, transition, or conclusion. An example may be found on p. 281.

> The lesson to be drawn from such an impudent monstrosity [we wrote] is not to avoid the complex sentence, or the simple sentence, or the compound sentence, or any other sentence but the bad sentence. Both independent and dependent clauses and all types of sentences should be used as the occasion demands, but with an ear for rhythm and with decent respect for the reader's ease, convenience, and powers of attention. Most of all, they should be used to make sense.

Without the two longer sentences that precede it, the concluding short sentence would lose its force.

The opposite device, similarity of sentence structure, has also been discussed already, in our paragraphs on balance, parallelism, and antithesis. We will just add here that similarly constructed sentences can be used to preserve the continuity of our discourse because they do point up likenesses and differences in meaning. The two following paragraphs provide a simple example:

> it was the speech that clung to the ears, the link that tingled in the blood; U. S. A.
>
> U. S. A. is the slice of a continent. U. S. A. is a group of

holding companies, some aggregations of trade unions, a set
of laws bound in calf, a radio network, a chain of moving picture theatres, a column of stockquotations rubbed out and
written in by a Western Union boy on a blackboard, a public-
library full of old newspapers and dogeared historybooks
with protests scrawled on the margins in pencil. U. S. A. is
the world's greatest rivervalley fringed with mountains and
hills, U. S. A. is a set of bigmouthed officials with too many
bankaccounts. U. S. A. is a lot of men buried in their uniforms
in Arlington Cemetery. U. S. A. is the letters at the end of an
address when you are away from home. But mostly U. S. A.
is the speech of the people.[34]

Each of the sentences in the second paragraph follows the same pattern:
U. S. A.—is—determiner—nominal; each states one element in the writer's concept of America; and the similarity in sentence structure carries
the reader smoothly through the enumeration. The concluding sentence,
of course, is further marked by its brevity and by the conjunction *but.*

REPETITION. It should be noted, finally, that not all the common means
of transition are structural. Some of them are lexical; that is, they do not
involve grammatical structures but the individual words that fill the various structural positions. Among the most important lexical means of
transition are the repetition of key words and the repetition of key ideas
in synonymous words. Both devices make for continuity of thought; the
repetition of key words adds likeness of sound to likeness of ideas; and
unwanted likeness of sound can be avoided by the use of synonyms.

Simple examples may be drawn from the preceding paragraph. The second sentence picks up the word *structural* from the first, repeats it once,
and varies it once with the word *structures.* Within the second sentence,
lexical is explained in a statement whose key phrase is *the individual
words. Words* is then repeated twice in the third sentence, which opposes
the repetition of key words to *the repetition of key ideas in synonymous
words;* and at the same time, *lexical* and *means of transition* are echoed
from the first and second sentences. The fourth sentence begins with *Both
devices* and uses both devices. *Devices* itself is a synonym for *means,* and
synonyms is a shorter way of saying *synonymous words,* which was used
in the third sentence to build a partly repetitive opposition; but the
phrase *the repetition of key words* illustrates its own meaning, and within

---

[34] From *U.S.A.* by John Dos Passos, Houghton Mifflin Co. Copyright, 1933,
1934, 1935, 1936, 1937, by John Dos Passos. By permission of John Dos Passos.

the fourth sentence *likeness of sound* is repeated and opposed to *likeness of ideas*. The verbal patterning of the whole paragraph is thus more complicated than it seems at first.

Various methods can be used, as we have suggested, to prevent even elaborate repetition from becoming objectionable. Most obviously, its extent can always be limited by the use of synonyms, but self-conscious refusal to use the same word twice is often more objectionable than direct repetition. Somewhat more subtle methods are to space the repeated words, so that they do not follow one another immediately, and to put them in different positions in the sentence, especially under different stresses, so that the verbal repetition will be matched by a calculated departure from an established repetitive pattern. The best way to make repetition effective, however, is to take care that it should always be meaningful.

Exercise two. Study the organization of the following theme carefully and in detail.

STUDENT ORIENTATION

1. When a person enters upon a new situation, he adjusts himself to that situation by the process of orientation. In the case of a student entering a college or University for the first time this process of orientation would involve his becoming acquainted with other students, learning the layout of the campus, and becoming adjusted to the type of work expected by the school.

2. The problem of meeting and learning to live with new friends is not a difficult one. In fact, this part of orientation is usually performed quite naturally by nearly all students. Since new students are, so to speak, "all in the same boat," the uneasy tensions, which are sometimes created when a new group is first forced together, are greatly alleviated.

3. After the student has met his new classmates, it is quite advantageous for him to become acquainted, also, with the layout of the campus grounds. This should include an understanding of where certain types of classes meet, where the libraries are located, and where any other buildings in which the student might be interested are situated.

4. The third and most important part of orientation is the adjustment to the work required in classes. The big change made in graduating from high school work to college work sometimes makes this part of orientation also the hardest. Adjustment to the work means first that the student assumes a serious attitude toward his work. Secondly he should have a well organized plan of study which will allow him to give sufficient time for study in each course. Also it is important for the student to realize that college work requires much more time and effort than high school work. It is easy to see that if this part of the orientation is neglected, the student will undoubtedly have great difficulty in keeping up his work.

5. The method employed by many colleges and universities in approaching the problem of student orientation is to set aside one week at the beginning of the fall term for this purpose. In many other schools the fraternities and sororities take care of the orientation program. Unfortunately, however, in some schools no effort of this sort is made either by the administration or by outside organizations of the school.
6. Orientation programs can do much to help a new student make friends, find his way around, and have "a taste" of the work which will be required of him. After this process of orientation has been completed he should then be better prepared to undertake his college program.

Answer the following questions.

1. What sentence provides an outline for the theme? What paragraphs develop the three topics suggested by the outline? Does the outline make any provision for the last two paragraphs?
2. In the first sentence of the first paragraph, should *it* replace *that situation?* Could we translate *by the process of orientation* as *by adjusting himself?* Is the first sentence of any use at all?
3. In the second sentence of the first paragraph, do you object to the repetition of *process of orientation?* Could *this* be changed to *the* without loss?
4. With what phrase in the first paragraph is the complete subject of the first sentence in the second paragraph intended to be synonymous? Would it be better to repeat *becoming acquainted with other students?*
5. *In fact* often introduces a stronger version of a preceding statement. Is this its function in Paragraph 2? Would it be better simply to get rid of the weaker statement?
6. In the second sentence of the second paragraph, *students* is not the subject, but the object of *by.* In the main clause of the third sentence, the students are not mentioned at all. In the first dependent clause of the third sentence, however, *students* has been used as subject of *are.* Do these shifts make the paragraph harder to follow?
7. What part of the first sentence in the third paragraph refers to Paragraph 1, and what part to Paragraph 2? What phrases in this sentence repeat earlier phrases, and what phrase is synonymous with a phrase in Paragraph 1 and a phrase in Paragraph 2? Does the change from *campus* to *campus grounds* serve any purpose?
8. Does *This,* in the second sentence of Paragraph 3, seem ambiguous to you? Do you approve the use of *are located* and *are situated?*
9. The first sentence in Paragraph 4 manages to include references to all three earlier paragraphs. How?
10. Paragraph 4 is in general very clumsy. What makes it so? Do you approve the repetition of *(this) part of orientation?* What about the repetition of *work?* In the second sentence, a *change* is first *made* and then *makes* something; does the shift bother you? Would anything be lost by the deletion of *Also it is important for the student to realize that* and *It is easy to see that?*

11. Be prepared to question your class, as you have been questioned, about the transitions in the last two paragraphs.
12. How would you advise the writer of this theme to improve his transitions?

Exercise three. Choose a passage of some two or three hundred words from a piece of exposition or argument that you think is good. Go over the passage carefully, and try to tell precisely how the sentences are held together. Don't be content with generalities; make your description as exact and full as you can.

Vocabulary and style

⟨ Relative importance of vocabulary

In most discussions of style, the choice of words gets far more attention than the choice of structural patterns. This is unfortunate. Though few students write badly because they do not have a vocabulary large enough to allow them to write well, many write badly because they have not mastered the structural devices of writing styles; and though most students are more ready and willing to discuss vocabulary than to discuss structure, they are apt to forget that the force and meaning of a word are governed by the words that go with it and by the structure in which it is placed. How do we know, for example, that the word *rat* is used metaphorically in the sentence *He's a dirty rat?* Without asking any questions about the situation in which the sentence is uttered, we know immediately that *rat* is metaphorical because *he* is not the pronoun which we normally use in referring to rodents. How do we know that /aɪ/ is *eye* and not *I* in *My* /aɪ/ *hurts?* Because the pronoun does not normally occur after a determiner as the subject of a verb like *hurts*. Words in isolation have many potential values, but particular values are selected and realized only when words are used in actual utterances.

It does not follow that the vocabulary is negligible in stylistic discussion—far from it. Writing is a single act in which the choice of words and the choice of structures are made together, and the effect of a piece of writing on its reader is determined by both choices. Most readers, in fact, if they give any conscious attention at all to style, are likely to notice the words before they notice the patterns. To underestimate the importance of vocabulary would be as serious a mistake as to neglect structure.

"COLLOQ." We must note at once that in vocabulary, too, the distinction between writing styles and conversational styles is fundamental. It is suggested by the much-abused term *colloquial*. For many of us, the abuse of the label *colloquial* consists in using it abusively. We think of colloquial expressions as at least naughty and perhaps sinful, maybe "illiterate" and certainly unbecoming the lips or pen of an educated man. Nice people, we may think, do not use colloquialisms in formal writing.

Words mean, of course, what people use them to mean, and in circles where *colloquial* is used as a synonym for *vulgar, low,* or *incorrect,* those are its meanings in those circles. Most educated people use the term quite differently. They use it to label words or structures which fitly and frequently occur in ordinary conversation but do not so occur in formal speech or formal writing. It is in this latter sense that we will use *colloquial,* and we will let it remind us once again that different selections of words and structural patterns are expected of us in serious writing and in casual talk. In practice, we must and do draw finer distinctions constantly. We all know that different styles are appropriate to different people, different subjects, different audiences, different situations, and different purposes; and we may be accustomed to talk about several different "levels of usage," such as *formal, colloquial,* and *illiterate.* The metaphor of *levels* is deceptive. Formal English, the English of serious prose, is no better in itself than colloquial English, the English of ordinary conversation; and in some situations neither is better than illiterate English, the English of uneducated people. For the word *levels,* the word *varieties* might be substituted, and the important point for us is simply that the varieties are different and that we must choose purposefully among them.

Among the differences between the vocabulary of serious prose and the vocabulary of ordinary conversation is the greater size of the writing vocabulary. It is true that many words are equally at home in plain talk and in formal writing and that in talk we use a good many words, perhaps surprisingly many, which we would hardly use in argumentative or expository prose. Conversation may have its own technical intricacies, as when a pair of farmers discuss the external anatomy of an ailing cow. On the whole, however, the writing vocabulary is probably the larger, partly because it includes more of the precise technical terms, the general and abstract words, that daily life does not require in such great numbers. We argue political and social issues more commonly than farmers discuss bovine diseases. The other side of this picture is that the words of daily life are nearer and dearer to us than technical terms are ever likely to be; but luckily most of our ordinary words are also used in formal writing.

⌘ Connotation and denotation

By saying that one word may be nearer and dearer to us than another, we have suggested another useful distinction, that between the *denotation* of a word and its *connotation*. If we say, for example, that a person is stupid, or that he is dumb, or that he is obtuse, we have said much the same unkind thing about our victim; the three words *stupid, dumb,* and *obtuse* can have the same denotation. Their *connotations,* however, are likely to be different. For many of us, *obtuse* is a fairly cool and bookish label; *stupid* is common in talk and in writing and ranges from moderate restraint to considerable violence; while *dumb* is conversational, not bookish, and seldom cool. In our sense, then, the denotation of a word is what it points to; its connotation is the suggestions that it carries as a result of the situations in which we have encountered it. *Obtuse* is cool and bookish for those of us who have coolly read it in books, but *dumb* usually carries some emotional overtone, suggests some strong attitude, because we have heard it used emotionally by people who were strongly disposed to act in some particular way toward the subject of their conversation. If we had encountered *dumb* only in restrained writing, its connotation would be entirely different.

⌘ Time, place, and social group

Because we do learn to use words by hearing them or reading them, both their denotations and their connotations vary with time and place and from group to group in a *single* time and place. This fact is so obvious when once we stop to think about it that examples are not much needed. Change with time is most strikingly illustrated in slang. During and after the second World War, *snafu* was popular, and a person who made a mistake had *fouled things up*. Ten years later, the same unfortunate was more commonly said to have *goofed* or *made a boo-boo*, and *snafu* had become quaint and antiquated. Change with place appears when we ask a New Englander and a Southerner to state the connotations of *bucket* and *pail*. For the Southerner, *bucket* is the ordinary, everyday word, and *pail* is likely to be old-fashioned and perhaps a little nostalgic; but the New Englander is likely to use the words in the opposite way, with *pail* as the more common of the two. Any college classroom, finally, provides examples of change from group to group. The writer of this book, until he took freshman English, used *quite* as he had heard his family use it, to mean "somewhat, moderately, rather"; but when he told his English instructor that a book which he had only moderately disliked was "quite disappointing," he was surprised to find that communication broke down. The instructor belonged to a more pedantic group and used *quite* to mean "very."

Because a lifetime stretches over many years and because we often move from group to group and place to place, each of us commands, as we have intimated, a number of overlapping but not identical vocabularies. Many of us know something of the technical vocabularies of literary studies, automobile manufacture and repair, and outdoor sports; we may be able to use the jargon of social scientists, language teachers, and fly fishermen; we understand and possibly may use one set of terms in church and another in the fraternity house or dormitory; and none of us can altogether escape the tough talk of TV cops and robbers, even if we hear it only out of the mouths of babes. A generation ago, we might have been able to write at this point that every man is his own Babel. Perhaps students from the Bible belt will still understand that statement.

❧ Clichés

In choosing among our various vocabularies, we cannot afford to forget that none of them is good or bad in itself. Though one word or set of words is likely to be more useful for one purpose than another is, every word is capable of good use, and there is no greater obstacle to the cultivation of a good style than the mere taboo. We are often told, for instance, that we should avoid trite expressions or clichés; and intentionally or otherwise, horrid examples are presented for our contemplation. Academic authors prepare such exhibits with some ease:

> The author believes that the young people who elect to enter the teaching field do so because they enjoy working with boys and girls.[35]

This sentence may be translated:

> I believe that young people choose to teach because they enjoy working with boys and girls.

Again:

> In this book the author discusses various types of teaching methods, methods by means of which the student teacher can achieve success in his teaching efforts.[36]

[35] Gilbert C. Kettelcamp, *Teaching Adolescents* (Boston: D. C. Heath and Co., 1954), p. v.
[36] *Loc. cit.*

The translation:

> This book discusses different ways of teaching well.

Finally:

> The concluding sections of the course first present a compari-
> son of the major national societies competing for dominance
> in the present-day world and a consideration of their implica-
> tions for social, economic, and political organization on both
> a national and international level.[37]

This sentence cannot be translated, because nobody can tell what it means.
To talk about the implications of societies for society ("social . . . organization") is to lose oneself in the empty spaces of too familiar words.

Though students are justified in flunking teachers who write like that,
even clichés like *the teaching field* and verbal fillers like *methods by
means of which* may have their uses. In talk, they may be notably useful.
At receptions and dinner parties, where silence is rude and conversation
is impossible, the lubrication of customary phrases on customary subjects
makes the wheels turn smoothly; and it is not only in the parlor and at
the table that clichés may come in handy. Political speeches and reports
of diplomatic conferences would be impossible without them, listeners to
radio and watchers of TV would be uneasy if the expected prefabricated
phrases did not emerge, and hurried writers of business letters and similar
documents in which neither personality nor scientific precision is essential
would never get through the day's work if they had to stop and look for
exact and lively words. Since the average mind can absorb only so much
information in a given time, in some kinds of speech and writing a certain
amount of waste motion is not wasted. Language itself may be viewed as
a very abstract set of prefabricated phrases.

❧ The grounds of choice

The preceding paragraph will not be taken, we trust, as recommending
the undiscriminating use of clichés like *precept and example* by precept
or example. It is rather an attempt to suggest the real problem of choosing
the right words: do they do the job we want them to do? The English
language has an enormous vocabulary drawn from unusually varied
sources. Some of our words have been English as long as English has ex-
isted as a separate language. Others have been taken into English from

[37] The note indicating the source of this quotation has been lost—fortunately.

Latin, the Scandinavian languages, French, Greek, Italian, Spanish, Dutch, German, and dozens of other languages which speakers of English have heard or read. As a result, even children have to choose from literally thousands of words which help us to map out the universe as we know it, to learn and teach, to tell other people what we want, and to work with them for things that they would also like.

Not only are the relations of likeness and difference among these words, in form and meaning, extremely complicated. There are also important limits on the kinds of situation and on the kinds of speech and writing in which particular words are customarily used, and any departure from these established customs is likely to produce a special effect. The problem of choice of words is therefore extremely complicated—too complicated to be solved by neat little rules. In an elementary discussion like ours, we can say only that the writer should acquaint himself as fully as possible, by wide reading, with the resources of the English vocabulary and that he should choose those words which seem to him best suited to his needs. On the occasions when he needs a cliché, he should grit his teeth and use it, conscious that if he has judged the occasion wrongly, his writing will suffer.

❧ Departures from custom

To the right judgment of occasions, custom is not an infallible guide. Departures from established customs, as we have repeatedly said, are recognized means to special effects. We may purposely use a word outside its normal social or literary context; or, within some context, we may give a word an unusual sense. The transference of a word to an unusual context is easily illustrated. An angry football coach might talk to a lazy team in a childish or even feminine vocabulary; the defeat of the team might be recorded, on the sports page, in words normally used in obituaries; or a mother might try to control a bumptious child by talking to him as she would customarily talk to an adult. The football coach would be using the normal vocabulary of a different kind of speaker, the sports writer the vocabulary of a different subject, the mother a vocabulary usually reserved for a different audience. Similarly, the vocabulary for one kind of situation may be used in another, or (more learnedly) the vocabulary of one literary kind, such as the lyric, may be transferred to quite a different kind, like the informal essay. The effect produced will depend on the nature of the words and of the two contexts involved.

⁀ Figures of speech

The use of a word in an unusual sense is often called a figure of speech. The reader or hearer understands the intended, *unusual* meaning from the usual meaning, the rest of the utterance, and the external situation. (In a book, of course, there is no external situation, only a longer utterance than we have to guide us in ordinary speech.) It would be possible, therefore, to describe and classify figures in terms of the clues which make the intended meaning clear, but the usual basis of classification is the relation between the literal and figurative meanings. Among the numerous figures which have been classified in this way, we will mention only four: understatement and overstatement, irony, and metaphor.

OVERSTATEMENT, UNDERSTATEMENT, IRONY. Understatement and overstatement are simple devices. A statement can be made weaker than the situation would justify, or it can be made stronger. Often the restraint of understatement results in quiet emphasis, sometimes in humorous diminution. Overstatement, which is a poor means to emphasis, had best be funny or it will grow tiresome. In either case, the effect of the figure depends on the discrepancy between the content and the way the content is expressed, and the same thing may be said of irony. An ironic statement is one in which the literal and figurative meanings are opposites, as possibly in the sentence, *The duty of the schools is to help everybody get ahead of the Joneses.*

The example rightly suggests that irony, like climax and anticlimax, presupposes a scale of values. If speaker and hearer, writer and reader share the same values, irony is easily used either in derision or in fun; but when values are so thoroughly confused as they are at the present day, irony can result in various complications. It may fall quite flat if the literal meaning is naïvely accepted; it may be used to puzzle an audience which does not quite know what is intended but smells a rat somewhere; it can startle and astonish if an audience can be brought to accept the literal meaning for a while and then suddenly forced to recognize the true intention. The possibilities for both success and failure are greater than with understatement and overstatement.

METAPHOR. Like irony, metaphor is a complex and powerful device, but the term has been so loosely employed and the thing itself has been so fancifully examined that sensible discussion is very difficult. Traditionally, metaphor has been defined as an implied comparison, the application to one thing of a linguistic form which literally means another thing. More commonly in recent years, any transfer of meaning and hence any figure of speech has been called a metaphor, and on the basis of this pretended definition elaborate theories of the importance of metaphor have been built. Metaphor, it is said, is not mere decoration or illustration but essential statement, shaping our attitudes, interpreting our experience, and giving us kinds of truth which we can get in no other way. Such theories often begin or end by contrasting the literal language of science with the metaphorical language of poetry—always to the advantage of poetry.

ITS POWER AND USES. We will not entangle ourselves in these complexities, which have little practical value in the teaching of exposition or argument. Undoubtedly, metaphor as traditionally defined can be used to enliven an otherwise dull piece of writing. An example is the last sentence of Sinclair Lewis's *Babbitt*. Ted Babbitt and Eunice Littlefield have slipped off from a dance one Saturday night and have got married without their parents' knowledge or consent, and the next morning the families have gathered to see what can be done about the marriage. Ted is surprised when his father takes him out of the room and tells him he was right to marry if that was what he wanted to do. The last sentence of the book describes Ted's return with his father to the living room:

> Arms about each other's shoulders, the Babbitt men marched
> into the living-room and faced the swooping family.[38]

Most readers remember this sentence because of the one metaphorical word, *swooping,* which suggests a comparison between the scolding, chattering adults and a noisy flock of smaller birds attacking a hawk. Very few of Lewis's sentences are so well remembered.

The same example indicates that metaphor may not only give life to otherwise dull prose. If we give the name of one thing, A, to another, B, we suggest so close a resemblance that our attitudes and feelings toward A are transferred to B: since a skunk is a smelly little beast, a man who gets called a skunk may be treated with wary contempt. Metaphor can thus be very moving. It can shape attitudes by implying and stimulating judgments of value, and the judgments can be all the more persuasive because they are not argued but assumed and are conveyed directly in the metaphoric word. During a recent governmental crisis, for example, a columnist wrote that the administration would be "free from the miasmic conniving which took place during the illness of Wilson." [39] To connive

[38] Sinclair Lewis, *Babbitt* (New York: Harcourt, Brace and Company, Inc., 1922), p. 401.
[39] *Chicago Sun-Times,* October 2, 1955.

is to work together sneakingly, and a miasma is a poison floating in the air, especially in the night mists. The metaphorical *miasmic* implied that when President Wilson was ill, sneaking plotters in the government were like a poison in the very air the nation breathed; in contrast, the present administration was represented as healthy and healthful, clean and honest. The metaphor directly conveyed a sweeping judgment on the two American parties and nudged the voter ungently away from one and toward the other.

Whether metaphor in this instance was wisely or foolishly used is a matter for the reader's own decision. The point is simply that metaphor can be used, with or without reasoned argument, to prepare an audience for reasonable or unreasonable action. It can also be used, in an equally a-rational way, to give the feel of direct experience, as when a poet spoke of "swallows with spools of dark thread sewing the shadows together": [40] reading the line, we get the feel of the thing as if we ourselves were watching the birds in the gathering darkness. Similarly, in the following lines, blowing and falling leaves in autumn are not so much described as presented:

> Leaves, summer's coinage spent, golden are all together whirled,
> sent spinning, dipping, slipping, shuffled by heavy-handed wind,
> shifted sideways, sifted, lifted, and in swarms made to fly,
> spent sun-flies, gorgeous tatters, airdrift, pinions of trees. [41]

METAPHOR AS A GUIDE TO INQUIRY. Metaphors like *summer's coinage, heavy-handed wind,* and *pinions of trees* would often be out of place in expository or argumentative prose, but there is another use of metaphor which is extremely important to the prose writer. When we try to explain something, we try to put it into a *class* of things, to say that it is like something else with which it shares some quality. That is just what metaphors do, and so they can serve not only as illustrations but as guides to inquiry, like the models which chemists use to represent molecules. Political scientists, for example, often talk of institutions as if they were living organisms. Their metaphor gives them a way of explaining the relations of one institution to another, since it allows them to talk about changes

---

[40] From "Bat" by D. H. Lawrence, in *Collected Poems of D. H. Lawrence.* Copyright 1929 by Jonathan Cape and Harrison Smith, Inc. Reprinted by permission of The Viking Press, Inc., New York. By permission also of the Estate of the late Mrs. Frieda Lawrence.
[41] From "Lapwing" by R. E. Warner in W. H. Auden and John Garrett, *The Poet's Tongue* (London: G. Bell & Sons, Ltd., 1937), II, pp. 78–79.

with environment; but it also invites them to pursue certain lines of inquiry. Are there parallels between organic evolution and the development of institutions, or between the development of institutions and the life cycle of organisms? Since many living creatures act from unreasoned habit, would it be just to say that formal law is less important to the conduct of a society than customs and traditions are? What are the illnesses of institutions, their symptoms, and their cures? Considering metaphor as an aid to reflection, we might very well insist that it is no more at home in poetry than in science.

The strength and the weakness of metaphor in exposition and argument is, as we have suggested, that the metaphoric use of a single word may embody or conceal a whole series of statements which need examination. An institution is not really a living organism; but to call it one, on the basis of a few obvious resemblances, is an invitation to hunt for likeness and to ignore plain difference. Metaphors are strongly persuasive, and not only to truth.

ABUSES OF METAPHOR. If that is the inherent strength and weakness of metaphor, there are also abuses of it which are not inherent but which result from the user's ignorance or disregard of linguistic differences between himself and his audience. Since we have defined a figure of speech as the use of a word in an unusual meaning, we cannot be quite sure what particular uses a particular individual will regard as figurative unless we know in advance what he accepts as the normal meanings of our words. For us, a metaphor may be *dead;* that is, what was formerly the unusual meaning may have become the usual meaning. This is what had happened for the city child who said, when she first saw a pig and learned its name, that it was very properly called a pig, since it was so dirty. The child's normal meaning for *pig* was not "swine" or "hog" but "dirty child, dirty beast"; and for her the use of *pig* which most speakers take as normal had become metaphoric. Similar explanations can probably be given for most *mixed* metaphors, of which the following is a somewhat gaudy instance:

> His whole picture will be a house of cards which will collapse at the first breeze of methodological rigor.

The writer of this sentence was not thinking about a real house of cards or a real picture. He was using *picture* to mean "explanation or account" and *house of cards* to mean "flimsy structure of argument." He did not stop to think that for many readers the literal meanings of his phrases would be so very different that the whole sentence would be absurd.

Exercise one. Ask five of your fellow students who are not members of your English class what they mean by *colloquial* and whether they take it as a favorable, unfavorable, or neutral term. Look up the word in the *Oxford English Dictionary* and in Webster's *New International*. How do the dictionary definitions differ from the popular definitions? How did you use the word before you looked it up? How does the phrase *levels of usage* illustrate what we have called the inherent weakness of metaphor?

Exercise two. In the same dictionaries, look up the terms *abstract noun* and *concrete noun*. Classify the following nominals under one heading or the other: *beauty, tree, book, truth, goodness, apple, height, giant, relationship, cigarette.* Classify the following nominals as specific or general: *frying pan, utensil, tool, shovel, building, bungalow, trout, fish, machine, typewriter.* Should a writer try always to use concrete and specific words and to avoid the abstract and general? If your answer is yes, write a paragraph of one hundred words to illustrate your principle.

Exercise three. What differences in connotation, if any, would *you* note within the following sets of synonyms?

1. beautiful, lovely, pretty
2. plain, homely, ugly
3. fat, fleshy, plump
4. rival, opponent, competitor
5. house, home, residence
6. undertaker, mortician, funeral director
7. dead, deceased, departed
8. face, visage, countenance
9. teacher, instructor, pedagogue
10. lie, fib, falsehood

Do any of these thirty words illustrate what is known as *euphemism?*

Exercise four. Look up *cliché, cant,* and *jargon* in a good dictionary. From the sports page of your local newspaper, make up a list of ten clichés. Make a similar list from political statements and discussions. Make a list of ten words from each of three technical vocabularies which you command (fishing, football, chess, golf, motoring, or the like).

Exercise five. Use a good dictionary to determine the origin of each word in the following sentence: *The problem of choice of words is therefore extremely complicated—too complicated to be solved by neat little rules.*

Exercise six. Clip the story of a football, basketball, or baseball game from your local paper. Rewrite it, using as few typically sporting words as possible. Is the rewriting better or worse than the original?

Exercise seven. Assuming that your audience consists of intelligent college freshmen, write a paragraph explaining and illustrating irony. Then rewrite the paragraph so that it would be suitable for eighth-graders. What linguistic differences do you make between the two paragraphs? Give your reasons for each difference.

Exercise eight. Look up the following words in the *Oxford English Dictionary* and explain how each might be considered a dead metaphor.

1. to ponder	6. career
2. pioneer	7. ferret
3. seminary	8. cancer
4. daisy	9. pedigree
5. muscle	10. temperament

Standards

We began our discussion of style with the assertions that style is the manner of saying what is said, that there is style in thought as well as style in language, but that we would be concerned mainly with style in language. Accordingly, we have organized the discussion around the linguistic choices, in structure and in vocabulary, which make style in language possible. The structural choices have been treated under the heads of clauses and sentences, the parts of clauses, sound and sound effects, and transition and sentence connection. The chief topics in the discussion of lexical choices have been the levels or varieties of usage within a single speech community, connotation and denotation, regional dialect, the special vocabularies of various social and professional groups, and figures of speech. Style in language is possible, we have emphasized, only because so great a variety of choices is open to the writer, who can say the same thing in many different ways.

❖ Circumstances and occasions

He can therefore adapt his style to a number of different circumstances. Not every style is appropriate to every subject, to every audience, to every situation and purpose; some styles may represent the writer himself as he does not wish to appear; and since linguistic choices are only one set among several which the writer must make, they must be adapted to his other decisions—for example, to those involving content and organization. The stylist must consider all these circumstances, both external (subject, audience, situation, purpose, his own character) and internal (content and organization); and his skill consists in shaping his language appropriately on the given occasions.

❖ Nature and purposes of student writing

In this chapter, we have been concerned with only a few of the infinitely varied occasions which may present themselves to writers. For example, we have said nothing and need say nothing of the different styles which might be demanded by different literary kinds, such as tragedy and comedy, epic and lyric. Much less ambitiously, we have assumed that the kinds of writing which college students can and should master and which college instructors can and should teach are exposition and argument, and even particular kinds of exposition and argument. We have assumed that students should learn to address an intelligent lay audience of responsible adults, on serious though not necessarily momentous subjects, in the usual range of day-to-day situations among American citizens, and that the purpose of such writing is to rationally promote mutual understanding and just action. Because we have limited ourselves in this way, we can set up fairly definite standards of stylistic choice.

❧ Standards

First of all, the writer should know and be able to use the full range of resources which are made available to him by the several varieties of the language at his command. Even within the limits which we have set, he cannot be content to write always in the same way. To be sure, he will consistently aim at clarity, precision, and movement, using enough verbals to keep his style from being clogged and making his transitions plain but not too obvious and insistent; but he must also remember that different occasions make different demands on his style. If he can adapt his writing to those various demands, he will make it convey a quiet sense of purpose that inspires confidence in his reader, and he will avoid the distressful sense of aimless fumbling and bumbling that much bad writing gives.

More particularly, the writer must know what is expected of him *as a writer*. We all know, from years of observation and practice, what is expected of us in various kinds of talk; as writers, we must learn to satisfy a rather different set of expectations; but again the only way to learn is to observe and imitate. By reading and writing, we learn the writer's art of using marks on paper to inform or persuade his reader. We learn the graphic devices which will control oral reading clearly and strongly, which will show the reader just what elements in our sentences go together, and which thus will rule out troublesome ambiguities and convey our precise meaning. Our success as talkers by no means guarantees success in these latter tasks.

A good talker, however, is more likely than his less articulate fellows to make a good writer; for normally, what we write should be fit and easy to read aloud. It follows that as writers we should not depart too far from speech. For example, though we should generally avoid contractions and sentence fragments and should take more care with our sentence structure and transitions than we usually do in conversation, we should not tamper much with a basic pattern like the order subject-verbal-complement. We should also pay some attention, as we write, to the possible sound of our prose if anyone should bother to give it an oral reading. The intended patterns of stress and pitch should be indicated as clearly as ordinary spelling allows and the sense demands; they should create a definite sense of considered movement without slipping into meter; and both aimless jingles and the unconscious building up of rare sequences of consonants should be avoided.

Jingles are more easily forgiven than jumbles. Of our speech and of our writing, our hearer or reader can reasonably expect that the natural and logical relations in our material will be made clear. Since he has no clue to these relations except our writing itself, our failures in this matter of clarity may take two forms. First, we may simply succeed in being totally obscure, so that the reader has no idea what the relations in our material may be. Second, we may be incoherent, showing the relations rightly at one point but obscuring them or even contradicting ourselves at another. The standards of clarity and coherence should guide our use of such linguistic devices as coordination and subordination, where style in language and style in thought come together.

❧ Style and morality

Ultimately, we must not only be willing to bring style in thought and style in language together again after their initial separation for purposes of study; we must go further. We have said that the stylist must know the full range of his available linguistic resources and use them flexibly, that he must observe the conventional differences between conversational and writing styles and yet take care that what he writes is fit and easy to read aloud, and that he must use his linguistic devices to achieve clarity and coherence, precision and movement. We must also recognize that the problem of style eventually merges with larger personal and moral problems. Of all the writing for which this book may serve as preparation, we will have to ask the final question, Does this piece of exposition or argument, in the given circumstances, do what a mature and responsible citizen would want it to do? A writer can no more escape his moral and social obligations in his style than he can escape them in any other aspect of his work, so that to some extent the judgment of style becomes a moral judgment. Ultimately, we have to face this consequence; but the evidence for our moral judgment, as far as style in language is concerned, is still the linguistic choice and rejection whose nature and extent we have discussed.

Exercise one. From a newspaper that you read regularly, select an editorial or a syndicated column dealing with a serious topic of national interest. Clip the editorial or column and submit it to your instructor along with an analysis and evaluation of its style. In your analysis, try to show how well or how badly the writer has adapted his style to the external and internal circumstances which we enumerated on p. 331 above.

Exercise two. From two newspapers or magazines whose policies and audiences are clearly different, select two editorials on the same subject. Compare and contrast the styles of the editorials, and suggest reasons why each editor wrote as he did. Turn in both editorials with your paper.

Exercise three. Write two accounts of a college course which you have recently taken. Assume that one account is for a faculty committee which is officially concerned with the evaluation of courses and the improvement of teaching. Assume that the other account is for a friend of yours who is thinking of taking the course. The two accounts may differ a little in content, perhaps *should* differ in outline, and certainly *must* differ in style.

Index

d

Correction chart

I. *Punctuation, mechanics, spelling*

M Correct the mistake in mechanics by consulting the section on punctuation and mechanics in a good desk dictionary.

Pn Correct the mistake in punctuation by consulting the section on punctuation in a good desk dictionary.

Sp Correct the mistake in spelling by checking the word in a good desk dictionary.

II. *Choice of words*

Cl Avoid the ineffective use of a cliché or of trite diction. Look up *clichés* in the index.

Colloq Avoid inappropriate colloquialism. Consult the entry *colloquial English* in the glossary.

Con Use language that is less abstract and more concrete. Consult the entries *abstract noun* and *concrete noun* in the glossary. You may be asked to do Exercise two, p. 330.

D Correct the mistake in diction.

Lev Choose your expression from an appropriate level of usage. Consult the entry *levels of usage* in the glossary.

MF Avoid mixed figures. See p. 329.

Rep Remove the aimless repetition. See pp. 310, 317–18.

Std Use standard English. Consult that entry in the glossary.

Wdy Avoid wordiness. Say it simply.

III. *Parts of speech*

Agr Correct the mistake in the agreement of a pronoun with its antecedent or of a verb with its subject. Consult the entry *agreement* in the glossary.

C Correct the mistake in case. Consult that entry in the glossary.

Ctr Avoid inappropriate contractions. Consult that entry in the glossary. Use the full form.

DC Consult the entry *double comparison* in the glossary. Avoid this usage.

DN Consult the entry *double negative* in the glossary. Avoid this usage.

FA Look up *flat adverbs* in the index. Use a form in *-ly.*

PA Do not confuse an adverb with an adjective in the predicate adjectival position. Consult the entry *predicate adjectival* in the glossary.

PP Use the proper form of the past tense or the past participle. Check the principal parts of the verb in a good desk dictionary.

Pron Correct the mistake in the use of a pronoun.

Ref Correct the mistake in the reference of a pronoun. Look up *reference of pronouns* in the index.

Seq Observe the sequence of tenses. Consult that entry in the glossary.

Spl Avoid ineffective split infinitives. Consult that entry in the glossary, and see pp. 270–71.

Subj Use the subjunctive mood. The subjunctive is the uninflected name form of any verb but *be,* which has a present subjunctive *be* and a past subjunctive *were.*

IV. *The sentence*

CF Correct the comma fault. Use a semicolon or a period here.

Coord Correct the faulty coordination. See pp. 275–85.

Frag Avoid the ineffective use of sentence fragments. Consult the entry *sentence* in the glossary.

Nr Set off a nonrestrictive clause by commas. Consult the entry *nonrestrictive clause* in the glossary.

Rst Do not set off a restrictive clause by commas. Consult the entries *restrictive clause* and *nonrestrictive clause* in the glossary.

Run-on Avoid the run-on sentence. Use a period or a semicolon here.

Subord Correct the faulty subordination. See pp. 275–85.

V. *Coherence*

Coh The sentence or paragraph lacks coherence, does not hang together. Rewrite it.

Correl Use syntactically equivalent constructions after correlative conjunctions. Consult the entry *correlative conjunction* in the glossary.

DM Avoid dangling modifiers. Consult that entry in the glossary.

Ill Avoid illogical comparisons. Choose the terms of your comparison logically and state them clearly.

MM Shift the misplaced modifier. If you frequently misplace modifiers, study the pages listed under *word order* in the index.

Par Avoid faulty parallelism. Look up *parallelism* in the index.

Sh Avoid unnecessary shifts of subject, number, person, tense, voice, mood. Do not shift back and forth between direct and indirect discourse without good reason. If the terms of this rule are not clear to you, look them up in the glossary.

VI. *Emphasis*

Act Use the active voice here. See pp. 302–03.

Anti Avoid unintentional anticlimax. See pp. 288–89.

Cli Use the order of climax. See pp. 288–89.

Emp Give due emphasis to important ideas.

Per Make the sentence periodic. See pp. 288–91.

VII. *Variety*

Var Vary your expression to prevent monotony. If your writing is frequently criticized as monotonous, study Chapter Eight.

VIII. *The paragraph*

¶ Begin a new paragraph here.

Tran Make transitions smooth and clear. See pp. 311–20.

TS Provide a topic sentence.

Un Preserve the unity of the paragraph by eliminating material that is not relevant to the topic sentence.